W9-AVC-841

Pseudoscience and Extraordinary Claims of the Paranormal

A Critical Thinker's Toolkit

Jonathan C. Smith

Roosevelt University

WILEY-BLACKWELL

A John Wiley & Sons, Ltd., Publication

This edition first published 2010
© 2010 Jonathan C. Smith

Blackwell Publishing was acquired by John Wiley & Sons in February 2007. Blackwell's publishing program has been merged with Wiley's global Scientific, Technical, and Medical business to form Wiley-Blackwell.

Registered Office
John Wiley & Sons Ltd, The Atrium, Southern Gate, Chichester, West Sussex, PO19 8SQ, United Kingdom

Editorial Offices
350 Main Street, Malden, MA 02148-5020, USA
9600 Garsington Road, Oxford, OX4 2DQ, UK
The Atrium, Southern Gate, Chichester, West Sussex, PO19 8SQ, UK

For details of our global editorial offices, for customer services, and for information about how to apply for permission to reuse the copyright material in this book please see our website at www.wiley.com/wiley-blackwell.

The right of Jonathan C. Smith to be identified as the author of this work has been asserted in accordance with the Copyright, Designs and Patents Act 1988.

All rights reserved. No part of this publication may be reproduced, stored in a retrieval system, or transmitted, in any form or by any means, electronic, mechanical, photocopying, recording or otherwise, except as permitted by the UK Copyright, Designs and Patents Act 1988, without the prior permission of the publisher.

Wiley also publishes its books in a variety of electronic formats. Some content that appears in print may not be available in electronic books.

Designations used by companies to distinguish their products are often claimed as trademarks. All brand names and product names used in this book are trade names, service marks, trademarks or registered trademarks of their respective owners. The publisher is not associated with any product or vendor mentioned in this book. This publication is designed to provide accurate and authoritative information in regard to the subject matter covered. It is sold on the understanding that the publisher is not engaged in rendering professional services. If professional advice or other expert assistance is required, the services of a competent professional should be sought.

Library of Congress Cataloging-in-Publication Data

Smith, Jonathan C.
   Pseudoscience and extraordinary claims of the paranormal: a critical thinker's toolkit/ Jonathan C. Smith.
      p. cm.
   Includes bibliographical references and index.
   ISBN 978-1-4051-8123-5 (hardcover : alk. paper) – ISBN 978-1-4051-8122-8 (pbk. : alk. paper) 1. Parapsychology. I. Title.
   BF1031.S635 2010
   130–dc22

                                                                                                        2009017134

A catalogue record for this book is available from the British Library.

Main cover image © Photodisc / Alamy; orange moon © Ghost / Fotolia; der Tod © Falco / Fotolia; tombstone © Paul Moore / Fotolia; evolution © imageZebra / Fotolia; om © Sibear / Fotolia; yin yang © Thorsten / Fotolia; bent spoon © TimurD / Fotolia; flying saucers © Geoffrey Holman / iStockphoto.com; witch © Andrew Howe / iStockphoto.com

Set in 10/12.5pt Sabon by SPi Publisher Services, Pondicherry, India
Printed in Singapore by Ho Printing Singapore Pte Ltd

1   2010

Praise for *Pseudoscience and Extraordinary Claims of the Paranormal*

"This book, particularly in regard to its discussion of memory errors and its insistence on the value of real science, takes a place of prominence on my personal library shelf."

James Randi, Chairman of the James Randi Educational Foundation

"I am astonished by the excellence of this book. Smith has produced a highly readable and very entertaining yet critical examination of virtually the entire gamut of paranormal claims, and he demonstrates an encyclopedic knowledge of the field in doing so. While drawing extensively from psychology, physics, logical analysis and history, he always manages to keep things clear and straightforward, so that one is never lost in complexity. Moreover, the tone is light-hearted throughout, and never becomes pedantic or condescending. And the book offers much more than an evaluation of extraordinary claims. It provides a refined set of critical thinking tools that the reader will find invaluable in everyday life. I strongly recommend this book to everyone who values the pursuit of truth in all things. And I can only wish that those who know that they already have the truth would read it as well, for they need it the most."

James Alcock, York University

"Can you be both a critical thinker and a believer in the paranormal? The 'reality checks' in Jonathan Smith's Critical Thinker's Toolkit will guide you to your answer."

Robert Todd Carroll, author of The Skeptic's Dictionary

"An excellent, engaging, and highly readable introduction to the paranormal and to the distinction between science and pseudoscience. A superb student-friendly guide to extraordinary claims. Chock full of interesting and fun examples, not to mention humor. Should become a favorite in undergraduate psychology courses."

Scott O. Lilienfeld, Emory University

Elmo, Gum, Heather, Holly, Mistletoe, Rowan, and Al

Contents

About the Author

Dr. Jonathan C. Smith has written extensively on stress, relaxation, meditation, and mindfulness as well as spirituality and skepticism. He is a Licensed Clinical Psychologist, Professor of Psychology at Chicago's Roosevelt University, and Founding Director of the Roosevelt University Stress Institute. Dr. Smith has published 17 books with major international publishers and has authored more than three dozen articles. His innovative approaches to relaxation, meditation, and mindfulness have won wide professional acclaim. Dr. Smith has taught his approaches to thousands and has served as consultant for government, business, educational, medical, and health organizations around the world.

For nearly a half century, Dr. Smith has had an enduring and deep interest in teaching critical thinking and exploring the paranormal. His doctoral dissertation, completed at Michigan State University in 1975, was one of the first professionally acclaimed double-blind placebo studies on the then popular transcendental meditation (he found no therapeutic effect). This work led to three APA articles and his first two books. In 1984 he founded the Roosevelt University Stress Institute primarily to combat pseudoscience and quackery in the field. His manuals and textbooks on meditation, mindfulness, and spirituality take a distinctly skeptical perspective toward popular extraordinary claims often associated with these approaches. More recently he has written reviews of paranormal books for the American Psychological Association journal *PsycCRITIQUES*. In addition he has created classroom and online classes at Roosevelt University specifically designed to teach critical thinking skills and evaluate extraordinary claims of the paranormal.

Preface

I confess I am a bit passionate about the paranormal. I truly believe that claims of astrologers, psychics, spiritualists, mind-readers, spoon-benders, practitioners of complementary and alternative medicine, acupuncturists, faith healers, and creationists should be taken very seriously. Not because these claims may be true or false. Instead, I believe that extraordinary claims can have extraordinary consequences.

Think about it. A paranormal event magically violates the laws of physics, what we know about matter and energy. If demonstrated true, a paranormal phenomenon could require rewriting the textbooks of science. Furthermore, it could require a massive emergency research effort that would dwarf historical efforts to create an atom bomb or land a man on the moon. Why? What would be the consequences if a rabbit's foot worked, *really worked*— and terrorists figured it out first? Seriously, what if people could indeed predict the future; influence the past; read minds; cure illness through touch, thoughts, and prayers; secretly observe hidden events; and move and manipulate objects and devices from great distances through simple intention? What if, as claimed by some paranormal researchers, they're *all* true? Think about it.

It is a mistake to discount the paranormal as the foolish obsession of tabloid newspapers. Seventy-three percent of Americans are paranormal believers (whereas 27% have no paranormal belief), and this number is growing. More people believe in astrology today than in the Middle Ages. In the United States, most of us belong to a religion, and for the vast majority faith is built on the rock of paranormal claims. However, this book is for a select audience, those who have chosen to step back and, for a brief precious moment, to question. I have written this book for:

> **College students.** This book is an appropriate core reading for three types of college courses: *Critical Thinking, Research Methods,* and

Pseudoscience and the Paranormal. Courses need not be restricted to the paranormal; the tools I offer work for evaluating a wide range of extraordinary nonparanormal controversies such as Freudian psychoanalysis, graphology, polygraphy (lie detectors), and conspiracy theories.

Health professionals. Nurses, social workers, counselors, psychologists, and physicians encounter paranormal claims in courses and workshops on complementary and alternative medicine (CAM). CAM includes nontraditional treatments such as those from nonwestern cultures (Chinese acupuncture, Indian yoga chakras, shamanistic healing, etc.), mind–body techniques (healing touch, tai chi, meditation and prayer), and bio-energy treatments. Health professionals need to know to what extent these treatments work because of claimed undetected energies and powers or through suggestion and the placebo effect.

Journalists. The paranormal is a perennial topic of great interest to the media. A responsible journalist often must consider extraordinary claims in face of pressing publication deadlines that preclude exhaustive investigation. This book is designed to be a useful quick guide.

Public officials. Yes, government officials must consider paranormal claims. Should taxpayer revenue be spent for energy treatments (acupuncture, healing prayer, tai chi) based on forces not detected by physics? Should the CIA and FBI investigate the national security implications of flying saucers and mind-reading (and worry about a possible "psychic gap" with Russia)? Should the state prosecute faith healers who, in the name of Jesus, charge huge sums for bogus cures? Should the law permit parents to give their children magical alternative treatments instead of standard medicine? Who is responsible if such treatments don't work and children are injured or die? Should biology classes be required to teach paranormal-based creation myths along with the science of evolution?

Religious seekers and educators. The spiritual journey is a search for transcendent realities and possibilities hidden in the fog of selfishness, superstition, and ignorance. Every major religion teaches the importance of avoiding "false gods," idols, and narrow-minded temptation. This book offers the seeker and educator assistance in evaluating the credibility of claimed divine revelations, magic relics, miracle cures, healing shrines, exorcisms, resurrections, reincarnations, prophecies, visions, spontaneous combustions, spontaneous creation of matter, virgin births, and so on. It should be noted that such paranormal claims are not the sole property of any one religion, but characterize most, if not all.

Paranormal investigators. Scientists who study paranormal claims face special challenges. It may not be easy to tease out a subtle paranormal effect from coincidence, suggestion, and ordinary natural phenomena. Perhaps even more challenging is the task of conducting a study that skeptics take seriously. This book summarizes scientific standards advocated by both skeptical and believing researchers.

The Critical Thinker's Toolkit

Here is my perspective and plan. Overall our goal is to consider and apply a systematic approach for performing **reality checks** on paranormal claims, **The Critical Thinker's Toolkit**. The **Toolkit** begins by asking "Why believe a paranormal claim?" We consider three basic types of support: Is the claim from a credible source? Is it based on clear logic? Is it the product of good scientific observation? Then we look at five alternative explanations for any apparent paranormal event:

1. Is this event an oddity of nature or the world of statistics?
2. A perceptual error or trick?
3. A memory error?
4. The placebo effect?
5. A sensory anomaly or hallucination?

For Toolkit practice I present a selection of paranormal claims. I deliberately focus on **claims of consequence**, phenomena with historical, individual, social, philosophical, and political significance. Astrology (Chapters 3–5) is important because it is the "grandfather" of paranormal beliefs, offers a prototype for prophecy and psychic readings popular to this day, and provides a vivid contrast to the view of the universe offered by the science of astronomy. Historically, spiritualism and channeling with the dead (Chapter 11) helped trigger and shape current interests in the paranormal. The best methodology for studying paranormal claims is used by parapsychologists. Indeed, they have come tantalizingly close to providing evidence for some extraordinary claims (Chapter 12). Energy treatments such as acupuncture and tai chi (Chapter 13) cost individuals millions of dollars each year and have attracted millions of government research funds. The healing power of prayer is by far the most popular paranormal belief and faith healers (Chapter 14) have persuaded critically ill patients to forgo life-saving medical treatment. The debates over creationism and evolution (Chapter 15) have influenced American politics for decades and provide a lesson in the importance of separating science and religion.

What This Book Is Not

You may not find your favorite paranormal topic in this book. There are simply too many and my goal has not been to write yet another encyclopedia of the paranormal (see Appendix B for a listing of some excellent online resources). We do not devote much time to the many paranormal curios found in Halloween shops or circus sideshows. These include pixies, fairies, ghosts, haunted houses, flying saucers, UFO crop circles, alien abductions, Atlantis, werewolves, Bigfoot, dowsing, the Shroud of Turin, the Bermuda Triangle, and tens of thousands of quaint everyday superstitions. Fun and popular as these topics may be, ultimately they are of lesser consequence and perhaps are best left to the tabloids, B movies, and cable television faux documentaries. However, even if you are a true believer in fairies, pixies, or whatever, I invite you to practice your reality-checking skills and apply the Critical Thinker's Toolkit. Once again, I have attempted to limit focus to *paranormal claims of consequence.*

Also, this is a book on the paranormal. We do not consider pop psychology, psychoanalysis, humanistic therapies, "New Age" philosophy, questionable or "crazy" psychotherapies, or debated assessment strategies such as the Rorschach inkblot test, graphology (handwriting analysis), or lie detectors. First, some are legitimate topics of scientific debate, with qualified scientists arguing for and against. This is particularly true for psychoanalysis, humanistic therapies, the Rorschach test, and lie detectors. Good scientists disagree, and they are not pseudoscientists or paranormalists. Also, to include such topics would require that we include a discussion of every current controversy in psychology, which is not the task of this book.

This Book's Perspective (and Bias?)

Studies of the paranormal are fraught with accusations of bias. Quickly you will find examples of skeptics and believers who unfairly discount each other's "prejudiced" work. In this climate, I suspect that my efforts will be tagged as tainted. But let me make this clear: Bias consists of ignoring or distorting reality. My commitment is to embrace fact over fiction, even when this proves discomforting. Unlike a few skeptics, I am more than willing to accept a solid finding that challenges what science tells us is "possible." Indeed, I would take some delight in thumbing my nose at prevailing popular opinion. Anyone who has read my work will discover that I've shamelessly done this in the past. However, we aren't there yet, and I take greater delight in living in the world as it is. I don't like to be tricked or fooled.

In sum, there is one point I hope my book makes:

> If we accept one extraordinary paranormal claim that fails to meet a few sensible reality checks, we are obligated to accept all paranormal claims that have equivalent support.

If you believe in ghosts, you must also believe in astrology, reincarnation, TV psychic superstars, prophetic pets, alien abductions, communication with the dead, fortune-telling, mental spoon-bending, and a Pandora's box of other treasures. Why? All have sincere, honest, sane, intelligent, educated, articulate, famous, and passionate proponents. All are based on the same types of support. And for all, the evidence might at first seem quite convincing. But rather than falling victim to an exploding box of troublesome surprises, I offer a systematic way of taking thoughtful pause.

A Look Inside

This book offers something new for students, scholars, and those who are simply curious. I share a few scholarly inventions which I hope my colleagues will pursue. In addition, I've done some things to make this book useful and engaging.

Conceptual Advances

This book attempts to integrate evaluative tools used by both paranormal believers and skeptics. Although key elements of our Toolkit are standard fare in careful considerations of the paranormal (logic, use of the scientific method), I introduce a few innovations not present in any other text. These include:

- The Continuum Mysteriosum, an eight-part hierarchy for organizing paranormal and supernatural claims (Chapter 1). The Continuum not only helps us rank paranormal claims but provides criteria for evaluating their implications if true.
- A detailed discussion of the costs of erroneously accepting (or rejecting) paranormal claims. I introduce an extended and novel approach to subjective relativism (Chapter 2).
- A discussion of criteria for evaluating sources, including why we should question sources even considered to be reputable (Chapter 3).
- A new and practical system for categorizing logical errors. There are many ways to organize fallacies of logic. This text presents an approach my students have found useful. I introduce the error of mistaking science with jargon, technobabble, and science fiction (Chapter 4).

- Elaboration of how scientific thinking is, as Einstein has suggested, common-sense thinking at its best (Chapter 5).
- Introduction to the **FEDS Standard,** an expansion of Carl Sagan's widely quoted advice, "extraordinary claims require extraordinary evidence" (Chapter 5). Here it is:

The FEDS Standard

To be fully credible, a paranormal study should include expert independent and impartial supervision and replication to minimize:

- ✔ **Fraud:** The investigator makes up or changes data, reports only positive results, fails to report compromising design features, or claims to have done something that was in fact not done.
- ✔ **Error:** The investigator misuses experimental tools, methods, or statistics.
- ✔ **Deception:** Research participants, assistants, or colleagues trick the investigator.
- ✔ **Sloppiness:** The investigator does not take into account the research problems outlined in this text.

- Introduction of the five major alternative hypotheses that must be considered when confronting a paranormal claim (Chapters 6–10).
- New research on perceptual errors. I offer five categories of cold reading techniques that enable a beginning student to perform as well as a TV psychic superstar (Chapter 7).
- Latest research on memory errors and déjà vu (Chapter 8).
- A new model of placebos that emphasizes the role of hypnotic suggestion, classical conditioning, the opioid system, and self-stressing (Chapter 9).
- Introduction to sensory anomalies, such as the pupil response, that may underlie possible paranormal experiences. Application of latest thinking of hallucinations to the paranormal (Chapter 10).
- The beginnings of a new theory of "paranormic propensity" that hypothesizes why some people get caught up in paranormal thinking (Chapter 16).

Instructional Highlights

I have attempted to make the **Toolkit** short, clear, and organized. For the Critical Thinker in a hurry, I recommend Chapter 2 (Why Study These

Things?), Chapter 5 (Evaluating Scientific Evidence), Chapter 7 (Perceptual Errors), and Chapter 10 (Sensory Anomalies and Hallucinations). For those facing a paranormal emergency, I recommend Chapter 2. Our final Chapter (16) outlines key points and suggests how to perform a full reality checkup using the **Toolkit**. I have attempted to keep things brief so that instructors can provide their own favorite supplementary readings or elaborate upon topics I note.

Although I am a psychologist, I recognize that many users and instructors come from other areas, including philosophy, religion, journalism, and the health professions. For this reason, I have attempted to minimize technical discussion of such topics as neurophysiology, cognitive theory, psychopathology, logic, and statistics. If a user requires elaboration of any of these or other topics, many excellent specialized texts are available. For example, a course on research methods could include this text along with a core text on statistics. Seminars on medical diagnoses could supplement primary medical texts with this book.

In addition, through Wiley-Blackwell I offer an extensive bank of multiple choice questions, PowerPoint chapter summaries, sample syllabi, links to online university instruction, current video links, and a variety of tested instructional aids. For a sample syllabus, course description, and free online video library, visit my website: http://faculty.roosevelt.edu/jsmith

I have favored content and quality primary sources that are readily accessible without charge on the internet. The reader who wishes to explore a topic I briefly note can readily explore my sources. These, supplemented by the many excellent DVDs available on topics such as astrology, psychics, healing, creationism, and the supernatural, should spark considerable discussion.

In sum, here you will find an assortment of scientific studies, discussions of history, philosophical debates, a touch of theology, and a bit of humor. I challenge you to take it all seriously. Whether I am explaining, philosophizing, joking, or attempting parody, my goal remains the same—to inspire and provoke critical thinking. Enjoy the journey!

Acknowledgments

I wish to thank the good and patient folk at Wiley-Blackwell, including Chris Cardone, Annette Abel, the marvelous art staff, and, alas, those forthright anonymous reviewers. It has been a unique pleasure working with Wiley-Blackwell. I thank my many colleagues and co-conspiring scientists, including André Aleman, Marjaana Lindeman, Scott Lilienfeld, and Samuel Moulton for their extensive and thoughtful feedback. Finally, I thank Jim Choca, Lynn Weiner, as well as friends, colleagues, and students at Roosevelt University. Their support made this project possible.

The author and publisher wish to thank the following for permission to use copyright material:

Figure 2.1	Jörn Koblitz, MetBase Library, Bremen
Figure 2.2	Oxford Science Archive/Heritage Image Partnership (HIP)
Figure 2.3	Bettmann/Corbis
Figure 2.4	Tony Korody/Sygma/Corbis
Figure 2.5	Marian Zygmunt/Franciszkanie.pl
Figure 3.3	NASA/JPL-Caltech/R.Hurt (SSC)
Figure 3.4	NASA/ESA/V.Beckmann
Figure 6.1	Paignton Zoo, Devon, UK
Figure 7.1a	NASA/Viking Project
Figure 7.1b	NASA/JPL/MSSS
Figure 7.1c	AFP/Getty Images
Figure 7.1d	Bill Steber/AP/PA Photos
Figure 7.1e	Scott Olson/Getty Images
Figure 7.1f	Marie Travers/www.ibrrc.org
Figure 7.1g	NASA
Figure 7.1h	NASA
Figure 7.1i	NASA

Figure 7.2   akg-images
Figure 11.1   Library of Congress Photographic Archive
Figure 11.2   AP/PA Photos
Figure 12.3   Figure 1 from *Using Neuroimaging to Resolve the PSI Debate* by Samuel T. Moulton and Stephen M. Kosslyn. JOURNAL OF COGNITIVE NEUROSCIENCE 20:1 pp 182–192 © 2008 Massachusetts Institute of Techology. Reprinted with permission of MIT Press Journals
Figure 12.4   Courtesy of James Randi Educational Foundation
Figure 13.2   Used with permission of Skeptic magazine at skeptic.com
Figure 14.1   Rex Features
Figure 14.2   Francis Miller/Time-Life Collection/Getty Images
Figure 14.3   akg images/Erich Lessing
Figure 15.1   Courtesy of Zach Strausbaugh
Figure 15.2   Library of Congress

Quotation in Chapter 7 from Hyman, R. (2003) 'How not to test mediums: Critiquing the afterlife experiments', Skeptical Inquirer, 27. Reprinted with permission.

'The Paranormal' by Susan Blackmore, from www.edge.org 2008. © Susan Blackmore. Reprinted with kind permission of the author.

Every effort has been made to trace copyright holders and to obtain their permission for the use of copyright material. The author and publisher will gladly receive any information enabling them to rectify any error or omission in subsequent editions.

Author photo by Bruce Jamieson

Part I

Introduction

1

The Continuum Mysteriosum

There are more things in heaven and earth, Horatio,
than are dreamt of in your philosophy.

Hamlet (I, v, 166–167)

All things bright and beautiful,
All creatures great and small,
All things wise and wonderful,
The Lord God made them all.

Famous Anglican Hymn (Monk, 1875)

'Extraordinary claims require extraordinary evidence'
Popularized by Carl Sagan (Truzzi, 1976)

Have you ever made a wish that came true? Perhaps you carry a rabbit's foot or read the daily horoscope. Maybe you avoid walking under ladders, stepping on sidewalk cracks, or spilling salt, comforted by the thought that you are still alive and kicking. Nearly everyone has a habit or belief that others might call a bit superstitious.

Then there are the bigger mysteries. People spend millions for energy manipulation cures, psychic readings, and faith healings. Terrorists commit history-altering acts of suicide and murder driven by promised rewards in the afterlife. What are we to make of this world of extraordinary and strange claims? Why do they persist in the face of science? Is it possible some are true? Does it matter?

Decades ago, I started looking into things paranormal and supernatural. I was a teenager and my interests were not quite those of a scholar. My childish and magical wish was to become famous, build time machines, develop superhuman powers, or find a secret way to get good grades or hot dates. Before long I realized I had opened a treasure chest of claims, too many to fully understand. Overwhelmed, I turned to the more manageable study of psychology. But my curiosity about the mysteries of life never completely went away. In fact, it is difficult to avoid the world of the paranormal and supernatural. Like the proverbial elephant, it sits conspicuously in the middle of the living room of life. If you ask the right questions, you will find that most of your friends, professors, doctors, or preachers harbor at least one secret superstition.

Making Sense out of Mysteries: The Continuum Mysteriosum[1]

This book tries to make sense out of the strange and unexplained. I have two goals, first to map the vast heavens of mysterious claims, and second to explore reality-checking tools for determining which are true or false. My mission is not to convert you into a true believer or true skeptic. Instead, the goal of this book is simple: **Question fearlessly and honestly.** I invite you to apply this challenge to all life's mysteries, bright and beautiful, great and small.

What is the realm of the paranormal? This is a question of considerable interest to scholars. Clearly, mind-reading, astrology, and seeing into the future are paranormal claims. But what about acupuncture? Yoga? Space aliens? I prefer to begin with a very simple definition: **paranormal claims contradict what we know about matter and energy[2] as discovered through the science of physics.** Put differently, a purely paranormal claim states that explanations consistent with the science of physics are not enough (see page 16).

Consider the following:

When playing the lottery, use the year of your birth and you are more likely to win. If this were to really work, with no tricks, it could not be explained in any way by science. The claimed event is paranormal.

A psychic can look at you and read what you are thinking. This is true, even if you are separated by a brick wall, the psychic doesn't know you, and you deliberately think of cards randomly selected from a deck. This claim appears to rule out natural-world explanations such as reading body language and making good guesses based on what you are wearing. So it's a genuine paranormal claim.

A nurse at a local hospital claims she can heal through therapeutic touch and cure your backache by gently waving her palm over your spine. Such cures could be due to many things. People get over backaches on their own. Expectation can play a large role. Once you rule out these other explanations, you may have something paranormal.

Some mysteries are bigger than others. Cherishing a magic rabbit's foot isn't as dramatic as going to war over an astrological reading. I find it useful to organize paranormal and supernatural claims into eight groups placed on a *continuum mysteriosum* (continuum of mysteries) according to the degree to which they challenge naturalistic views of matter and energy identified through physics. Minor or *low-level paranormal claims* are on the left while *high-level paranormal claims* are on the right. You can see that higher-level claims are more encompassing, complex, and organized. More aspects of the natural world are brought into question, with greater diversity, and organized into an abstract belief system, itself divorced from the natural world. Claimed low-level processes have limited impact on our world, whereas high-level claims have greater potential impact.

It should be noted that all truly paranormal claims by definition involve a fundamental violation of what we know about matter and energy. In that sense they are all equal. However, high-level paranormal claims are more elaborated than low-level claims. They more fully elucidate the implications and applications of a paranormal assumption, and posit additional parallel, perhaps equally improbable, assumptions. The belief that possessing a rabbit's foot will help you win the lottery violates what we know about matter and energy. Nothing about the chemistry and physics of a disembodied and dried piece of mammal anatomy should affect the random selection of winning lottery tickets thousands of miles away. If this could happen, then why not assume that lines in the disembodied foot say something about your personality and future? Or that the foot possesses an energy that can cure warts? Or that the foot is indeed conscious and wants you to win the lottery and be wart-free? Or that the dead foot possesses the ghost of the recently deceased rabbit, a reincarnation of an ancient sage who is now your guardian angel and who wants you to be healthy, wart-free, and rich? All of these are equally improbable. All violate what we know about the properties of matter and energy. They differ primarily in their elaboration.

Flying saucer

Table 1.1   The Continuum Mysteriosum

Lower-level paranormal claims ———————————————————————————

Borderline/gratuitous paranormal claims	Simple superstitions	Paranormal patterns	Paranormal powers
• Bigfoot	• Magic charms	• Palmistry	• ESP
• Loch Ness Monster	• Rabbit's foot	• Tarot cards	• Psychokinesis
• Flying saucers*	• Stepping on cracks	• "Reading"	• Fortune-telling
• Acupuncture*	• Number "13"	entrails	• Astral projection,
• Tai Chi*		• Tea leaves	out-of-body
• Firewalking		• Some astrology*	experience
• Moon madness		• Numerology	• Dowsing
• Many types of yoga and meditation*		• Bible code	

* Many paranormal claims come in several varieties each of which might be classified differently. For example, the claim that acupuncture evokes brain endorphins is not paranormal. A vague claim that acupuncture triggers nebulous body energy can be classified as a simple energy claim. A claim that the arrangement of stars at the time of one's birth contains information about one's personality and future is a paranormal pattern. However, it is an energy claim to state that the stars contain some mysterious force that can influence life on earth.

Borderline and Gratuitous Paranormal Claims

Borderline paranormal claims concern mysteries that need not violate the world of physics; however, true paranormal explanations are not ruled out and are often entertained. For example, we have no clear evidence that flying saucers have visited the earth, but nothing in physics says that flying saucers from a different planet could not visit us. It might take a spaceship thousands of years using conventional rocket propulsion. Perhaps such a ship would be directed by robots or beings in hibernation. Or, to entertain a paranormal explanation, space aliens might slip from their home in the 13th dimension and instantly (and invisibly) appear on earth. Such a paranormal explanation invokes a claimed phenomenon (travel from the 13th dimension) that runs counter to the physical world we know.

Closer to home, acupuncture is an ancient Chinese medical procedure that involves inserting needles in precisely defined points on the body. Acupuncture patients claim relief from a wide range of problems ranging from pain to hypertension. The traditional paranormal explanation is that acupuncture

Higher-level paranormal claims

Simple energies	Intelligent forces/entities	Afterlife entities	Supernatural entities
• Qi/Chi • Magnet therapy • Homeopathy • Early Chiropractic • Traditional tai chi • Traditional Acupuncture • Healing touch	• Yin-Yang theory • Spirits • Werewolves • Witches • Karma • Fate	• Reincarnation • Ghosts • Communication with dead	• Flying saucer cults • Faith healing • Organized supernatural religion with complex theologies incorporating a literal heaven, hell, devil, angels, saints, virgin births, resurrections, and fantastic miracles

frees the flow of a mystical vital energy, qi (or chi), resulting in healing. Qi has never been detected and does not operate by the known laws of physics. A variety of contemporary nonparanormal explanations exists, including that the slight discomfort of inserting needles distracts one from pain, triggers the release of peaceful brain endorphins, reinforces expectations of cure, and so on. Thus, acupuncture represents a borderline paranormal claim.

Cryptozoology is the study of "hidden animals" ("cryptids"), claimed creatures whose existence is controversial (Heuvelmans, 1962). Examples include the Loch Ness Monster, Bigfoot, and various dragons of antiquity. Strictly speaking, there is nothing paranormal about cryptids because their existence would not violate the laws of physics. However, a few psychics have made additional paranormal claims, for example, that Bigfoot and Nessie are from some other dimension and can be conjured up psychically (Bauer, 1996). In such cases one might classify cryptozoology as a borderline paranormal claim.

Gratuitous paranormal claims offer a nonphysical explanation when there is no mystery to be explained. Why do leaves fall from trees? Because little fairies pluck them off. Why did you fail your exam when you didn't bother to read the textbook? Because Fate is punishing you for your irresponsibility. Why did your headache go away when you took the aspirin tablet? Because you unblocked the qi flowing to your brain. In each case there is nothing to be explained, no need for a paranormal hypothesis.

Rabbit's foot

Note the difference between pure, borderline, and gratuitous paranormal claims. Pure paranormal claims imply that an extraordinary event can be explained only by going beyond current basic science. No alternative explanations are sufficient. Borderline and gratuitous paranormal claims accept that current scientific explanations may work just fine and paranormal explanations are simply alternatives. The remaining claims we consider are purely paranormal.

Simple Superstitions

Simple superstitions refer to everyday events that seem to violate the laws of physics. Generally, they are based on *coincidence, folklore*, as well as "*similarities*," or "*contagion*" (Frazer, 1911–1915). If you coincidentally won a card game while wearing a red shirt, you might wear this lucky shirt whenever playing cards. If your great-grandmother warned you never to peek at birthday presents, you might honor this rule because it is a bit of family folklore. Perhaps you think you are a bright and sunny person because of this similarity—you were born on a bright and sunny day. Maybe you shouldn't wear your great-grandfather's ring. After all, he wore it just before falling into the well, and you don't want to "catch" his unfortunate luck. Simple superstitions are not encompassing, complex, and organized. Generally their broader implications are ignored or not elaborated. People do not devote careers to the risks of stepping on sidewalk cracks or avoiding the number "13." There are no rumors of secret Russian labs studying the feet of rabbits.

Paranormal Patterns

Are there secret messages embedded in the creases of your palm, tarot cards, tea leaves, entrails of sacrificial lambs, I Ching symbols, special combinations of numbers, the Bible code, and heavenly constellations? A relatively simple

Open palm with lines (for palm-reading)

paranormal claim asserts that certain patterns contain special information that cannot be explained through any means consistent with contemporary physics. Palmistry claims that the wrinkles in the palm of your hand contain vast information about your history, personality, and future. There is no physical way this could be the case. Similarly, ancient tarot picture cards, particles of tea at the bottom of a tea cup, and the arrangement of intestines in a slaughtered lamb can be equally revealing. And of course astrology claims that the patterns of heavenly bodies present at the moment of your birth can say much about your life and future. Although such patterns may possess paranormal information, typically an individual with no paranormal ability can "read" the messages contained. Anyone with a book on palmistry can discover the secrets hidden in the wrinkles of a hand, and the message of a long "life line."

Paranormal Powers

Paranormal powers are limited human (and possibly animal) capacities that violate physics. However, few people possess or have cultivated such powers

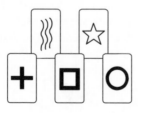

Zener cards

and these gifted individuals appear to be able to use them only in highly restricted circumstances. Examples include reading thoughts through extra-sensory perception or bending spoons (or influencing the roll of a casino slot machine) through psychokinesis. People have devoted their careers to these topics. Libraries of books and articles have been written.

Simple Life Energies

Unlike paranormal powers, which may be limited and appear in select individuals at select times, simple life energies are enduring and more pervasive.

Acupuncturist inserting needles in patient

Furthermore, they have the potential for affecting physical health and biological processes. For example, many practitioners of acupuncture believe that a mysterious paranormal energy, qi (chi), permeates the human body and can be "unblocked" through the strategic insertion of needles. Unlike fate or karma, such forces do not guide, direct, or provide a purpose for actions. And unlike ghosts or spirits, they lack psychological characteristics such as thoughts, feelings, and intentions. However, simple life energies can be tapped and directed by individuals with paranormal powers. A skilled acupuncturist claims to use qi to heal.

Intelligent Forces and Entities

Intelligent forces are also enduring and exist beyond the natural world. However, they have a complexity not possessed by life energies—an "intelligence" of their own that does not require the assistance of someone with a

Witch

paranormal power. Such forces may be impersonal sources of guidance or direction, such as fate, yin/yang, the powers of prophetic astrology, karma, some nonphysical evolutionary principle that pushes toward "goodness" or "higher consciousness." Alternatively, intelligent forces may have psychological characteristics, such as consciousness, thoughts, feelings, and intentions, all internal complexities that enable us to call them **entities**.[3] Examples include living objects possessed by spirits that wish us well.

Afterlife Entities

Afterlife entities are intelligent forces with one spectacular additional characteristic—they exist in this world and the world after death. They

Ghost over tombstone

might include reincarnated souls as well as ghosts and some spirits. The existence of such entities permits communication with the dead.

Supernatural Entities

Supernatural claims are "superparanormal" and go beyond challenging naturalistic views of matter and energy identified through physics. As we

Some World Religions (Judaism, Islam, Christianity, Hinduism, Taoism)

have noted, they are encompassing, complex, and organized. More aspects of the natural world are brought into question, with greater diversity. Supernatural beliefs are often organized into an abstract conceptual system, itself divorced from the natural world. Supernatural entities have vast potential impact on our world. What does this mean?

The natural world consists of things we can conceivably detect with our senses, or sense-based tools like telescopes, microscopes, or x-ray machines. So, everything you see, hear, touch, smell, or taste is part of the natural world. And anything you could conceive of someone else seeing, touching, smelling, or tasting is also part of the natural world. Apples on the trees of Maine are part of the natural world. Apples on a planet in a different solar system are also part of the natural world, because they could conceivably be detected if we were there.

Is there anything else? Anyone with a fertile imagination can conceive of many types of possible supernatural entities, including the Pantheon of ancient deities, universe-sized supercomputers, beings in the 13th dimension, time-traveling voyeurs, the Flying Spaghetti Monster, and so on. (Curious? See page 17.) Each is equally possible.

Note that some supernatural entities may never intrude in the observable universe. Such a being would never make itself known, and would be forever unknowable. We may never know the private life of the great entity in the 13th dimension, why we've been dumped in a cosmic lunatic asylum, or who set the clockwork universe into motion and stood aside. Such *purely supernatural ideas* are off limits to science, but discussed extensively in various forms of literature, including personal accounts and diaries, Holy Scriptures, theology texts, science fiction and fantasy novels, and comic books. In contrast, some supernatural ideas claim a specific and measurable impact on the observable world. Claims of such miraculous phenomena are fair game for questioning.

REALITY CHECK   Do you have a friend or relative with a paranormal belief? Where does it fit on the continuum? How seriously does it challenge what we know about the physical universe?

Extraordinary, Nonparanormal Mysteries

One type of claim does not merit placement on our continuum of mysteries. *Extraordinary mysteries* include scientific anomalies, strange observed events for which currently there is no scientific explanation. However, scientists assume that an explanation is possible once science develops. Sometimes an event seems mysterious simply because of our ignorance. I do not understand how laser pointers work, but I choose not to invoke a *premature paranormal explanation*. Other phenomena are mysterious even to experts.

Consider the notion of *dark energy*. Recently, astronomers discovered that the universe is expanding more rapidly than expected. No existing form of matter or energy, no existing physical process, can explain this anomaly. So scientists use a special term, a **causal placeholder**, as a kind of **sticky note** to remind them that there's a mystery here that needs to be explained. The term "dark energy" is such a sticky note. The mysterious cause of the universe's expansion isn't actually *dark* and it may not actually be *energy* as we know it. However, it is easier to give it a name, "dark energy," rather than some boring code like "unexplained phenomenon # 325.112A."

For another famous example, we turn from the universe to the world of atoms. Quantum physics is one of the most powerful theories ever created and has led to television and hydrogen bombs. However, much of quantum physics is very strange. For example, electrons are both particles and waves. Even more strange is the notion that some attributes of particles can appear to exist in several places at the same time. Under certain circumstances, if a particle of light, a photon, is split, each half will have an opposite polarity ("vertical" vs. "horizontal"). Now imagine you split a photon in such a way that one part stays in your home lab and the other shoots off into the universe. If you check the polarity of the home photon, then you automatically know the polarity of the distant photon, even without checking. In itself this might not seem particularly odd. After all, if you split a bag of 13 marbles so that one part has 4, you immediately know the other part has 9, no matter where it is. But quantum particles aren't marbles. **Quantum characteristics exist at all possible states until the moment they are observed.** Every photon, whether or not it is split, is like a spinning little slot machine, with all possible scores, or polarities, whizzing by randomly. But the moment you look at a photon, it freezes, the slot machine stops, and you know the result, that is, whether its polarity is "horizontal" or "vertical." It gets even stranger. After you split your photon, the distant photon may be millions of miles away. However, its polarity is fixed at the very moment you check the polarity of the home photon. Checking the polarity of the distant photon won't "fix" it, because it was fixed, apparently the instant you checked the polarity of its home partner. This is called "entanglement," which Einstein mocked as "spooky action at a distance" (Einstein, Podolsky, & Rosen, 1935). Remarkably, research has actually demonstrated entanglement and shown Einstein to be wrong. The term "entanglement" is a placeholder, a label for complex mathematical equations that seem to apply to the subatomic world, and not the everyday "macro" world of molecules, bacteria, cats, chimpanzees, or us. There's a reason why I have burdened you with this strange and complicated explanation. If my explanation doesn't make much sense, good. The smartest physicists don't fully understand entanglement either. More important, physicists don't make the mistake of thinking their causal placeholder fully explains what they have observed.

There is a risk in labeling mysteries. Sometimes a causal placeholder has excess meaning that is actually irrelevant. For example, a string of unsolved murders might involve a common clue—the murderer leaves a magic token, usually a rabbit's foot, horseshoe, or four-leafed clover, in the hand of the victim. For convenience, the police name the suspect "The Magic Killer." This name is simply a convenience, something easier to discuss than "Suspect No. 32-881-B." If you were to ask someone who the suspect is, they might reply, "Oh, the Magic Killer." That might conjure up all kinds of surplus meaning, such as someone who delves in the occult. People might suddenly become very suspicious of local psychics and astrologers, but when pressed, "Who is the Magic Killer," the only answer would be "That killer who leaves magic tokens at the crime." Thus, a careful reality check reveals that place-setters are by definition circular.

One can get into considerable trouble by counting too much on the excess meaning of causal placeholders. Once again, the terms "spooky action at a distance" and "entanglement" are simply ways of describing complicated mathematical equations that work in describing what happens to some subatomic particles, not objects in the everyday world. One famous example of reading too much into a placeholder is Dean Radin's (2006) claim that psychics can transfer thoughts because their minds are "entangled" at the quantum level. As we shall see throughout this book, notions of "quantum consciousness" are currently in vogue in paranormal circles. However, such ideas are like saying that ghosts use "spooky action" to open doors in haunted houses or that psychics use "dark energy" to bend spoons.

Causal placeholders and paranormal claims illustrate a difference between the scientist and the paranormalist true believer. A scientist can tolerate the ambiguity of not knowing an answer; indeed, if there were no mysteries there would be no science. The journey of science is paved with promises and sticky notes. A scientist has faith that the methods of reasonable and scientific inquiry can conceivably uncover the truth. The true believer takes a bigger step and has faith in a specific explanation beyond science, even though natural-world explanations may eventually emerge.

Finally, I do not include as paranormal the millions of mistaken claims that stay within the boundaries of normal science. For example, you may believe that your Hummer gets 100 miles per gallon. As long as you do not claim your Hummer uses a special miracle fuel, or runs on ghosts, you are simply mistaken. You may claim that eating nothing but rice and beans will cure all illness. For a known biological process to achieve this, a few laws of physics would have to be broken and your claim would be paranormal. However, if you claim that the human body, and the physics on which it is based, can currently explain the curative powers of rice and beans, your claim is not paranormal. It is simply wrong.

There are many extraordinary claims that are the center of considerable controversy. Freud thought all men had latent homosexual urges. Is this true? How would you ever test this? Is Freud's long and tedious approach to psychoanalysis any better than simple 10-session therapies based on learning theory? Should evidence from lie detectors, and hypnosis, be accepted in courts? Can graphologists really read your personality from your handwriting? Is the government really conspiring to hide the truth about UFOs, the Kennedy assassination, or 9/11? Is the medical community conspiring to hide evidence of simple and inexpensive cures available to everyone? Controversial as these claims may be, none are paranormal. None require that we abandon physics. (However, all can be evaluated using the tools of this text.)

An Invitation

In this book we take a strange journey into the unknown. In Part II we introduce a Critical Thinker's Toolkit and use it to perform reality checks on a variety of examples, most prominently astrology and psychic readings. It is fitting that we start with these paranormal topics, given their popularity and persistence over the millennia. In Part III, The Paranormal Files, we review the main categories of paranormal claims. At the end of the Civil War, spiritualism and its concern with the afterlife and ghosts marked the beginning of contemporary interest in the paranormal. We move to scientific parapsychology, a field of study that evolved from spiritualism to focus on basic paranormal powers to read minds and move or alter objects with thoughts. Then we switch to the practical and consider the application of healing life energies in complementary and alternative medicine, and healing through faith and prayer. Our final topic is perhaps the most controversial paranormal debate of our time: Darwin, creationism, and intelligent design (with honorable mention to the Flying Spaghetti Monster). Our journey concludes with a tutorial on performing a formal **reality checkup** using the Critical Thinker's Toolkit.

The Paranormal, Ontological Fusion, and Category Errors

Paranormal claims can also be viewed as category errors (Ryle, 1949). You make a category error when you give something a property which it cannot logically have. "Colors" are properties of objects. "Ideas" are mental phenomena. Consider this famous illustration:

Colorless green ideas sleep furiously

This statement has no meaning because it makes a category error. Ideas can't be green.

Lindeman and Aarnio (2007) offer a useful elaboration. At an early age children acquire ideas on what the world is like. These ideas constitute "core knowledge" and apply to the worlds of physics, psychology, and biology. These worlds are also termed "ontological categories." The physical world consists of material objects that have volume, occupy space, and can affect (technically, transmit physical energy to) each other if they touch (collide and bounce, for example). The psychological world is one in which living beings have choice, make decisions, and have a conscious mind. The mind has "content" such as thoughts, beliefs, and desires that are not "substantial" and objective. Biological entities are living, require food, reproduce, transmit disease, get sick, and die. The characteristics of these three ontological worlds are distinct and separate. Rocks do not have thoughts. Thoughts can't move rocks. You can't get sick by standing next to a broken rock, or make a person sick by thinking about them. During an eclipse the sun does not eat the moon. The setting sun does not die.

A paranormal claim mixes ontological categories, and inappropriately applies attributes that belong to one world or ontological category to another. Your thoughts and intentions can move and change physical objects (psychokinesis) or cure disease. The ancient Chinese system of feng shui teaches that arranging furniture (physical world) can affect your health (biological world) and psychological well-being (psychological world).

This ontological fusion (or confusion) perspective shows some promise. Young children also mix ontological categories, and talk to thinking frogs, wish problems away, and so on. Perhaps studying the core ontological confusions of children will yield insights for adults.

The 10 Gods of Planet Paranormia: A Fable

Supernatural claims are "superparanormal" and go beyond challenging naturalistic views of matter and energy identified through physics. In addition, they are encompassing, complex, and organized. More aspects of the natural world are brought into question, with greater diversity, and organized into an abstract belief system, itself divorced from the natural world.

People sometimes have the narrow view that their preferred supernatural entity is the only one. In fact, hundreds of supernatural entities are possible beyond the currently popular local deity. Virtually every ancient culture had a great family of colorful and lively higher powers. The famous myth-writers of the past have enriched our universe with additional ideas. Today's science fiction or comic book author might be tomorrow's prophet or mystic. Scientology, a government-recognized religion, was invented by a science fiction author. Today the phrase (from the *Star Wars* series) "May the force be with you" is sometimes used as a spiritual invocation. It can be enlightening to contemplate the full range of supernatural entities, each equally possible. Let me share with you a brief fable that attempts to make this point.

Not so far away in a rather ordinary solar system Planet Paranormia orbits a modest sun. Planet Paranormia serves as home for no fewer than 10 continents, each completely isolated by ocean. The inhabitants of the continents are unaware of their neighbors and have developed separate cultures and beliefs. In some respects, their religions are remarkably similar. Religious insights came from a single visionary who had direct contact with the supernatural. This visionary was martyred, although his followers eventually prevailed. Common core beliefs include the importance of compassion, helping the less fortunate, self-control, free inquiry and choice within the framework of faith, and total obedience. Although disbelievers were once put to death or ostracized, now they are simply prohibited from running for political office. In spite of these similarities, each continent's vision of the supernatural is unique. Indeed Planet Paranormia has no fewer than 10 gods, one for each continent. Here they are:

1. **God the Great Supercomputer.** A huge supercomputer encompasses the entire universe. Everything is just a computer simulation, and the universe is a great computer game on some gigantic laptop. We can never figure this out because we are "programmed" to be not quite intelligent enough.

2. **God the Universal Mind/Consciousness.** A great mind or consciousness underlies and unites everything. You can't detect it because it is everywhere, and is everything. Here's why. If Mind is everything, there's nothing left for it to observe; because Mind is everything, you are Mind; therefore there's nothing left for you to observe; therefore you can't see Mind. Get it?

3. **God in Another Dimension.** A 13th dimension is inhabited by powers and entities that often communicate with powers and entities in the 12th dimension. They could control our lives, but aren't interested.

4. **God Beyond the Edge of the Universe.** Beyond the edge of our universe is another universe populated by wise and ancient beings. They are more powerful than we can imagine. However, we can never see them because they are outside of our universe.

5. **God the Infinitely Small Entity.** Smaller than the smallest atom, and smaller than we can ever detect, is another world of strings. String-beings think about us a lot. They keep subatomic particles together and control everything. But we can't see them because they slither between atoms.

6. **The Time-Traveling Voyeur Gods.** Far in the future is a race of time-traveler voyeurs. Their laws forbid interfering in the past (except for entertainment). However, it is OK to peek. For amusement they observe what's happening in our world. Shades are useless. Don't even think about calling the police.

7. **God the Great Invisible Spirit.** Invisible ghostly entities walk through us every day. We can never measure them, because they are clever enough to avoid detection. However, they scare us, play tricks, and randomly do things in the world that can't be studied scientifically (like cracking mirrors and making strange noises in empty houses).

8. **God the Fleet-Footed Entity.** There are entities amongst us who travel so fast that we can never detect them. Actually, they aren't particularly intelligent. However, what they lack in sophistication they make up in speed.

9. **God the Shape-Shifting Entity.** A huge shape-shifting creature walks and rules the earth. Whenever someone is about to notice her, she changes shape to avoid detection. She can instantly become a frog, tree, or university professor. We are sometimes mystified, but remain clueless.

10. **God the Super-Smart Prankster Entity.** A very intelligent being reads and controls our thoughts. He lets us ask probing questions, but tricks us into getting the wrong answer.

I end this fable here. It could go in many directions. What wars might erupt when the inhabitants of Continent #2 meet and try to convert the inhabitants of Continent #9? What if they all met at once and tried to convert each other simultaneously? Perhaps a grand cosmic visionary discovers a universal truth that binds them all together.

Note: Kuhn (2007) has offered a less colorful, and perhaps more scholarly, catalog of nonphysical causes beyond the constraints of physics: The Theistic Person, The Ultimate Mind, The Deistic First Cause, The Pantheistic Substance, Spirit Realms, Causal Consciousness, Being and Non-Being as Cause, Causal Abstract Objects/Platonic Forms, and Principle or Feature of Sufficient Power.

2

Why Study These Things?

The unexamined life is not worth living.

(Socrates, Apology 38a)

Why study the worlds of the paranormal? First, if you believe in such things you are not alone. Most people (73–76%) have at least one paranormal belief not derived from Judeo-Christian tradition (Moore, 2005; Newport & Strausberg, 2001) and 80–96% hold a religious-based paranormal belief (Bader, Froese, Johnson, Mencken, & Stark, 2005). More people believe in astrology today than in the Middle Ages (Gilovich, 1991; Vyse, 1997). Belief in the Devil appears to have increased over the decade (Table 2.1). At the very least it is important to understand what our friends, neighbors, politicians, doctors, and preachers believe.

If you have a paranormal belief, surely it is valuable to know more about it. If you read the daily horoscope, do you really know how it was calculated? If you enjoy a good ghost story, do you know why some Christians are so opposed to Halloween (and Harry Potter), and why the United States government has officially recognized a witchcraft-based tax-exempt religion? If you go to an acupuncturist, did you know that this treatment is based on a form of energy which, if detected, could revolutionize physics?

There is a deeper reason for exploring strange and extraordinary claims. They might be true. History shows us many cases of disputed beliefs once considered crazy and then accepted as true. Two such phenomena are meteors and hypnosis.

Meteors

In 1492, the year Christopher Columbus arrived in America, a 12-year-old boy in Ensisheim, Austria heard a loud thunderclap and saw a stone fall from the sky and land in a field of wheat. He led townsfolk to the fallen rock, and quickly the excited crowd began chipping away the relic

Table 2.1 Percentage of population who believe paranormal claims

Claim	Percentage
Superstition and witchcraft	
Witches	28%[1] 26%[2] 26%[3]
Superstitious ("very or somewhat")	24%[4]
Spiritualism and ghostly experiences	
Ghosts	40%[1] 38%[2] 39%[3] 42%[4] 32%[5]
Haunted houses	42%[2] 40%[3] 37%[5] 37%[6]
Spirit possession	15%[2]
Communicating with dead	28%[2] 16%[3] 21%[5] 20%[6]
Reincarnation	21%[1] 25%[2] 14%[3] 25%[4] 5%[7]
Fortune-telling and psychic readings	
Psychics (etc.) foresee future, clairvoyance, prophecy	32%[2] 13%[6]
Astrology	25%[1] 28%[2] 17%[3] 33%[4] 25%[5]
Astrology impacts one's life and personality	12%[6]
Dreams foretell future/reveal hidden truths	52%[6]
Déjà vu	69%[4]
Scientific parapsychology	
Telekinesis	28%[6]
Extrasensory perception	50%[2] 28%[3] 60%[4] 41%[5]
Telepathy	36%[2] 24%[3] 31%[5]
Clairvoyance, (psychic seeing)	24%[3] 26%[5]
Healing energies and faith cures	
Psychic/spiritual healing	54%[2] 56%[3] 59%[4] 55%[5]
Efficacy of alternative treatments	75%[6]
Personally had illness cured by prayer*	34%[4]
Space aliens and monsters	
UFOs	34%[1] 41%[4] 25%[6]
Aliens have visited Earth	33%[2] 17%[3] 35%[4] 24%[5]
Bigfoot, Loch Ness Monster	18%[6]
Traditional religious beliefs	
"God" (ambiguously defined)*	82%[1] 86%[9]
God (anthropomorphic plus non-anthropomorphic, see below)*	96%[6]
God (anthropomorphic – with human characteristics)*	70%[6]
Authoritarian paranormal entity involved in daily life and world affairs; God is quite angry and punishes unfaithful or ungodly*	31%[6]
Benevolent paranormal entity involved in daily life and world affairs; mainly a positive force and less willing to condemn or punish*	23%[6]
Critical paranormal entity who does not interact with the world; observes the world and views the current state of affairs unfavorably; justice is applied in the afterlife*	16%[6]

Table 2.1 *(cont'd)*

Claim	Percentage
God (distant nonanthropomorphic paranormal (?) entity who is not active in the world and is not especially angry; God is a cosmic force which set the laws of nature in motion; God does not "do" things in the world or hold clear opinions about our activities or world events)	24%[6]
"Heaven" (ambiguously defined)*	70%[1] 81%[9]
A person not of your religion can go to heaven	79%[7]
Hell*	59%[1] 69%[9]
Devil Possession*	41%[2] 40%[3] 59%[4] 42%[5]
The Devil*	61%[1] 70%[9]
Angels*	68%[1] 75%[9]
Creationism (Biblical account literally true)*	54%[1] 56%[4] 44% 47% 44% 47% 45% 45% 46% 43%[8]
Miracles*	73%[1]
Virgin Birth of Jesus*	58%[1]
Resurrection of Jesus*	66%[1]
God literally answers prayers (most popular paranormal belief)*	83%[4]
Life after death*	70%[1] 72%[4]
Traditional religious beliefs and nonreligious paranormal beliefs	
Believe in paranormal claims from traditional religion; do not believe in paranormal claims not from religion	36%[4]
Believe in paranormal claims both from traditional religion and paranormal claims outside of religion	40%[4]
Do not believe in paranormal claims from traditional religion, but do believe in paranormal claims outside of religion	12%[4]
Do not believe in paranormal claims, both those from and outside of traditional religion	10%[4]

* Traditional religion.

[1] Harris Poll, 2005 (Harris, 2005), 1,000 Nationwide telephone poll.

[2] Gallup Poll, 2001 (Newport & Strausberg, 2001).

[3] Farha-Steward Poll, 2006 (Farha & Steward, 2006).

[4] Rice Poll (Rice, 2003), 1,200 random telephone interviews. Nationwide sample.

[5] Gallup Poll, 2005 (Moore, 2005), 1002 nationwide sample, telephone interview.

[6] Baylor/Gallup Poll, 2005 (Bader, Froese, Johnson, Mencken, & Stark (2005), 1,721 telephone and mail.

[7] Newsweek/Beliefnet Poll, 2005 (Newsweek/ Beliefnet, 2005), 1004 Americans.

[8] Gallup Poll (Gallup, 2008), Summary of Gallup polls from 1982, 1997, 1999, 2001, 2004, 2006, 2007 all involving about 1,000 Americans each.

[9] Gallup Poll (Newport, 2007), 1,003 Americans.

Figure 2.1   The Ensisheim meteorite

sent from God. Maximilian I, King of Austria, believed it was God's message that his battles against the French would succeed. (The Austrians did win.) This belief was typical. For millennia people had believed that meteorites were rocks from heaven and signs from God. Three hundred years later, about the time of the American Revolution, this thinking was to change.

In 1772, Europe's leading "think tank," the French Academy of Sciences, asked Lavoisier to take part in an investigation of rocks from the heavens. Lavoisier was an excellent choice, having rejected the superstitions of alchemy and created the foundations for modern chemistry. He concluded that meteorites were produced by lightning (explaining their burned surface) and were not objects from the sky (Glenday & Friedman, 1999). Quickly the consensus among enlightened scholars was that meteors were impossible. Indeed Thomas Jefferson scoffed that rocks could not fall from the sky because there were no rocks up there (Hall, 1972). Museums throughout Europe tossed out their meteorites as superstitious rubble. The Austrian rock survived, probably because it was too heavy (280 pounds) to dislodge and survives to this day in a museum in Ensisheim (faithfully guarded by "The Brotherhood of St. George of the Meteorite"). Of course, today we know that meteors come from space and burn as they fall through the atmosphere. Incidentally, Lavoisier lost his head to the guillotine during the French Revolution, but that is a different story.

Figure 2.2   Mesmer's tub

Hypnosis

Some still think of hypnosis as a paranormal phenomenon. However, today scientific hypnosis is respected and serious research has explored the application of hypnosis for treating problems such as pain, obesity, and smoking (Lynn & Kirsch, 2006). The lingering negative reputation of hypnosis can be traced again to 17th and 18th century France (with links to Lavoisier and the guillotine).

When people speak derisively of hypnosis, they often call it "Mesmerism," after Franz Anton Mesmer. Mesmer was a Viennese physician who won notoriety and popularity with his flamboyant sessions of "animal magnetism" (Pattie, 1994). In a darkened and colorfully draped chamber Mesmer would utter hypnotic suggestions to willing female subjects as they touched magical iron rods embedded in large tubs of iron filings. These rods transmitted a special magnetic fluid, causing one to faint and fall into convulsions. Although many of Mesmer's subjects claimed spectacular cures, King Louis XVI was not impressed. The king appointed a learned panel that included commissioners from the Academy of Sciences, notably Lavoisier, Guillotin (responsible for the appliance used on Lavoisier), and the American Ambassador to France, Benjamin Franklin. Through a series of clever experiments, the commission concluded that Mesmer's treatment was nothing more than mere imagination requiring no special fluids. Mesmer was soundly discredited, and "Mesmerism" became synonymous with fraud and fakery, a connotation hypnosis carries even today. It is ironic that today the recognized clinical potential of hypnosis is often attributed to the healing power of imagination. As with meteorites, a phenomenon once discounted is now a legitimate topic of research (Gordon, 1967; Kroger, 1977).

So what if claims of the paranormal are true? The Parapsychological Association (www.parapsych.org) has listed a number of possibilities:

- The current scientific view of the universe, space, time, energy, and information may be incomplete.
- Human capacities for perception and memory have been underestimated.
- Beliefs about the mind and body may be wrong.
- Supernatural assumptions that form the foundation of traditional religion may be wrong.
- There may be a greater, nonmaterialistic spiritual world.
- There may exist a nonmaterial human soul.
- Mental and prayer-based healing may work.
- Paranormal abilities may enhance human decision-making.
- Paranormal abilities may assist in locating missing personas and variables.
- Paranormal historians and forecasters may obtain information by directly traveling to or viewing the past or future.
- Paranormal skills may assist psychotherapy and counseling.
- Paranormal market investors could help people make stock choices.
- Paranormal archeologists could locate hidden treasures.

If one paranormal claim were to be demonstrated beyond doubt, this could well be the most important discovery in the history of science. Such a discovery could easily justify the most massive international research effort ever, much larger than the program to create an atomic bomb or land a man on the moon. Obviously, prematurely embracing such a project would be very costly. There are other potential harms that are a bit more realistic.

REALITY CHECK What if all of the claims of the Parapsychological Association were true? Can you see any logical contradictions? How might the implications of one claim conflict with another?

The Dangers of Unexamined Paranormal Claims

One premise of this book is that extraordinary claims can have extraordinary consequences. Undeniable proof of a single superstition or single mysterious event that cannot possibly be rationally or scientifically explained could mean that the worldview of science has a defect. This in turn could require a new physics, a new astronomy, and perhaps even a new appreciation of the ultimate mysteries of the universe. Yes, if your rabbit's foot worked, *really worked*, everything could change.

Let me share with you an observation. In recent years we have witnessed an avalanche of books promoting paranormal claims. Books on psychics, astrology, the Bermuda Triangle, and faith healing often become bestsellers. This has spawned over a hundred books on critical and skeptical thinking, as well as a few very popular television productions (Penn and Teller's "Bullshit" for example). After viewing, reading, and studying this body of work, it is hard to miss one important difference. Paranormal works are generally cheerful and enthusiastic, even a bit giddy. However, more often than not, those who question these claims come across as very serious, often angry and upset. I have no reason to think that skeptics are by nature disagreeable folk (except for the one or two who don't appreciate my humor). So what's their problem?

For many years, I have been something of a recreational paranormalist. The paranormal has been a hobby, a treasure chest of curiosities. Then something happened. Perhaps I encountered too many self-righteous psychic frauds, read too many foolish horoscopes, or encountered too many casualties of misapplied alternative medicine. Perhaps it was the never-ending drama of medieval religious warfare and terrorism in the 21st century. Eventually it became abundantly clear that paranormal claims can do great harm. Perhaps my glittering treasure chest was a dark Pandora's box. I see four potential dangers.

Danger #1: Costs to Society

It is easy to find disaster stories of paranormal beliefs gone wild. Fanatical bombers kill thousands for bizarre supernatural beliefs and flying saucer cultists cheerfully commit suicide to prepare for promised alien rescue. However, murderous catastrophes in the name of the paranormal are nothing new. Perhaps the most spectacular examples in recent history are witchcraft trials and the Nazi holocaust, both frequently cited in scholarly discussions of the paranormal.

Witchcraft

In the early 11th century, the Catholic Church considered belief in witches to be heresy. Witches simply did not exist. Gradually, the Church decided they did exist but were powerless in the face of God. However, in the 15th century, doctrine took a deadly turn. In 1494 Pope Innocent VIII issued a bull pronouncing that witches cavorted with demons, destroyed crops, and aborted infants. He commissioned a study which yielded a text, the *Malleus Maleficarum* ("Witches' Hammer"). This document included stories of women having sex with demons, murdering babies, and stealing penises. The *Malleus* made it clear that Christians were obliged to hunt and destroy witches and gave judges and prosecutors torture-based tests. For the next three centuries it is estimated that over 200,000 witches were killed. With the dawn of the Enlightenment in the 18th century (about the time of Jefferson, Lavoisier, Franklin, and Guillotin), persecution of witchcraft subsided (Robbins, 1959). Scholars of the Enlightenment argued that there was no evidence for witches and that torture to elicit confessions was inhumane.

The most famous instance of witchcraft hysteria in America is the witchcraft trials in Salem Village, Massachusetts. In 1692 a group of young girls started behaving strangely, going into convulsions, screaming, and wandering about in trance states. Physicians could find nothing wrong, so city leaders concluded the girls were witches (today they would be rock stars). Village people began praying to chase the witches away. Eventually, the girls were forced to confess and 19 victims were tried and hanged. In addition, an 80-year-old man was crushed to death for refusing to be brought to trial.

One might discount witchcraft as a relic of unenlightened times. However, today roughly a quarter of Americans believe in witches and witchcraft. It wasn't until 2000 (on Halloween) that the state of Massachusetts officially

Figure 2.3 Salem witchcraft trials (hanging of a witch—Bridget Bishop)

exonerated the Salem witches, finally responding to centuries of tireless petitions of their desperate descendants (*New York Times*, November 2, 2001). Today Wicca is a recognized earth-based religion that uses (only for good) some of the same paranormal practices of early witches.

Nazi Holocaust

The degree to which paranormal thinking influenced Hitler and the Nazis in World War II is debated. Some of Hitler's top advisors consulted astrologers and used swinging pendulums over maps to locate enemy ships. The Nazis did hold a fanatical belief in a superior Aryan race, which was defiled when mixed with other inferior groups (Niewyk & Nicosia, 2000). The claimed superiority may be derived from a fallacious borderline paranormal belief that Aryans were toughened by their harsh life in Northern Europe. Nazi beliefs supported the Holocaust and the extermination of six million Jews and countless minorities, disabled people, gay men, Jehovah's witnesses, non-Jewish Poles, and political prisoners. Again, most of these groups were reviled because of fictitious and borderline paranormal claims of blood inferiority.

Danger #2: Misguided Complementary and Alternative Medicine

Complementary and alternative medicine (CAM) includes a wide range of treatments not generally accepted as part of traditional medicine or taught in traditional medical schools (see Appendix A). This includes a truly diverse assortment of approaches ranging from vitamin supplements, herbal treatments, and massage to yoga, acupuncture, tai chi, homeopathy, chiropractic, therapeutic touch, fasting, prayer, healing shrines, faith healing, and urine therapy. Saher and Lindeman (2005) sort these into approaches based on (a) paranormal claims, (b) inadequate or erroneous evidence, and (c) sound science. Up to 75% of the population believes alternative approaches are as effective as traditional approaches (Table 2.1) and over half the population uses alternative medicine (Barnes, Powell-Griner, McFann, & Nahin, 2004).

The medical establishment frequently warns of the dangers of alternative medicine (Angell & Kassirer, 1998; Fontanarosa & Lundberg, 1998) and questions their effectiveness (Bausell, 2007). Risks include the cost of ineffective interventions, safety (alternative approaches are generally unregulated), dangerous side effects, unexpected interactions with conventional treatments, and avoidance or delay in seeking traditional treatment.

An understanding of the paranormal helps us understand and evaluate many of the claims of alternative medicine. Indeed it may be the paranormal association that attracts many to such treatments (Saher & Lindeman, 2005). In chapters to come we will discover that often the same types of rationale given for voodoo spells, palm-reading, and magic rabbit's feet have also been used to justify acupuncture, tai chi, and homeopathy. Proponents of alternative medicine often make the same logical and scientific mistakes made by those who claim to have been abducted by flying saucers, or believe they are reincarnations of Cleopatra.

Unfortunately, alternative medicine is a catch-all category that lumps paranormal and borderline paranormal approaches with simple nutritional supplements, exercise, and relaxation. A patient may experience benefit from a relatively benign approach involving vitamins or exercise and conclude that alternative medicine has value. He or she may then feel comfortable exploring more risky borderline paranormal and paranormal alternative treatments. Knowing what's paranormal, and what's not, can help us navigate this medical minefield.

It is unethical and potentially dangerous for licensed health professionals to naively and uncritically accept paranormal treatments. Yet I have seen physicians and therapists embrace the mystery energies of qi, the curative power of prayer, and the healing magic of shamans—and pride themselves for their openness to alternative cultures, and sensitivity to non-Western wisdom. My wish is that all health professionals at least buy this book.

Danger #3: Superficial and Aggressive Religiosity

Organized religion plays an important part in people's lives. Throughout history paranormal claims have been sources of religious controversy. Jesus rejected temptations from Satan to turn stones into bread and fly off mountains to impress the masses. Buddha warned against meditation distractions of psychic powers. Mohammed condemned magic as deceptive evil contrary to God's will. Yet virtually every major world religion has devotees that are passionate advocates of the paranormal. Psychic powers are sometimes viewed as miraculous signs of God's intervention or of spiritual growth.

Bestselling polemics such as *The End of Faith: Religion, Terror, and the Future of Reason* (Harris, 2004) and *God is Not Great: How Religion Poisons Everything* (Hitchens, 2007) argue that supernatural paranormal beliefs breed fanaticism, war, and oppression. Typically they cite the Crusades, ethnic cleansing, and a variety of religious wars. People of faith counter with examples of genocide in atheistic countries such as the Soviet Union and Cambodia. Skeptics respond that in such atheistic countries, leaders had become like gods, convinced of their god-like significance and privilege. At the very least, Stephen Jay Gould (1999) has suggested we note "… the stunning historical paradox that organized religion has fostered, throughout western history, both the most unspeakable horrors and the most heartrending examples of human goodness." And Christopher Hitchens (2007) notes that throughout history atheists have been every bit as generous and self-sacrificing as believers.

Let me offer some hypotheses: (1) Paranormal beliefs become dangerous when embraced with dogmatic fervor, without honest and fearless questioning. (2) High-level paranormal beliefs are more risky than low-level beliefs. More generally, I propose that religions tend to get combative when they apply paranormal claims of the supernatural to earthly politics and social policy. God wants your group to own or conquer this plot of land. God wants you to kill infidels. God wants you to love others by showing off your religion. God wants you to wear a hat in church, as long as it is not red or made of cloth of mixed fibers. It helps us gain perspective to realize that many of these holy injunctions are justified by the same type of thinking used to justify astrology, flying saucer cults, witchcraft, and urine therapy.

I am not suggesting that religion is a fraud. Many books on critical thinking and the paranormal are critical of conventional religion. Let me make it clear that I respect religion. (Note that I have published practical manuals on prayer and meditative technique.) However, I believe a sincere and careful contemplation of God must acknowledge and genuinely accommodate the tools of critical thinking. A truly religious person can question honestly and question fearlessly. An adult spirituality need not fear the reality check.

> **REALITY CHECK**   Consider a religion you do not agree with. Do followers make any questionable paranormal claims? Now consider your favorite religion, perhaps the one in which you were born. Have any of its followers made similar claims? What's the difference?

Danger #4: Paranormal Cherry-Picking: The Paranormal Firewall and Subjective Relativism

Many feel comfortable having one paranormal belief, reassured by the thought that they reject others. You may believe in the power of acupuncture to modify qi, but reject astrology and ghosts. You may accept the biblical miracle of the virgin birth, but consider Noah's Ark to be a myth. However, such paranormal cherry-picking can have disastrous consequences. If you accept one extraordinary paranormal claim that fails to meet a few sensible reality checks, you are obligated to accept all paranormal claims that have equivalent support. If you believe in ghosts, you must also believe in astrology, reincarnation, TV psychic superstars, prophetic pets, communication with the dead, fortune-telling, mental spoon-bending, and a host of other treasures. All are based on equally substandard evidence. None have met the threshold of fact: truly scientific, public, and replicable observation.

Of course, you could assert that ghost-believers have some special exemption from the rules, whereas mere astrologers, reincarnationists, and the like must prove their claims. This might seem like crude hypocrisy, but it's been tried quite often throughout history.

The paranormal firewall

There are two somewhat more credible ways you might attempt to deal with your cherry-picking problem. First, you might erect constraints on your beliefs, a **paranormal firewall**. Such a firewall states: "Although I may have some beliefs that run counter to science, I will not abandon science when making important decisions." The constitutional separation of church and state is perhaps the most famous example of an institutionalized paranormal firewall. Your religion may require acceptance of a variety of paranormal claims. However, keep your religion separate from your vote. Many advocates of paranormal health treatments frequently admonish users to use these alternatives to "complement" traditional medicine. You may believe that drinking urine will cure bronchitis. However, you should still go to the physician when you have a serious cough.

Paranormal firewalls can work quite well. However, they ultimately postpone an uncomfortable moment of reckoning. Which is more important and real, your cherished paranormal belief or the firewall that keeps it in check? There is another way to hide from the paranormal cherry-picking problem.

Subjective relativism

Consider the following hypothetical blog between Amy (a nurse) and her friend Jim:

AMY: I believe that when I touch people I can cure their arthritis.

JIM: Why do you believe that?

AMY: I took a nursing course on therapeutic touch and got continuing education credit for it. I've tried touching arthritic patients and they report they've been cured.

JIM: Did you get any medical confirmation?

AMY: No. I believe what my patients say. They're honest people.

Amy is making a simple paranormal claim involving healing touch. It is typical of those who use this approach. Now the blog gets interesting:

JIM: My grandmother is a nurse trained in voodoo and she says she can cure arthritis by sticking pins in dolls owned by her arthritis patients.

AMY: Why does she believe that?

JIM: Because her patients report they've been cured, and they are honest people.

AMY: That's nonsense! Sticking pins in dolls can't cure arthritis.

JIM: I think you're being hypocritical. You accept the fantastic claims of your patients, but don't except the same claims of my grandmother's patients. You have a double standard.

Here we see that Amy has cherry-picked a paranormal claim. Therapeutic touch can cure arthritis, but pin-sticking cannot, even though both are equally plausible. Now examine how Amy escapes her problem:

AMY: You know, each of us creates our own reality. My reality is what I create. When I touch my patients, I think positive thoughts about them. They become positive and lose their negativity, their arthritis.

JIM: So I'm thinking that your belief is totally false. I'm thinking "positive thoughts will make people sick."

AMY: OK ...

JIM: That means you're having fun creating the universe using your thoughts. Then all of a sudden I destroy the entire universe by thinking the opposite thought.

AMY: Huh ...

JIM: You said your thoughts create the universe. So there's a dollar bill in your pocket because you're thinking it. And I'm thinking that there's no dollar bill in your pocket. It's in my pocket. I'm thinking I took it. This could get ugly.

Amy's solution to her cherry-picking dilemma is called **subjective relativism** (or postmodernism). Here all truth is relative and personal. Reality depends on what you believe, not how the world is. It's OK to cherry-pick your paranormal beliefs as long as you grant others the same right to selectively believe what they want. Prominent researchers of the paranormal often embrace this as a perspective that promises to uncover paranormal mysteries that have eluded science and logic (Irwin & Watt, 2007). However, such a fantasy begs for a reality check. First, subjective relativism has yet to produce a verified fact. More seriously, if we follow subjective relativism to its logical conclusion, we fall into an inevitable pit of absurdity. Consider these problems:

- Subjective relativism is *self-defeating*. If you can will something to be true, someone else can just as easily will it false. In our world it is logically impossible for something to exist and not exist at the same time.
- Subjective relativism is a logical contradiction and is *self-refuting*. The subjective relativist believes that in the real world there are no absolute truths because everything's subjective. If subjective relativism is a part of the real world, then it too is not absolutely true. If subjective relativism isn't always true, then there are indeed some absolute truths. But because everything is subjective, there aren't any absolute truths ...
- If you are a subjective relativist, congratulations—*subjective relativists are gods*. (Add your name to the supernatural entities listed in Chapter 1 (p. 17).) If you can make anything exist simply by thinking or wishing it, you have superhuman god-like powers. Even Superman can't do that.

- Subjective realism can be a *science stopper*. Let's imagine that you have decided that the natural worldview is relative, and that one must consider alternative worldviews not based on physical notions of matter and energy. So, what's the harm of being open-minded and accepting an alternative worldview? Imagine you believed that studying the livers of butchered pigs enables you to tell the future (some cultures once believed this). When it comes to liver-based fortune-telling, your alternative worldview may prohibit you from ever discovering for sure if it doesn't work. Every time a liver forecast fails, your alternative worldview can explain it away (evil spirits got in the way, the universal mystery energy blocked the forecast, you were fated to get a defective liver).

There is a second way subjective relativism can be a science stopper. Consider this statement: "It works for everyone in different ways." At first this might seem like a perfectly reasonable claim. However, on close examination it comes close to stating that any effect, even opposite effects or no effect, is evidence of efficacy. If everything is to be considered positive evidence, then there is no way of proving a claim wrong. You can't lose with such pragmatic relativism. See if you can figure out how these examples illustrate this problem:

Does herbal tea make you healthy? Some people may feel more energized. Others may have a more restful sleep. Some may not experience an effect for years. And for others the tea may sustain healthy things that are going on in your body. For each person the effect may be different.

Does it matter just where an acupuncturist inserts acupuncture needles? Very much so. Needles must be inserted in precise energy points in the body. However, different practitioners of acupuncture have different systems for identifying where these energy points are. So different experts may end up inserting needles in completely different parts of the body, even though they are trying to evoke the same cure. Acupuncture is a very individualized system, one that depends very much on the person applying it.

Consider the controversy

An argument similar to subjective relativism takes no stand concerning the validity of conflicting claims, but suggests that in the spirit of open-mindedness we consider them all. We will encounter such quasi-relativist thinking in our discussion of the debate between creationism and evolution (Chapter 15) and retroactive healing prayer (Chapter 14). Darwin's theory of evolution is taught in biology classes. Should we also teach the six-day biblical creation myth as theory? What about creation "theories" offered in other cultures, for example, the ancient Romans, Native Americans, Northern Europeans, and so on? Similarly, it might seem reasonable to study the claims that a prayer group can secretly cure strangers at a distance. If so, then why not the claims of certain meditation groups that they can influence the stock market through chants, shaman priests can cure by entering special states of mind, or that my nephew can cure by drawing pictures of those who are suffering? Again, a critical thinker has to evaluate when to draw the line.

But there are more things in heaven and earth …

A subjective relativist might complain that the questions we present reveal narrow-mindedness. After all, surely there are *realities* science cannot detect. Just because something can't be measured by science doesn't mean it's not *true*. Science doesn't have all the *answers*.

Of course, there are many "realities," "truths," and "answers" beyond the domain of science. Among these are subjective states such as emotions and urges; judgments of beauty and morality; and symbolic expressions of metaphor and myth. Anyone can claim that their feelings of love, opinions concerning what is beautiful or righteous, or favorite fairy tale are "real," "true," or some sort of "answer."[1] Evaluating such claims simply isn't the job of science. Indeed such utterances may well involve a degree of subjective relativism. Beauty is in the eye of the beholder (Shakespeare, 1598).

However, here is where such questions get into trouble. Words such as "reality," "truth," and "answers" have a certain ambiguity in that they can also refer to objective facts as determined through the scientific method. An "objective fact" is by definition based on reliable and public observation. The only way to show that something is publicly and reliably observable is to *subject it to public and reliable observation*, that is, scientific inquiry.[2]

So when someone says, "Paranormal Phenomenon X (God, qi, the wisdom of the stars, a ghostly presence, the eternal now, the magic energy from crystals, fate, universal mind, quantum interconnectedness, etc.) is real, true, the answer" and tries to shut down any discussion by asserting "there is more to the world than science," it is not impolite to ask for clarification:

> Is this Paranormal Phenomenon X some sort of inner feeling or urge, like love or feeling "high"? Is it a metaphor or story? Perhaps it's an aesthetic or moral "reality, truth, or answer"? If so, you're right and science has nothing to say, but my perspective is just as valid as yours. But if you are claiming that Paranormal Phenomenon X is objective fact, then by definition you are

claiming that it is scientifically demonstrated. Objective facts are scientific facts. So we are entitled to a civilized discussion of the evidence.

If an advocate friend persists by asserting that Phenomenon X is not something that can be subjected to scientific scrutiny, yet is not a subjective emotional state or urge, metaphor or fairy tale, or something of beauty or a moral principle, you can rightly wonder if your friend knows what he or she is talking about.[3]

REALITY CHECK See if you can find a website that promotes a health treatment that appears to have a paranormal basis. Can you find any examples of subjective relativism?

The Risk of Paranormal Passion and the Critical Thinker's Toolkit

Paranormal claims are potentially risky because of their potential to thrill, excite, and prompt extraordinary missionary enthusiasm. They have the power to evoke the paranormal passion of the true believer. Try this simple thought experiment. Imagine an aging relative who has difficulty writing legibly. She sends you a letter which, unfortunately, is indecipherable. After an hour of study you suddenly "get it" and realize you can read her words. You discover an unexpected ability to read sloppy handwriting.

Now imagine a slightly different scenario. You close your eyes and press the unopened letter against your head. Suddenly you realize you can read your relative's thoughts, without even looking at the letter. You discover an unexpected ability to read minds. Which discovery, the ability to read sloppy handwriting or the ability to read minds, is more likely to prompt you to quit your job and spend time and money exploring your fantastic new-found potential?

Strong emotion and motivation can prompt us to abandon common sense and good everyday thinking. People are "blinded by love" and commit "crimes of passion." If you have been blessed with a paranormal experience, this extraordinary event would likely stir your feelings—and possibly compromise your capacity for clear, cool-headed thinking. Freed from caution, you may be more likely to erroneously discover more evidence of the paranormal, further fueling your enthusiasm. You may join a group of believers. Perhaps you write a book. Maybe appear on Oprah.

Let me introduce you to a Critical Thinker's Toolkit. When we uncritically accept paranormal claims we run the risk of carelessly ignoring some basic tools of critical thinking and becoming victims of confusion, trickery, and error. To counter this we must become **detectives** and engage in **reality checking**.[4] This involves asking two types of questions: *Why believe this? Are there other explanations?*

Why believe a paranormal claim? Often when we claim something is true we base our claims on three types of support:

- reports from various sources;
- logic; and
- observations (scientific tests and theories).

Reality checking involves evaluating the validity of such support.

In our detective work, we may explore blind alleys. Source reports may be the result of trickery. Logical arguments may be based on distorted evidence. Observations, tests, and theories may be flawed and compromised by error. For these reasons, when performing a reality check on an extraordinary claim, we need to be alert to sources of error and consider five **fundamental alternative explanations**:

- oddities in nature and the world of statistics;
- perceptual error or trickery;
- memory error;
- the placebo effect;
- sensory anomalies and hallucinations.

Together our reality-checking detective tools and questions constitute a broader view of the **scientific method**. Misused, they become **pseudoscience**. A scientist is a smart detective. A pseudoscientist is a bumbling detective, seduced by the flashy jewelry and intoxicating perfume of false leads. Good science appropriately uses sources, logic, and observation (texts and theory) and systematically considers alternative explanations. *Pseudoscience is the claimed application of the scientific method in a way that misuses sources, logic, and observation (texts and theory) and fails to systematically consider alternative explanations.*

To summarize, our Critical Thinker's Toolkit prompts us to ask eight reality-checking questions. Together they form The Critical Thinker's Toolkit (or "Pseudoscience Detection Kit").

Eight Reality Checks: The Critical Thinker's Toolkit

Support for a Claim

1. Are the *sources* credible? We learn about the world by listening to the reports of others. Experts and authorities describe and explain what we might not discover on our own. We run into trouble when our sources are flawed. (Example: Based on hearsay accounts, the now defunct tabloid newspaper, the World, claimed that Osama Bin Laden and Saddam Hussein were married, and had a child—a space alien.)

2. Is the *logic* valid and sound? We use logic to figure out what is true or false, possible or impossible. It is easy to make logical errors and make false conclusions about the world. (Rose petals are pink, smooth, and soft. When my skin is healthy, it is also pink, smooth, and soft. Similars cure similars. Therefore, I should use skin lotion made out of rose petals.)

3. Are claims based on *observation* (scientific tests, and theories)? Science involves making observations, carefully setting up experiments to test hypotheses, and integrating observations and test results into theories. Pseudoscience pretends to be scientific, but actually misapplies scientific techniques. (Your friend hypothesizes that eating chocolate will cause you to get rich. So you try it out and conduct an experiment. You eat five chocolate bars and, yes, find a lucky penny. Hypothesis confirmed? Any sane person can think of alternative explanations for this terrible pseudoscientific experiment.)

Fundamental alternative explanations

4. Are we misinterpreting *oddities of nature and the world of numbers*? Most people don't understand statistics, and as a result have mistaken ideas about what is probable and what is unlikely. (One day, after playing the lottery many hundreds of times, you finally win a dollar. You figure this is your lucky day and purchase many more lottery tickets. Was this a real "string of luck," or simply chance?)

5. Is there a potential for *perceptual error* or *trickery*? Is what you see for real, or are you noticing just what you want (or someone else wants you) to notice? (One night your friends drag you out of your bedroom for a flying saucer citing. The night is a little cloudy and city lights a bit distracting. In great excitement, one friend points to a fuzzy light shining in the sky. Everyone shouts "There it is, a flying saucer!" And you realize that if you look at it in just the right way, the light looks something like a saucer. Maybe they're right.)

6. Is there a potential for *memory error*? The brain's perceptual and memory processes can automatically distort and make things up. (Last month you watched a television documentary on the White House. This week you are taking a vacation in Washington, DC and visit the White House. Forgetting the documentary, you comment on how "familiar" things seem, almost as if you have been there before.)

7. Might the *placebo effect* be at work? A placebo is a worthless dummy treatment, the proverbial "sugar pill." The placebo effect can evoke genuine psychological and physiological changes through nothing more than suggestion. (You suffer from a headache, and a friend plays a CD containing "music vibrations" specially tuned to brain frequencies in order to cure headaches. You listen to the CD and enjoy its peaceful music, accompanied by soothing reassurances from a speaker. Your headache goes away. Was it the vibrations? Perhaps the music just made you happy?)

8. Are we misinterpreting *sensory anomalies or hallucinations*? The human brain and nervous system are quite capable of conjuring up false percepts that appear convincingly real. (You are in bed in a twilight state slipping between sleep and wakefulness. Strangely, you notice your pet poodle Rover at the end of your bed. You stare in wonder, because Rover passed away years ago. You stare for several long minutes, and then go back to sleep concluding that you had been dreaming.)

Is Science Bad?

Unfortunately, calling something "science" can cause problems. Believers in the paranormal and supernatural often display hostility toward science, accusing scientific thinkers of narrow-mindedness and rigidity. Christian creationists warn against the "godless religion" of science. Non-Christian advocates of complementary and alternative medicine speak of deep mystical energies that science cannot detect. Movies and television often portray scientists as sexless geeks wearing white lab coats, isolated from the real world in windowless laboratories. Scientists are eccentric, if not outright mad.

It is easy to test the depth of this misperception of science. The next time you are with a group of friends, say at a party, wait for someone to utter an extraordinary paranormal claim. (You can "stir the pot" by mentioning the latest TV or movie hit on ghosts, miracles, flying saucers, or psychic detectives.) A friend comes up with this:

"Last week I was thinking about you, and you called! I think I can see into the future! I'm psychic! I'm going to be famous!"

Imagine what would happen if you replied:

> "Let's be scientific and systematically apply the scientific method to your extraordinary claim. How many times do you think about your friends? Probably many times. Psychologists would say that it is highly likely you forgot most of the times. When I call, you are more likely to remember that you just thought about me. It's just chance and selective recall."

I think your friend would be rather annoyed, and not inclined to pursue this line of discussion. Now imagine you made the same observation without using the "S word" (or "P word").

> "Get a grip, friend! Let's do a reality check. You use your phone a lot. Eventually you are bound to think of me just before I call. That's simply an everyday coincidence."

As biologist Thomas H. Huxley, perhaps the most important defender of Darwin's theory of evolution, remarked (1880): "Science is simply common sense at its best—that is, rigidly accurate in observation, and merciless in fallacy in logic." More recently, Albert Einstein said pretty much the same thing: "The whole of science is nothing more than a refinement of everyday thinking" (Einstein, 1936; Paydarfar & Schwartz, 2001).

This is a book on good common sense, everyday thinking at its best. When confronting claims of the paranormal, we will perform two types of reality check and ask two types of question. First, is the claim based on sound methods for seeking and evaluating support? Second, are there alternative explanations? When you do this well, you are a scientist. When you claim to do it well, but are in fact misapplying reality checks, you are not a scientist.

The Critical Thinker's Pocket Survival Kit

This book covers a lot of material and our journey will take time. Lest you get lost in the jungle, let me share with you two simple tools you can use right away for protection against most infectious and dangerous forms of trickery. This is your **Critical Thinker's Pocket Survival Kit**. The kit consists of two fundamental questions to ask about an extraordinary claim.

1. Extraordinary Claims Require Extraordinary Evidence

Astronomer and skeptic Carl Sagan popularized this rule (often called "Sagan's Balance.") It can be extremely useful because it is sensible and

Figure 2.4 Carl Sagan

reflects many of the rules that make civilized life possible. For example, it would be wasteful and foolish for courts to spend as much time and effort investigating parking violations as murders. An accusation of murder is an extraordinary claim, a parking violation is not.

2.   Consider Alternative Explanations. Then Apply "Occam's Razor" and *Reductio Ad Absurdum*

Try to think of possible alternative explanations for a claimed paranormal phenomenon. If you don't have time to use the entire Critical Thinker's Toolkit to test them out, simply applying Occam's razor and *reductio ad absurdum* can serve you well.

William of Occam was a 14th century English logician and Franciscan friar who, according to lore, is said to have proposed that an explanation should assume as little as possible (actually there is little evidence that Occam actually invented the razor bearing his name; however, it's a great story). Superfluous assumptions should be discarded or "shaved off" (as with a razor) because they add nothing. Put differently, avoid using one unexplained/unobserved phenomenon to explain another unexplained phenomenon.

Figure 2.5 William of Occam. Fourteenth century portrait located in the cloisters of the Monastery of St Francis of Assisi, Krakow, Poland

Imagine a church group performs a rain dance, and the next day it rains. One explanation might be that the Rain Gods were pleased by the dance performed in their honor, and granted rain as a gift. Another explanation might be that the rain was a random event, perhaps expected because of the changing seasons. Which is simpler? Count the assumptions. This can be a little tricky. After all, it might seem simple to say the Rain Gods did it. However, this claim makes many questionable assumptions. Do supernatural entities exist? How do we know Rain Gods exist? Are they invisible? Why don't they make their presence known? How do we know this is true? Do the Rain Gods create rain out of thin air, or do they manipulate global weather patterns to eventually create rain over your dry field? What if all the churches prayed for rain at the same time, how could it possibly rain everywhere at once? Who gets the rain and who doesn't? How do we know? We could go on and on for centuries, or simply apply Occam's razor, conclude that the rain was a random weather event, and go on with living.

> ✓ **REALITY CHECK** Noted paranormal researcher Gary Schwartz (2003) claims that scientific experiments have shown that psychic mediums can accurately retrieve messages from the dead. He argues that there are two interpretations: (a) there's an afterlife, or (b) mediums use trickery, are good guessers, or have been studied in poorly designed experiments. Professor Schwartz reasons that explanation (a) is simpler, so, applying Occam's razor, we should conclude there's an afterlife. Discuss.

One powerful way to supplement Occam's razor is to assume, for the sake of argument, that a claimed extraordinary explanation is true. Then think of all of the inevitable implications and consequences of this claim. If you eventually uncover an impossible implication or consequence, then the claim itself is questionable. This technique of logic is sometimes called *reductio ad absurdum* (Latin for "reduction to the absurd").

Let's assume that dancing a rain dance pleases the Rain Gods and causes it to rain. Imagine this is absolute, verified fact. Then what? What kind of predicament are we in? Well, we should create a committee to list the specific types of dance that most please the Rain Gods. Maybe they prefer belly-dancers or strippers. Perhaps classical ballet. And we should attempt to determine the level of dancing skill that is required. Perhaps we could have novices do rain dances on some weeks, and experts on other weeks, and see when it rains most. Surely rain dancing could be used to modify the environment. We need to determine where we want lakes, and send lots of dancers there (so it will constantly rain and create a lake). When it doesn't rain after a dance (which surely will happen sometime), we need some clue as to what we did wrong. To find answers, we need to establish special Rain God questioning days in which we ask the God a question ("If we are virtuous, please make it rain after the dance."). You can see where this is going. If applying *reductio ad absurdum* opens a ridiculous chain (indeed, another Pandora's box) of absurdities, then perhaps your claim needs to be reconsidered.

If you don't have time to do a full *reductio ad absurdum*, try this short version. Simply replace complicated and confusing jargon with straight talk. I call this *reductio ad veritas* (reduce an argument to its core absurd truth). To illustrate, the Parapsychological Association (www.parapsych.org) has offered this insight concerning one implication if psychics could read minds and move objects:

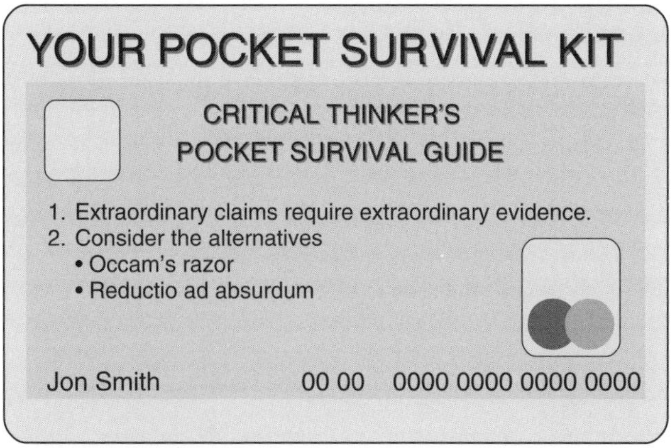

YOUR POCKET SURVIVAL KIT

CRITICAL THINKER'S
POCKET SURVIVAL GUIDE

1. Extraordinary claims require extraordinary evidence.
2. Consider the alternatives
   • Occam's razor
   • Reductio ad absurdum

Jon Smith   00 00   0000 0000 0000 0000

Figure 2.6   Your Pocket Survival Kit

[M]odern machines based upon sensitive electronic circuits, such as copiers and computers, may at times directly interact with human intention, and as a result, inexplicably fail at inopportune times. Of course, the converse may also be true. That is, the possibility exists to repair, or to control sensitive machines solely by mental means. Such technologies would significantly benefit handicapped persons.

Translation?

Copier isn't working? Maybe it's haunted by a ghost. Better call a ghostbuster. If we find a ghost, perhaps we could use it to propel wheelchairs.

Part II

The Critical Thinker's Toolkit

Evaluate Support for a Claim

3

Reality Check

Are the Sources Credible?

Perhaps the easiest way to support a claim is to accept what others report. In most cases this involves trusting their logic and testing and evaluation of hypotheses and theories, or perhaps their sources. A good source can be a powerful scientific tool. A misused source can contribute to pseudoscience. In this chapter we will examine some reality-checking precautions one needs to take when considering support from sources.

Before we start our journey, we need to take a brief detour into the stars. It is fitting that we begin our Critical Thinker's Toolkit with the world's oldest and most popular paranormal belief system, astrology. Astrology will provide our first opportunity to practice critical thinking skills, and provide a model for evaluating many additional paranormal claims in Part III. More important, astrology gives us a dramatic opportunity to contrast the awe and wonder of scientific discovery with that of dogma and superstition.

Astrology

Astrology is an ancient form of divination, a way of acquiring information, seeing into the future or seeking interpretation. It is based on the idea that the positions and movements of the stars, planets, sun, and moon are associated with personal, political, and even geological events on earth.

History of Astrology

Let's look at some history first. Astrology can be traced to the Babylonians more than 4,000 years ago. At first they made use of omens such as dreams, disemboweled animals, and heavenly bodies. Many people also worshiped the sun, and to a lesser extent the moon. Eventually nontheistic astrology won out over other omens and the sky gods, perhaps because of the obvious links between seasonal warmth and the positions of the sun and moon (Culver & Ianna,

1984; Hoskin, 2003; Tester, 1989). Although the Babylonians developed many astrological concepts, at the time of Alexander the Great the Greek geographer, mathematician, and astronomer Ptolemy was responsible for creating the system familiar today. Ptolemy viewed the universe as enormous spheres within spheres, an erroneous notion that persisted for centuries.

In Europe astrology grew in popularity during the renaissance, because of interest in science and astronomy. In the 16th and 17th centuries Christian theologians and popes condemned astrology as challenging free will and the prevailing views of an all-powerful God. Even the founders of modern astronomy, Copernicus, Tycho Brahe, and Galileo, held astrology in high esteem (van Gent, 2004).

The Zodiac

Look into the sky any night. All the visible stars arrange into 88 recognized constellations (some, of course, are hidden on the other side of the Earth). Imagine these are on a huge glass bubble that surrounds the earth. Now think of a window or belt arching overhead from horizon to horizon. Some constellations reside in this window, while others are outside. The window is relatively narrow at 16 degrees wide (the entire bubble is 360 degrees; there are 360 degrees in a circle). Its precise placement is called the "ecliptic," the limited band of sky where eclipses occur.

This horizon-to-horizon window is called the zodiac and is divided into 12 window panes called *houses* or *signs*, each defined by one of 12 (out of a possible 88) constellations of stars it contains. Constellations are named for the animals or people they seemed to resemble. In fact, the word "zodiac" means "circle of animals" and is based on the same root as the word "zoo"; both the zodiac and zoos are filled with animals.

Your *sun* or *natal sign* or *natal astrology* (the type used in newspaper horoscopes) is the house or window pane that the sun is in at the moment of your birth. If the sun is near the constellation of stars that define the house of Sagittarius ("The Archer"), you would be called a Sagittarius. Almost of equal importance is the *ascendant* or *rising sign*. This is the zodiac house rising on the Eastern horizon at the moment you are born. So if the constellation of stars that defines Sagittarius appears on the Eastern horizon, your rising sign is Sagittarius.

Each sign (and its sun sign date) is associated with a different set of attributes, some of which are described below:

Aries (The Ram; March 21–April 19): Free, assertive, impulsive ...
Taurus (The Bull; April 20–May 20): Resourceful, patient, affectionate, stubborn ...

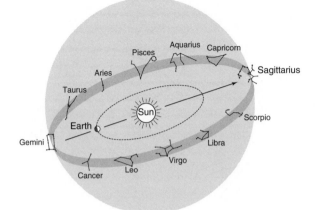

Figure 3.1   The zodiac

Gemini (The Twins; May 21–June 20): Logical, lively, sociable …

Cancer (The Crab; June 21–July 22): Protective, clinging, nurturing, crabby …

Leo (The Lion; July 23–August 22): Generous, proud, noble …

Virgo (The Virgin; August 23–September 22): Practical, modest, fussy, lovable …

Libra (The Scales; September 23–October 22): Cooperative, fair, charming …

Scorpio (The Scorpion; October 23–November 21): Passionate, secretive, sadistic …

Sagittarius (The Archer; November 22–December 21): Free, careless, optimistic …

Capricorn (The Sea-Goat; December 22–January 19): Cautious, rigid, competent …

Aquarius (The Water-carrier; January 20–February 18): Democratic, humanitarian, objective …

Pisces (The Fishes; February 19–March 20): Imaginative, spiritual, lazy …

These attributes were not obtained through any sort of scientific observation but simply reflect the shapes ancient people thought they saw in various patterns of stars, and popular associations to these shapes. So the house of Sagittarius is defined by a set of stars thought to look like a centaur, a half-human half-horse creature wielding a bow and arrow. The centaur was an untamed beast characterized as "free, careless, and optimistic." If you were born under Sagittarius you may also possess these attributes.

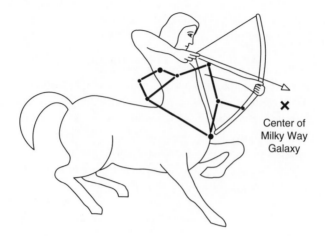

Center of
Milky Way
Galaxy

Figure 3.2   Sagittarius (the centaur)

Astronomy vs. Astrology

Now for a reality check. First, the houses of the zodiac are not of equal size. It takes the sun 7 days to pass through Scorpio and 44 days for Virgo. In addition, there are not 12, but 13 constellations in the zodiac. Ophiucus (the "serpent bearer") has been left out. Also, Earth slowly wobbles over thousands of years. This process, called precession, means that the apparent positions of the sun and constellations on January 1, 2007 were not the same as their positions on January 1, 2,000 years ago. If you are an Aries, you should read the Pisces horoscope. When astrology was developed 2,000 years ago, the sun was in the house of Pisces, not Aries, when you were born.[1] Newspaper horoscopes routinely ignore or use strange ad hoc explanations to discount this odd fact.

But there is a bigger problem. The science of astronomy has made discoveries about our universe, some involving the same constellations considered by astrologers. I am particularly fond of one finding because it teaches us how the awe and wonder of science can outshine the fantasized mysteries of the paranormal. Indeed, for those so inclined, there may be something of a spiritual message in all of this. But back to our story.

For thousands of years astrologers have written about the constellation Sagittarius. Unknown to astrologers, most of the 20 stars of Sagittarius aren't stars at all, but huge clusters of stars. However, one "star," *Sagittarius* *A*[*2] (pronounced "A-Star"), is a mysterious invisible object that occupies a strangely unique position – the exact center of our galaxy. Indeed, the entire Milky Way is an enormous disk that rotates round Sagittarius A*.

In 1999 astronomers made an astonishing discovery (Melia, 2007). Sagittarius A* is a supermassive black hole more than four million times more massive than our sun. It may well be the closest black hole to earth. A black hole is one of the most mysterious objects in the universe, with gravity so massive that not even light can escape. Although black holes can be as small as an atom, or huge like Sagittarius A*, generally they are of "stellar mass," about 10–20 miles in diameter, and having the mass of at least 3.8 suns. Sagittarius A* is not alone. Incredibly, it may well be surrounded by a gigantic swarm of hundreds of thousands of stellar-mass black holes (Irion, 2008).

There is another story of Sagittarius A.* This enormous black hole and its companions may have been pivotal to the very formation of our galaxy and may well contribute to the complete destruction of humankind, the sun, the solar system, and neighboring stars (when it gobbles up the neighboring Andromeda galaxy in a few billion years). Indeed this process has begun and the Milky Way, with the help of Sagittarius A*, has already destroyed several galaxies.

There are important lessons in these contrasting stories from science and astrology. Astrologers had no idea of the significance of the little spot of light tagged as Sagittarius. Sagittarian horoscopes have provided no insight concerning our long-term cosmic fate. And the claims of astrology have remained fossilized for thousands of years. In contrast, astronomy has revealed a breathtaking trove of discovery in less than a single decade. The story science reveals is truly one of immense and searing beauty, far more awesome than some fairy tale of a horse with a human head.

In spite of such apparent fatal problems, astrology still has an impact. Wars have been influenced by astrological forecasts. Presidents and popes have consulted astrologers. Horoscopes remain very popular and appear in nearly every newspaper. Hundreds of astrologers belong to serious international organizations and have their own serious, professional journals.

Questionable Sources

Is astrology true? In Chapters 4 and 5 we consider the logical and scientific support. However, many believe in astrology because of various sources.

Ancient Wisdom

Astrology is true because it is old, over 4,000 years old. It has survived the "test of time" and must be valid. The fact that it has not changed is additional evidence that the early creators got it right.

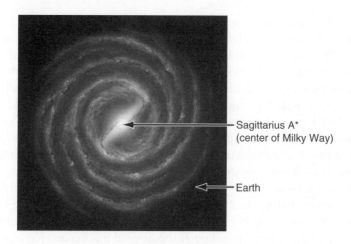

Sagittarius A*
(center of Milky Way)

Earth

Figure 3.3   Sagittarius A* in the Milky Way: artist's rendering shows a view of Milky Way Galaxy and its central bar as it might appear if viewed from above

Figure 3.4   Sagittarius A* supermassive black hole

Just because an idea is very old doesn't mean it's true. Some old ideas are downright silly. After all, we no longer talk to rocks or consult volcanoes for political advice. Some erroneously liken survival of an idea over time as a sort of informal "scientific test." Presumably over the millennia people have tested astrological predictions and found them valid, otherwise they would abandon astrology. However, I doubt non-Babylonian systems such as Mayan astrology failed to gain worldwide acceptance because people over time found them less effective. As we will see throughout this text, there are many ways in which vast numbers of people can be fooled, even for millennia. And the survival of a belief system over history often has to do with the charisma of its proponents, and how well they wage war. If you accept astrology as valid because it is ancient, then you also have to accept the wisdom of witchcraft, the sadistic injunctions of the Old Testament, and voodoo, because all are equally ancient. And you would have to suspect more recent human efforts such as the writings of Shakespeare, Lincoln, and Einstein.

The world overflows with a special type of ancient wisdom, venerable inspirational texts rich with poetry and moral instruction. Such works have guided humankind for millennia and are often embraced without careful thought. Before accepting such sources wholesale, it is wise to ask a few questions:

- Are insights ambiguous and subject to various and contradictory interpretations?
- Do contradictory passages permit one to "cherry-pick" those that fit one's preexisting biases?
- Are there passages that make sense even in light of current knowledge?

Testimonials and Anecdotal Evidence

If you ask enough friends, eventually you will find one who can testify to the accuracy of horoscopes. Such testimonials are often called anecdotal evidence. Testimonials and anecdotal evidence can be persuasive, especially if they are from credible and honest sources you know personally.

Even intelligent and honest people can be fooled. One case proves nothing. For every glowing testimonial, there may be thousands, even millions, of disappointed users (we may never know how many, given they probably don't speak out).

Carroll (2005) has offered a succinct evaluation of anecdotal and testimonial evidence:

Anecdotes are unreliable for various reasons. Stories are prone to contamination by beliefs, later experiences, feedback, selective attention to details, and so on. Most stories get distorted in the telling and the retelling. Events get exaggerated. Time sequences get confused. Details get muddled. Memories are imperfect and selective; they are often filled in after the fact. People misinterpret their experiences. Experiences are conditioned by biases, memories, and beliefs, so people's perceptions might not be accurate. Most people aren't expecting to be deceived, so they may not be aware of deceptions that others might engage in. Some people make up stories. Some stories are delusions. Sometimes events are inappropriately deemed psychic simply because they seem improbable when they might not be that improbable after all. In short, anecdotes are inherently problematic and are usually impossible to test for accuracy.

Popularity (and Common Use)

Astrology is very popular around the world. A Google search reveals over 30 million hits for astrology. Thirty million hits can't be wrong.

Again, the popularity of an idea doesn't mean it's true. Women used to be (and often still are) viewed as property. Various racial groups were once viewed as subhuman. Amazon.com lists twice as many books for astrology (70,000) as for the Ten Commandments (35,000). The number of books on astrology, the Old Testament, and the New Testament are about equal (70,000–90,000).

Mass Media and the Internet

Some of the best newspapers and magazines in the world have published positive articles on astrology. Of the 30 million internet hits, some are pretty impressive.

Again, popularity isn't proof. Mass media and internet sources may or may not reflect authentic expert opinion. When considering articles and websites, use the criteria we considered for evaluating the qualifications of an expert. Note that the standards for getting something in the mass media are lower than for professional publication. And anyone can post any claim on the internet. Among the worst sources are slickly produced paranormal "documentaries" on cable networks that feature documentaries. Having subjected myself to over 100 shows on ghosts, flying saucers, psychic detectives, miracles, angels, and communicating with the dead, I must report that for every 10 unacceptable programs you may find 1 of quality. Programs on the paranormal are notorious for editing out disconfirming evidence, interviewing questionable and fraudulent sources, and engaging in outright deception. Remember that such programs are designed to be entertainment.

The Question of Authority

Some of the most famous scientists in the world, indeed, even the founders of science, believed in astrology. If it was good enough for Copernicus, Tycho Brahe, Galileo, it's good enough for me.

Just because someone is an expert in one field doesn't mean they are an expert in another. You wouldn't go to a "doctor" for cancer treatment if this "doctor" has a doctorate in insect physiology. Famous actors may know how to act, but they aren't necessarily experts in health and living. Just because a politician or religious leader is popular doesn't mean he or she is all-knowing. Everyone is ignorant about something.

When evaluating whether someone is an expert it is useful to consider if they:

- have education and training from a relevant and up-to-date program or school;
- are experienced and have accomplishments in their area of claimed expertise;
- are current (ancient experts may no longer be relevant);
- are respected among peers, other experts in their area.

Generally, when an authentic expert rejects a claim, or several experts disagree, there is good reason for us to doubt the claim.

In my experience the mainstream scientific community is often suspicious of claimed experts who:

- make exaggerated and unqualified claims and, for example, conclude that paranormal phenomena are conclusively and unambiguously supported by research (look for unqualified superlatives, like "breakthrough," "revolutionary," "proven," or "pioneering");
- have a record of gullibility, for example, accepting as credible demonstrations of the paranormal clearly shown to be fraudulent or in error;
- fail to differentiate well-designed studies from those compromised by poor design, error, and the possibility of fraud;
- have a record of failing to report breaches in good design; and
- resort to ad hominem arguments (Chapter 4) when rejecting sincere criticisms of skeptics (accusing critics of being mean-spirited, narrow-minded, dogmatic, and the like). It is misleading to divide paranormal researchers into two groups, dogmatic believers and dogmatic disbelievers. There are many who are inclined to believe or not believe who are nonetheless willing to take an honest look at the evidence. Furthermore, I see absolutely no reason to question the openness, objectivity, or honesty of any of the skeptical resources listed on page 62.

Finally, when considering the miraculous claim of a paranormal expert, it is useful to apply **Hume's Maxim**. David Hume was an 18th century Scottish philosopher famous for his book, *An Enquiry Concerning Human Under-standing*. He argued: "That no testimony is sufficient to establish a miracle, unless the testimony be of such a kind, that its falsehood would be more miraculous than the fact which it endeavours to establish" (Hume, 1758/1958, p. 491). In other words, which is more miraculous? (1) That someone making a paranormal claim is deceiving or deceived, or (2) the claimed paranormal event actually happened. After making up your mind, reject the testimony of the greater miracle.

> **REALITY CHECK**   Which of the eight levels of the Continuum Mysteriosum is more likely to rely on authority as support for para-normal claims? Why?

When Experts Get It Wrong

Imagine you have identified sources that meet the criteria we have just outlined. Can we put aside our questioning and accept their claims? Unfortunately not. One problem is simple sloppiness. Those responsible for carefully evaluating studies for publication note that researchers often simply do not report flaws and mistakes in their work. Indeed, an entire project may have been conducted by relatively novice assistants. Even though the primary researcher ends up publishing a study, he or she may be completely unaware of unreported problems (Bausell, 2007).

Most obvious is the problem of fraud. We have no reason to believe that paranormal researchers are less honest than other researchers. However, there are scientists in all professions who sometimes lie and make up data (Broad & Wade, 1983; Kohn, 1988). Generally when many studies are involved, a single fraudulent study may not make that much difference. However, in paranormal research support for an extraordinary claim may be based on a handful of studies, and a single fraudulent study can have considerable impact. Furthermore, science is not equipped to police fraud. It is easy to get away with it. Our best protection is independent replication of research.

Even when outright fraud is not involved, bias can influence and distort what gets published. In drug studies, research supported by pharmaceutical companies reports more positive results than research supported by public funds. Ninety-eight percent of Chinese studies on Chinese acupuncture report positive results compared with 53–60% of studies conducted in the

United States, the United Kingdom, and Scandinavia. Journals with lax publication standards are more likely to publish positive results than more rigorous journals (Bausell, 2007).

The very publication process has built-in sources of bias that favor positive results (Bausell, 2007). Let's walk through the steps involved in getting a study published. First a scientist, usually employed by a university or medical establishment, conducts a study. He or she may have several under way. Grant funding, promotion, prestige, and even tenure may ride on publishing positive results. Given such incentives a researcher could easily "put off until later" completing and writing up studies that seem to be producing negative results. (In other words, these studies die from neglect and end up in the recycle bin.)

Once a study is submitted for publication, a journal has incentive to publish positive results. The editors may well have honorable intentions. Perhaps they want to encourage research in an unexplored area. Perhaps they want to help others recognize a positive result as having potential benefit for those in distress. Maybe they want to sell more copies of their journal, and unexpected positive results sell, especially when the paranormal is involved. Publication bias has been demonstrated in research. In one study (Atkinson, Furlong, & Wampold, 1982), researchers sent two versions of the same study to journal reviewers. One version reported positive results while the other reported negative results. The reviewers recommended publication for the version with positive results.

An Invitation to Question

We could not function without taking the word of others we respect. We trust our drinking water is not poison, our vehicles will not collapse into piles of nuts and bolts, and our groceries will be stocked with food. We hope our children obey our rules not to play in streets, take candy from strangers, or eat yellow snow. However, there are times when we have to think for ourselves, ask questions, and perform reality checks. There are times when we have to take on the burdens of adulthood and not live as children. Perhaps one of the most important lessons of this book is that respected, honest, sincere individuals can get it wrong. Your professors, doctors, politicians, and preachers can suffer profound delusions. These delusions can persist for thousands of years. Never assume that the claims of your favorite authority are always based on the best of sources, logic, or science, or that their claims are immune from the errors of misinterpreting the oddities of nature, perception, memory, the placebo effect, or sensory anomalies and hallucinations. To begin, look at the logic and examine the science, topics we will consider in the following chapters.

REALITY CHECK

Your author suspects that investigations of the paranormal, compared with studies of more mundane topics such as fruit flies and efficacy of various flu vaccines, may be at greater risk for reliance on questionable sources. What do you think?

Useful Links

Much more can be said about evaluating the quality of sources. I have found the following websites useful and entertaining. See Appendix B for a more complete list.

Skeptical Websites

skepdic.com

This site contains *The Skeptic's Dictionary*, the most useful online source of definitions, arguments, and essays on paranormal claims. Its primary focus is skeptical. The site includes many useful links and a large bibliography.

www.randi.org/site/index.php/encyclopedia.html

Encyclopedia of claims, frauds, and hoaxes of the occult and supernatural. Online version of James Randi's encyclopedia.

csicop.org

This is the official website for the Committee for Skeptical Inquiry (CSI). The CSI encourages the responsible, critical, and scientific investigation of paranormal claims and the dissemination of factual information about paranormal research. The site includes useful links and a large bibliography. The SCI publishes the *Skeptical Inquirer*, a very readable journal of paranormal claims.

A transnational umbrella organization, the Center for Inquiry, encompasses the CSI as well as the Council for Secular Humanism and the Center for Inquiry—On Campus.

skeptic.com

This is the official website of The Skeptics Society, "a scientific and educational organization of scholars, scientists, historians, magicians, professors and teachers, and anyone curious about controversial ideas, extraordinary claims, revolutionary ideas, and the promotion of science." Its official journal, *Skeptic*, provides a thorough and readable inquiry into various paranormal topics. The website has a free reading room with interesting articles and essays, as well as a free collection of podcasts and video downloads.

skepticreport.com

This is Chris Larson's compendium of news articles, essays, and links on paranormal topics. Skepticreport contains much information, including transcripts of psychic cold readings, difficult to obtain elsewhere.

quackwatch.org

Quackwatch, Inc., is a "nonprofit corporation whose purpose is to combat health-related frauds, myths, fads, fallacies, and misconduct. Its primary focus is on quackery-related information that is difficult or impossible to get elsewhere." It offers useful links to other sites and a forum where experts can answer questions.

randi.org

The James Randi Educational Foundation was founded by author, magician, and skeptic James Randi. It promotes "critical thinking by reaching out to the public and media with reliable information about paranormal and supernatural ideas so widespread in our society today." The Foundation offers classroom demonstrations and educational seminars, supports and conducts research into paranormal claims, maintains a library of print, audio, and video resources, and assists those critical of paranormal excesses who have been the victim of attack. To increase public awareness of paranormal issues, the Foundation offers a $1 million prize to anyone demonstrating "any psychic, supernatural or paranormal ability of any kind under mutually agreed upon scientific conditions." The website has many useful links and audio and video downloads. It is not shy about presenting heated discussion from both skeptics and non-skeptics. For recent video clips see The James Randi Foundation Channel on YouTube: youtube.com/user/JamesRandiFoundation

Non-Skeptical Websites

www.answers.com

On this website you can find the *Encyclopedia of occultism and the paranormal: 5th edition* (Shepard, L. A. 2003). This two-volume encyclopedia contains more than 5,000 entries which cover recent phenomena, concepts, cults, personalities, organizations and publications. For controversial topics, evidence for and against is presented. The specific link is: www.answers.com/library/Occultism+&+Parapsychology+Encyclopedia-letter-1S-first-151

parapsych.org

The Parapsychological Association is an "international professional organization of scientists and scholars engaged in the study of '*psi*' (or 'psychic') experiences, such as telepathy, clairvoyance, psychokinesis, psychic healing, and precognition ('parapsychology')." This website describes the organization, discusses how to conduct parapsychological research, and provides links to groups conducting such research. Try out the fun do-it-yourself online psi game/experiments.

www.koestler-parapsychology.psy.ed.ac.uk/

The website of the Koestler Parapsychology Unit of the University of Edinburgh consists of scholars and students interested in parapsychology. Their site provides useful information on research and links to journals and other laboratories doing research on the paranormal.

Urine Therapy

Note: And now for something completely different. This faux promotional piece integrates the best points made by advocates of urine therapy. I made none of it up. Can you find any problems or any questionable sources? Maybe you can detect errors in logic or scientific thinking, topics we will consider in future chapters. Please recognize that in fact urine therapy is unproven and potentially dangerous. I do not practice or advocate it. For a thoughtful analysis of this presentation using concepts from the Critical Thinker's Toolkit, see Chapter 16.

The Miracle of Urine Therapy
Jon Smith

Drink water from your own cistern, flowing water from your own well.
(The Book of Proverbs 5:15)

He that believeth in me ... out of his belly shall flow rivers of living water.
(John 7:38)

Urine therapy involves drinking your own urine for health, beauty, or spiritual growth. This practice originated as a yoga technique in India 5,000 years ago where Hindus called it **Shivambu Kalpa** ("waters of the God Shiva.") [1] People have benefited from urine therapy throughout history. The Romans valued and even taxed urine produced in public reservoirs [1]. Roman naturalist Pliny the Elder extolled the powers of urine from a virgin boy [2]. Aristocratic French women bathed in it [1]. Ancient Arabic writings praise the healing powers of urine from white elephants [2]. In the 18th century famous scientists and physicians, including Pierre Fauchard, the French founder of modern dentistry, and the great British scientist Robert Boyle, described the numerous medical (and dental) benefits of urine consumption [2].

Today, urine therapy is gaining respectability. On his 99th birthday, India's former prime minister Morarji Desai attributed his longevity to drinking his own urine [3]. Mohandas Gandhi was also a practitioner and advocate [3]. Other famous users include Jim Morrison, John Lennon, and Steve McQueen [4]. Three million Chinese are practitioners [5]. Even scientists take urine therapy seriously. Since 1996 there have been three professional World Conferences on Urine Therapy [6].

The benefits of this simple treatment are amazing. Indeed, famous advocate Michael Braunstein recommends it: "If health is what you *urine* for ..." [7]. Patients and physicians report it's good for many things, including:

Aging, AIDS, allergies, asthma, birthmarks, baldness, bloody urine, broken bones, burns, cancer, chicken pox, common cold, cold sores, congestion, constipation, diabetes, depression, dry skin, dysentery, eye irritation, fatigue, fever, gastric ulcers, gastritis, gonorrhea, gout, foot fungus, flu, hangover, heart disease, hypertension, infections, infertility, insomnia, jaundice, hepatitis, Kaposi's sarcoma, leprosy, lumbago, morning sickness, obesity, Parkinson's disease, parasites, poisoning, pneumonia, psoriasis, rheumatism, smallpox, snake bites, strokes, tetanus, tooth aches, typhus, and tuberculosis. [5]

How to Do It

When engaging in urine therapy, it is important to use the correct procedures. Drink early in the morning, when hormonal secretions are at their highest (because the body has been relaxed during sleep repairing itself) [1]. Aim for the intermediate, rather than initial or end flow. Don't eat for at least 15 minutes. Be sure you get enough sleep, meditation, and exercise, and maintain a balanced, preferably vegetarian, diet free of sugars, caffeine, nicotine, and preservatives [1]. It is fine to mix urine with orange juice [8].

One can also place 1–5 drops of fresh morning urine under the tongue, gargle it, snort it, spray it into one's nostrils, use it as ear or eye drops, foot baths, enemas, as a massage lotion, a skin moisturizer, and nose drops to clear congestion [9]. Urine therapy guru Dr. Beatrice Bartnett [10] appropriately advises uttering a prayer before treatment.

When starting urine therapy, you may well experience a "healing crisis" [1] involving various forms of discomfort when the body releases toxins. Symptoms include headaches, nausea, rashes, fever, diarrhea, vomiting, and sweating. Do not worry. These are just part of the natural release process and well worth the final results.

Scientific Evidence

The power of urine should come as no surprise. During World War I troops covered their eyes with urine-drenched swabs when exposed to chlorine poison gas. During World War II urine was collected from soldiers receiving penicillin in order to reuse this antibiotic in short supply. Today, urine is used to make Pergonal, a powerful fertility drug, and Urokinase, a drug for unblocking coronary arteries. Urea is used in cosmetics. Given the many approved medical uses for urine byproducts, it makes sense that urine itself has powerful healing properties. After all, a manufactured substance is no match for your body's own natural medicine [1].

Urea itself has scientifically-proven antibacterial effects [11], so urine has to be good for you. But this is just the beginning. The amount of nutritional ingredients in Urine will "knock your socks off" [12] including: Alanine, Arginine, Ascorbic acid, Allantoin, Amino acids, Bicarbonate, Biotin, Calcium, Creatinine, Cystine, Dopamine, Epinephrine, Folic acid, Glucose, Glutamic acid, Glycine, Inositol, Iodine, Iron, Lysine, Magnesium, Manganese, Methionine, Nitrogen, Ornithine, Pantothenic acid, Phenylalanine, Phosphorus, Potassium, Proteins, Riboflavin, Tryptophan, Tyrosine, Urea, Vitamin B6, Vitamin B12, Zinc [9].

But urine is more than a vitamin shop. The body excretes only what it doesn't need at any moment [12]. However, needs naturally vary throughout the day, so you can maintain the balance of these substances by consuming urine. When urine does contain small amounts of toxins, these actually stimulate the intestines and lymphatic system to flush other toxins from the body. So both the good and bad things in urine are therapeutic [8].

How It Works

Urine therapy may be a very powerful form of self-homeopathy. Homeopathy is a venerable and popular treatment that involves ingesting very small amounts of pathogens or substances that have come in contact with pathogens. When water comes in contact with a pathogen it acquires an unmeasurable memory of the pathogen that can be used to inoculate one against the very same pathogen. Using this very same process, the flu vaccine contains a tiny amount of a flu virus which triggers the body's immune system to build a defense against the flu. Similarly, urine acquires a memory of viruses, bacteria, and toxic substances it contacts in the body. This memory gives consumed urine its therapeutic power.

Recently a new idea has excited and inspired the urine therapy community. *Holographic urine theory* proposes that urine contains an exact holographic picture of the body's fluids and tissues, both healthy and ill. Therefore, bio-feedback from this holographic information informs the body's energy to restore health and balance [13, 14].

It is exciting to contemplate what the future may bring. Once urine therapy is accepted by medicine, politics, and religion, stigmas concerning urine excretion may be flushed away. This golden elixir may be shared in public celebrations and human fountains of healing and hope. (OK, I made this point up. But prove it isn't true!) Perhaps the ancient Hindus are right and urine is indeed a divine manifestation of cosmic intelligence [8].

Testimonials

Most urine therapists have not looked for a scientific reason for how their treatment works. Their personal experiences are proof enough [8]; no science is needed. Christy [12] has collected a large number of impressive medical testimonials:

> J. P., MD: "urine acts as an excellent and safe natural vaccine and has been shown to cure a wide variety of disorders including hepatitis, whooping-cough, asthma, hay fever, hives, migraines, intestinal dysfunctions, etc. It is completely safe and causes no side effects."

> D. S., MD: "a patient with intractable ovarian cancer was treated with Human Urine Derivative and is now completely well and enjoying the rest of her life."

> C. W. W., MD: "It was rapidly appreciated that undiluted urine administered orally was therapeutically effective for Immune Therapy and was initiated when it became obvious that an allergic condition had become uncontrollable."

> L. M., MD: Urea has been used for the treatment of various infected wounds and it has been found to be extremely efficient ... even the deepest wound can be treated effectively.... Urea treatment has been successful where other treatments have failed. For external staph infections we found urea preferable to any other dressing ... there are no contra-indications to its use."

Testimonials from patients are equally impressive. Perhaps the most famous case is that of author J. W. Armstrong [9]. Armstrong was suffering from TB at a time when there was no treatment. After reading the Bible ("Drink water from thy own cistern") he started drinking his own urine. He was completely cured, and started promoting urine therapy as a treatment. He eventually treated over 40,000 patients. Here are more testimonials [9]:

> Boy (age 9) suffering from enuresis. Treated by many physicians using all available methods. Failed. Fasted on urine for 11 days and completely cured.

Woman (40) suffering from severe kidney disease. Given two days to live by doctors. Difficult breathing, blood in urine. Started urine therapy, and as much tap water as she desired. Cured in about a month.

Woman (40) with gangrene in right leg. Amputation recommended. One week of urine therapy and no sign of gangrene and completely cured.

Male (45) with gangrene in thumb. Surgeon's decision to amputate rejected. Fasted 14 days. Body rubbed with urine. Improvement after three days of treatment. Cure complete after twelve days.

Male (40) with leukemia, three months to live. Faithfully drank urine for six months. Unfortunately, resorted to bad diet and died six years later.

Woman (17) with malaria. Cured after three days of urine therapy.

The medical community has known of urine therapy for decades. Why isn't it used widely in hospitals in clinics? Perhaps there is no profit for doctors and drug companies to use a treatment available to everyone for free.

Conclusion

When Magellan set his fleet of ships around the world in 1519, each ship contained 50 casks of water. This was not enough for crew needs, and it was assumed water would be discovered at sea. However, 18 months into their voyage, Magellan's crew was out of water and desperate. They decided to drink their own urine. As one crew member commented, "It was surprisingly not unsavory, having no worse a taste than a flagon most foul with rancid port, as many I have tasted before" [7]. If Magellan's crew can do it, so can you. Urine expert and advocate Braunstein offers a tempting invitation: "Welcome aboard. Coffee, tea or pee?"

1. More, B. (1996). Drink to your health. *Yoga Journal, 127*. Retrieved April 1, 2008 from: snakelyone.com/URINE.htm
2. Thorndike, L. (1923). *History of magic and experimental science during the first thirteen centuries of our era*. New York: Columbia University Press.
3. Gardner, M. (1999). Urine therapy. *Skeptical Inquirer,* May–June.
4. Rao, A., Omar, A., Karim, O., Motiwala, H., & Das, S. (2007). *Urine, the white gold*. 22nd Annual Congress of the European Association of Urology, March 22–24, *Abstract 145*.
5. Carroll, R. T. (2007). *Urine therapy*. Retrieved March 29, 2008 from: www.Skepdic.com
6. Newman, A. (1999). *Health and body*. Salon.com, June 7. Retrieved March 29, 2008 from: www.salon.com/health/feature/1999/06/07/urine/index.html

7. Braunstein, M. (1999). *Urine therapy*. Heartland Healing Center featured column. Retrieved March 29, 2008 from: www.heartlandhealing.com/pages/archive/urine_therapy/

9. Armstrong, J. W. (1971). *The water of life: A treatise on urine therapy*. Essex, England: Health Science Press.

10. Bartnett, B. (1989). *Urine-therapy: It may save your life*. Hollywood, FL: Water of Life Institute.

11. Kaye, D. (1968). Antibacterial activity of human urine. *Journal of Clinical Investigation, 47,* 2374–2390.

12. Christy, M. M. (1994). *Your own perfect medicine: The incredible proven natural miracle cure that medical science has never revealed*. Scottsdale, AZ: Wishland.

13. Van der Koon, C. (n.d.). *Transmutation and the healer within*. Lightbalance. Retrieved March 29, 2008 from: www.lightbalance.com/articles/urine05.htm

14. Van Der Kroon, C. (1998). *The golden fountain: The complete guide to urine therapy*. Scottsdale, AZ: Wishland.

4

Reality Check

Is the Logic Valid and Sound?

Why do people believe in astrology? For many, astrology must be true because it is popular, ancient, and used by friends, celebrities, and authorities. Such thinking reflects a logical error, one of basing a conclusion on an unacceptable premise (the unquestioned truthfulness of what someone else says). Much pseudoscientific thinking is based on logical errors. In this chapter we will take a deeper look at logic, or the process of drawing conclusions from premises, and examine how it can be a very useful reality-checking tool.

Basic Logic

First we need to define some terms. A **conclusion** is a claim that something is true. Conclusions are often based on **premises**. Together, conclusions and premises comprise a logical **argument** (not to be confused with a heated dispute). Here are some arguments for astrology:

Premise		Conclusion
Astrology is very ancient.	therefore	astrology is true.
Many people believe in astrology	so	it must work for them.
My priest says astrology's true	thus	it must be true.

Crude Logical Errors: Unfounded Assertions and Contradictions

Our first logical error is the simplest, the **unfounded assertion**, or "conclusion" that isn't a conclusion. People sometimes utter conclusions without any justification whatsoever. Such statements might superficially look like arguments, but they are not. No matter how interesting or informative, they prove nothing. Even when proclaimed with messianic passion in front of huge cheering crowds, they still prove nothing. For example:

> Astrology is very ancient. Many people believe in astrology. Astrological horoscopes can explain much of history as well as today's events.

This comment is interesting and possibly true. But it simply asserts various claims, without any support. One way to tell if someone is trying to make an argument is to look for *indicator words*, like "prove," "because," "therefore," "so," "thus," and "leading one to conclude." These words tell you that there's a conclusion present. The above statement can be written so that it attempts to argue or support claims:

> Astrology is very ancient. Many people believe in astrology. Astrological horoscopes can explain much of history as well as today's events. *Therefore*, there must be something to astrology.

Another crude logical error is the **contradiction**, opposite claims that can't possibly be true at the same time. Contradictions are typically hidden and implied, requiring careful and thoughtful consideration of the entire claim.

Types of Logical Arguments

There are two types of arguments, **deductive** and **inductive**. Examine this classic deductive argument:

> *Premise*: If something's a vegetable, then it's a plant.
> *Premise*: A carrot is a vegetable,
> Therefore
> *Conclusion*: A carrot is a plant.

Note that if we assume the premises that all vegetables are plants and carrots are vegetables, then carrots must be plants. As long as we accept the premises, there is absolutely no room for debate, no need for further research or argumentation. A carrot is a plant, case closed. This is a characteristic of all **deductive arguments**. For example,

> *Premise*: If a person is born when the sun is the house of Pisces, he or she is athletic.
> *Premise*: You were born in March and the sun was in the house of Pisces.
> Therefore
> *Conclusion*: You are athletic.

As long as you accept the premise, then the conclusion necessarily follows. Deductive arguments that correctly take this form are said to be **formally valid**. Note that the term "valid" has a very specific meaning—a deductive argument's logical structure has been correctly presented. A deductive argument may be internally valid, but not represent the real world. It may have false premises.

The following is a *valid* deductive argument that is *not true*.

Premise: If a creature is an animal, it can engage in abstract reasoning.
Premise: Socrates, my cat, is an animal.
Therefore
Conclusion: Socrates can engage in abstract reasoning.

Here the first premise is wrong: some living animals cannot, as far as we know, engage in abstract reasoning. But the argument is valid in that it follows the formal rules of deduction.

Here is an invalid deductive argument.

If someone believes in ghosts and witches, they believe in a reality beyond the physical world.
Bertha believes in a reality beyond the physical world.
Therefore
Bertha believes in ghosts and witches.

In fact, Bertha is a practicing Roman Catholic, very much believes in a higher power, and rejects the idea of ghosts and witches as heresy. The problem with this deductive argument is that it breaks the rules. The first premise is an "if/then" claim with two parts, (A) If someone believes in ghosts and witches, (B) then they believe in a reality beyond the physical world. The first "if" part is called the **antecedent** and the second "then" part the **consequent**. We have already seen that by affirming the "if," that is the antecedent, the consequent is automatically true. Every valid argument we have considered has done this. However, that's not what the Bertha argument does. It works backwards by initially **affirming the consequent**, and arguing that the antecedent is true. Because it breaks the formal rules it is not valid. To summarize, a valid argument **affirms the antecedent**, like this:

If A is true, then B is true.
A is true.
Therefore
B is true.

Affirming the consequent proves nothing.

If A is true, then B is true.
B is true.
Therefore
A is true.

Arguments that affirm the consequent often appear in discussions of the paranormal. For example:

If the stars and planets are aligned properly (A), you will recover quickly from your cold (B).
You recovered quickly from your cold (B).
Therefore
The stars and planets are aligned properly (A).

If a psychic can read your thoughts (A), he can tell if you are skeptical (B).
The psychic you are visiting correctly observed that you are skeptical (B).
Therefore
The psychic can read your thoughts (A).

If a mystic has truly supernatural powers (A), she can perform stunts you cannot explain (B).
Maria, the mystic, has bent a spoon without touching it, a stunt you can not explain (B).
Therefore
Maria has supernatural powers (A).

There is a different way of describing the mistake these examples illustrate. Whenever you affirm the consequent you have proven nothing because alternative explanations must be considered.

An **inductive argument** bases a conclusion on a set of observations. Unlike deductive conclusions, inductive conclusions are not absolutely true or valid, but simply supported or not supported. If you conduct a survey of 1000 Pisces and find that 80% are athletes (versus 20% of the general population), you would have some evidence that Pisces are athletic. It is important to note that you have not proven anything, but simply acquired **strong**, or **weak**, support for a conclusion or claim. Inductive claims are always probabilities, not certainties.

An **inductive generalization** starts with a premise about a sample of cases and leads to a conclusion about the population of all cases.

Premise: 80% of the Pisces I randomly interview happen to be members of sports teams.

Therefore
Conclusion: 80% of the Pisces in the general population are probably members of sports teams.

Informal Logical Fallacies

Philosophers have listed hundreds of logical fallacies in terms of faulty premises. Technically these are "informal fallacies" because their error has nothing to do with their "form" as described above. I find it useful to sort informal logical fallacies into five overlapping groups:

- confusing fact with fiction;
- fallacies of ambiguity;
- irrelevant characteristics;
- argument from temporal contiguity;
- self-terminating or fatal assumptions.

Confusing Fact with Fiction: Pointless Jargon, Technobabble, and Science Fiction

One of the simplest logical errors is to introduce a premise that confuses fact with fiction. Later we will see that this is a type of fallacy of ambiguity. Just because A shares some superficial characteristics with B doesn't mean that A and B are alike in other ways. Apples are red and sweet. That doesn't mean that all red fruit are sweet. More to the point, a piece of pointless esoteric jargon can look like a deeply sophisticated scientific term. Indeed, both may involve a multisyllabic word or two and require a dictionary to decipher. However, just because a claim uses scientific language doesn't mean it has scientific support. It may well be pure pseudoscience. "Quantum entanglement" is a legitimate technical phrase with precise meaning. "Dental oscillatory friction device" is a pointlessly complex phrase for an electric toothbrush. Pointless jargon can be introduced into an argument (valid or invalid) to make it appear more plausible and respectable even though it may be weak or meaningless.

Technobabble goes further and incorporates jargon in an extended argument. Often those who use technobabble do not understand the very point they are trying to make, or are deliberately trying to be unclear or deceptive. Technobabble has been used to intentionally convey the idea that a claim has a scientific explanation when in fact it has not.

Two parodies make the point. Isaac Asimov's short story, "Endochronic properties of resublimated thiotimoline," is actually a fake chemistry paper, based entirely on technobabble. In it he argued that the more "hydrophilic" (water-loving) a chemical is, the faster it will dissolve in water. Chemicals, like the fake substance "thiotimoline," increase hydrophilism and speed up dissolving time. Asimov went on to claim that thiotimoline is so hydrophilic that it dissolves in water before it touches water (perhaps anticipating parapsychological work on retroactive psychokinesis; see Chapter 12). This remarkable characteristic exists because the thiotimoline molecule contains one carbon bond to the future and one to the past. Asimov eventually published four articles on thiotimoline, and claimed that its remarkable properties could be used to travel faster than light or study hidden objects through remote viewing (Chapter 12). Although published in a science fiction magazine, *Astounding Stories*, many people were convinced that thiotimoline existed and flooded libraries with requests for further information (Asimov, 1969).

In a more recent and relevant example, Alan Sokal fooled the prestigious professional journal, *Social Text*, into publishing as a serious article his technobabble spoof, "Transgressing the boundaries: Towards a transformative hermeneutics of quantum gravity" (Sokal, 1996, 2008). This parody is so good that it provides a more convincing quantum-based rationale for parapsychological phenomena than the currently popular notions of "quantum consciousness" (see below). But it is pure and deliberate nonsense.

My all-time favorite example of pseudoscientific technobabble is holographic urine (Chapter 3). In case you forgot, because human urine initially resides in the body, it comes in contact with healthy and diseased or damaged tissue and thereby acquires a holographic memory of health and disease. Thus, by consuming one's one urine, one can activate the body's natural healing potential. You may note that throughout this text I apply holographic urine theory as the gold standard for evaluating technobabble.

Science fiction goes one step beyond technobabble. Here one begins with scientifically accepted fact and theory and then extrapolates new scientific-appearing fictions that have no bases in reality. For example, science fiction writers often have their characters travel from galaxy to galaxy in a matter of hours. This is physically impossible. To get around this inconvenience, writers may invent wormholes that serve as rapid long-distance transit portals. The rationale may begin with the correct observation that black holes exist throughout the universe (fact supported by theory) and that the laws of physics may not apply deep within black holes (also proposed by current science). When two black holes in different parts of the universe connect, what happens between them also violates the laws of physics (so far this also fits current theory) so they form a tunnel (yes, this indeed would also violate the laws of physics; but it's science fiction) through which people can travel nearly instantaneously (science fiction).

The notion of quantum consciousness (Radin, 1997, 2006) is a popular explanation for many claimed paranormal phenomena, including reading thoughts at a distance and influencing objects through thoughts. Here is a reality check. The notion of quantum consciousness begins with the accurate observation that under certain conditions some subatomic particles seem "entangled," that is, at the subatomic level an esoteric characteristic of one may immediately appear in a sister particle far away. (See Chapter 1.) This may seem strange, but it is fact. Quantum consciousness states that the human brain is made of atoms, which in turn are made of subatomic particles (fact). The subatomic particles in the brain follow the rules of quantum physics (fact). Human thought is generated by the human brain (fact) and may follow the same quantum rules as subatomic particles in the brain (science fiction). Therefore, the thoughts of one person can immediately influence the thoughts of another far away (science fiction), a process that may seem like thought reading or thought control.

However popular, quantum explanations of thought reading and control make no more sense than various other possible science fiction explanations. Let me offer a few. String theory, a popular notion that says that subatomic strings permeate the universe, requires the existence of almost a dozen dimensions (actual theory). One might then reflect one's thoughts off a fifth or sixth dimension in order to communicate telepathically with someone else (science fiction). Here's another. Some quantum theories state that gravity is the only force that can leak between dimensions. All atoms possess some gravity (fact). Our brains are made of atoms (fact). Thoughts are generated by activity in the brain (fact). One might then imagine that thoughts travel by means of gravity waves (science fiction) through other dimensions and return to our dimension instantaneously (science fiction), resulting in telepathic communication. And another: A mysterious dark energy forces some galaxies apart, at times approaching and maybe exceeding the speed of light (an apparent fact). When human thoughts come in contact with dark energy, they can travel very rapidly to others, permitting telepathy (science fiction). Obviously science fiction explanations are partly based on fact. However, those who believe in such make-believe typically have a very poor understanding of underlying science and therefore make the logical error of confusing fact with fiction.[1]

Fallacies of Ambiguity

An argument can be weak or pseudoscientific because it manipulates language or ideas in misleading ways. Sometimes this simply involves playing tricks with words. Other examples involve confusing the logical relationships between words.

Weasel words

A weasel is a thin squirrel-like mammal known for its ability to slither out of trouble and sneak into the burrows of tasty victims (Nowak & Walker, 2005). A weasel word enables you to make an apparently strong claim on what is actually weak evidence. It gives you an "out" in case your claim is challenged. For example, examine the claim: "Some scientists challenge global warming." Here the word "some" is a weasel word. On close examination, we find that "one percent of scientists challenge global warming." Another example: "Three out of four dentists surveyed recommend sugarless gum." This sounds dramatic until we discover that only 12 dentists were actually "surveyed."

Paranormalists sometimes engage in weaseling by their use of the word "healing." "Healing" generally means "return to physiological health." When a broken leg is healed, you can walk again. Healing can also mean "return to psychological well-being." Even if your leg is broken, you are "healed" if you have recovered from the initial distress of breaking your leg and are more or less happy. Because of these two meanings, faith healers can weasel out of promises. They may claim to "heal" your arthritis, take your "donation" ("healing" your wallet of excess weight), and then praise the Lord that your "spirit" has been healed. Who are you to challenge such a demonstration of piety? A similar and clever weasel word is the construction "dis-ease." Of course, when spoken, it sounds like "disease," a medical condition, whereas "dis-ease" should refer to something like "discomfort." A healer can claim a worthless potion cures your "dis-ease" and convey the impression of offering a medical treatment when in fact he is simply making you feel good. What is clever about this weasel word is that the healer has a backup rationalization, the idea that psychological well-being ("ease") is important for physical health, and that his nostrum removes obstacles to such good feelings ("dis-ease").

Just as weasels can sneak into uninvited places, weasel words can introduce unintended and confusing meanings into a discussion. The words "controversial" and "debatable" are popular weasels in paranormal literature.[2] Let's take a simple example. Uri Geller is one of the best-known contemporary psychics (Chapter 7), world-renowned for his claimed ability to bend spoons with thought alone. However, magicians routinely bend spoons through simple sleight of hand (Randi, 1982). Randi has claimed that whenever Geller attempts to bend a spoon in the presence of a magician, he fails. In addition, he can bend spoons only in settings where deception or sleight of hand cannot be ruled out. In sum, few credible scientists question the overwhelming rejection of Geller's spoon-bending claim. Here there is no serious "debate" or "controversy" (Randi, 1982).

Yet, consider what Irwin and Watt (2007) conclude in what is perhaps the most widely respected serious paranormal textbook written by believers:

> The authenticity of Geller's performance is a matter of much debate (as it must be with folk who derive their living from such performances). (p. 119)

To be fair, Irwin and Watt duly note the challenges of skeptical magicians. However, they try to have it both ways. They do not conclude that Geller's claim that he uses thought to bend spoons is "not taken seriously by the mainstream scientific community," and has been labeled by many magicians who perform spoon-bending to be "a magic trick." Instead, it is "a matter of much debate." Furthermore, the primary reason given for the "debate," the only reason honored by its position in the very same sentence, is the potential for financial gain, a potentially compromising circumstance that must be faced by many paranormal researchers and skeptics, including myself.

Weasel words can have consequences. Weaseling can mean the difference between a recommendation to stop or continue researching a topic. Surely, a logical assessment of the scientific consensus concerning Geller would lead to a recommendation to stop inviting him to participate in expensive scientific studies. This is not what Irwin and Watt conclude. Instead:

> Without adequate testing in properly controlled conditions it is impossible to validate Geller's psychic talents. (p. 119)

Implication? If we could only amass sufficient resources for adequate testing, then perhaps we could attempt to finally validate Geller's talents. This implies that the "controversy" or "debate" is far from settled, the evidence at hand is not sufficient to challenge Geller's claims, and future research on Geller is merited. See where this innocent bit of weaseling gets us?

Let me put this in a slightly different way. The words "controversial" and "debatable" can also imply that there is good evidence on both sides of a question, or that a plausible claim has minimal evidence. John claims that he can turn rocks into gold through touch. This claim is "controversial" and "debatable" because he has never demonstrated it to others. John believes, others do not. Joe claims that eating chocolate reduces blood pressure. His claim is also "controversial" and "debatable" because one or two studies offer suggestive support, whereas others do not. In other words, there are two ways in which a claim can be controversial or debatable. It might not be supported by evidence, but stir argument. Or it might have inconsistent empirical support. A careless scholar may report that a paranormal claim is "controversial" or "debatable," meaning "no support, much argument." He or she may then engage in weaseling and treat the claim as having achieved at least a limited level of respectability (implying "mixed support").

| ✓ REALITY CHECK | Can you think of examples where subjective relativism (Chapter 2) might encourage the use of weasel words? |

Here's another example. Consider the word "faith." Physicist and cosmologist Paul Davies (2007) argues that both science and religion rely on faith. The religious believer accepts God without evidence. The scientist accepts an unexplained set of basic physical laws as "just there." Nobel Prize winner Charles Townes (2005) agrees that many people don't realize that science basically involves faith. From this one might conclude that a scientist risks hypocrisy when he or she chides a supernaturalist for accepting paranormal claims without logic or evidence. But as Park (2008) has explained, this oversimplifies things. A scientist is perfectly open to testable explanations for physical laws, even though none may be present. Yes, he or she may have "faith" that such laws will eventually be found. But this "faith" is different from the "faith" of a God-fearing individual.

To elaborate, the word "faith" has at least two meanings: (1) Confident belief in the truth, value, or trustworthiness of a person, idea, or thing, and (2) Belief that does not rest on logical proof or material evidence (*American Heritage Dictionary of the English Language*, 2003). A scientist may claim confidence in the "truth, value, or trustworthiness" of the idea that explanations for basic physical laws will eventually be found through logic and empirical investigation. This confidence is based on the success of scientific explanations over history. However, such confidence or "faith" is not chiseled in stone. If some future observations show that current perspectives of physics are inadequate, the faith of the scientist would change. In direct contrast, the faith of the religious does not rest on and simply cannot be challenged by logic or evidence. Yes, the true believer may have "faith." But the faith of a scientist is a different animal.

Straw man argument

In military training soldiers might practice combat skills on straw men, or dummy soldiers' uniforms filled with bags of straw. Such opponents are cheap, easy to defeat, and don't talk back. (Of course, defeating a straw-stuffed soldier is not a real victory because the enemy is still standing.) A straw man argument distorts an opponent's position so it is easy to refute.

One can render an argument easily refutable by exaggerating it (or making it universal), presenting it incorrectly, ignoring key contextual elements essential to the argument, or oversimplifying the argument. Like a military dummy, a straw man argument is easy to build, and requires little familiarity with the facts.

Category errors, ontological fusion, and reification

Sometimes words are misused and given meanings that do not apply. In most general terms, a **category error** involves giving something a property it cannot logically have (Ryle, 1949). Rocks can't have "feelings." One way of elaborating this idea is to think of the world as consisting of three basic types of entities or "ontological categories," each with their own attributes: psychological (thoughts, feelings, intentions), biological (life), and physical realities (matter, energy). **Ontological fusion** involves applying an attribute of one type of reality to another (Lindeman & Aarnio, 2007). Rocks (a physical entity) think (a psychological attribute). Emotions (psychological) can be transmitted through electrical wires (physical).

Reification is a category error that involves taking an abstraction, belief, or hypothetical construct, and treating it as if it were a concrete entity, something real. ("Reify" is based on the Latin word "res," which means "thing.") For example, "government" is an abstract idea. The statement "Government wants you to prosper" treats government as a person. "The universe guides every action" reifies the universe as a being with intentions. "Religion tries to lead people down the path of virtue" again treats religion as a person. The notion that "Good and evil are the two forces driving the universe" treats ideas as forces.

Reification can be particularly confusing when it involves the use of jargon-sounding weasel words. To elaborate, when we reify, we turn something that is not a thing into a thing, an object or process that can be scientifically measured.

In Chapter 2 we briefly noted confusions that can arise when we consider the world of subjective states, moral and aesthetic judgments, and symbolic expressions (Chapter 2). In most general terms, these are "thoughts," entities that ontologically belong in the world of psychology. One can legitimately use words like "real," "true," and "answer" when describing thoughts:

> I'm feeling energized (subjective state). This is very real to me. It is a true feeling. It is my honest answer to the question "How are you?"

> I believe you should treat others as you wish to be treated (moral judgment). This rule is real to me; I live my life accordingly. It is my personal "truth." It is the answer to my question, "How should I live my life."

I am a tiny and insignificant piece of dust in an infinite universe (metaphor). This symbol works for me, it really depicts how things are. It's true. It's the answer to the question, "What is the meaning of your existence?"

Words like "real," "true," and "answer" can be weasel words that mean quite different things to different people. As we have seen, they can refer to thoughts. However, they can also refer to objective facts. Hydrogen and oxygen really do combine to form water. This is true. This is the answer to the question "What is water?" We get into trouble when we claim that a specific thought is "real," "true," or "the answer," and pretend we are referring to something objective rather than something psychological. Take this claim:

When I touch this magic crystal I feel energized. Crystal energy is real and truly in my body. That's how I feel.

So far this claim is purely psychological and breaks no logical rules. An unscrupulous or confused psychic may take your words and turn them around to mean something quite different:

Yes, that demonstrates the mystical paranormal energy in crystals. You have confirmed that this energy is real. It's truly in you.

Fallacy of similarity or analogy

An argument based on similarities assumes that if two things are similar in one way they are similar in other ways. This is also called an analogy. For example, Cush and Nimrod both have red hair. Cush is irritable; therefore Nimrod is irritable.

Sometimes analogies are indeed useful if they are based on close similarities.

Last week I was sick. I had a cough, but no fever. It turned out I had a minor illness, a common cold, and got better.

Today my throat is sore, but like last week, I have no fever. There's a good chance I have a minor throat problem and will get better quickly.

When similarities are far-fetched or irrelevant, then we may have a risky premise:

"Taurus" is a constellation of stars that looks like a bull. Bulls are aggressive. So the constellation "Taurus" is associated with aggressiveness.

Or consider this:

Any system that looks like the science of astronomy must be true.

Astrology looks like astronomy because it is complicated, mathematical, and considers the stars.

Therefore astrology must be true.

Technobabble and science fiction often use inappropriate scientific analogies. For example, an acupuncturist may claim to free the flow of your qi "energy" along paths or lines in the body called "meridians." This sounds scientific, but it isn't. Energy is a term from physics, and a meridian is a geological term that refers to a precise line running from pole to pole around the earth. However, other than a superficial similarity, qi energy and meridians in acupuncture have no resemblance to their counterparts in science. For example, they cannot be detected or measured.

Sometimes the fallacy of similarity or analogy takes the form of a colorful and metaphorical explanation. Always be suspicious when you encounter a **dangling analogy** that is not grounded in a solid logical argument. Here are some examples:

Students are like horses. They learn best when subjected to strong discipline.

Prayer is like soap. Its bubbles lift you up and burst into a different realm.

You can travel faster than light across the universe. Einstein says the space-time continuum can be warped (true). So, the space-time continuum is like a giant sheet of paper, which you can fold over on itself. This way, two spots, which might be at opposite ends of the sheet, are now adjacent. So instead of traveling a vast distance, one only need jump a little distance to move from one end of space to another, apparently faster than the speed of light. In the center of black holes the laws of physics break down (apparent fact), so two black holes adjacent on a folded space-time sheet should easily punch through and connect, forming a tunnel.

When my priest blesses a glass of wine it turns to blood. Of course it still tastes and looks like wine, but it is really blood. It's like this. When we have an infection, we take an antibiotic. We can't see what the drug is doing to the bacteria in our bodies, but it still works. There are things that are true that we cannot see. (Carroll, 2006)

Here are some questionable analogies presented by various paranormal advocates. See if you can figure out the problems. (If you give up, check www.skepdic.com):

Research on psychics is like studying baseball players. When Mickey Mantle gets one hit out of three, that's good. So when a psychic guesses what you're thinking one time out of three, that's equally good.

The body reacts to medicine like a piano string resonates to the vibrating string of another piano. If you strike "C" on one piano, the "C" string of a nearby piano will resonate and vibrate.

Homeopathic medicines involve extremely small dilutions of substances that supposedly have an impact on the human body. Medical science says the substances are so diluted that they couldn't conceivably have any effect on the body. However, small things can have big effects. Just because atoms are very small doesn't mean that they have no effect when they collide in an atomic bomb.

Fallacy of composition

Arguments based on composition start with a premise that what is true for the component parts must be true for the whole:

The church has a few priests who are immoral. Therefore the church is immoral.

Fallacy of division

Division is the opposite of composition. Here we start with the premise that what is true for the whole must be true for all component parts. The Noah family line is notoriously irritable. Nimrod is a member of the Noah family. Therefore, Nimrod is irritable. Here are some more:

The church is immoral. Therefore our local priest is immoral.

The Academy of Astrology is known to be honest and law-abiding. Madame Phoebe, member of the Academy of Astrology, must be honest and law-abiding.

Irrelevant Characteristics

When juries consider guilt or innocence, they try to keep personal issues and feelings out of consideration. Similarly, your annoyance with astrologers says nothing about whether or not astrology is true. Your respect for a kind and loving preacher does not extend to his or her proclamations of who is going to hell. And your blind prejudice against any particular sect or ethnic group is no evidence of how group members actually behave.

Appeal to emotion

An appeal to emotion uses emotion as a premise for an argument. The arguer attempts to arouse intense fear, pleasure, or desire, when making a case. Such pleas and manipulations are usually easy to detect:

> I know astrology is true because it is so beautiful. Something that fills me with such inspiration and joy must be true.

> You want to be part of a larger and infinite universe, one with meaning and purpose. Belief in extrasensory perception suggests a larger universe. Therefore ESP must be true.

Appeal to the person/ad hominem

An *ad hominem argument* (Latin for "to the man") rejects a claim because of presumed negative characteristics of the person making the claim, rather than the claim itself. A claim may or may not be true, regardless of who is making it:

> Those who criticize astrology are often cold-hearted scientists who are closed to deeper human potentials. They realize that astrology threatens their livelihood. And we can't accept the criticisms of people of faith. The gods and rituals they believe in are just as much a "superstition" as astrology. Therefore they're wrong.

Appeal to ignorance

You hope something is true. Yet there is an absence of evidence on which to base your hope. How might you cope with such "ignorance"? I believe that this issue is especially salient for students of the paranormal, some of whom strongly desire their claims to be true, yet must face an enormous lack of evidence. Under such conditions perhaps it is understandable that one might commit the logical fallacy known as the *appeal to ignorance*. The most popular version of this fallacy asserts that the lack of evidence against something proves (or makes it reasonable to believe) that it is true. For example:

> There's a lot we don't know about the brain. Therefore, I believe in ESP. ESP exists.

> There is no evidence that God did not create the universe. Therefore, it is justifiable to believe he did.

> No scientist has shown that rubbing moss on your head doesn't grow hair. So you might as well try it.

Superficial newspaper horoscopes may be worthless, and most self-proclaimed "astrologers" use the wrong system or are poorly trained. Somewhere there are true masters of astrology who can generate horoscopes of astonishing accuracy. Otherwise, how could astrology have lasted for thousands of years? There is no evidence that all masters of astrology are fakes. I have to believe that some are genuine.

An appeal to ignorance is both irrelevant and ambiguous. It is irrelevant because the claimant is responsible for providing evidence for a claim.[3] The questioner need do nothing. This is only fair. Think of the consequences (applying *reductio ad absurdum*) if the opposite were the case, and we had to accept all crazy or foolish assertions as true until proven otherwise. Courts would immediately be clogged with frivolous cases. Physicians would have no way of selecting treatments. Such an approach to truth-finding would indeed be akin to relativism gone wild (Chapter 2).

More seriously, an appeal to ignorance is ambiguous. Consider these claims:

There is no evidence that God doesn't exist. Therefore I accept that he does exist.

Here there is no evidence one could conceivably examine. There is no test one could possibly perform to validate the claim. If you test God by asking him to answer a prayer, his response, or failure to respond, could both be argued to be consistent with his claimed existence. The God claim is unfalsifiable.

Of the thousands of reported sightings of unidentified flying objects (UFOs), a small percentage remains unexplained. Therefore they must exist.

Simply because science has yet to find an explanation does not mean that it will never find one. This history of science can be described as a journey of discovering explanations for phenomena that initially appear to defy explanation (and tempt one to believe in the paranormal). Absence of a normal explanation does not require an extraordinary explanation.

There is no evidence that all dark moving shapes in haunted houses are not ghosts. Therefore there are ghosts.

Again, there is plenty of evidence. Many people have looked. Every careful scientific examination of dark moving shapes in abandoned houses has found an alternative to the ghost explanation. Dark moving shapes are routinely found to be shadows of objects like drapes, reflections of moving lights, or rodents. However, note that this claim is a *universal negative* (*all dark moving shapes*). Logically, one would have to perform a scientific test on every dark moving shape everywhere in the universe until the end of time. It is impossible to disprove a universal negative.

There is no evidence that eating clams does not increase intelligence. Therefore I can accept that eating clams increases intelligence.

There is no evidence to examine. No scientist has bothered to ask the question so obviously we have no evidence to support the claim. The claim has not been examined.

In sum, the statement "there is no evidence that a claim is false" can have four meanings:

- The claim is unfalsifiable.
- Currently an explanation does not exist.
- The claim is a universal negative.
- The claim has not been examined.

Often an appeal to ignorance is based on an irrelevant **personal characteristic,** personal ignorance. Almost always it can be restated: "Because I can't imagine or understand x, x must be true." One of the most popular arguments for the existence of an all-powerful, all-knowing, thinking and willing human-like deity who has plans for everyone can be called the **argument from design: ignorance version**. It states:

The universe is so complex it could not have been the result of natural and evolutionary processes; it must have been designed by a deity.

I propose that a more honest statement of such an argument might be:

The universe is so complex that I can't understand how it could have been the result of natural and evolutionary processes; it must have been designed by a deity.

So stated, arguments from personal ignorance have a ready reply.

I accept you might believe you are ignorant. That's OK. There are many things in life about which I am ignorant, for example, how lasers work.

But perhaps there are people who are more knowledgeable who understand what you find mysterious.

The opposite of an *appeal to personal ignorance* is the *appeal to personal knowledge*. Basically it begins with this premise:

Because I know so much, I am right about everything.

I like to call this the **first-year theology student's error** because of the distressing frequency with which it appears in discussions about theology. Here's how it usually goes:

SKEPTIC: I doubt your idea of God exists because of XXXX (the reason is irrelevant because it will provoke the same response).

TRUE BELIEVER: I won't give your claim the dignity of a discussion. Any first-year theology student can see the foolishness in your argument.

This is very similar to what I call the **argument from complexity**. Here it is:

SKEPTIC: I've read my sun sign horoscope and it doesn't fit me at all.

TRUE BELIEVER: Of course. A true horoscope is an extremely complex computation based on hundreds of variables. It takes a highly qualified professional to understand.

The gist of the argument to complexity is that one's criticism is invalid because it is based on an overly simplistic understanding.

The grand conspiracy theory (argument from ignorance—suppressed information variant)

Some paranormal claims are supported by grand conspiracy theories. We might think of a conspiracy theory as a variation of an argument from ignorance. However, instead of simply claiming that the lack of evidence concerning a claim is support for its truthfulness ("There is a lot we don't know about the brain. Therefore, I believe in ESP"), one begins with an unsupported premise that some individual, agency, or force is actively suppressing evidence ("The government doesn't want you to know all the proven powers of the human brain because such knowledge could lead to people challenging the government; therefore, I believe in ESP."). Here are some other examples:

Information that flying saucers have visited earth would cause mass panic and social chaos.

The government hides information that could cause mass panic and social chaos.

Therefore the government is hiding evidence that flying saucers have visited earth.

Another example:

There are some everyday herbs that can cure many illnesses, and eliminate the need for physicians and expensive treatments.

The medical community hides any information that could do damage to the livelihood of physicians.

Therefore the medical community is hiding evidence of the curative potential of everyday herbs.

Argument from Temporal Contiguity

Some arguments are questionable because they require or presume something that may be untrue. In most general terms, this is the **fallacy of presumption**. One of the most common examples is the **post hoc** or **post hoc ergo propter hoc** (after this, therefore because of this) fallacy. Here one argues that just because event X comes before event Y does not prove that X caused Y. The false presumption is that correlations prove causality.[4] Temporal contiguity can be caused by many other factors. For example, astrology may well have developed when early humans figured out that when the stars appear in a certain part of the sky, spring will soon arrive. Of course, the stars do not cause the seasons to change. But this did not prevent the development of astrology.

Similar to the post hoc fallacy is the **pragmatic fallacy**, the belief that because something appears to work, the presumed assumptions must be true.

Whenever I get my horoscope read, I feel better, like I understand my universe better.

Therefore, there must be something to the ancient idea that the positions of the sun, moon, planets, and stars can affect us.

Self-Terminating or Fatal Assumptions (Additional Fallacies of Presumption)

One type of premise is a show-stopper. If accepted, no further consideration is permitted. I call these *fatal* or *self-terminating assumptions*. Together they represent a type of fallacy that presumes "that's all there is to consider."

Closed-mindedness (blind faith)

I suspect that the most common self-terminating assumption is a simple refusal to honestly question a claim. It is acceptance of a conclusion without a premise. A closed-minded individual asserts such things as "I believe it and refuse to talk or think about it anymore. I take it on faith alone." The implicit assumption is that one's belief is true, self-evident, and needs no justification. It is the death of curiosity and thoughtfulness. A closed-minded individual may well pretend open-mindedness, and then automatically reject or even fail to notice challenges. For further discussion of open-mindedness, see the excellent work of William Hare (2009).

Begging the question

When one begs the question, the conclusion is the same as the premise (although perhaps put in different words). Consider this argument:

> Astrology is an infallible system of divination.
>> How do we know this?
>> Because astrological predictions come true.

Let's pick this apart. Here the premise is that astrology is an infallible system of divination. But that's essentially what the conclusion says. So the conclusion does nothing more than repeat the premise. More to the point, the premise is simply asserted twice without supportive evidence. You are left begging for more support.

Sometimes arguments that beg the question are difficult to identify. Here's one that Carroll (2003) has offered:

> Past-life memories of children prove that past lives are real because the children could have no other source for their [past-life] memories besides having lived in the past. (p. 51)

A past-life memory is by definition a memory that comes from having lived as a different person in the past. So this utterance is again nothing more than a restatement of the assertion "past-lives are real." So again we have an argument that begs the question. Simplified, it reads:

> Past lives are real.
> Because past lives are real.

An argument that begs the question is actually not an argument, but an assertion masquerading as an argument. Consider this:

Generally dogs are more friendly and sociable among people than are
cats.
Therefore
Cats, when compared with dogs, generally are more stand-offish and
solitary.

This is a simple statement, which may be true, false, or something in-
between. You can either accept, reject, or question it as it stands. But it is
not an *argument*. The conclusion adds nothing to the premise. The following
is an argument (inductive):

I have examined over 1,000 cats and dogs at animal shelters. Here, dogs
are more friendly and sociable than cats.
Therefore
I conclude that dogs in general are probably more friendly and sociable
than cats.

Begging the question is fatal to productive argumentation. You either
accept the claim or ask for support because none has been supplied. One is
stuck in a terminal loop, a black hole of circular reasoning, with no way
out.[5]

False dilemma

A false dilemma is an argument based on the premise that there are only two
alternatives, when in fact there are more. Usually one of the alternatives is
clearly unacceptable, forcing us to accept the remaining assertion. Accepting
a false dilemma kills a discussion by prematurely restricting the range of
alternatives that might be considered.

You are either for us or you are an enemy. (We know you aren't an enemy,
so you must be for us. Unconsidered alternative: you're neutral.)

You either believe in astrology or you have a closed mind. (Surely you
do have a closed mind, so astrology must be true. Unconsidered alternative: You have an open mind and are willing to consider all the evidence, pro and con. You have concluded that the case for astrology is
weak.)

Either God exists or the world is entirely without meaning and morality.
(Clearly the world must have meaning, and morality. Therefore God
exists. Unconsidered alternative: there are other sources of meaning and
morality in life.)

Those round lights in the night sky were flying saucers, or you were mentally ill and hallucinating. (We know you are of sound mind, and not inebriated, so you weren't hallucinating. So flying saucers must be real. Unconsidered alternatives: Weather balloons are real and sometimes look like flying saucers).

Premises, Logic, and Hypothesis Testing

The capacity for logic and reason is an impressive human achievement. However, these tools of critical thinking can take us only so far. It is instructive that many of the greatest philosophers sometimes made great mistakes in actually explaining how things really work in the world. A premise or conclusion about the real world requires public and replicable observation, the task of science.

The Logic Cheat Sheet

Sometimes everyday phrases contain nuggets of wisdom. Below are some simple challenges one might use in daily conversation. For each I've suggested which logical error they might convey. Can you see how? What other logical errors might they represent?

Taken together these phrases can come in handy and enable you to challenge the logic of an assertion simply and directly. Hopefully they might stimulate a more serious discussion in which you can introduce formal concepts of logic.

Just because it's scientific-sounding doesn't mean it's true.
   Confusing fact with fiction
Just because it's complicated doesn't mean it's true.
   Argument from complexity
You're mixing apples and orangutans.
   Affirming the consequent
   Straw man argument
   Category errors
   Fallacy of reification
   Fallacy of similarity
Just because it feels good, doesn't mean it's true
   Appeal to emotion

Don't judge a book by its cover (or) don't judge someone by the company they keep.
   Fallacy of similarity
   Fallacy of composition
   Fallacy of division
   Ad hominem
Lack of negative evidence doesn't mean it's true.
   Appeal to personal ignorance
Just because things happen together doesn't mean they're connected.
   Post hoc ergo propter hoc
   Pragmatic fallacy
Just because you believe it (or say it's so) doesn't make it true.
   Closed-mindedness
This isn't black or white, either/or
   False dilemma

The Star Trek Technobabble Generator

Technobabble is a standard tool in science fiction, a literary genre that frequently violates the laws of physics for entertainment purposes. To make such violations believable, a science fiction writer may invent scientific-sounding explanations. Bob Yewchuck (2008) has created an online Star Trek technobabble generator. With a simple click you can create a fresh sample of meaningless scientific-sounding discourse tailored on the famous Star Trek series. I clicked and found this discussion between blind Lieutenant Geordi LaForge (LeVar Burton) and Data (Brent Spiner), an android second officer and chief operations office. (I've taken the liberty of slightly modifying some of the babble, but rest assured that my adjustments in no way change the meaningfulness of the discussion.) (For a similar technobabble generator based on the British TV series *Dr Who*, see www.shockeye.org. uk/technoblab/TBG.php)

GEORDI: Data, come here and take a closer look at these readings: I think there's something wrong with the personal sensor grid.

DATA: The grid appears to be functioning normally, Geordi. Perhaps you were referring to the personnel dampening bay, right here, beside this quantum uncertainty improbability inverter. If we use the communication reserve operation to align it with the bipolar maintenance platform, then ...

GEORDI: Yes, of course! Then by modifying this secondary electrical conducer, we can make it work in conjunction with the guidance access impulse thruster. That would ...

DATA: I believe that this will increase the efficiency of the personal coil chamber 3 percent. Thus reducing the load on the ship's organic deflector.

GEORDI: Data—you're a genius!

Correlations and Causality

Just because two events appear together and are correlated doesn't mean that one caused the other. Events A and B might occur at the same time for four reasons: (1) A may cause B, (2) B might cause A, (3) some unknown variable C might cause A and B, or (4) the paired appearance of A and B was a fluke. (See Chapter 6.) Professor Jonathan Mueller has posted some wonderful articles from the popular press that illustrate the need to think clearly about correlations (Mueller, 2007). I've screened his many examples and have added some. For each of the following, perform a reality check and see if you can identify an alternative explanation.

Pill changes women's taste in men (BBC News, 2003)

Women who take contraceptive pills are more likely to prefer "macho types" with strong jaw lines and prominent cheekbones. Women who do not take contraceptive pills like sensitive men with traditional masculine features. Explanation: Women taking the pill can't become pregnant and are therefore subconsciously liberated to feel sexually attracted to men. If they marry someone while on the pill, they might realize they made the wrong decision when they are off the pill.

> ✓ **REALITY CHECK**   What's your alternative explanation?

Alternative explanation: Perhaps women who take the pill are already more assertive, and prefer assertive men. But then do assertive men have strong jaw lines and prominent cheekbones?

Nightlight may lead to nearsightedness (CNN, 1999)

Children who go to bed with a night light on in their room are significantly more likely to be nearsighted when they get older. Nightlights cause eye strain and eventual nearsightedness.

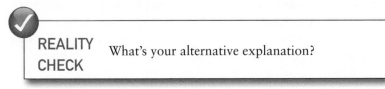

REALITY CHECK   What's your alternative explanation?

Alternative explanation: Nearsighted parents leave a night light on in their children's bedroom so they (the parents) can see more easily. Nearsighted parents are more likely to have children who grow up nearsighted.

Video games improve surgery skills for surgeons (Science Daily, 2007)

A study of 33 surgeons and surgical residents finds those who had more experience playing video games did better at performing laparoscopic surgery on a simulation test. The authors concluded that medical schools should consider including video games in their training.

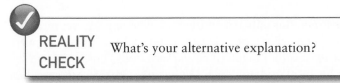

REALITY CHECK   What's your alternative explanation?

Alternative explanation: Surgeons who have good visual-motor skills (skill at using their eyes and hands) will naturally enjoy using these skills, at video games and in surgery. Because they already possess these skills, they are probably better surgeons than those who lack the skills.

Housework cuts breast cancer risk (BBC News, 2006a)

Research on 200,000 women from nine European countries found that housewives who did housework were less likely to contract cancer than those playing sports or having a physical job. Housework included 16–17 hours a week cooking, cleaning, and doing the wash.

REALITY CHECK   What's your alternative explanation?

Alternative explanation: Housewives who are already sick are likely to be less physically active, and unlikely to do lots of sports, cleaning, or cooking.

Sexual lyrics prompt teens to have sex (Tanner, 2006)

Teens who say they listen to music with degrading sexual messages are almost twice as likely to have sexual intercourse the following two years as teens who say they listen to music with little or no sexually degrading content. The music makes them less inhibited.

> **REALITY CHECK**   What's your alternative explanation?

Alternative explanation: Teens who are drawn to kinky sex in the bedroom might be expected to be drawn to kinky sex elsewhere—in comics, music, and so on.

Sex cuts public speaking stress (BBC News, 2006b)

Sex helps reduce stress. But only penetrative sex works. Forty-six men and women kept diaries on when and what they did in bed. Then they were asked to take a stress test that involved public speaking. Those who had the most penetrative sex displayed more rapid reductions in blood pressure than those who did not. Abstainers had the highest blood pressure during stress. Penetrative sex may stimulate the vagal nerve, which can produce relaxation.

> **REALITY CHECK**   What's your alternative explanation?

Alternative explanation: some extremely shy people may find any type of human interaction anxiety-arousing, whether it is public speaking or private sex. Some very extroverted people may have no "performance anxiety" and feel very comfortable with public speaking and sex (private and public).

Eating breakfast makes girls slimmer (Peer trainer, 2007)

In a 10-year study of 2,400 girls, girls who ate breakfast every day had lower average body mass than those who did not. It didn't matter what the girls ate. Not eating breakfast is the worst thing you can do for your weight.

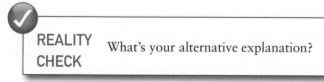

REALITY   What's your alternative explanation?
CHECK

Alternative explanation: Some people just don't gain weight. Such naturally thin people can eat breakfast without fear of gaining weight. Some people with weight problems more readily convert what they eat into fat, so eating a breakfast can increase weight.

Your name influences your future (Brooks, 2007)

People named Dennis and Denise are more likely to become dentists. Those named Lawrence and Laurie are more likely to become lawyers. People are drawn to professions that remind them of their names.

REALITY   What's your alternative explanation?
CHECK

Alternative explanation: Out of thousands of names there are bound to be some coincidental connections between name and profession, just by chance.

Panic attacks may raise women's heart, stroke risk (Johnson, 2007)

A panic attack is often characterized by rapidly pounding heart, sweating, trembling or shaking, and shortness of breath. The symptoms are very similar to those of an actual heart attack, although just having a panic attack doesn't mean you are having a heart attack. A study of more than 3,000 older women found that women who reported at least one full-blown panic attack during a six-month period were three times more likely to have a heart attack or stroke over the next five years than women who didn't report a panic attack. Perhaps having a panic attack releases stress hormones that can cause a heart attack.

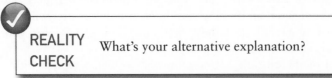

REALITY CHECK   What's your alternative explanation?

Alternative explanation: Perhaps the "panic attacks" reported were actually small heart attacks (the symptoms are similar). If so, then women who reported at least one heart attack during a six-month period are more likely to have another heart attack later on. This is a pattern previous research has established.

"Make your bed, save your brain" (Springen, 2007)

In 1994 researchers studied 997 older Catholic priests, nuns and monks (average age: 75) who did not have dementia. The subjects rated themselves on a "conscientiousness scale" answering such questions as "I am a productive person who always gets the job done." Over the 12 years of the study, those who developed Alzheimer's had initially rated themselves as less conscientious.

REALITY CHECK   What's your alternative explanation?

Alternative explanation: Early symptoms of Alzheimer's includes occasional inattentiveness and forgetfulness. Perhaps those who rated themselves as less conscientious were actually displaying the initial symptoms of Alzheimer's which seemed to them like lack of conscientiousness ("I forgot to get the job done ... I wasn't paying attention, was less productive ... how unconscientious of me!").

"Societies worse off 'when they have God on their side'" (Gledhill, 2005)

According to *The Times*: "Religious belief can cause damage to a society, contributing to high murder rates, abortion, promiscuity and suicide, according to research published today."

"According to the study, belief in and worship of God are not only unnecessary for a healthy society but may actually contribute to social problems. The study counters the view of believers that religion is necessary to provide the moral and ethical foundations of a healthy society."

In the largest study of its kind, using the best survey data available, researchers looked at all of the world's 18 most prosperous democracies (with a combined population of 800,000,000) and found a nearly perfect correlation between negative societal health/societal dysfunction and religiosity (belief in God, frequency of prayer, church attendance, biblical literalism, and creationism).

REALITY CHECK   What's your alternative explanation?

For more see Burns (1997) and Carroll (2007).

5

Reality Check

Are Claims Based on Observation (Scientific Tests and Theories)?

Scientific observation is one of our best reality-checking tools. When you test an idea, often you use science. When you try to find out what works and what doesn't work, you use science. When you take a pragmatic or practical approach to solving a problem, you use science. Doctors use science to diagnose illness and prescribe treatment. Detectives use science to solve crimes. Auto mechanics use science to fix cars. Students use science to decide on courses, career paths, and even weekend dates.

We have seen that sources and logic can provide impressive support for a claim. However, all are trumped by scientific observation, tests of hypotheses as well as explanations and theories. The famous expert can be proven wrong. A logical argument may be sound, but based on false premises.

Science (for the sake of simplicity, we will shorten "scientific observation" to "science") is not technology or the production of devices and gadgets. Science is not religion because science holds no dogmas. Indeed science is no more religious, or atheistic, than dentistry. But science is not without values; a scientist treasures discovering things as they are, and questioning honestly and fearlessly.

Here are some everyday scientists in action:

Gloria is a basketball player looking for a new pair of shoes that let her perspiring feet breathe during a game. She notes that the best brands are not made of cloth, but of real or synthetic leather. Her friends recommend real leather. Her coach wears synthetic leather. She decides to find out for herself which is best and goes to the sports store. There Gloria picks the best real and best synthetic leather shoe, wears each for 10 minutes and walks around the store, jumps a few times, and stretches. After each trial she asks herself if the shoe was comfortable and seemed to fit right for a good game.

Jose (a carnivore) is cooking a special dinner for his vegetarian friend Josh. He is trying out a new soup made with water, soy beans, onions, celery, salt, and garlic. The problem is that this concoction tastes terrible. Something is missing. Jose guesses that the soup is too bland and needs something to add spice and tang. So he adds a tomato and a green pepper. This time the soup passes the taste test, and Josh is happy. (Jose secretly plops some shrimp in his serving.)

Tony is very excited about the new DVD player he has just acquired. Unfortunately, it is not working. The front panel simply flashes the time, and the remote does nothing. Perhaps the remote needs a new battery. So Tony pops in a new battery, pushes the "start" button, and nothing happens. Maybe the DVD player is like a computer and can be automatically reset by switching it off and on.

How are these examples of the scientific method? Although philosophers disagree as to the precise elements of scientific investigation, most would agree that a narrow definition includes the following: observe, test, and explain through theory. By applying these tools, ideas are added and rejected, and knowledge grows. When these tools are not applied, our knowledge is likely to remain static and unchanging. Indeed, one of the best signs of whether a theory is scientific, or pseudoscientific, is whether it has changed and grown over time.

Observations

Observation is at the heart of scientific inquiry. All observation involves collecting data in a way that is **public** and **replicable**. Decades ago, as part of my doctoral dissertation, I conducted an extensive study on the effects of meditation on anxiety. Part of the design involved observing how meditators and non-meditators responded to various anxiety questionnaires. Near the end of the study I met with the meditation organization who agreed to provide free instruction and asked how my participants were doing. Without hesitation, their leader closed her eyes and after a few thoughtful seconds reported, "You have nothing to worry about. They are doing fine." I assumed she was recalling her meeting with my trainees. I was wrong. She was using her presumed psychic powers to contact each participant and psychically assess their well-being. I was not convinced. Her observations were not public because I could not see what she was doing in her head. And they were hardly replicable because there was no way I could do exactly the same thing in my head.

Our measures must be **reliable** and **valid**. Reliability and validity have precise scientific meanings which may differ from everyday use. In science, a reliable test yields a similar score over and over. A valid test agrees with other tests of the same thing, or works well in testing out hypotheses. A set of scales that yields the same weight at different times is reliable. Scales that are cheaply constructed may give you scores that vary. A valid set of scales will give you the same weight as, say, the scales used in your doctor's office. Invalid scales may be calibrated incorrectly and consistently under- or overstate your weight.

Tests

When we make observations, we may encounter a problem, something we don't know or understand. A scientific statement of an observed problem is also public and replicable. Others should be able to see the same problem if they use the same observational tools. In our beginning examples, Gloria's problem was deciding whether real or synthetic leather shoes were better for perspiring feet. Jose's problem was how to create a soup Josh would publicly praise as tasty. Tony wanted the DVD player to work. Of course, Gloria, Jose, and Tony performed simple personal experiments; their reports are simple anecdotal accounts. If they wanted to publish findings about which shoes are generally best for perspiring feet, how to make a vegetarian soup generally palatable, or the first thing to try when fixing a DVD player, they would have to test many people under careful conditions using procedures described below. They would start with a hypothesis, a proposed answer to a question, cause for an effect, or correlation between variables.

Ask the Right Question

A useful hypothesis specifies a type of observation or replication. It states specific things that should be observed if the hypothesis is true. In addition it proposes how we might change a replication to rule out alternative hypotheses. In our example, Gloria was comparing two hypotheses: real leather shoes are best for her perspiring feet vs. synthetic leather shoes are best. Jose hypothesized that adding tomatoes and green peppers would add spice and tang to a bland soup. Tony's hypothesis was simple: turning off a DVD player will reset it and make it work.

Most hypotheses are a bit more complicated and are tested by examining their logical implications or consequences. Recall that deductive reasoning starts with premises (All men are mortal, Socrates is a man) and ends with a necessary conclusion (Therefore, Socrates is mortal). Inductive reasoning also starts with a premise (Most men are married, Socrates is a man) but ends with a probable conclusion (Therefore, Socrates is probably married). Detectives use deductive and inductive reasoning when trying to figure out a crime:

> One night Josh discovers his DVD player has been stolen. He calls the police and names Tony as a suspect. Detective Grissom is assigned to the case and, using logical reasoning, generates some hypotheses. Does Tony have a new DVD player at home? If so, does it have the same serial number as Josh's player? Do any of the local pawn shops have a record of a recent transaction with Tony involving the stolen player? Did any of Josh's neighbors see Tony the night of the theft? Each of these is quite testable.

Doctors use such reasoning in attempting to diagnose a disease:

> Josh has a stomach ache. His physician has two hypotheses: a food poisoning or a viral intestinal infection. If Josh has an infection, he should have a fever and pumping his stomach shouldn't help. If Josh has food poisoning, perhaps he can report eating a questionable meal the previous day.

If a hypothesis can't be tested, or disconfirmed, it is generally useless for establishing the facts. This is the **falsifiability (or testability) criterion**, one of the most frequently cited tools of critical thinking. Philosopher Carl Popper (1959) proposed that no hypothesis can be considered scientific if there is no way of proving it false. For example:

> Freud says that all men have latent homosexual tendencies. If you are male, and have no homosexual urges, then you are repressing them. If this claim irritates you, your irritation is evidence of your underlying homosexual urges. If you're getting confused, that's evidence that your repressed homosexual tendencies are interfering with your brain. You can't win. There's no test to show this idea is wrong.

Basically a hypothesis is not falsifiable if there is no conceivable way of showing that it is false.

Sometimes a hypothesis is effectively not falsifiable if its proponent simply refuses to accept any evidence, no matter how good. Put differently, the proponent uses **ad hoc** (improvised "for this purpose") reasoning to explain away any observed empirical support:

ASTROLOGER: You are a Pisces. Therefore, you are sensitive.
SKEPTIC: But my friends tell me I am tough and unfeeling.
ASTROLOGER: That's because the moon and sun are in conflict for your sign.

Often ad hoc hypotheses are unfair manipulations of science. Another unfair tactic is to shift the burden of proof away from the person making a claim. If someone claims that you stole their DVD player, it is up to them (with police and the courts) to prove it. It would be unfair to require you to prove that you didn't commit the theft. If you apply *reductio ad absurdum* you will see the insanity that could result if you were responsible for disproving every charge leveled against you. The same rule applies to science. **The burden of proof is with the claimant.** If someone claims that little pixies pluck leaves off trees each autumn, it is not up to the scientific community to spend millions of dollars showing that this is not true. That's the responsibility of the person who believes in pixies. Sometimes we see advocates of the paranormal use this strategy. Can you see how the following claims do not play by the rules?

I can read my grandmother's thoughts. Prove I can't.
Astrological horoscopes can predict the future. Prove they can't.
Drinking urine is good for you. Prove it isn't.
God is female. Prove this isn't true.

Rule Out Alternative Explanations

We have noted that a good test specifies how we might perform observable public replications that rule out alternative explanations. This is often done through careful experimental design, which often involves **control groups, double-blind procedures,** and **controls for stimulus leakage.** Imagine you are testing the effects of green tea on memory. You give a group of people green tea and then test their memory. If memory scores improve, there could be alternative explanations. For example, perhaps their belief that tea increases memory resulted in their improved scores. The tea-drinkers became so motivated and enthusiastic that their performance improved. To control for this, one would have to test a control group designed to rule out the explanation that expectation and motivation improved performance. Such a control group would be identical to the experimental group in every way except that green tea would not be used. They might get green tap water spiked to taste somewhat bitter, like tea. Such a fake treatment designed to look exactly like an experimental treatment, but with the active ingredient removed, is called a **placebo** (Chapter 9). If the placebo control group scored worse than the tea group, then one has support for the hypothesis that green tea improves memory.

Often the enthusiasm and beliefs of an experimenter can rub off on participants. Perhaps the experimenters who gave the real green tea were excited about the powerful memory elixir they were about to test. Perhaps the participants unconsciously picked up on this excitement and became more motivated and excited. The only way to absolutely control for this alternative explanation is to introduce a **double-blind** control. In a double-blind study, neither the experimenter nor the participants know what treatments they have. Those giving and receiving the green tea or green tap water have no way of knowing which. Therefore, one group has no reason to be more enthusiastic or motivated than the other.

When a study has inadequate double-blind controls, the possibility exists for **stimulus leakage**. Here key elements of a research design may be detected by participants, biasing their results. An individual receiving a genuine medication may recognize its taste, and conclude that it is not the placebo. A psychic attempting to detect the thoughts of a sender may actually detect subtle facial expressions, and present a convincing reading. Stimulus leakage can be very difficult to detect and may require the assistance of an expert trained in deception, distraction, and subliminal control—a magician. This suggestion is actually now accepted by the majority of paranormal researchers (Irwin & Watt, 2007).

Test the Right People

Finally, a study might have an excellent experimental design and fail because research participants were poorly sampled. It is impossible for a researcher to include everyone in a study, so a **representative sample** must be selected that resembles the population in which one is interested and is not biased to favor a preferred research outcome. A study about the female population should include women. A study about heart patients should include heart patients. In our green tea study, imagine that the sample happened to include people who loved tea and hated water. So those who received tea would understandably enjoy what they got and the water-drinkers would be disappointed, a bias that might help explain differences in memory scores. This problem would not even arise if the sample had been representative. One way to increase representativeness is to select a **random sample** from the population. One might pick names out of a giant hat, have a monkey point at names in a phone book, or use more systematic statistical tools.

> **REALITY CHECK**
>
> One source of knowledge about the physical world is your own anecdotal evidence, that is, your personal experience and intuition. Can you think of times when personal experience and intuition cannot conceivably pass the test of science? Does this mean that your personal experience and intuition are worthless? Why? Why not?

Theories

Once you have made observations and tested a hypothesis, or series of hypotheses—again, all public and replicable—you might generate an encompassing theory that explains an observed phenomenon. A good theory shows how different ideas are related and thereby systematizes and unifies what we know. "Green tea can improve memory" is a simple explanatory hypothesis. A theory is encompassing and complex, and includes confirmed hypotheses. This would be a green tea memory theory:

> The antioxidants in green tea help prevent the deterioration of brain cells, and stimulate the flow of blood to the brain. This combined effect results in improved memory.

Many philosophers and scientists have proposed long lists of rules for judging the adequacy of theories (and hypotheses). The essentials can be reduced to four criteria (Schick & Vaughn, 2005).

Falsifiability (Testability)

Falsifiability (or testability) is one of the most frequently mentioned criteria for theory adequacy. It is also one of the most hotly debated (Hartshorne & Weiss, 1932). Imagine that you have a stomach ache and you go to the doctor. She says that your ailment is caused by blockage of energy flow in your spine. You would not be happy with this theory because it is nonsense; such energy has never been demonstrated and cannot be tested. In contrast, a diagnosis that you are suffering a hangover from last night's binge is testable. An unfalsifiable explanation is a string of empty words. As Vaughn (2008) has quipped: "It is equivalent to saying that an unknown thing with unknown properties acts in an unknown way to cause a phenomenon—which is the same thing as offering no explanation at all" (p. 351).

There is another way of saying all of this: a good testable theory predicts something we don't already know. We might not know if something's false; a theory should enable us to increase our knowledge of the universe a bit by finding out if it is indeed false. In the 15th century, witches were hypothesized to be possessed by the devil. If you admitted (after augmented interrogation) that you were a witch, the case would be closed and you would be burned at the stake. If you denied being a witch, this would be evidence that the devil was causing you to lie, and again you would be burned at the stake. We know you are either going to deny or admit to being a witch.

Hypothesizing that you are a witch adds nothing because our minds are already made up. We already know you're guilty.

Some paranormal theories are falsifiable, whereas others are less so. Although there are many systems (or theories) of astrology, any one can usually generate a testable hypothesis based on the time of your birth. In contrast, quantum theory of extra-sensory perception (ESP) states that thoughts are interconnected at a subatomic level (see Chapter 1). How could this be falsified? If everyone is connected, shouldn't everyone have access to everyone's thoughts all the time? Or are connections between thoughts random, like the flickering of electrons? If so, we could never predict when any one person randomly picks up the thought of another, and when this does appear it would be indistinguishable from a non-paranormal random coincidence. And then there is the creationist theory of the origin of the universe which states that the story of Genesis is factually correct. God created the universe 6,000–10,000 years ago. This would seem to permit some easy tests. We can determine the age of rocks and fossils through carbon dating and the age of stars through an analysis of the light they emit. Unfortunately, creation theory permits a convenient additional feature—God may hide evidence of His handiwork in order to test our faith.

Unfalsifiable theories have caused considerable mischief and misery throughout history. Today they are as pervasive as air pollution and global warming. The Nazis believed that they were a race with superior blood. God wills that a particular plot of land belongs to our people, and we must die (and commit genocide) to keep it. God doesn't directly answer our prayers because that would compromise our free will. Mind-reading works only when negative scientists (and skeptical magicians) are kept away. Ghosts are shy and tend to hide when ghost-detecting equipment (or scientists and magicians) are present. Many paranormal phenomena in this text are unfalsifiable.

Unfalsifiability is not always undesirable. Aristotle correctly hypothesized that all material was comprised of atoms. However, because he didn't have a cyclotron or nuclear reactor, he couldn't test it out. (Aristotle also incorrectly proposed that all elements were combinations of four basic elements, fire, earth, air, and water, another untestable idea that contributed to hundreds of years of alchemy.) So, a theory that can't be falsified may not be wrong, but simply ahead of its time.

Furthermore, in real science, researchers at times go to great lengths generating ad hoc hypotheses so that preferred theories can survive assaults of falsifying evidence. Sometimes, as with the case with many paranormal phenomena, such patchwork represents a refusal ever to discard a theory. The theory is embraced with dogmatic fervor. However, at other times such efforts stimulate good research. At first, those who postulated that the earth orbits the sun didn't know how to test this idea against the prevailing and apparently obvious notion that the sun orbits the earth. But they persisted and eventually won out. How do we know when it's time to give up a theory? We need to see how it stands the tests of productivity, comprehensiveness, and simplicity.

Productivity (Predicting Something New)

How do you select between two theories that are testable? Two of the greatest scientists of the world had different theories about gravity. Newton thought that gravity pulled masses together and kept planets in orbit. Einstein thought that gravity was a curve in space and time that bent the movement of whatever passed through. Newton's theory worked well. By examining the tug of planets, astronomers could predict the existence of the planet Neptune. Something was pulling on Uranus, probably an undetected planet. Einstein's theory also worked to predict planets. However, it predicted something extraordinary that Newton never considered. Heavy objects could actually bend light like a lens. Indeed, massive galaxies far away bend space and time so much that, like a telescope, they magnify what is beyond so that we can see what might otherwise be too small to detect. Einstein's theory of gravity is more **productive** than Newton's theory. It predicts the unexpected.

Because good theories are productive, they are always changing and growing, always on the move. One good way to determine if an explanation is not science is to ask if it has evolved over time. Astrological explanations have remained fixed for thousands of years, as have Christian claims that surrender to a deity is the only path to happiness, Buddhist notions that the ego is the source of all misery, and that special people can communicate with the dead. One might rightly question if such notions are fixed theological dogmas and truths, not science.

Comprehensiveness

How much of the world does the theory explain? Good theories have wide scope. Einstein's theory of relativity explains not only why heavy objects bend light, but the fact that time slows down when one travels very fast. This hypothesis has actually been verified in research. Clocks in fast-moving satellites actually run slower than clocks on earth. (Yes, this is true. You can test it out. All you need is a $1 million atomic clock and a jet.) His theories also state that as objects go faster, they get heavier. A particle moving at the speed of light would get extremely heavy. This too has been shown in carefully controlled experiments. (To test this you need a particle accelerator, costing millions of dollars.)

Simplicity

We have already encountered this exceptionally useful criterion in Chapter 2. Recall that **Occam's razor** states that the best explanation is the one that requires the fewest assumptions. To elaborate, a weak theory implies additional untested questions (often answered with **ad hoc** assumptions). In addition, the links between parts of a theory are not simply explained. And the theory conflicts with "background knowledge," what we already have observed to be true.

Lack of simplicity is not always undesirable. As stated by Thomas Kuhn (1970) in *The Structure of Scientific Revolutions*, science progresses when one discovers a certain type of complexity, an **anomaly** that does not fit the prevailing **paradigm** or worldview of facts and investigative methods. When anomalies persist and cannot be explained away, the scientific community is forced to change what it believes is true. Such changes are called **paradigm shifts** and have occurred throughout history. For example, there was a time when people believed that diseases arose spontaneously (Black, 1996). This seemed to fit everyday observations that people fall ill for no apparent reason. However, some observations could not be explained. People living in isolation from those suffering an epidemic were less likely to fall ill. People living under hygienic conditions seemed more protected from disease. A new investigative tool, the microscope, enabled scientists to discover the presence of microorganisms in spoiled food and diseased tissue. Eventually these observations led to a paradigm shift in medicine that linked disease with germs, and used microscopes as an investigative tool (Metchnikoff & Berger, 1939).

Patchwork and Implicit Theories

Sometimes discussions of the paranormal do not formally present a theory explaining their claims. Instead, you may find bits and pieces of theory scattered throughout a presentation. Here, you will have to play the role of master "quiltmaker" and weave together a patchwork of explanations. Also, you may discover theories that are implied, leaving it to you to elaborate. For example, "We have found evidence of dinosaurs roaming the earth 6,000 years ago, which is consistent with what we know of God's plan." The implicit theory here could well be creationism, the notion outlined in the book of Genesis that God created the earth 6,000 years ago in a week.

REALITY CHECK

One of the more challenging tasks facing students of the paranormal is figuring out what implicit theoretical notions underlie a paranormal claim. Astrology is a good example. You will not find a single, coherent, agreed-upon "theory" of how astrology might work. However, if you browse through various astrology websites, you can collect bits and pieces of theory. What can you find? Do any of these notions contradict each other? How could this be a logical problem?

Astrology

Perhaps astrology, and paranormal phenomena in general, are anomalies that challenge contemporary physics. However, in order for them to be truly anomalous, their existence would have to be as undeniable as germs. We aren't there yet.

Astrology fails the test of simplicity. *First, it raises many unanswered questions.* By what forces do celestial bodies influence human affairs? Gravity? Electromagnetism? Something related to dark energy? If the influence is through some unknown force, why do we have no evidence of it, especially if it is so strong as to produce accurate horoscopes, even for nations? Why is the Sun sign so important? Why is the Zodiac divided into 12 sections, and not 13 (as a few astrologers have actually proposed)? When is upbringing more important than the positions of the stars?

Second, the theory of astrology has a huge number of parts which are not integrated or explained. Heavenly bodies travel the zodiac and enter and leave various houses. Some bodies appear together, and then separate. Indeed, taken together there are potentially thousands of patterns of constellations, sun, and the moon. Astrology presents no sensible theory explaining which are important and why.

Third, astrology conflicts with many facts already demonstrated by careful science. Distant stars have no measurable impact on the inhabitants of earth. How could they have an astrological effect? The electromagnetic and gravitational forces of the gravity of the book you are now reading are millions of times stronger than the force of Mars on you, so how can the movement of Mars in the zodiac have any effect? Some heavenly objects once thought to be stars are actually galaxies combining billions of stars. Should they have greater astrological effect? Two stars that appear in the same constellation may not be close by, but huge distances apart. How could they possibly have an equal impact? Perhaps the greatest set of facts that conflict with the claims of astrology is direct empirical tests of horoscope predictions.

Sagan's Balance and the FEDS Standard

In Chapter 1 we introduced Carl Sagan's Balance: "*Extraordinary claims require extraordinary evidence.*" This is an idea that skeptics and many believers accept for evaluating paranormal claims. With paranormal claims, the stakes are high; falsely accepting a claim as true, a "Type 1 Error," can be very costly. However, so far we have considered the rules of **ordinary evidence** that apply to all research. What additional precautions might Sagan's Balance require? Before offering my suggestion, let's begin with a few observations.

First, this book presents a number of remarkable cases in which highly qualified scientists have been fooled by magicians. We will also encounter psychics who have used the same manipulations deployed by professional magicians, quite likely fooling themselves (and scientists) into believing that their inadvertent tricks are evidence of the paranormal. Sincere investigators of the paranormal routinely warn us that scientists are utterly unqualified to detect sleight of hand. This is not part of their training. Even though I have a PhD in the science of psychology, see myself as fairly rigorous, and have studied paranormal claims for half a century, I am not a trained magician. I am still amazed by tricks I simply cannot explain. I have acquired immense respect for the sophistication and depth of training required to become a professional magician.

In addition, it is relatively easy to conduct and publish a marginally acceptable parapsychological study that generally follows the rules of scientific inquiry. Over 30 scientific journals readily accept such research (see Appendix B). However, after publication, the mechanisms of science are not well suited for identifying potential sources of sloppiness, error, and fraud (Bausell, 2007). Laboratories may have closed, making direct inspection impossible. Researchers may have misreported what they actually did, offering their recollections as their only evidence. In chapters to come we will see that out of the thousands of experiments done on paranormal claims, few provide enough evidence to check for potential sloppiness, error, and fraud. Furthermore, the number of paranormal studies accepted for publication greatly exceeds the number of studies subjected to careful *post-publication* scholarly review.

As noted in Chapter 1, if one paranormal claim were to be demonstrated beyond doubt, this could well be the most important discovery in the history of science. Such a discovery could easily justify the most massive international research effort ever, much larger than the program to create an atom bomb or land a man on the moon. It is truly remarkable that many paranormal researchers have concluded that paranormal phenomena have already been demonstrated beyond doubt (Irwin & Watt, 2007). In contrast, independent and impartial reviewers (who are not employed by paranormal institutes, or do not make money promoting paranormal books, products, or services) have concluded that the evidence is virtually nonexistent.

Extraordinary claims require extraordinary evidence. In my opinion this means *expert independent and impartial supervision and replication to eliminate fraud, error, deception,* and *sloppiness.* I call this the **FEDS Standard** (see page 114). Once a test of an extraordinary claim meets this standard, we can justify more extensive inquiry.

Science and Alternative Hypotheses

Science is always on the move. Once a basic phenomenon is discovered, subsequent research explores nuances, implications, and ramifications of underlying theory. Consider the germ theory of disease. As we noted earlier, diseases were once thought to emerge spontaneously. In the 1800s, about the time of Charles Darwin, Italian entomologist Agostino Bassi (2008) discovered that microorganisms caused fungal infections of silkworms. This led him to propose that many human illnesses were also caused by microorganisms, not spontaneous generation. Once the disease-causing potential of microorganisms was identified, research took off as scientists asked a flurry of productive questions. Which microorganisms caused what diseases? Under what conditions are people most likely to be infected? How are microorganisms transmitted from one person to another? Why do some people resist and others succumb to infection? What agents can destroy and protect against microorganisms? Today, the germ theory of disease is part of the foundation of modern medicine.

This same pattern of growth characterizes most of science. Once a phenomenon can be publicly observed and replicated, new questions can be asked and theories developed. The picture is quite different for paranormal research. Paranormal science is as old as other lines of scientific inquiry, yet it still faces the same initial question: Do paranormal phenomena exist? Those in the psi community have concluded that psi's existence has been demonstrated beyond doubt (Irwin & Watt, 2007), but have failed to persuade mainstream researchers. It would be as if medical researchers were still debating whether germs exist. Indeed, studies of the paranormal may well be the only area of long-term scientific investigation that is still at the starting gate. Paranormal researchers must rule out five alternative explanations: oddities of nature and the world of numbers, perceptual error, memory error, the placebo effect, and sensory anomalies and hallucinations. These are the fundamental alternative explanations that we will consider in the following chapters.

The FEDS Standard

To be fully credible, a paranormal study should include expert independent and impartial supervision and replication to minimize:

- **Fraud**: The investigator makes up or changes data, reports only positive results, fails to report compromising design features, or claims to have done something that was in fact not done.
- **Error**: The investigator misuses experimental tools, methods, or statistics.
- **Deception**: Research participants, assistants, or colleagues trick the investigator.
- **Sloppiness**: The investigator does not take into account such research problems as stimulus leakage, submission of positive studies for publication (the file drawer bias), untrained and careless assistants, arbitrarily stopping a study when positive results emerge (arbitrary stop points), or failing to rule out any of the five "alternative explanations" discussed in this text.

Science and Astrology

How does astrology fare when subjected to scientific questioning? First, the fact that the basics of astrology have changed little for thousands of years suggests a system that is not particularly productive. This has not been for a lack of research (for summaries, see Blackmore & Seebold, 2001; Culver & Ianna, 1984; Dean, Mather, & Kelly, 1996; Eysenck & Nias, 1982; and Jerome, 1977). Indeed, there's so much research on astrology that even the summaries have been summarized (Hines, 2003; Schick & Vaughn, 2005).

Extroversion and Introversion

Many of the studies on astrology have focused on the personality traits of introversion and extroversion, the compatibility of couples, and nonpsychological attributes of people (Hines, 2003).

Introversion and extroversion are excellent candidates for astrological research on personality. These are two of the most studied traits in psychology. Furthermore, these traits are readily understood by nonpsychologists, and are clearly quite different from each other. There are many excellent psychological tests of introversion and extroversion, and people generally have a good idea of how introverted or extroverted they are even without aid of psychological assessment.

Astrological horoscopes frequently refer to introversion and extroversion, often directly and in terms very similar to those used by psychologists. For example, if you look at the signs reviewed in Chapter 3 you will see that an Aries is "free, impulsive, and assertive." A more extensive horoscope lists these traditional attributes: "adventurous, energetic, pioneering, courageous, enthusiastic, confident." On the dark side, attributes include "foolhardy and daredevil." Similarly, psychologists define extroverts as people who are "gregarious, assertive, and excitement-seekers."

Are those born in Aries extroverted? The way to test this is simple. Give a large number of people a standard psychological test that measures extroversion and introversion, and determine their sun signs by looking at date and time of birth. Forlano and Ehrlich (1941) examined 7,527 college students and found no relationship. Eysenck and Nias (1982) conducted at least one study that appeared to find a relationship. However, subsequent research suggests that such positive findings are often an artifact of preexisting bias. That is, if you know you are a Pisces, and know the presumed characteristics of a Pisces, you may well complete a personality questionnaire on the basis of reflecting these presumed attributes. Indeed researchers have found no relationship between one's sun sign and objective physical characteristics such as body build, height, weight, and neck size (Culver & Ianna, 1984). Astrologers might respond by hypothesizing that sophisticated and accurate horoscopes must also take into account the positions of the planets. Again, research does not support this reasonable ad hoc hypothesis (Crowe, 1990; Kelly, 1998).

The Gauquelin Study

Astrologers frequently cite the apparently supportive research of Michel Gauquelin, a French scientist who looked at astrological signs of various professions (Gauquelin, 1974; Irving, 2003). His most famous claim was that, after examining 2,000 champions and thousands of non-champions, champions are more likely to be born when Mars is rising (the planet Mars appearing at the horizon at the time of one's birth). Examples include Babe Ruth, Mohammed Ali, Tiger Woods, and Venus Williams (but not her sister,

Serena). Indeed, this observation has been called the "Mars Effect" or "Gauquelin effect," as if it were a fundamental law of physics.

Actually, some type of link between Mars and athleticism makes sense to astrologers. Mars was the god of war. Warriors are active and aggressive. Athletes are also active. So where the planet Mars appears in the sky at the time of one's birth should be associated with athleticism. Is it?

There are problems (Dean et al., 1996). First, it is misleading to claim that Gauquelin looked at Mars as a rising sign. More precisely, he divided the path that Mars travels from rising to setting into six equal parts, or sectors (a strange strategy typically not used by astrologers). Sectors 1 (the actual point of rising over the horizon) and 4 (Mars is in mid-sky) are most associated with athleticism. Why is this a problem? There are thousands of possible astrological patterns. The sun, moon, and all of the planets have their rising signs. If we include additional sectors, the possible signs multiply quickly into the tens of thousands. If you have enough time (Gauquelin devoted much of his life) and enough subjects (Gauquelin had thousands), eventually you will find a sign somewhere that fits what you expect. This is fishing in a cosmic sea of possibility, a phenomenon we will meet in Chapter 6 when we consider the law of very large numbers.

Second, Gauquelin did not deploy double-blind procedures. From a huge list of subjects (whose signs he knew), he selected those he considered to be champions. He should have had someone blind to his hypotheses and the signs of athletes make the selection. One wonders why he included ordinary basketball and soccer players, and even Italian aviators, as athletic champions. Strengthening the criticism is the failure of most researchers to agree on his selection of champions (Nienhuys, 1997), or to replicate these findings when more controlled procedures are used.

Most seriously, Gauquelin's findings could have been an artifact of biases in recording times of birth (Dean et al., 1996; Dean, 2002). Much of Gauquelin's birth data was obtained at a time when parents, and not medical professionals, recorded birth times, the belief in astrology was common, and occupations ran in families. Parents could easily have made errors consistent with astrological expectations for family professions. For example, a family of athletes might be motivated to report a time of birth consistent with an astrological chart for athletes. This interpretation is consistent with two findings: (a) astrological patterns do not appear for children whose time of birth was recorded by someone other than a parent (a nurse, for example), and (b) there is a deficit of births for what people likely considered to be "unlucky times" not specified in astrology, for example the thirteenth day of each month, and midnight (which common superstition tagged the "witching hour," a time for massive witch hunts centuries earlier).

The Carlson Study

Carlson (1985) conducted what is one of the best and most extensive studies on astrology. One of the most frequent ad hoc critiques leveled at astrology studies has been their use of simplistic and mechanical horoscopes. Astrology is a complex enterprise, and casting a horoscope can indeed be as sophisticated as performing a complete medical assessment. A horoscope is only as good as the person creating it.

REALITY CHECK "Studies on astrology are flawed because they use simplistic horoscopes that do not resemble professional horoscopes." Does this claim reflect a logical flaw (Chapter 4)?

To meet objections that previous studies involved superficial and unprofessional horoscopes, Carlson sought the assistance of the National Council of Geocosmic Research (NCGR: www.geocosmic.org/). The NCGR is the nation's most prestigious professional astrological organization. It includes serious astrologers, medical professionals, and scientists, and offers a certification program as well as a scientific journal. With the advice of the NCGR, Carlson incorporated prominent American and European astrologers, all of whom agreed that his research procedures were fair before the study began.

In one test, professional astrologers constructed horoscopes for 177 subjects recruited from newspaper ads. Then, each participant was given three horoscopes and asked to pick theirs. They could not. In a second test, 166 subjects took the California Psychological Inventory (CPI), a widely used and accurate questionnaire that measures a full range of personality traits traditionally accepted by psychologists. Most of the personality traits mentioned in the CPI have clear parallels in astrology. Each astrologer was given one natal chart and three CPI personality profiles. One profile was for the subject whose natal chart was computed. Astrologers could not match the correct natal chart and personality profile. Thus, an international study involving highly respected and highly trained professional astrologers, using methods approved by professional astrologers, and published in *Nature*, one of the most respected scientific journals, failed to support astrology. These findings are consistent with the vast body of research already conducted on astrology.

Consider Alternative Explanations

In the previous section of our Critical Thinker's Toolkit we examined three reality-checking tools for finding support for a claim. We considered how to select sources, think logically, and test and evaluate scientific observations. We now turn to how evidence itself can be confusing. When considering paranormal claims, our reality checks must rule out five alternative hypotheses. Sometimes things aren't what they seem because of a misunderstanding of unexpected oddities of nature and numbers, perceptual errors and trickery, memory errors, the placebo effect, and sensory anomalies and hallucinations. Good science rules out alternative explanations; pseudoscience fails to do so.

6

Reality Checking for Oddities of Nature and the World of Numbers

The world is full of surprises. You need only consult the latest edition of the *Guinness Book of World Records* or *Ripley's Believe It or Not* to uncover a wealth of bizarre and unusual facts. Lizards that walk on water, frogs with two heads, fish that rain from the sky, housewives lifting automobiles—there's enough to entertain for hours. In a previous age, many of such oddities might be viewed as evidence of the paranormal. Today, paranormal researchers do not embrace the *Guinness* and *Ripley* books as evidence. Most people recognize that their contents are natural phenomena.

Yet the world serves up too many oddities to fit the record books. Many tempt us to consider paranormal interpretations. A slender slimy form bobs above the surface of Loch Ness. Is it the Loch Ness Monster (perhaps from another dimension) or a log? A hand placed on an electrically charged photographic plate leaves a glowing hand-shaped image. Is it a photograph of spiritual energy or an artifact of electrical discharge? A digital camera records a shining orb in a haunted house. Is it a ghost or a lens reflection? A marble statue of the Virgin Mary weeps. Or is it condensation of water drawn from humid air to cold stone? Years ago, Native Americans witnessed gigantic paranormal entities (gods) arriving on their shores. Or were these simply Spanish ships?

UFO (unidentified flying object) sightings are perhaps the best known and most enduring examples of wide-scale misinterpretation of natural oddities as paranormal or borderline paranormal phenomena. The UFO era began in 1947 when Kenneth Arnold, a private pilot, reported seeing nine airborne objects that looked like saucers. Around the world others began seeing flying saucers. Then came the famous alleged 1947 UFO crash near Roswell, New Mexico, later revealed to be a government crashed balloon radar array. To this day UFO sightings persist, complete with expert anecdotal accounts and photographic evidence, and repeatedly broadcast in television "news" documentaries. All can conceivably be explained as natural phenomena (planets, stars, reflections of the moon, ball lightning, aircraft, missile launches, satellites, balloons, searchlights, test clouds, flares, St. Elmo's fire, optical camera distortions, simple fraud) as well as examples of perceptual and memory error and sense anomalies (McGaha, 2009). For an excellent review, see the January, February 2009 issue of *Skeptical Inquirer* (Frazier, 2009).

It is beyond the scope of this book to catalog all of the unusual natural phenomena that have at one time or another inspired paranormal beliefs. Our concern is more basic: the world of numbers and how a misunderstanding of statistics can fool us and lead us to make pseudoscientific mistakes.

Probability Estimates and Bias

We misjudge probabilities because of lack of experience with the unusual. Sometimes this simply involves not knowing an esoteric statistic. Here are some examples. Are you more likely to die on a motorcycle or on a bicycle? The odds of dying on a motorcycle are 1 in 938, and on a bicycle 1 in 4,472. What about on a bus or train? Answer: your odds on a bus are 1 in 94,242 and in a train 1 in 139,617 (www.NSC.org). Drowning in a swimming pool or bath tub? 1 in 6,031 vs. 1 in 9,377. What about winning the jackpot in a slot machine vs. a "mega millions" lottery? 1 in 16,777,216 vs. 1 in 175,711,536 (casinogambling.about.com/). For more odds see www.veegle.com.

However, people tend to make consistent errors when estimating probabilities. A simple example is the **availability error** in which one notices and remembers evidence that stands out (Tversky & Kahneman, 1973). For example, imagine you could not get to sleep last night because the new neighbor's dog barked twice. The next morning, tired and upset, you complained to your neighbor that the dog was barking all night. Your frustration made two barks stand out, leading you to overestimate the actual frequency of barks. A friend shares with you a remarkable newspaper horoscope. It says she will come upon some money, and the same day she finds $5. This event sticks in your mind, prompting you to comment on "all the evidence for astrology." Because of the availability error, we often make hasty conclusions and over-generalize from a few cases.

Conversely, people underestimate the probability of rare negative events, for example, the likelihood that they will get injured in a car accident, or experience an illness from smoking, until the unexpected actually hits and they have an accident or get sick. Ask someone who is not reading this book the following question: "Compared to others, how likely is it that you will get sick next month? Less likely, equally likely, or more likely?" Most people will answer "less likely" even though the law of averages states that the probability that the average person will get sick next month is, of course, average. Try asking the same question to a group of 50 people. Statistically, the mean answer should be "average"; in fact researchers find that "less likely" is what most people will claim. This common mistake illustrates **unreasonable, or illusory optimism** (Weinstein, 1980; Weinstein & Klein; 1996), the tendency to perceive yourself as more likely than your peers to have something good happen to you (a raise, new friend, solve a problem, win the lottery), and less likely than your peers to have something bad happen to you. Similarly, gamblers tend to overestimate the probability of winning, especially when the stakes are high (Sanbonmatsu, Posavac, & Stasney, 1997).

Unreasonable optimism can be one example why smokers think they are less at risk than other smokers, why teenagers think they are less likely than others to contract AIDS, why many people do not use seat belts, or stay in relationships that aren't working. Fortunately, there are strategies to minimize the risk of such distorted thinking, including having an unfortunate experience. Those who have been in a car accident are more likely to wear seat belts (McKenna & Albery, 2001). Nonetheless, unreasonable optimism is a general process in which we misjudge probabilities. An unscrupulous psychic or astrologer who knows this human tendency can comfortably predict that you will have more good fortune, and less misfortune, than others. It is likely you will agree.

Math Ignorance

Psychic Madam Phoebe is very popular on the lecture circuit. Each week she addresses groups of about 75 eager listeners. She begins each lecture with a dramatic demonstration of her paranormal abilities. As the lights dim, she closes her eyes, stretches her arms upward, and in a hushed tone pronounces, "I hereby determine that there are two people in this room who have exactly the same birthday. The same day and month." She then asks everyone to write down their birthday, and has three audience volunteers tabulate the results, to be announced at the end of her hour-long presentation. Remarkably, Madam Phoebe has made this prophecy for hundreds of groups and her success rate is nearly 100%. Recently a local newspaper reporter decided to check the psychic out. Convinced the Madam was a fraud, he attended several sessions in disguise, and each time volunteered to tabulate the collected birthday reports. He was astonished to discover that indeed her success rate was 99%. Before publishing his findings, he went to a local junior college and found a professor interested in paranormal phenomena. After explaining Phoebe's claims and his experiences, the professor offered several hypotheses. Perhaps the psychic had retroactive psychokinetic abilities (Chapter 12), a claimed paranormal power to use one's thoughts to change events in the past. That is, perhaps Madam Phoebe used her psychic skills to change the actual birthdays of two audience members. Alternatively, he suggested she may have used her psychokinetic powers to attract two people with the same birthday to her sessions. Or perhaps she used mind control to make two participants unconsciously write down the same birthday. The professor suggested testing Madam Phoebe in controlled conditions in which she would perform for random groups of 75 students at his college. Phoebe was more than willing to comply. As a check, birthdays would be obtained from university records before students attended the psychic's lecture. Astonishingly, the psychic maintained a near perfect hit rate. In just about every group, two participants had exactly the same birthday. Which hypothesis is supported? Have we missed anything?

Sometimes we misjudge probabilities because we are unfamiliar with a mathematical rule or haven't done our math homework. Let's begin with a popular example. In a room of 23 individuals, what is the probability that two will have the same birthday (day and month)? Most people guess that the probability of this should be low, maybe one out of 20. Actually, the chances are 50/50. Furthermore, the probability that two in a group of 75 will have the same birthday is 99.9%, a probability often called the **birthday paradox**. In other words, there was nothing spooky going on in Madam Phoebe's sessions. To understand, you need to understand a little about statistics.

Imagine there is only one person in a room. What is the probability that the birthday of this person is unique in that room, and there is no one else in the room with the birthday? This question is actually a little silly; because there is no other person in the room, logically she can't share a birthday. The probability is 365/365, 100%. If there are two people in the room what is the probability that person No. 2 does not have the same birthday as Person No. 1? If No. 1 has taken one birthday, there are 364 left, any of which would be different from No. 1's birthday. Therefore, No. 2 has 364 chances out of 365, or 364/365, of having a birthday different from that of No. 1.

When we get to person No. 3, let's assume for the sake of argument that two birthdates have already been taken, so there are 363 birthdays left untaken and the probability that No. 3's birthday will be one of these is 363/365. Following this logic, each time we add a person, we reduce by one his or her chances of having a birthday not already taken. Now, to obtain the overall probability that none of the three share a birthday the statistical rule is to multiply the individual probabilities, 365/365*364/365*363/365.

The answer is .992. It's almost certain that in a room of three, no two will share birthdays. Note that the statistical multiplication rule yields the very result you might have predicted. You can trust the rule, it works fine.

Now, for a room of 23, we simply apply the same rule 23 times:

$$365/365*364/365*363/365*362/365*361/365*360/365*359/365*358/$$
$$365*357/365*356/365*355/365*354/365*353/365*352/365*351/365*$$
$$350/365*349/365*348/365*347/365*346/365*345/365*344/365*343/365$$

and get 0.493. Rounding things out, the chances are about 50/50 that in a room of 23 people, no two will share the same birthday. But we were interested in the probability that two people would share the *same* birthday. If the chances are 50/50 that no two have the same birthday, logically the chances are 50/50 that two will indeed share the same birthday. Using the same process, the probability is 99.9% that two people in a group of 75 will have the same birthday.

Here's another question. Take the large sheet of paper and fold it in half. Once again, fold the folded paper in half. Now imagine folding it 25 times. (Obviously this is an imaginary experiment because the laws of physics prevent you from folding it more than 8 times. So imagine you have paranormal paper.) If you do this 25 times, how thick will the resulting paper wad be? Here's a hint. The paper is 0.1 millimeter thick. Write down your guess before proceeding. The answer: After 25 folds, your folded wad would be a mile thick. Do the math. Each time you fold the paper, you double the previous thickness.

Coincidences

Coincidences involve events that unexpectedly occur together in a meaningful way, without any apparent causal link. A present–future coincidence might be seen as a prophecy, an event that correctly follows an omen or prediction. A present–present coincidence might suggest a set of events that are remarkably linked by some paranormal process outside of the world of causality. The best way to explore what is going on is to contemplate a variety of remarkable coincidences.

Popular paranormalists have made much of coincidences. Carl Jung, Freud's famous breakaway disciple, invented a term, **synchronicity**, to refer to remarkable coincidences. Confusingly, he defined two synchronous events as not causally determined, yet not completely random. I have yet to figure that out. Similarly, Redfield (1993) in *The Celestine Prophecy* counsels us to look at strange coincidences as somehow fated and willed, and to use them as spiritual guides. SQuire's [sic] silly but very popular *God Winks* books argue that there are no coincidences because all are messages from the divine. And then there's Deepak Chopra (2003) who advises that coincidences enable us to connect with the underlying field of infinite possibilities, *synchrodestiny*, where it becomes possible to achieve the spontaneous fulfillment of our every desire. Such a notion begs for a reality check.

In fact, coincidences happen all the time and usually mean nothing. If you want meaning, go to Shakespeare (see page 138). For just about any topic, if you look hard enough, you will find a coincidence. Those intrigued by such things often point to presidents (Leavy, 1992), starting with Lincoln and Kennedy. Examine these strange facts. Lincoln was elected in 1860, Kennedy in 1960; both were assassinated on a Friday while with their wives; both were involved in civil rights; both had lost a child while in office; both were killed by a bullet shot to the head; Lincoln was killed in Ford's theater, and Kennedy was killed in a Lincoln, a card made by Ford. According to some, Booth (Lincoln's assassin) was born in 1839, Oswald (Kennedy's assassin) was born in 1939. There seems to be a lot of synchronicity going on with Lincoln and Kennedy. What are the deep forces of life trying to tell us?

Why stop with Lincoln and Kennedy? Why not look at two other assassinated presidents, William McKinley and James Garfield? Sure enough, both were Republicans, both born and raised in Ohio (as was the author of this book!), both were veterans of the civil war, both served in the House of Representatives, both supported the gold standard, both names have eight letters, both were replaced by vice-presidents from New York City, both of their vice-presidents had mustaches, both were shot in September at the onset of their terms, Garfield named his cat "McKinley" and McKinley named his cat "Garfield" (this latest claim is hotly disputed; Schick & Vaughn, 2005).

One could write a small volume on coincidences involving the terrorist attack of 9/11. Both New York City and Afghanistan have 11 letters. The terrorist who first threatened the Twin Towers, Ramsin Yuseb, has 11 letters. George W. Bush has 11 letters. The 11th state is New York. Two flights hit the twin towers, Flights 11 and 92; 9 + 2 = 11. Flight 77 has 65 passengers (6 + 5 = 11).

What most people don't realize is that if you look deep enough, you can always dig up a coincidence for just about anything. If you take all of the words in the Bible, and circle every tenth letter, some of the circled letters would form words, and some of the words might seem to convey a message, a sort of Bible Code. For another example, consider the Reformed Church of the Flying Spaghetti Monster (Chapter 15). It would be truly remarkable if there were no coincidences. Two processes involved are the inherent **clumpiness of randomness** and the **law of very large numbers**.

The Clumpiness of Randomness

Random lists rarely appear random. You will always find clumps or streaks that seem unexpected, and even meaningful. This contributes to the **clustering illusion**. Imagine you tossed a coin 51 times and your sequence of heads (H) and tails (T) was spread evenly, like this:

HTHTHTHTHTHTHTHTHTHTHTHTHTHTHTHTHTHTHTHTHTHTHTHTHTHTH

Does this look random? Of course not, it's too regular. You can see that any random sequence has to have a few clumps to be convincing.[1] What people underestimate is the frequency and size of clumps that will appear in a random sequence. For example, Myers (2004) flipped a coin 51 times and got this sequence of heads (H) and tails (T):

HTTTHHHTTTTHHTTHTTHHTTHTTTHTHTTTTTTHTTHTHHHHTHHTTTT

Remember, this is a purely random sequence, nothing more. Now imagine I told you that this sequence contained a secret and profound message. Once I planted this seed, what could you find? I discovered there are 19 "TT" pairs but only 8 "HH" pairs. In addition, there are five "TTTT" combinations and only one "HHHH" combination. And "TTTTT" appears twice while "HHHHH" never appears. There is even one "TTTTTT" combination. The Myers Randomized Sequence prefers even-numbered T combinations. "T" stands for "Tails." It can also stand for "Truth." "H" stands for "Heads." It is clear that if you are looking for truth in your life, don't use your head too much. To discover truth you must turn what you think about probabilities on its "tail." It's obvious I did a bit of manipulation to fit my biases (see Chapter 7).

We see such clumpiness all the time in gambling. A poker player wins three times in a row. Friends conclude he has a *hot hand* or *winning streak*, and bet on him. Conversely, a gambler might identify a slot machine that hasn't paid out for a full day. It's time for a win, so she plays the machine. This too is a mistake. If the slot machine isn't defective, your chances of winning are the same with other similar machines. To believe that the chances of a random event are influenced by, or can be predicted from, other independent events is the **gambler's fallacy**. Imagine you purchase three lottery tickets today. Your first, second, and third tickets win. Should you assume you've been blessed with a winning streak and buy more tickets, or stop buying tickets because you figure the probability of winning again after three wins is reduced? The only reasonable answer is to realize that you misunderstand probabilities and that your chances of getting a fourth ticket have nothing to do with your previous winnings. It's pure chance.

Statisticians refer to a phenomenon called **regression to the mean** (Gilovich, 1991). Put simply, it means that if you have an extreme run of bad or good luck, chance alone says this won't continue. In the long run, scores average out. In Chicago, the average temperature for March may be 50 degrees. Some days will be warmer, and some colder. And there will always be a few extreme days. But generally, temperature will average out to 50 degrees. So if it is freezing in Chicago in March, and you pray for warmer weather, the odds are that the extreme temperature will not continue—just through regression to the mean.

> **REALITY CHECK**   How might the clumpiness of randomness illustrate the notion of regression to the mean? Consider a winning streak in a game of poker.

The Law of Very Large Numbers

Death Premonitions

Holt (2004) has calculated the probability of having a death premonition, just by chance. Let's walk through the logic. Think of all the living people you know, know of, and have thought about at least once over an entire year. This includes your family, friends, distant relatives, authors, teachers, movie actors, politicians, and so on. Of this long list, perhaps 10 will die each year. (If this seems excessive, do a Google search for "people who died this year" and pick a year. How many do you recognize? Probably more than 10.) So we start with the reasonable premise that 10 of the people on your list will die each year. This includes distant relatives, former acquaintances, movie actors, politicians, etc.

We started with the assumption that over a year you have at least one thought about each of the people on the list (while they are still alive). That's a given. So, if the pope is on your list, we would assume that you thought about the pope at least one time over the last 12 months. How long is a thought? For the sake of argument, let's say a thought lasts five minutes. In a year there are 105,120 five-minute intervals. Statistics show that there are 10 chances in 105,120 that you will have a "thought" about one of these people five minutes before you hear of his or her death. Put differently, that's about one chance in 10,000, not very likely.

Now look at the big picture. There are over 300 million people in the United States, and each person has one chance in 10,000 of thinking about the passing of someone they know of five minutes before their death. That changes the numbers considerably. Specifically, over 25,000 people a year, over 70 a day, will think of someone dying five minutes before their death. This is by chance alone, with nothing spooky going on. In this day when most people have access to the internet, what is remarkable is that there are so few premonitions of death reported. We should be hearing about hundreds every month. Psychics should be enjoying a nonrandom run of field days.

Prophetic Dreams

Most people can remember a dream that came true. Perhaps you had a dream of meeting a friend, and the next week you met your friend. Perhaps you had a dream of getting a raise, and you got one. Are prophetic dreams coincidences, or extraordinary evidence of the paranormal? (For an interesting discussion of how our motivations affect the extent we think our dreams are prophetic, see Morewedge & Norton, 2009.)

Paulos (2001) has looked at the numbers. Most people have about 250 dreams a night. This is not so hard to believe if you consider how many thoughts you have during the average day. After all, dreams are thoughts we have while sleeping. Of course, we remember very few of these dreams. However, a memory cue might help you remember. Perhaps last week one of your 1,750 ($7 \times 250 = 1,750$) dreams involved a small furry dog. There is no reason you would remember such a trivial dream, unless you nearly drove your bicycle over a small furry dog. This could readily trigger a memory of your furry dog dream, and provide you with false evidence for your paranormal powers, at least concerning small furry dogs. A much more conservative estimate of dreams leads to the same conclusion. Imagine that everyone remembers only one dream every day, or 365 dreams a year. In a country of 300 million, there are 109,500,000,000 remembered dreams a year. By chance alone, some are bound to coincidentally precede some remarkable event (Schick & Vaughn, 2005). Statistics suggest that for every dream that comes true, there are billions that don't.

To actually test if dream prophecies come true, one would have to actually obtain dreams before a prophesied event. Furthermore, the prophecy and event would have to be unambiguous, not fortune-cookie platitudes. One remarkable study pulled this off. In 1937 Charles Lindbergh's baby was kidnapped, causing national outrage. Murray, at the Harvard Psychological Clinic, placed a newspaper advertisement asking people to send in their dreams concerning the fate of the baby. Of course, the baby's body was eventually discovered. But before this gruesome event, Murray (Murray & Wheeler, 1936) had obtained about 1,300 dreams and could analyze them for unambiguous predictions, such as whether or not the baby was dead. Many dreams simply repeated speculations that had appeared in newspapers. Only 5% indicated the baby was dead and only 7% predicted concrete conditions associated with the murder. Only four people correctly predicted that the baby was dead and buried near trees.

Littlewood's Law of Miracles

These examples illustrate Littlewood's Law of Miracles (Bollobás, 1986): *a person can by chance expect one miracle a month*. How can this possibly be? For the sake of argument, Littlewood begins by defining a miracle as an extraordinary event of extraordinary significance, whose probability is one in a million. How often have you heard someone use that informal statistic, "A miracle ... one chance in a million"? Also, for the sake of argument, let's assume that a human will experience one thing per second (this sentence, the next sentence, the sound of a fan, the binding of a book, the color of the sky ...). If this typical person is alert 12 hours a day, in 35 days they will have experienced 1,008,000 things. (Do the math.) We have just defined a miracle as something that will occur one time out of a million. Well, that's 35 days, a little over a month. We have just defined a miracle as something that has a probability of one in a million.

> **REALITY CHECK** One person's trivial coincidence might be another person's divine message. List all the things that happened yesterday that seemed like a coincidence. When done, spend a day carefully noting coincidences. How might someone view your coincidences as evidence of the paranormal? Save your list for Chapter 7 (Perceptual Errors) and see if that chapter offers additional interpretations for your discovered coincidences.

Pi

It is fitting that we end with pi. Pi is the ratio of a circle's diameter to its circumference:

3.14159265358979323846264338327950288419716939937510582097494459230781640628620899862803482534211706798214808651328230664709384460955058223172535940812848111745028410 27

01938521105559644622948954930381964428810975665933446128
47564823378678316527120190914564856692346034861045432664
82133936072602491412737245870066063155881748815209209628
29254091715364367892590360011330530548820466521384146951
941511609 ...

This number is a constant and never changes no matter the size of the circle. Anyone computing pi will obtain the exact same number. What makes pi useful is that it is a very large number (actually it is infinite) available to anyone. Furthermore, it has some of the properties of a random number; as far as we know, knowing one number in the pi sequence is useless in helping us predict the next number. Therefore any message you see in pi is meaningless. But the law of very large numbers says that surely there are messages to be found.

To find meaning in pi we need to create a pi number – letter key, associating each letter of the English alphabet with a different letter. 0 = a, 1 = b, 2 = c ... 23 = x, 24 = y, and 25 = z. So the first five digits after the decimal point, "14159," would correspond to "OPJ," because 14 = O, 15 = P, and 9 = J. Note that when two digits can refer to either a single letter (15 = P) or two letters (1 = B, 5 = F), we go with the two digits in combination, "3–14–15–9."

Now we can search for meaning. Given that the complete number pi is more than trillions and trillions and trillions of digits long (remember, it is actually infinite), how can one go about looking for mysteries? Fortunately, Dave Anderson (1996) has created an internet pi-search page. Convert your desired words into numbers, and then search for these numbers.

Using this system, I decided to ask pi one of the deepest questions I can think of. Does God exist? There are two answers I was willing to consider: "GOD IS" and "NO GOD." The pi translation for the phrase "GOD IS" is "6143818" which occurs at position 3,973,885. The number of "NO GOD" is "13146143" which occurs at position 28,330,853. Therefore, the very first answer the pi code gives to the God Question is "GOD IS." Apparently one of the core mathematical patterns of the universe has no doubt about this question.[2] However, being cautious, I decided to check the validity of this answer. So I decided to convert the first 100 digits to letters and look for messages. Here are the letters of pi:

D.OPJCGFDFIJHJDXIEGCGED**DID**CHJFA**CII**ETHQJDJJDHFKF
ICAJHEJEEFJX**AH**IQEA GCIGUIJ**JIGCIA**DEIZDEV**RAG**

Can you see the first five words to appear in pi? The most obvious are:

DID, AH, JIG, CIA, and RAG

Pi speaks simply, in monosyllables. But this should not distract us from the simple truths that may be hidden. First, we note that there is no reason to be limited to current dictionary definitions of terms. After all, pi is eternal. So, consulting dictionary.com, I found the following definitions:

DID
Past tense of do

AH
An exclamation of pain, surprise, pity, complaint, dislike, joy, etc.

JIG
A machine for holding a tool
A lively irregular dance
A joke, prank, or trick ("The jig is up")

CIA
Central Intelligence Agency

RAG
A musical composition in ragtime
A worthless scrap of cloth
A worthless scrap of anything
A shabby-looking or exhausted person
A tabloid sensationalizing newspaper
A piece of untrimmed roof
To scold
To subject to teasing
To play a crude practical joke
The act of teasing, or playing a crude practical joke
To break up lumps of ore for sorting

So what is the message here? To me the following arrangement conveys the combined meaning of the first five words of pi:

AH! Jig? Did CIA rag?

After considerable contemplation, I have arrived at this interpretation:

This is pi's answer to my inquiry concerning the existence of the deity. Clearly, pi is surprised and astonished at my theological efforts ("AH!"). It immediately questions whether this is some sort of joke or trick ("Jig?").

And it prompts us to ask if my claimed discovery of evidence for God is actually part of a massive CIA conspiracy ("Did CIA rag?"). It is unclear why the CIA would go to the trouble of inserting evidence for God in pi, presumably using retroactive psychokinesis (see Chapter 12). Is it to "scold," "tease," or simply to play a "crude practical joke" ("rag")? Alas, we would have to look deeper into pi, far beyond the first 100 digits. Regardless, I am troubled that pi thinks my spiritual efforts are some sort of joke.

Science and Chance

Scientific experiments are designed to rule out chance as an alternative explanation. Informally, we can use the same methods. In statistics and research we have a system of rules, procedures, and "checks and balances" to help us sort things out.

Replication and Sample Size

It is illogical and unfair to generalize from one example. The bad apple you got from the store might be an exception. Similarly, one scientific study does not convincingly prove a claim. Too much can go wrong. Researchers can be dishonest. Sometimes the unexpected happens. To guard against this, scientists require additional studies (from different unbiased researchers and labs) to confirm any finding. Any single study must include a sufficient number of participants to be powerful enough to yield a significant result. Generally, data from one or two individuals are not enough, and are akin to anecdotes (Chapter 3).

Control Groups

A good way of ruling out random fluctuation as an explanation is to include a control group. Perhaps students generally pass their first driving test after drinking green tea for a week. In itself, this finding says little because we do not know the baseline. We need a control group of students who take their first driving test without drinking green tea. Good control groups enable us to answer the question, "Compared to what?"

Arbitrary Stop Points

We have seen that purely random phenomena happen in clumps or streaks. If you were studying a purely random phenomenon, for example the relationship between foot size and grades, you would inevitably run into a streak of cases of short-footed individuals with high grades. This would likely even out in the long run, possibly by a streak of short-footed individuals with low grades. So what would happen if you stopped your study right after your first streak of short-footed, low-grade individuals? This would be cheating, and your study would seem to confirm that foot size is related to IQ. So you can't run a study over and over, and apply an arbitrary stop point once you get the results you want. For example, one might suspect that Gauquelin (1974), the noted astrology researcher, continuously worked his data until he finally found a pattern, a somewhat obscure relationship between two appearances of the planet Mars in two points in the sky and athleticism (Chapter 5). What makes this appear to be an arbitrary stop point is that the obvious astrological predictions for athleticism did not pan out, and the pattern he did find was not one that astrologers would typically hypothesize.

Publication Bias

We have already seen (Chapter 3) that researchers tend to submit exciting and positive results for publication. They aren't interested in their failures. Journals do the same thing and tend to publish positive results. If you did a very careful experiment and found that shouting at clouds had no effect on whether or not it rained, I doubt you would send this off to a scientific journal. If you did, the journal certainly would not publish it. The fact that positive results are more likely to find their way into scientific journals is called publication bias, and is probably an explanation for many scientific demonstrations of paranormal phenomena. In terms of probability, one might expect by chance 5 out of every 100 studies on the paranormal to yield positive results. This would be the chance rate if the paranormal indeed did not exist. Of these 100 studies it is likely that the 5 positive results would eventually be published, giving a misleading impression of support for the paranormal. To rule out publication bias, researchers and journals must scrupulously publish both negative and positive results. Journals that focus on the paranormal are beginning to do this, and are requesting that researchers put on record intended studies before they are conducted. Another strategy is to conduct a meta-analysis of many studies and calculate how many nonsignificant studies would have to have been carried out to nullify the effects of an overall significant result. Because meta-analysis is a very popular tool in research on parapsychology, we consider it in Chapter 12.

It is frequently noted that one of the strongest findings in scientific research on the paranormal is a negative correlation between study quality and obtained support for the paranormal (Bausell, 2007; Hines, 2003). Poorly designed and inexpensive studies are more likely to yield positive results. Good studies are much less likely to yield positive results. This is the opposite of what is found in all other areas of research. Ordinarily, the better the study, the more likely it will find an effect.

Summary: Psychic Bias

Yes, it is easy to be tricked by the numbers. Nearly everyone has mistaken ideas about how probable various events are. We may perceive a perfectly ordinary coincidence as something more than random, perhaps as evidence of the paranormal. Some people are more prone to this type of error than others. Blackmore and Troscianko (1985) have found that people who believe in paranormal abilities are especially prone to make mistakes in probability judgments, a phenomenon we might call *psychic bias*. One study involved an automatic coin-flipping test in which believers and nonbelievers were instructed to use their thoughts to influence the results of automated coin-flipping. In one part of the experiment, the researchers asked paranormal believers and disbelievers to guess the number of "heads" one might expect by chance alone. Believers, but not disbelievers, displayed an interesting bias called *chance baseline shift*. Specifically, they *underestimated* the number of heads one might get from chance alone. Why is this important? Because when Blackmore and Troscianko asked participants to use their thoughts to influence the outcome of coin tosses, and got perfectly random results, paranormal believers thought they were nonrandom (of course they were from the believers' distorted perspective). Because of their bias, they were more likely to believe they had used their paranormal powers to influence the coins. In more general terms, such a bias illustrates how our beliefs and expectations can influence perception, a topic we consider in the next chapter.

> **REALITY CHECK** How might availability error, illusory optimism, math ignorance, and the clustering illusion enhance psychic bias?

How to Tell When a Scientific Finding is "Significant"

When do you take a scientific finding seriously? When is it "significant"?

Paranormal events are by definition extraordinary and go beyond the world depicted through normal science. If you erroneously conclude an effect is due to a cause rather than chance, you've made a *Type I error*. (Erroneously concluding that a real effect is just chance is a Type II error.) Put simply, a Type I error is concluding that "there's something special going on" when in fact "there's nothing special going on." In this text we conduct reality checks to identify Type I errors.

A scientist performs an experiment to determine if there is some special phenomenon beyond what one might expect by chance, perhaps a remarkable ability to win the lottery, read minds, or predict the outcome of elections. Simply by chance our scientist will get positive results a few times. By chance a poker player will get a winning hand, with nothing mysterious going on. And people do sometimes win the lottery.

Fortunately, there are statistical procedures for estimating the likelihood of making a Type I error. For example, we assume that a lottery is a purely random and fair game and whether or not you win is due purely to chance. Yet some people do win. If more people win than might be expected, we might suspect that the lottery isn't purely random. Perhaps someone's cheating, or maybe there are paranormal forces at work. To explore what is happening, lottery statisticians compute how many people would have to win before we conclude that something strange is going on. Perhaps by chance one might expect 10, 100, or maybe 1,000 winners out of a million. Any number larger than 10, 100, or 1,000 would be suspicious. But how do you pick which number? It depends on how much risk you are willing to take. To what extent are you willing to risk a Type I error?

This "risk level" of making a Type I error is called the *alpha level*. By convention, many scientists accept an alpha level of .05 (or occasionally .01 or .10). That means they are willing to conclude that the lottery is indeed suspicious if their confidence level is .05, that is, their chances of being wrong are 1 out of 20. Sometimes scientists use a shorthand by denoting the letter "p" for this level, where "p" stands for "probability of a false positive." Frequently you will see statements like this in scientific reports (again, note that "p" is actually better, lower, than .05, meaning the results are significant):

> We compared the success rate of predictions of 50 psychics and 50 nonpsychics. Psychics were correct 45% of the time and nonpsychics 41% of the time. The psychic predictions were accurate significantly more often than nonpsychic predictions ($p = .02$). We conclude there is evidence that psychics can predict the future.

If this study found no evidence for the accuracy of psychic predictions, it might read like this:

We compared the success rate of predictions of 50 psychics and 50 nonpsychics. Psychics were correct 44% of the time and nonpsychics 43% of the time. The accuracy rate of psychic predictions was not significantly higher than nonpsychic predictions ($p = .12$). This study does not support the conclusion that psychics can predict the future.

Note that scientists say a finding is "statistically significant" if the obtained alpha "p" level is better (lower) than .05. The statement "This result is statistically significant, $p = .02$" can be translated "We are confident that this result is not a fluke or due to chance. Our statistics show that the likelihood of us being wrong is only 2 out of a 100, better than the risk of 5 out of 100 accepted by most scientists."

The way one computes the alpha level for a statistic is beyond the scope of this book. However, it can be tricky. For example, conducting the same study many times can pose a special problem, sometimes ignored by paranormal researchers. Any study in itself is like a throw of dice. Eventually by chance alone you might get a hoped-for result. In the hypothetical psychic prediction study we just mentioned, a few psychics (and nonpsychics) made accurate predictions by chance alone. We have explained that statisticians can estimate the chance rate and take it into account. Similarly, if one repeated this study hundreds of times, each on a different group of 50 psychics and 50 nonpsychics, by chance alone in some of the studies the psychics would score higher. At the very least, you should adjust your alpha level to reflect the increased risk of a false positive.

Researchers who repeat a study many times (or look at many variables in one study) up the ante to rule out a false positive. Some apply a test invented by Carlo Emilio Bonferroni (1935) and divide .05 (or .01) by the number of studies (or analyses) to compensate for the increased likelihood of spurious results. The new alpha reflects a stricter confidence level that compensates for the fact that you are increasing the chances of winning by repeatedly tossing dice. For example, if you conducted 100 studies on psychic predictions, or conducted one study in which you had your participants make separate predictions on 100 groups of events (sports games, winning lottery numbers, weather events, etc.), your new alpha threshold would be .0005 (.05 divided by 100). Thus, if after conducting your study your statistics showed that your confidence level is only .05, this would now indicate that the results were not significantly different.

You may not understand the statistics described. However, Bonferroni gives you a handy tool for evaluating whether a paranormal researcher is raising false hopes with a finding. Count the number of actual experiments they report. Or look at the different "outcome" variables they examine.

Divide .05 by the number of experiments done, or number of variables. The new "p" value is your threshold. The research you are examining must show an alpha level equal to or lower than this before you can be confident in the significance of the results. Below is a hypothetical report of a study on green tea. Can you see why it is misleading?

> We examined the effects of green tea as a way of increasing classroom performance. In a double-blind placebo study, 20 students were given green tea, and 20 flavored water made to look like green tea. Participants drank their tea or water every day for a month. We looked at 5 variables: grade point average, grades on final exams, grades on written reports, classroom participation, and class attendance. On written reports, green tea drinkers received an average grade of "A" whereas water drinkers received an average grade of "B." The difference is significantly different, $p = .02$. We conclude that green tea improves classroom performance.

Here's the same report applying the Bonferroni correction:

> We examined the effects of green tea as a way of increasing classroom performance. In a double-blind placebo study, 20 students were given green tea, and 20 flavored water made to look like green tea. Participants drank their tea or water every day for a month. We looked at 5 variables: grade point average, grades on final exams, grades on written reports, classroom participation, and class attendance. Green tea worked best on written reports. Here green tea drinkers received an average grade of "A" whereas water drinkers received an average grade of "B." We found that the grades were different at $p = .02$. However, the Bonferroni correction specifies an alpha level of .01, which was not met. We conclude that green tea does not improve classroom performance.

Monkeys Typing Shakespeare: The Infinite Monkey Theorem

The infinite monkey theorem is one popular application of the law of very large numbers. You may have heard the saying that if you give an infinite number of monkeys an infinite number of typewriters and lots of time, eventually they will type the complete works of Shakespeare. Believe it or not, this claim has stirred some controversy. Believers state that it has to be true. Skeptics use evidence and logic.

Figure 6.1 Monkeys typing Shakespeare

Critics cite a 2003 grant-funded study conducted by students at Plymouth University in England. Six Sulawesi crested monkeys (Elmo, Gum, Heather, Holly, Mistletoe et al., 2002) were left alone with computers for a month to see what they would type. None produced Shakespeare. Instead, the lead monkey got a stone and started bashing away. Most spent much time peeing and defecating on the keyboard. Eventually the monkeys produced five pages of text, consisting mostly of the letter S, and the letters A, J, L, and M. The entire work has been published as "*Notes towards the complete works of Shakespeare*" (Elmo et al., 2002) and is available online for your pleasure.

Kittel and Kroemer (1980) argue that in any practical sense the monkey claim cannot be true, because it would require more monkeys than could fit in the entire universe and a period of time longer than the age of the universe. But what about multiple universes filled with monkeys from different dimensions? It's time to apply the holographic urine theory test.

Regardless of whether or not the monkey-Shakespeare claim is eventually demonstrated empirically, the law of very large numbers still applies. You can wait around or take my word for it.

7

Reality Checking for Perceptual Error and Trickery

The fact that you are reading this book says something about you. Quite likely you're a college student curious about critical thinking and the paranormal. You may be surprised that surveys of other readers and students have revealed an interesting and remarkably detailed portrait. See how well it fits you:

> You have a need for other people to like and admire you, and yet you tend to be critical of yourself. While you have some personality weaknesses you are generally able to compensate for them. You have considerable unused capacity that you have not turned to your advantage. Disciplined and self-controlled on the outside, you tend to be worrisome and insecure on the inside. At times you have serious doubts as to whether you have made the right decision or done the right thing. You prefer a certain amount of change and variety and become dissatisfied when hemmed in by restrictions and limitations. You also pride yourself as an independent thinker, and do not accept others' statements without satisfactory proof. But you have found it unwise to be too frank in revealing yourself to others. At times you are extroverted, affable, and sociable, while at other times you are introverted, wary, and reserved. Some of your aspirations tend to be rather unrealistic.

Time for a reality check. If you found these assessments uncomfortably close to the mark, you're not alone. In 1948 psychologist Bertram R. Forer gave his students a personality test, and a few days later personality profiles presumably based on the results. Students rated the accuracy of their profiles on a 5-point scale (0 = "very poor," 5 = "excellent"). The average rating was 4.26. However, the whole demonstration was a trick. In fact, Forer gave all students the same generic personality profile based on horoscopes he had read. The profile Forer used is actually the same as the "detailed portrait" presented above. It has nothing to do with your personality. The Forer demonstration has been given hundreds of times and the average accuracy score is always about 4.2, or 84% accurate (Carroll, 2003). Try giving it to friends at a party. Chances are they will marvel at your psychic powers.

Top-Down Processes and Perception

Yes, often things are not what they seem. Our eyes can fool us. Others can trick us. In this chapter we consider these two types of trickery, perceptual error and the manipulations of magicians and psychics. We begin with perception.

Perception is fundamentally biased and constructive. We do not see exactly what is "really out there," but a selective and distorted picture. At any moment the real world provides far too much information to be assimilated. Our attention is something like a *spotlight* (Crick, 1984) that targets and intensifies some stimuli and ignores others. Our *emotions and motivations* guide this spotlight; we perceive what is consistent with how we feel as well as our wants and needs. A starving person notices food. Our *past experiences, beliefs, and expectations* guide us to notice some things, ignore others, and even conjure up perceptions that may not accurately reflect reality. At times we *monitor* our perceptions in an attempt to evaluate their accuracy. In Chapter 2 we noted that this involves reality checking. The attentional spotlight; emotions and motivations; past experiences, beliefs, and expectations; and reality checking constitute *top-down* (or "internal cognitive") *processes* that mold perception.

The Barnum Effect (Forer Effect)

The Barnum effect (also called the **Forer effect, personal validation fallacy,** or **subjective validation**) is the tendency to rate a statement as personally accurate even though it could apply to nearly anyone.[1] Studies (Dickson & Kelly 1985) show that this effect can be aggravated if (a) you are misled to believe that a statement applies only to you (if you read a newspaper horoscope or see one on television, it's fairly obvious that it wasn't written just for you), (b) you believe the authority of the person making the statement, and (c) the statement lists mainly positive traits.

I propose that the Barnum effect may be enhanced by the *transparency illusion* (Vorauer, 2001). We tend to overestimate the extent to which our internal states and characteristics are obvious to others. In studies in which participants are asked to negotiate, 60% of the time they believed that observers could tell what their hidden goals were, when in fact observers could correctly guess 26% of the time (Vorauer & Claude, 1998). In other studies, participants instructed to deliberately lie incorrectly believed that observers could see through their attempts to hide deception. Similarly, anxious public speakers unrealistically believed that audience members could see through their calm facades (Gilovich, Savitsky, & Medvec, 1998). Perhaps when we believe that a psychic reads our internal states, traits, and future, we again are assuming too much personal transparency.

Confirmation Bias

Confirmation bias is a special type of selective thinking in which one looks for and notices what confirms one's beliefs, and ignores or does not look for or undervalues what contradicts. Confirmation bias is a preference for supportive over conflicting information (Nickerson, 1998; Watson, 1960). It can be a powerful factor reinforcing prejudice and discrimination. In reading a long horoscope, one might skim past a list of statements until one chances upon one that appears to fit. When confronting a mass of information, we tend to notice what appears to fit our expectations. This process can be quite automatic, and partly explains why you can quickly pick out a friend's voice in a noisy crowd, known as the **cocktail party effect** (Cherry, 1953).

We see examples of confirmation bias every day. A fervent advocate of the value of a college education will notice all the job notices for college graduates. An advocate of entering the workforce without a college degree will notice all the job notices for those with experience, not education. Those advocating support for gays adopting children will selectively notice reports of successful gay adoptions (and perhaps heterosexual child molestation), whereas those opposing will notice examples of gay couples breaking up and gay child molestation. Those supporting abstinence before marriage will notice all the singles couples in taverns who go home alone. Those who believe otherwise will notice all the couples going home together. Chicago fans of the Chicago Cubs will notice all the people wearing Cubs hats. Chicago Sox fans will not. Obviously one way to directly counter our automatic tendency for confirmation bias and selective attention is to deliberately seek contrary evidence. As we say again and again throughout this book, look for alternative explanations.

Denial is the refusal to accept the facts. One of the most dramatic historic instances of this is that of the Millerites, a religious group in the 1800s who, on more than one occasion, predicted the end of the world. In 1818, William Miller figured out mathematically that the Bible predicted the world would come to an end between March 21, 1843 and March 21, 1844. This was refined to January 1, 1844. With the help of some newspaper publicity, Miller attracted a flock of eagerly awaiting followers. However, when the end date came and went, his followers awaited March 21, the final date. Again, nothing happened. Miller redid his calculations and concluded a new date, October 22. Of course, nothing happened. The Millerites eventually founded the Adventist movement and Jehovah's Witnesses, groups that exist today. (See religioustolerance (2007).)

Reasons for the Barnum Effect and Confirmation Bias

I suspect that the Barnum effect and confirmation bias persist for many reasons. Confirming evidence provides apparent **positive reinforcement**. When such evidence is professed by a group we might experience communal reinforcement, a desire to accept claims because of others who are important to us. Confirming evidence requires the least effort to understand and assimilate because it fits what we already think we know. Such evidence is least likely to evoke **cognitive dissonance** (Festinger, 1957; Stone, 2001), the discomfort coming from having two conflicting thoughts at the same time, or from engaging in behavior that conflicts with personal beliefs (Dissonant thoughts: "I am an intelligent person; yet an astrologer fooled me into paying good money for a bogus horoscope." Dissonance resolution: "Actually, the horoscope looks like it could eventually be true, if I wait a few weeks."). Cognitive dissonance can prompt one to accept what one expects to see and rationalize away disconfirming evidence. For a good discussion see Carroll (2007a). Finally, people tend to believe that their own perceptions and introspections are based on what is "really out there," but believe that others are more vulnerable to the distortions of bias. Such a **bias blind spot** (Pronin, Lin, & Ross, 2002; Pronin, Gilovich, & Ross, 2004) might lead you to question the accuracy of horoscopes of others, and yet accept a horoscope as true for you.

What happens when you give believers and skeptics information that seems to challenge, or support, their paranormal beliefs? Studies have compared those who believe in astrology with those who are skeptical towards it. When both groups are presented with fake scientific studies that challenge the accuracy of horoscopes, believers tend to be rigid and unchanging in their belief and fail to reconcile the negative evidence with their beliefs. As you might expect, skeptics view the negative evidence as not supporting astrology. Are skeptics equally rigid and unchanging when presented with fake evidence that appears to *support* the validity of horoscopes? Surprisingly, skeptics are more likely to change their preexisting attitudes when they see evidence that appears to show their beliefs are false (Glick, Gottesman, & Jolton, 1989; Glick & Snyder, 1986). Such important findings contradict the claims of many paranormal believers that skeptics are unchanging and rigid in their beliefs. It also highlights what I see as a defining goal of critical thinking: to question honestly and fearlessly.

Everyday Illusions

We have seen that the Barnum effect and confirmation bias can contribute to false and distorted perceptions. We conclude with an everyday process that is happening right now as you read this paragraph.

Perception is constructive. We unconsciously adjust ambiguities in our world by filling in missing details, connecting the dots, sometimes blatantly hallucinating something that just isn't there – often to fit our expectations (Sternberg, 2006). Perhaps the most familiar examples of this are optical illusions and magic.[2] Less familiar is **pareidolia,** seeing recognizable forms in an ambiguous object. For example, many see a man in the moon. East Indians see a rabbit in the moon, Samoans see a woman weaving, and the Chinese a monkey pounding rice (Schick & Vaughn, 2005). And of course, people see Jesus Christ or the Virgin Mary in window reflections, shadows, grilled cheese sandwiches, wood doors, tree stumps, and urine stains on freeway embankments. See our inspiring *Galleria Pareidolia* on the next page. Similarly, through the process of **apophenia** we see connections and find meaning in unrelated things. The ancients connected the stars to form meaningful constellations. The Chinese and Indians have named constellations quite differently from western astrology.

✓ REALITY CHECK	How might an unscrupulous psychic use any of the examples of pareidolia (in our Galleria Pareidolia) as evidence for the paranormal?

One of the simplest examples of constructive perception is the phenomenon of **perceptual constancy**. We tend to see objects as having a certain expected shape, size, color, and place regardless of whether they are close or far away, brightly or dimly lit, viewed directly or from an angle, and so on (Goldstein, 2007). For example, if you were on an open plain and saw some buffalo grazing a few miles away, they would appear very small. Are they really small? Of course not, and you would probably observe that the buffalo are about the size of large cows. But what if you brought along someone from an African tribe who had no experience with vast plains or buffalos? Anthropologist Colin Turnbull (1961) actually did just that. He was in Africa studying the MaBhuti, a people who live their entire lives in the dense Ituri Forest of the Ruwenzori Mountains. Turnbull had a companion, a 22-year-old youth named Kenge, who introduced him to various tribes.

The Galleria Pareidolia

Figure 7.1a NASA photo of the face on Mars

Figure 7.1b Mars smiley face

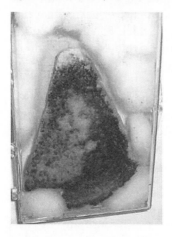

Figure 7.1c Virgin Mary in a grilled cheese sandwich

Figure 7.1d The nun bun

Figure 7.1e Motorway Madonna. Image on Chicago Expressway underpass.

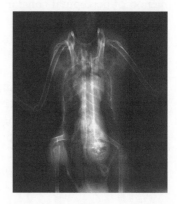

Figure 7.1f Alien in a duck

Figure 7.1g   Moon

Figure 7.1h   Man in the moon

Figure 7.1i   Rabbit in the moon

One week they both traveled farther than before, to an area cleared by a missionary group. From there they could see things Kenge had never witnessed before. Of particular interest were some strange forms in the distance. Were they clouds? Turnbull explained that they were mountains, and to the mountains they drove. Then they viewed buffalo miles away. Kenge asked what kind of insects they were, because they appeared so small. Turnbull explained they were in fact buffalo, twice the size of the animals back home. Kenge laughed in disbelief and told him not to tell "such stupid stories." When Turnbull persisted, his companion started talking to himself "for want of more intelligent company." However, as the two approached the buffalo, the apparent size of the animals magically grew, and Kenge was frightened. Eventually Kenge accepted the actual size of the buffalo, but his overall view of the world had not changed. When returning home, Kenge observed "This is bad country, there are no trees." Perhaps it is stretching things only a bit to say that Kenge speaks the anxiety we all experience when we stick to our false and distorted perceptions and fail to entertain challenging hypotheses.

Manipulations of Magicians and Psychics: The Cold Reading Toolkit

Through basic perceptual processes, we often trick ourselves. In addition, trickery can be a deliberate manipulation of a magician or psychic. Magic is an ancient practice in which skilled sleight of hand evokes convincing errors in perception. From the simple card trick to escaping locked jails, magicians never cease to amaze. Indeed, unscrupulous magicians can and have convinced PhD physicists under laboratory conditions that they can bend metal rods locked in Lucite and read pictures sealed in envelopes through presumed paranormal powers (see Chapters 11 and 12). When confronting what appears to be a paranormal phenomenon, a critical thinker needs to perform perhaps the most basic of reality checks and ask: Is this a magic trick? (Martinez-Conde & Macknik, 2008)

One of the easiest manipulations to achieve is the psychic reading. Here a seer appears to use paranormal powers to supply a willing stranger with personal information. Readings can describe a deceased relative, personality observations, predictions, and identification of objective facts in one's life and history. Of course, the Barnum effect and confirmation bias increase the likelihood that readings will fit personal expectations and appear accurate. However, the reader can do much to augment the apparent accuracy of observations. Indeed, once reinforced by client praise and payment, such a psychic might be quickly "shaped" to use the reading strategies that work best and firmly believe that his or her psychic powers are real.

Let me share with you one of the most widely cited examples of this very process. Psychologist Ray Hyman is one of the most outspoken critics of those who profess to have psychic powers of perception. In a recent review of research on psychic mediums, he recalls an experience he had as a student (Hyman, 2003a).

Now it so happens that I have devoted more than half a century to the study of psychic and cold readings. I have been especially concerned with why such readings can seem so concrete and compelling, even to skeptics. As a way to earn extra income, I began reading palms when I was in my teens. At first, I was skeptical. I thought that people believed in palmistry and other divination procedures because they could easily fit very general statements to their particular situation. To establish credibility with my clients, I read books on palmistry and gave readings according to the accepted interpretations for the lines, shape of the fingers, mounds, and other indicators. I was astonished by the reactions of my clients. My clients consistently praised me for my accuracy even when I told them very specific things about problems with their health and other personal matters. I even would get phone calls from clients telling me that a prediction that I had made for them had come true. Within months of my entry into palm reading, I became a staunch believer in its validity. My conviction was so strong that I convinced my skeptical high school English teacher by giving him readings and arguing with him. I later also convinced the head of the psychology department where I was an undergraduate.

When I was a sophomore, majoring in journalism, a well-known mentalist and trusted friend persuaded me to try an experiment in which I would deliberately read a client's hand opposite to what the signs in her hand indicated. I was shocked to discover that this client insisted that this was the most accurate reading she had ever experienced. As a result, I carried out more experiments with the same outcome. It dawned on me that something important was going on. Whatever it was, it had nothing to do with the lines in the hand. I changed my major from journalism to psychology so that I could learn why not only other people, but also I, could be so badly led astray. My subsequent career has focused on the reasons why cold readings can appear to be so compelling and seemingly specific.

A **cold reading** is a prophecy, observation, or interpretation of a total stranger (whereas a **hot reading** involves simple cheating, such as secretly obtaining information on the "stranger" ahead of time). For the best discussion of cold reading techniques, see Ian Rowland's (2005) *The Full Facts Book of Cold Reading*, *4th Edition*. Michael Shermer (2005) shares an exhaustive and entertaining application.

I like to organize cold reading techniques into five groups. First are attempts to maximize the Barnum effect and confirmation bias. Second are sneaky strategies for tricking a subject into telling you things about themselves, which you can then feed back as a "reading." Third are ways of drawing inferences from information other than what a subject tells you. Fourth are ways of making less than perfect readings seem accurate. Fifth, and most important, make a good show. Let's consider each.

Techniques for Enhancing the Barnum Effect and Confirmation Bias

Multiple out

This is simply a vague statement that can have several interpretations or "outs." Make the statement. Elaborate based on your subject's response. Avoid elaborations that seem not to be true, pursue elaborations that seem to evoke a positive response. Finally, offer a complex statement; clients will tend to ignore what doesn't fit and notice what does fit.

> PSYCHIC: You seem to be at a crucial junction in your life, a time of transition that involves significant other people, finances, and a major medical decision.
> CLIENT: Yes, I'm worried about what to do after school.
> PSYCHIC: Just as I thought. You have concerns about career, education, marriage—those things that confront us at this time of life.
> CLIENT: Yes! I'm looking for a wife!

Double-headed statement

Make a prediction or observation that includes its opposite:

> PSYCHIC: At times you are a bit shy and sometimes surprise yourself with how forward you can be.
> PSYCHIC: You will find riches, but for each silver lining there will be a cloud.

Here a statement contains a claim and its opposite. One has to be true, so you can't lose. And if you appear genuine enough, your subject will selectively ignore the part of your statement that is wrong.

Shotgunning

This is similar to using a double-headed statement. However, you inundate your subject with so many questions and claims that some are bound to be true. Again, if you appear sincere and knowledgeable, your "misses" will be ignored (especially if you talk quickly).

Drop and return

This bit of deception works best with shotgunning. While pelting your subject with questions and claims, make a mental note of any that seem to evoke a positive reaction (a fleeting smile, a glance up, a blink, or shake of the head). Give your subject time to forget your shotgunning. Then, with solemn certainty utter the claim that seemed to evoke some interest.

> **REALITY CHECK**   Explain how each of these cold reading techniques might enhance the Barnum effect and confirmation bias.

Have the Subject Feed You Facts

Questions (direct, incidental, and veiled)

Once you establish rapport and cooperation it is amazing how much personal information a subject will tell you if you simply ask. You can do this **directly**, providing you talk quickly and distract the subject from thinking about the fact that they have actually given you personal facts. When you feed this information back, disguise it a bit so you aren't caught.

You might obtain information on the sly by slipping in a quick **incidental question** after a lot of talk.

PSYCHIC: In this day and age we're all working harder ... I can tell that you are not immune from the pressures of today ... how does this relate to you?

CLIENT: You are sure right. I'm working harder at home and school. Dealing with three kids is a bit much!

Try asking a **veiled question** by making a question sound like a tentative reading. Here's a relatively direct question that might evoke suspicion:

PSYCHIC: Is there stress between you and a certain significant other?

Turn this into a reading:

PSYCHIC: I am picking up a very faint impression that there might be some heat, no, maybe some type of tension in your life, perhaps between you and a certain significant other? ...

CLIENT: Yes, my boyfriend and I are discussing breaking up.

Encourage cooperation

Make it clear that doing a reading is a cooperative venture, and that readings work only to the extent that the reader and subject "connect." To do this "both you and your reader have to be very honest and open, hiding nothing."

Ask for interpretation of an esoteric reading

Give a vague, jargon-laden reading that sounds very mystical. Offer a vague interpretation. Ask the subject to elaborate.

PSYCHIC: I'm picking up something strange, and maybe very important. But it's very weak. It involves a large mythological creature who lives in a strange land. Help me out. Is there someone or something new in your life?

CLIENT: Yes! I just started college, and it is the threatening "beast" in my life!

Draw inferences

If a subject gives you any facts ("I am a student, married, live alone, busy shopping"), think about logical inferences one might make from these facts. For example, students have to buy books and deal with schedules. Those who live alone are responsible for a lot of finances. Then feed back these inferences, first as abstract generalizations, and then as specific readings. For example, for a subject who has earlier shared that he has been busy shopping, you might later observe:

PSYCHIC: I sense your awareness of your limitations (Inference: a shopper often has to be concerned about not spending too much) ... perhaps of a financial nature (getting more specific, a shopper has to be concerned with finances).

Twenty questions

Twenty questions is a childhood guessing game in which one systematically narrows one's options through the process of elimination. See how Josh figures out what Tony is thinking of:

JOSH: Are you thinking of something living or inert?

TONY: Inert.

JOSH: Is it man-made or natural?

TONY: Man-made.

JOSH: Is it larger than a chair, or smaller?

TONY: It's smaller than a chair.
JOSH: Is it a high-tech device or a mechanical device?
TONY: A high-tech device.
JOSH: Is it an appliance or entertainment device?
TONY: Entertainment device.
JOSH: Ah, is it a DVD player?
TONY: Yes.
JOSH: Do you have the purchase receipt?

This can easily be transformed into readings that sound astrological:

PSYCHIC: You are thinking of something ... inert ...
CLIENT: Not quite ...
PSYCHIC: Yes, I can tell, it is a living thing that sometimes is inert, possibly an animal.
CLIENT: Yes!
PSYCHIC: The animal is wild ...
CLIENT: Not quite ...
PSYCHIC: I know, you misunderstand, in the past the animal was once wild, and now has a wild streak in it. Of course, it is domestic, like a pet.
CLIENT: Yes.
PSYCHIC: I know you are the kind of person who would have either a dog or a cat, am I right?
CLIENT: Yes.
PSYCHIC: Which is it?
CLIENT: A dog.
PSYCHIC: Yes, it is a dog. That is what I was thinking of.

Drawing Inferences from Other Sources of Information

You don't have to wait for a subject to tell you personal information in order to make informed readings. There are many other sources of information you can tap.

Read subtle cues and body language

A good observer will note that clothes, demeanor, posture, and gestures can be very revealing. A devout person may wear religious jewelry. A student may carry books. Someone with money may have expensive clothes. However, do not directly state your immediate conclusions ("You are devout," "You are a student," "You are rich."). Instead, start with observations that are logical inferences if your observation is true. So, if your subject has a book bag and several pens in his pocket, do not blurt out "you are a student" (which may arouse suspicion); say "I sense you are often tired at the end of the day, perhaps because you are doing many things at once and using your brain a lot." (Probably true if the subject is a student.) Indirect inferences protect you from being found out, and make it seem as if you are struggling to make your observations correct.

Base prediction on a probable but unexpected statistic

Here you will have to do your homework and find some fact that is unexpectedly common. Rowland (2005) provides a catalog of good high-probability guesses. For example, people generally do not realize that in most homes one would likely find (p. 54):

old unsorted photographs;
some toy or book that dates to childhood;
jewelry from a deceased relative;
a pack of cards (with one or more cards missing);
some electronic device that no longer works;
a note that is significantly out of date;
some books or instructions on a hobby or interest one no longer has;
a drawer or door that sticks or doesn't work properly;
a key no longer used (or you don't know what lock it works on);
a number "2" in their home address, or they know someone who does.

Rowland suggests that most men:

have tried learning a musical instrument as a child, but quit;
have had a beard or moustache at least once;
have a old suit that doesn't fit.

Most women:

have an item of clothing which they have never worn;
have more shoes than they need;
wore their hair longer as a child;
have at least one lost earring.

Most people:

have or have had a scar on their left knee;
have been in a childhood accident involving water.

Psychics often acquire vast listings of unexpected statistics that apply to most people. In a pinch, almost any reading can be pulled out of the hat and a client is impressed with the uncanny specificity of a reading. You might take the probable fact that one has unused medical supplies or outdated drugs somewhere at home. With a little flair, this can be woven into a plausible psychic reading:

> I detect at home energy from an old, and possibly ongoing medical concern. You have stopped using those pills, or that medical device. It or they are just sitting around gathering dust. Maybe they are dated. Perhaps you no longer need them. Am I right?

Predict a body change that is probable (but unexpected)

When most people breathe deeply and rapidly they feel a bit dizzy. This is called hyperventilation, a normal physiological process resulting from rapid decreases in carbon dioxide in the brain. You could have someone breathe deeply, and then predict "The spirits are making your head light. Do you feel it?" Or have someone stare at a candle flame without blinking. In time their eyelids will get heavy, a simple physiological process of fatigue. Describe this in psychic terms: "The spirits of the flame are pulling your eyelids closed. You can actually feel the heaviness as the spirits work."

Base a prediction on pareidolia or apophenia

Find a simple ambiguous object that you know can readily evoke pareidolia or apophenia. Quickly show this object to your subject. Then, using a ritualistic incantation, suggest how this object is really something else (something which can be readily seen by most people). Show the object again, suggesting the vision. This works especially well with visions of Jesus or the Virgin Mary. Find any oddly shaped sidewalk stain, reflection of light, or pattern of wood grain. With great sincerity and emotion, proclaim your vision.

Dealing with Less Than Perfect Readings

Divert attention

Do anything to prevent your subject from generating alternative hypotheses, or looking more deeply into what you are doing. Divert attention by talking continuously, chanting, introducing a colorful environment, performing interesting rituals, evoking emotion, etc.

Shoehorning

Simply force the facts to fit your claim. If you are creative enough, you can make a claim fit nearly anyone. Shoehorning is the same as using ad hoc hypotheses.

Turn misses into hits

If you have made a prophecy or interpretation that is off the mark, reinterpret it so it fits. You can see this in the following:

ASTROLOGER: You are an Aries. You are very assertive and impulsive.
SUBJECT: No I'm not. I am very shy. I have no friends.
ASTROLOGER: I was picking up on your mood right now. Right now you are very assertive, assertive enough to challenge me!

An easy way to turn a miss into a hit is to claim that your claim refers to something that will happen in the future. Of course, that can never be verified at the moment, and can be made to appear very profound.

ASTROLOGER: You have many friends.
SUBJECT: I am alone.
ASTROLOGER: Let me reassure you that I see a time in the near future when you will have many friends.

Blame the subject

If you get something wrong, blame your subject. "Help me out. We need to work together on this. I sense a certain negativity and skepticism in you, which is getting in the way. You are thinking too much, which is blocking my reading."

Make a Good Show

Create a context conducive to confirmation bias and the Barnum effect

Take care to create a setting that is appropriate to and suggests the validity of the psychic claims you are making. Use soft, mysterious music; incense; photos of ancient saints; globes and crystals; strange animals; and perhaps a cat.

Make a few errors

Getting everything right arouses suspicion. Make a few errors, and then claim that because your powers are not magic tricks, they come and go (depending on certain astrological factors, etc.).

Flatter the subject and tell them what they want to know

"You have more creative talent than you give yourself credit for." "Your friends respect and love you more than you might expect."

Hypnotic Suggestion Enhancers

We have seen how cold readings and expectations can alter how we view ourselves and the world. In its simplest form, hypnosis is just a verbal suggestion, a verbal "command" to do or experience something. Hypnosis is not a zombie-like trance state. You cannot be forced to do something against your will during hypnosis. You don't even have to be told you are participating in hypnosis in order to respond to a hypnotic suggestion (Baker, 1990).

There has been much debate as to how to define hypnosis. I prefer a simple behavioral definition: hypnosis is responsivity to a set of standardized suggestions (Baker, 1990) as presented in various scientific scales including the Harvard Group Scale of Hypnotic Susceptibility (Shor & Orne, 1962) and the Stanford Hypnotic Susceptibility Scale (Kihlstrom, 1962). In measuring how hypnotizable one is, a researcher often begins with a pre-induction ceremony in which hypnosis is defined as heightened suggestibility and proceeds to instructions to close one's eyes, focus, and relax. Suggestions are then read, progressing from easy to difficult. A person "responds" to a suggestion if he or she involuntarily experiences the suggested effect, that is, without deliberately willing it. One's hypnotic susceptibility score is defined in terms of the number of suggestions that "take." Simple suggestions, passed by most people, include:

Postural sway (your body is slowly swaying).
Eye closure (your eyelids are getting so heavy they cannot stay open).
Hand lowering (your hand (stretched in front of you) is getting so heavy you can't hold it up).
Mosquito hallucination (you hear a mosquito buzzing).
Taste hallucination (you can taste lemon in your mouth).

Slightly more challenging are:

Arm immobilization (your arm is so stiff you can't bend it).
Waking dream (right now you will have a dream).
Age regression (you are going back to your grade school days. Giggle and talk like a little kid).

Most challenging are:

Hallucinated voice (you hear someone calling your name).
Insensitivity to ammonia (inability to smell a glass of ammonia placed under nose).

Finger lock (you can't separate hands clasped together).

Verbal inhibition (can't say your name).

Amnesia (you can't remember something simple, like your address).

Post-hypnotic suggestion (time-delayed suggestion in which you auto-matically and unconsciously do something, like change chairs).

Perhaps the simplest suggestion is the **ideomotor effect** in which one sug-gests a minor body movement (swaying, for example), which then uncon-sciously takes place. This effect is so powerful that the simple expectation that one might make a movement can be enough to evoke the movement.

It is important to realize that these scale items have been developed through careful research on thousands of individuals. This means that if someone passes a few highly challenging suggestions, it is very likely they will also pass other suggestions, especially those that are easier. Conversely, if someone displays no response to simple suggestions, it is very unlikely that they will respond to those that are more challenging.

This is a useful piece of information for students of the paranormal. For example, imagine that you have a headache and are participating in an elab-orate "psychic healing ritual" complete with exotic music, incense, and a psychic dressed in a flowing lavender robe. As part of the ritual, the psychic suggests that you will hear the sound of a bell in the distance. There is no bell, and what you hear is a minor hallucination. However, the fact that you hallucinated reveals that you will probably respond to other suggestions, including that your pain will go away, and will respond to a post-hypnotic suggestion to speak favorably of your psychic to your friends. Indeed, research shows that the best predictor of such susceptibility is not personal-ity, mental health, or brain functioning, but simply whether or not one responds to suggestions (Kirsch & Braffman, 2001).

Remarkably, most of the easier hypnotic behaviors can be evoked without initially closing one's eyes, focusing, or relaxing. A growing body of research on alert (or waking (Wark, 2006)) hypnosis shows that one can respond hyp-notically while fully aware, even while riding an exercise bicycle (Bányai & Hilgard, 1976). Suggestions to focus (probably required for inducing more advanced suggestions) can be woven into various eyes-open activities, such as preparatory stretching and breathing exercises.

Hypnosis is augmented when one is instructed to (a) close one's eyes, (b) focus on a simple stimulus (ideally in an environment of restricted stimulation, such as a quiet and dim room), and (c) relax. Furthermore, I propose that any suggestion, whether explicit or implicit, to suspend reality checking (Chapter 2) is an essential ingredient. It may help estab-lish a suggestive environment (an elaborate "hypnotic chamber" or pres-ence of a crowd that reinforces suggestions) and select a suggestible recipient (an imaginative person who can be completely "absorbed" in something such as a book or movie).

I find it useful to consider such "hypnotic suggestion enhancers" as ways of boosting the effects of expectation and manipulation considered in this chapter. For example, a psychic could perform a cold reading by simply looking at your palm and saying something like "Your life line indicates that this year will be very challenging, but you will grow from your difficulties." This might be moderately persuasive. Another psychic may give you the same reading, augmented to enhance expectation:

I am about to perform a deep psychic reading. You need to come into my special silent-reading chamber. Close your eyes. Focus on the mysterious powers of the fragrances flowing from the candles. Attend to the soothing music and with every breath relax more and more deeply. Let me hold your hand. Your life line indicates that this year will be very challenging, but you will grow from your difficulties.

Perceptual Bias in the Mental Health Professions

The possibility of perceptual bias exists throughout the mental health professions (Garb, Lilienfeld, Wood, & Nezworski, 2002). It is beyond the scope of the book to consider pop psychology, psychoanalysis, humanistic therapies, "New Age" philosophy, questionable or "crazy" psychotherapies, or debated assessment strategies such as the Rorschach inkblot test, graphology (handwriting analysis), or lie detectors. First, some are legitimate topics of scientific debate, with qualified scientists arguing for and against. This is particularly true for psychoanalysis, humanistic therapies, the Rorschach test, and lie detectors. Here good scientists disagree and they are not pseudoscientists or paranormalists. Also, to include such topics would require we include a discussion of every current controversy in psychology, not the task of this book. See Lilienfeld, Ruscio, & Lynn (2008).

That said, let me indulge in few observations. Clinical psychologists and other helping professionals must entertain hypotheses about their clients. What is the cause of a student's depression? What might be the best strategy to help a suicidal war veteran talk about her traumatic experiences? Should this patient receive medication or behavioral treatment for his anxiety? Hypotheses are evaluated on the basis of theory, research, and practice. However, uninformed fictional accounts of therapists often portray the act of generating hypotheses as something similar to that of making a psychic reading. Your dream about a bear reveals your fear of your father. The fact that you see blood in a red ink blot suggests you have concerns about death. If your doodles include a tiny human figure next to a big house, you have low self-esteem. Such psychic reading is bad psychology, and is not taught in any credible clinical training program approved by the American Psychological Association.

Nostradamus: 16th Century Astrology Superstar

Nostradamus was a 16th century French physician and perhaps history's most famous astrologer. I found 8,450,000 Google hits on Nostradamus, and 3,887 books. He is most known for his 942 prophetic quatrains, or four-line poems.

Nostradamus wrote his quatrains claiming to use ideas from astrology. He made them a bit vague so as not to provoke attacks from religious fanatics. People continue to read astonishing prophecies from the quatrains of

MICHEL NOSTRADAMUS.
Médecin,
Né à S.ᵗ Remy, en Provence, le 14 Décemb. 1503.
Mort le 2, juillet 1566.

Figure 7.2   Portrait of Nostradamus, French astrologer, Copper engr., 17th century, by Boulanger

Nostradamus. He is claimed to have predicted Napoleon, World War I, World War II, aircraft fighters, the French Revolution, the atom bomb, submarines, the deaths of both John F. and Robert Kennedy, the nuclear destruction of Hiroshima and Nagasaki, the moon landings, the death of Princess Diana of Wales, the Space Shuttle *Challenger* disaster. Perhaps his most famous is his prediction of the rise of Hitler (Randi, 1993):

> Beasts ferocious from hunger will swim across rivers:
> The greater part of the region will be against the Hister,
> The great one will cause it to be dragged in an iron age,
> When the German child will observe nothing.
>
> (II, 24)

Believers claim that "Hister" refers to "Hitler," a lawless leader, and that the "Beasts" refer to Nazi armies crossing rivers, hungry for conquest. This is shoehorning at its best. Hister is actually the name of the Danube River. "German" at the time of Nostradamus did not refer to any country, but to an ancient region of Europe, or possibly part of the Roman Empire.

Imagine the mischief you could get into if you had all 942 of the Nostradamus quatrains to play with! Indeed I found one internet website that will randomly give you a genuine Nostradamus prophecy. All you have to do is type in a question and press the button (www.getodd.com/stuf/nos tradamus.html).

For your edification, I typed in: "Will the reader of this page find true love this year?" After six attempts, I found your prophecy:

> When the lamp burning with an inextinguishable fire
> Over the walls to throw ashes, lime chalk and dust
> It will be seized and plunged into the Vat
> Drinking by force the waters poisoned by sulfur

My apologies. I hope next year turns out better for you.

On the Web: 21st Century Psychic Superstars

Throughout history, thousands of people claiming psychic powers have gained fame and fortune. However, our record of past psychics is primarily through word of mouth, print media, and venerable religious texts. In the 21st century this has changed dramatically. We now have available a lasting record of psychics caught in the act of doing their thing, with transcripts, videos, and firsthand accounts duly posted on the internet. These are the

21st century psychic superstars. I invite you to search the web and see for yourself the tools they use. Here are the stories of six internet psychic superstars. As a rough indicator of their relative popularity, I list the number of Google hits for each (as of 27 November, 2007).

John Edward (1,040,000 Google hits). John Edward McGee Jr. (www. johnedward.net/) was born in 1969 and raised a Roman Catholic. At age 15 a psychic convinced him that he could become a famous medium (Edward, 1998, 2001, 2003). As a young adult he was a phlebotomist, studied health-care administration, and pursued work as a ballroom dance instructor. His first book (Edward, 1998) and resulting appearance on the *Larry King Show* launched Edward's career as a TV medium. Edward has subsequently published five books, has been featured in TV programs such as *Crossing Over*, *John Edward Cross Country*, and *Phenomenon*, and appeared as guest on numerous others.

On television Edward does cold readings of audience members, focusing on deceased friends and relatives. Perhaps because of what many see to be crass attempts to profit from the misery of the grieving, Edward has been the frequent target of television comedy. He was branded "the biggest douch in the universe" in South Park, fights (and loses to) Miss Cleo on *Celebrity Deathmatch*, and was mercilessly skewered in the first episode of Penn and Teller's *Bullshit!* series. The cartoon comedy *Family Guy* has parodied Edward's use of cold and hot reading (Memorable Quotes, 1999):

> In this episode Peter Griffin (the beer loving and portly head of the Family Guy household) is in the audience of *Crossing Over with John Edward*.

JOHN EDWARD:	I'm sensing an 'A'. Does your name begin with an 'A'?
PETER:	No.
JOHN EDWARD:	A 'B'?
PETER:	No.
EDWARD:	C? D? E, F, G, H, I, J, K, L, M, N, O, P ...
PETER:	P! Peter! My name's Peter!
JOHN EDWARD:	Is your name Peter?
PETER:	Wow! You are some kind of sorcerer.

Gary Schwartz has studied and enthusiastically validated Edward, reported in his book *The Afterlife Experiments* (Schwartz, 2003a). This research has been severely criticized for methodological weaknesses (Hyman, 2003a; Hyman, 2003b; Schwartz, 2003a; Schwartz, 2003b). Critics such as James Randi claim that Edward uses (crudely) simple magician's tricks such as cold and hot reading (cheating). Studying an unedited two-hour tape of readings, Randi found that only 3 of Edward's 23 readings were actually correct (Randi, 2006). There is evidence that TV editors delete Edward's misses, providing a distorted picture of his success rate (Endersby, 2002), a practice that may permeate TV "documentaries" of the paranormal.

Uri Geller (555,000 Google hits) was born of Jewish parents in 1946 as Gellér György in Tel Aviv, Israel (www.uri-geller.com). According to his autobiography (Geller, 2007), Geller claims to have discovered his paranormal abilities at age 5, a year after encountering a mysterious sphere of light while gardening. During a meal, he picked up a spoon and it broke without effort. Uri then developed these powers by displaying them to his playmates. Incidentally, his mother thought Uri inherited his powers from Sigmund Freud, a claimed distant relative.

As an adult, Geller worked as a paratrooper in the Israeli army and as a model for watches, towels, and underwear (Beloff, 1999). In 1969 he started to demonstrate his powers to audiences, and in 1971 became a well-known psychic performer. At this point Geller's autobiography and other accounts differ significantly. Geller, for example, claims to have been contacted by NASA to fix a satellite antenna, and recover (through thought power) a camera left on the moon by astronauts; other accounts disagree (Randi, 2007).

In 1973 psychologists and computer experts at Hebrew University duplicated Geller's feats using simple sleight of hand. Geller left Israel (*Time*, 1973). In the 1970s Geller became an international TV psychic star, using his presumed psychic powers to bend spoons, start dead watches, and read drawings in sealed envelopes. Puthoff and Targ, researchers at the Stanford Research Institute (SRI; no connection with the university), tested Geller and proclaimed him genuine. They even invented a special term for his powers, the "Geller Effect."

Geller is perhaps one of the most thoroughly challenged psychics, and skeptics point to numerous descriptions and actual videos that appear to show how sleight of hand can replicate his feats (Carroll, 2007b; Randi, 1982a, 1982b). Publicly challenging Geller can take a bit of courage, given his propensity to sue critics. (Note the extremely cautious choice of words in this paragraph.) Perhaps the most famous test was Geller's legendary 1973 performance on the Johnny Carson show, where he attempted and failed to bend spoons and find hidden objects. Unknown to Geller, Carson (an accomplished magician) worked with James Randi to set up cheat-proof tests. After his failure, Geller has refused to perform when magicians are present, citing interference from their negative vibrations. Nonetheless, magicians claim to be able to replicate Geller's feats. It is truly amazing that such a controversial psychic still commands a huge audience. Incidentally, Gary Schwartz has tested Geller and concluded that his skills are authentic.

Sylvia Browne (523,000 Google hits). Sylvia Browne (www.sylvia.org) was born in 1936 in Kansas City, Missouri as Sylvia Celeste Shoemaker. Her father was Jewish and mother Episcopalian and soon after Browne's birth the entire family converted to Roman Catholicism. In 2001 Browne professed to be Jewish (King, 2001). Browne started having visions when she was 3 (Browne, 2005), which her grandmother saw as encouraging signs that Sylvia was a psychic medium. Browne gave her first reading in 1974 (Dulin, 2005) and has over the years given thousands of individual and group readings (sometimes charging $750 for a half-hour telephone reading). Browne has married four times and claims that her son, Christopher, is psychic (Novus Spiritus).

Browne is known for her television appearances, primarily on *Larry King Live* and the *Montel Williams Show*. She has made frequent predictions (mercilessly checked out by internet reporters), worked as a psychic detective in up to 35 cases (King, 2001; Carroll, 2007b) and claims (unsubstantiated) to have worked with 350 doctors (King, 2001), often as a psychic healer. Browne is the founder of a Gnostic Christian church, the Society of Novus Spiritus (Novus Spiritus) that incorporates teachings from Judaism, Islam, Buddhism, and Hinduism (Browne, 2006). Browne has been indicted on several charges of investment fraud and grand theft, explaining that she is unable to apply her powers of psychic prediction to herself (Nickell, 2004).

Although many know of Browne's psychic readings, few are aware of her other assertions. She claims to know what heaven is like (Browne & Harrison, 2000). The temperature is a constant 78 degrees F, there are no insects (unless you want some), pets go to heaven, and one can build one's house anywhere, providing it doesn't obstruct someone else's view (special permission is required). The "other side" exists three feet above ground level, but is difficult to perceive because it exists at a higher vibrational level. Browne claims to have the ability to perceive a wide range of vibrational frequencies (which enables her to see angles and speak with her spirit guide, "Francine").

James Randi has frequently confronted Browne in print, on television and the internet, and Robert Lancaster has maintained an exhaustive online record of Browne's failed predictions, distortions, and criminal activities (Lancaster, 2007).

Allison DuBois (165,000 Google hits). Allison DuBois (www.allison dubois.com) was born in 1972 in Phoenix, Arizona and claims to have acquired mediumship abilities at age 6. She graduated from Arizona State

University, majoring in Political Science. DuBois's life is the basis of the TV show *Medium*.

Allison claims to have a "100% hit record" as a psychic detective and research medium. In her first case the Texas Rangers asked for assistance in solving a child disappearance (The Two Percent Solution, 2005). She also claims to have solved crimes for the Glendale, Arizona police. Both the Rangers and the Glendale police have denied any help (The Two Percent Company, 2005). For four years she participated in Schwartz's mediumship research and has been validated by Schwartz as authentic (Carroll, 2006; McClain, 2005).

According to DuBois, heaven is a flawless place where people live a life of perpetual youth and happiness. Hell is solitary confinement in a stew of a dark energy. One might surmise that Gary Schwartz may well find himself in a dark stew given that DuBois accuses him of misleadingly gaining profit from her research participation, and violating her confidentiality. Unfortunately, at this time we do not have a public record of DuBois's readings.

James van Praagh (142,000 Google hits) was born in 1958 in Bayside, New York (www.vanpraagh.com). He was raised a Roman Catholic and entered the seminary at 14 where his interest in communicating with dead spirits grew. After an impressive encounter with a medium (who informed van Praagh that he would be a medium in two years), he started receiving messages from the beyond. His popularity as a medium and expert on life after death began with the NBC talk show, *The Other Side*. He has since made many television appearances on shows such as *Oprah*, *Larry King Live*, *Maury Povich*, *20/20*, and *48 Hours*. Van Praagh has authored five books and worked on the CBS series *Ghost Whisperer*.

We are fortunate to have numerous eyewitness accounts of Van Praagh's readings, and clear evidence of his use of psychic tools. Michael Shermer debunked him on *Unsolved Mysteries*, although one audience member complained that Shermer's behavior inappropriately destroyed the "hope" of the grieving. (Shermer, 2002).

To my knowledge, van Praagh has yet to be tested by Gary Schwartz, although van Praagh has lavishly praised Schwartz's work.

Rosemary Altea (39,000 Google hits) was born in 1946 in Leicester, England. At an early age she claimed to have heard voices and had visions of the departed. Abandoned by her husband in the 1970s, she began work as a spiritual medium. She is the author of five books (www.rosemaryaltea.com). Rosemary claims a spiritual guide from the other side, "Grey Eagle," who has assisted her writing efforts. She has invented a "soul system" that organizes the souls of all living beings into five soul types (fire, earth, air, water, and sulfur), an astrology-like system she uses to counsel others. She has also founded the Rosemary Altea Healing and Educational Foundation (www.rahef.org) dedicated to spiritual healing using her techniques. Although a relative newcomer to the television psychic circuit, she has appeared on national television, including *Larry King Live*, *The Oprah Show*, and *Prime Time Live with Diane Sawyer*. Altea earns a place among the superstars because of her featured performance on the 2003 premiere episode ("Talking with the Dead") of Penn and Teller's *Bullshit!* Here viewers could observe her use of cold and hot reading techniques, including the shotgun technique, multiple out, and obtaining information ahead of time before giving a "reading."

Honorable Mention

Miss Cleo
Kathlyn Rhea
Maureen Flynn

Other Contenders

Derek Acorah
Doris Collins
Sue Dobbs
Mia Dolan
Colin Fry
Lamar Keene (partially reformed)
Diane Lazarus
Sally Morgan
Derek Ogilvie
Chris Robinson
Charles J. Sibley
Craig Shell
Gordon Smith
Tony Stockwell
Doris Stokes
David Thompson
Stephen Turoff (psychic surgeon)
Deb Webber
Lorraine Warren
David Wells

Reality Checking for Memory Errors

Many television documentaries have featured psychic pet detectives. From my recollection, they offer pretty strong evidence for the paranormal.

The first time I visited Paris, I had the strong sensation I had lived there before. Indeed, when I visited the Eiffel Tower I could recall details before seeing the tower for the first time. I knew what was on top, and how it was lighted at night.

I'm amazed at the psychic experiences I can remember, especially if psychics are present to help me focus. My memory is even better if psychics present pictures of paranormal phenomena to stir my memory.

Most of the world of the paranormal rests on such claims of memory. I came to this realization after reading hundreds of accounts and talking to thousands of friends and students. In the majority of cases the best evidence is a recollection of specific events. In Chapter 7 we considered how various top-down processes can affect our perception of outside events. In this chapter we examine how the process of memory can add distortions. Pseudoscientific observations often do not take into account the errors of perception and memory.

Few things are as precious as our personal memories. Yet, few things are so immune from accurate review. Rarely do we need to check if personal cherished memories are entirely correct. It simply doesn't matter. You remember your dear Aunt Mimi, maybe her warm embraces, pink hat, green shoes, yellow flowers, and that awful sofa. All of this could be embellishments, and no one would ever know.

Memory Myths

Let's begin by debunking a few memory myths. First, many people believe that everything we experience is recorded in memory, as if we carried around a personal security camera that is always on. The fact is that very little of our experience is committed to memory. Our memory capacity is limited, and new memories can replace and corrupt old ones. This myth is perhaps a variant of a larger myth, that we use 10% of our brain. This myth may well have respected sources, perhaps one of the founders of psychology, William James, or even Albert Einstein. However, it is still false. Neuroscience shows that over the course of a day we use 100% of our brains. This should not be surprising. The brain is a relatively small organ, but it has much to do. It comprises 3% of the body's weight but uses 20% of its energy (Boyd, 2008; Radford, 1999).

The second myth is more serious. People believe that memory is accurate, like a video recording or photograph. The surprising finding of years of cognitive research is that memory is *reconstructive*, more like a historical fiction or docudrama than fact. Each memory may have nuggets of truth, but these are embellished by mental creations. Compare a memory with a movie of historical fiction, perhaps Cecil B. de Mille's *The Ten Command-ments* starring Charlton Heston. The movie was great entertainment, and even inspiring to those of faith. Is it based on fact? Very little.

Memories are more like such historical fictions than replays of the latest ball game. If you want to demonstrate the reconstructive nature of memory, try recalling your most recent encounter with a good friend. Close your eyes and conjure up as many details as you can. What was this brief mental snap-shot like? Specifically, does it show what things were like as seen through your own eyes (called an **observer memory**)? Or did you picture this encoun-ter as if you were looking at it from the outside (called a **field memory**)? Most people respond to this type of question with field memories. But if you think about it, field memories cannot be accurate because at the time of the event you were not hovering outside looking at what is happening. Your field memory has to be your own invention.

What Is Memory?

"Memory is the means by which we retain and draw on our past experi-ences to use that information in the present" (Sternberg, 2006, p. 157). The things we remember include personal experiences (our last date), facts (the ideas in this chapter), as well as skills and habits (how to tie our shoes, how to program a DVD player). To do this we must encode, or process, what we want to remember, store, and retrieve, or bring back memories or skills in response to a cue or command (Sternberg, 2006).

The traditional perspective considers three "memory stores" (Atkinson & Shiffrin, 1968; Squire, 2004). First, **sensory memory** is the fleeting registra-tion of what we immediately experience. We look at something and for no longer than half a second a memory of it lingers, and then immediately fades. Second, some of what's in sensory memory gets transferred to **short-term memory**, where it lasts from a few seconds to as long as a minute. If our initial perceptions are in error (Chapter 6), clearly their registration in sensory and short-term memory will also be in error.

Third, with repetition and rehearsal, short-term memories can be transferred to **long-term memory**, the capacity of which is more extensive and enduring. Current memory theory focuses on **working (or active) memory**, the most recently activated portion of long-term memory. Here short-term memory is seen a little differently as a temporary storage place. Working memory theory provides a metaphor for how information moves in and out of memory:

> Information remains within long-term memory; when activated, information moves into long-term memory's specialized working memory, which actively will move information into and out of the short-term memory store contained within it. (Sternberg, 2006, p. 170)

Long-term memory can be declarative (explicit) or nondeclarative (implicit; Squire, 2004). Declarative or explicit memory consists of facts and event sequences we can deliberately and consciously recall. This includes **episodic memory**, or sequences of events such as the steps you took to get from home to school, and **semantic memory** or abstract knowledge and facts (Tulving & Wayne, 1972).

If you are currently pondering the possibility that you have the paranormal ability to read thoughts, you are probably drawing upon your working memory of experiences. This may include recollections of times when you appeared to have read others' thoughts (episodic memory) as well as definitions and studies you have read about this psychic ability (semantic memory).

To continue, nondeclarative or implicit memory involves automatically remembering something without being aware where you learned it or even that you are remembering it (Schacter, 1996). These can be simple procedures, like riding a bicycle, or emotionally conditioned memories.

Although you may not know you have nondeclarative or implicit memories, they can influence your actions and experiences through a process called **priming**. To elaborate, in a **priming experiment**, you might be asked to identify words on cards briefly flashed in front of you. However, if you were previously flashed the word "hospital" you might more quickly recognize when the word "nurse" is flashed, whereas prior priming with the word "vehicle" would have no such effect. What is remarkable is that priming works even when you do not remember (and can't even recognize from a list) any of the priming words ("hospital" or "vehicle"). The entire effect is implicit, or unconscious. Advertising is often based on implicit memory. We are continuously exposed to ads and think we ignore them or tune them out. But in fact we are more likely to buy products featured in ad campaigns we might not even remember! And consider the many "documentaries" and "reality shows" on cable television. Many present psychics, mediums, ghosts, flying saucer chasers, blurring fact and fiction. At the very least, such shows prime you to notice paranormal claims.

Implicit memory is not like Freud's notion of the unconscious. According to Freud, we automatically bury memories of traumatic events through a process called repression. Such events presumably are threatening to the ego. Freud claimed that repressed traumas create anxiety and depression, influence behavior, and are one source of nightmares. There is considerable debate about whether Freud was right. In fact, traumatic experiences are very much more likely to be remembered. Implicit memories are simply poorly encoded memory traces that still have a residual impact.

REALITY CHECK How is priming like selective perception? How are they different? Can you think of a case where both might work together?

Memory Errors

Memory, like perception, is reconstructive (Sutton, 2003). Indeed, many of the same processes that lead to perceptual distortion (Barnum effect, confirmation bias, etc.) can apply to our perception of memories (Moskowitz, 2005). An important point of this chapter is that when asked to recall a fact or event, you actually remember only bits and pieces and automatically fill in the missing details and add embellishments. Your final recollection is rarely a completely accurate record, but a partial fiction based on relevant fact, incidental information, suggestion, and sheer imagination.

False Memory

The term *false memory* describes a wide range of episodic memory distortions (Hyman & Pentland, 1995; Wade et al., 2006). Generally a false memory is an inaccurate recollection based on selective forgetting as well as mixing memories or memory fragments, dreams, fantasies, information from television or the movies, interrogations, or suggestions and manipulations of others. All these are potential sources of error accentuated by repetition, using imagery to "enhance" memory, and recalling in the presence of others who reinforce false recollections as true. Recent research suggests that those who believe in the paranormal and claim paranormal experiences are especially prone to display false memories (Wilson & French, 2006). As we shall see, research shows how surprisingly easy it is for distortions to occur.

Source monitoring error (or cryptomnesia)

If you could accurately determine the source of each part of a memory, you might determine to what extent the memory itself is false. Unfortunately, memories do not come with identification tags. Library books and emails generally have some record of where they came from, perhaps a return address or purchase record. Instead, in the process of recall, we evaluate our memories and attribute (accurately or inaccurately) what we think the sources are (Hicks & Marsh, 2001; Johnson, 2006; Johnson, Hashtroudi, & Lindsay, 1993). We create source tags as needed, greatly compounding the difficulty in assessing the accuracy of recollections.

One widely cited example involves former president Ronald Reagan (Schacter, 1996). During a presidential campaign, Reagan told a heart-rending story of a WWII pilot who ordered his crew to bail out of their damaged bomber. One gunner was wounded and couldn't jump. Reagan, barely holding back tears, recalled the heroic pilot's promise: "Never mind. We'll ride it down together." A very touching memory, except it never happened—it's the ending of the 1944 film *A Wing and a Prayer*.

It is important to note that a memory might have any of a number of sources, including actual fact, a dream, someone else's claim or dream, our desires, and our imagination. Without outside corroboration it can be impossible to determine whether your vivid memory of your Aunt Mimi's pink hat is accurate, based on what a friend claimed, a movie about an aunt, your wish that she wore clothes you prefer, a dream you had about your aunt, or simply your imagination. Furthermore, the degree of detail or vividness of your memory (although sometimes helpful) does not guarantee accuracy of its source. The best we can do is carefully consider our memories, for example, by reviewing their plausibility and objectivity (not part of what we want or expect).

Forgetting the source of a memory is more serious when we forget a source that might not be credible. A psychologist might claim to have conducted a research study that demonstrates that people can communicate with the dead. Later he might be exposed as a complete fraud. We might recall, "I remember a researcher who once demonstrated the validity of communication with the dead," completely forgetting the fraudulent source and recalling only the claim.

Cryptomnesia (from the Greek "Kryptos" for hidden, and "mnesia" for memories, as in "amnesia") is another name for source memory error. As a nonparanormal phenomenon, cryptomnesia can lead to charges of plagiarism. The famous Beatle, George Harrison, moved millions with his song, "My Sweet Lord," a deeply spiritual anthem for the Hindu Hare Krishna church. "My Sweet Lord" was the first hit by a Beatle after the group disbanded. Harrison was sued (and lost) when a competing record company claimed that his hit resembled another hit, "He's So Fine," composed by Ronald Mack and sung by the Chiffons. Harrison's plagiarism was likely unintentional; he fully believed his tune was new. In the literary world there are many examples of cryptomnesia. Hellen Keller's "The Frost King" was an unintentional plagiarism of Canby's "The Frost Fairies." Bits of Robert Louis Stevenson's *Treasure Island* were taken from other books (Stevenson, 2004). Cryptomnesia is not an acceptable legal defense against accusations of plagiarism. If you're a student, don't try it on your professor. However, it is perfectly legal to remember your former life as an Egyptian queen (even though you have forgotten the book on Egyptian queens you read as a child). Many claims of reincarnation and alien abduction are quite likely examples of cryptomnesia.

Misinformation and pseudomemories

Researchers have conducted over 200 studies involving over 20,000 individuals on the **misinformation effect**, in which exposure to misleading information can lead to the distortion of recollections (Loftus, 1996). In a typical study, one might observe a simulated event such as a crime or accident and, after a delay, be exposed with post-event information, some of which is accurate and some inaccurate. Later accuracy of memory for the event is measured.

In a famous study (Loftus, 1996), participants watched a simulated auto accident that involved a crossing with a stop sign. Then, half received a suggestion that there was a yield sign, not a stop sign. Later, those who were given the false suggestion falsely remembered a yield sign rather than a stop sign. Participants in other studies have falsely remembered a suggested conspicuous barn in a scene that actually had no buildings, a white instead of a blue vehicle at a crime scene, and Minnie Mouse instead of Mickey Mouse. Loftus (1996) concludes that misinformation is especially likely to distort recollection when it comes from discussions we have with others, leading to aggressive interrogations ("did you steal the *six raisin oatmeal cookies in the glass jar over the refrigerator?*"), and exposure to media coverage about the event we have experienced.

The misinformation effect typically refers to the distortion of one or two details. It is possible to create more extensive memory errors with **implanted pseudomemories**. In one study Loftus (1996) created personalized information pamphlets for each of 24 participants. Each pamphlet described four childhood incidents, three of which actually happened to the participant (as determined from previous interviews with parents, older siblings, and close relatives). Unknown to the participants, the fourth event was fake, specifically a traumatic experience of getting lost in the shopping mall for an extended period of time.

Weeks later, participants were asked to recall and describe actual childhood experiences. Brief cues from each pamphlet story (real and fake) were presented to help cue and prod memory. About a quarter recalled as real the details presented for the shopping mall fiction. They were not just identifying a fake event as actual, but were recalling what they felt were real memories. Fake memories had been implanted. This effect occurs even when subjects had earlier correctly stated they did not recognize a fake event as having happened ("Getting lost in the shopping mall ... this is news to me."). In later interviews, 20% actually claimed remembering the fake event as factual, and actually provided details (all made up, of course).

Again, we can consider such memory errors as alternative hypotheses for what might seem like remarkable paranormal memories. For example, you and a friend attend a group reading featuring a famous psychic. The psychic gives one audience member a detailed personal reading, including: "you are a student, you have a respiratory disorder, your two pets miss you, and you are thinking about buying a new car." Immediately after the session, you and your friend go out for coffee. You recall the four specifics. Your friend adds, "but don't you remember that she correctly guessed that person's name, Bill?" You respond, "I don't recall this." In fact, your friend is in error. However, the stage has been set for an implanted pseudomemory. Months later you may well recall, and even remember details of, the psychic guessing one participant's first name.

As you might imagine, the implanted pseudomemory effect has the potential for compromising much eyewitness testimony in courts. Indeed, some have suggested that up to 10,000 individuals have been wrongly convicted because of such memory errors (Cutler & Penrod, 1995; Loftus & Ketcham, 1994). I am deeply skeptical of retrospective accounts of the paranormal, no matter how credible a witness may be.

Familiarity (from repetition) is truth

We are more likely to believe a memory if it seems familiar and has been formed on the basis of repeated experience. However, familiarity is not a logical basis for truthfulness. This **illusion of truth effect** (Hasher, Goldstein, & Toppino, 1977) has been demonstrated in a number of startling experiments (Begg & Armour, 1991; Begg, Anas, & Farinacci, 1992). In a typical study, you first might be asked to study a list of general information statements, some of which happen to be true and some false. For example, the list might state that "Boston is the capital of Massachusetts" (true), "Los Angeles is the capital of California" (false), "Adams was president before Lincoln" (true), "Franklin was president after Jefferson" (false), "Edison invented the light bulb" (true), and "Einstein invented the television" (false). Note that in this case you are simply presented the statements, and not told that any are true or false.

If later on you are presented a larger list of statements, some repeating the true and false statements already presented, you are more likely to rate the previously presented statements as true—*regardless of whether they are true or false*. Furthermore, this effect is implicit and occurs even if subjects do not recall the actual previous statements. What happens if the initial statements were tagged as true ("It is widely known that …") or false ("Few people believe that …")? This makes little difference. Previous exposure to a statement, *even when labeled as true or false*, is enough to increase the likelihood that it will be subsequently rated as true.

There are many explanations as to why claims that seem familiar seem true (Begg et al., 1992). Perhaps once you have been exposed to a claim, it takes less time to process (and comprehend) when you encounter it again. The first time you read about "retroactive intercessory prayer," it may take you some time to learn that this actually refers to the claim that we can pray that people in the past be cured of illness (Chapter 15). When you again encounter a claim of "retroactive intercessory prayer," you are familiar with it, and therefore more likely to feel it is true. In addition, we may erroneously believe that a quickly recognized claim is more likely to be true. Alternatively, when an event is clearly factual it may well be repeated with greater frequency. After living through dozens of cold and snowy winters in Michigan, you come to learn that this is a fact of life in Michigan. The one mild winter was never repeated and cannot be described as typical. From such experiences we may come to automatically label any repeated experience, factual or not, as based on actual evidence.

It is easy to identify many real-life examples that may well illustrate the familiarity-truth effect. Our media is saturated with advertisements claiming various "facts." Toothpaste X whitens teeth best, a specific diet works, and so on. Some of these claims may be challenged and thoroughly discredited by journalists. However, such debunking may have little effect. Simple repetition of the claim makes it seem familiar, and therefore true, regardless of whether it is presented as true or false. Indeed, in one study, warning older adults that a consumer claim is false can make them later mistakenly remember it as true (Skurnik, Yoon, Park, & Schwartz, 2005).

Can you think of any paranormal claims that have been repeated so often that they are familiar? This might include flying saucers at Roswell, Uri Geller's psychic ability to bend spoons, ships lost in the Bermuda Triangle, sightings of the Loch Ness Monster, the Amityville haunted house, scientific studies proving the efficacy of prayer or healing touch, or the Nostradamus prediction of Hitler. The list grows if we add figures from antiquity and reports of individuals walking on water, levitating, turning water into wine, bringing the dead to life, and so on. Over time, the simple repetition of these claims (regardless of accompanying caveats or even disproof) contributes to their recollection as factual.

Imagination inflation and saying is believing

Asking someone to imagine or engage in a fantasy about an event that never happened increases the likelihood that later on they will remember the same event as having happened. This is called *imagination inflation* (Loftus, 1996). To elaborate, when we recall an experience, we are more likely to be confident that our memories are accurate when the perceptual details are vivid and detailed. Recalling a memory (false or otherwise) may well strengthen its vividness and detail, especially when relaxation and visualization strategies are used. One might as a consequence be increasingly convinced of the accuracy of one's recollection (Sternberg, 2006).

Sometimes *saying is believing* (Higgins, 1992; Ackil & Zaragoza, 1998), especially when we are addressing friends who agree with us. Consider this example. A politician who once supported the Iraq war proclaims to a cheering crowd of supporters that she opposes it. Another politician who derided extremist televangelists as "agents of intolerance" speaks glowingly of fundamentalists in front of warmly appreciative conservative Christians. Politicians are frequently accused of "flip-flopping" and adjusting their positions to fit those of their supporters. Nearly 30 years of research suggests that under certain conditions, we, and our politicians, actually come to believe what we say.

When we tune our message to fit our audience's beliefs, our later recollection and belief is of the tuned (and possibly distorted) message. Our perception of reality has been molded by our communications with others. This effect is strongest when there is an emotional and trusting connection between the speaker and the audience (Echterhoff, Higgins, Kopietz, & Groll, 2008). This is the glue that "fixes" the distorted memory. However, under some conditions this effect is much less pronounced, for example when trying to persuade skeptics, entertain, or simply comply mechanically with instructions.

Apply this to a paranormal belief. Imagine that you are an acupuncture buff in the company of other friendly believers. You are describing news reports of research on acupuncture. In fact the news accounts are complex and include observations from believers as well as scholarly skeptics. In your excitement you tune your report to what your listeners want to hear—the apparently supportive evidence. Later, when asked to describe the news reports, your honest recollection is distorted—you recall only the support for acupuncture.

Déjà vu

French for "already seen," déjà vu is the uncanny sense that you have experienced something before, when in fact you are experiencing it for the first time. About 60% of the population has had at least one déjà vu experience, and most people have them about once a year (Brown, 2004). This feeling is typically accompanied by an intense and convincing feeling of familiarity as well as a sense of "eeriness," "strangeness," or "weirdness." Such otherworldly feelings can readily suggest otherworldly interpretations. Given the prevalence and persuasiveness of déjà vu experiences in the paranormal literature, we will devote substantial space to this topic.

Let's imagine that you can remember specific details of a famous castle you have never visited. Why might one experience this strange and remarkable event? In a previous life, did you reside in the castle as a king or queen? Perhaps in sleep your spirit left your body and traveled to the castle. Is some supernatural entity, or worldly ghost, trying to communicate to you about the castle? Maybe one of your descendants traveled to the castle far in the future, and is telling you about it using time travel. Perhaps something very unfortunate, or fortunate, is going to happen in the castle, triggering a timely premonition. Could it be that the castle is on a quantum energy meridian that also connects to your house, giving you an occasional direct view? Maybe in an alternative universe you actually live in the castle, and this information is leaking through dimensional cracks to your mind. Could it involve wormholes? Maybe space aliens took you to the castle for their experimental probes, and then returned you, having botched the job of erasing your memory of the castle.

What does research say? Researchers have identified a few consistent patterns. Déjà vu is often associated with stress and fatigue (Brown, 2004). Logically, if you go to many places, the likelihood increases that you will evoke a déjà vu feeling just by chance. Stress, fatigue, and laws of probability may explain why soldiers going into battle and travelers are particularly likely to have déjà vu experiences since both face new environments and are under some stress and fatigue.

A few other patterns are worth noting. Those who recall their dreams are more likely to have déjà vu experiences. Zuger (1966) has suggested that some déjà vu experiences may be dream states intruding into waking consciousness. Also, a dream memory fragment may evoke a déjà vu experience when one encounters a similar situation while awake. Déjà vu is not consistently associated with psychopathology or brain-related illness; however, it is more common for head injury patients (who have lost consciousness). Finally, déjà vu has been associated with abuse of amphetamines, toluene-based solvents, use of mind-influencing medications (amantadine and phenylpropanolamine), and withdrawal from medication for bipolar disorder and herpes simplex encephalitis.

The déjà vu experience is very difficult to study scientifically because it typically occurs spontaneously without an identifiable stimulus trigger. Generally one has to accept the word of the person reporting a déjà vu experience, and the credibility of their memory-based claims. In spite of this limitation, four groups of theories have emerged (Brown, 2004).

Dual-processing explanations

Dual-processing explanations propose that déjà vu experiences emerge when two memory processes that are generally coordinated are temporarily disconnected, or one works in the absence of another. For example, Gloor (1990) has suggested that the retrieval of memories and the experience of familiarity are linked to two different cognitive functions. Typically these are coordinated, so that when one retrieves a memory, say of Aunt Mimi, the memory is experienced as familiar. However, either process may temporarily operate independently. With no basis in memory, a "familiarity response" may be triggered, and experienced as déjà vu.

Neurological explanations

Some have suggested that déjà vu experiences are associated with minor brain seizures or changes in how the brain operates. Indeed, déjà vu experiences sometimes (1–6%) precede seizures in those with temporal lobe epilepsy. Direct electrical stimulation of portions of the brain involved in seizures can artificially evoke déjà vu. However, déjà vu is not a sign that one suffers from a brain disorder.

Another set of neurological explanations are based on the assumption that information from the outside world simultaneously reaches the brain through several nerve pathways. When you visit a friend's house, perceptions of the house do not travel to the brain through one link, like cable television, but take several routes, and are then reassembled into what is experienced as a single perception of a house. When, because of stress or fatigue, one pathway "cable" is delayed, one signal may arrive early, and another a millisecond later. When the second part of the "house signal" arrives, it is experienced as "familiar" because a memory has already been established (based on the signal just received).

Attentional explanations

You are about to visit a bakery for the first time. It is on the other side of the street and you wait for the light to let you cross. The light turns green, you start walking, and notice many racks of bread through the bakery window. In a blink, a car runs a red light, honks loudly, and barely misses you. Startled, you jump aside, completely forgetting your fleeting first impression of the bakery window. However, when you enter the bakery you observe the racks of bread and have a strong sense of déjà vu. Brief initial perceptions, even those of which you are only dimly aware, can lead to déjà vu experiences in situations that immediately follow.

Implicit and source memory explanations

Recall that forgotten past events can still influence present experiences and actions. You may not recall the amusing television ad for a particular brand of cola; however, it can still **prime** you to notice the same cola on a supermarket shelf of many soft drinks. You may find the packaging of the brand strangely amusing, forgetting that in the forgotten commercial the same packaging was woven into a cleverly funny story. Here, your amusement reflects a **source memory** error (you find it funny, but may not know why). To use another example, you may not remember that you had at one time visited a particular temple. However, your previous temple encounter was enough to prime you to feel a strange sense of familiarity when you visit the temple again. Indeed, you may interpret this as a divine message that you are "coming home," one a priest might eagerly reinforce.

What about déjà vu experiences concerning a place you are absolutely sure you have never visited? A single element in a previous experience is enough to evoke déjà vu. For example, years ago you briefly visited a forest. Deep in the forest was an old wooden cabin. Today you visit a lake for the first time. You notice an old wooden canoe, and are filled with a feeling of déjà vu. You are convinced you have visited the lake before, perhaps in a previous life. The forgotten memory of the cabin on the lake was enough to trigger your déjà vu experience.

A sense of familiarity may be evoked by a memory that has nothing to do with a current novel situation. A dream, story, or movie episode of a similar setting is enough to trigger déjà vu. Remarkably, the similarity does not have to involve actual events, as illustrated below.

Imagine you visited a bakery last year:

> Upon entering you are struck with the strong delightful aroma of fresh bread. You look ahead and are astonished to see an enormous rack of hundreds of loaves. Suddenly the baker turns to you and surprises you with the question, "Is something wrong?" Confused, you explain that

this is the first time you have visited a bakery. However, you remain a bit uncomfortable and make a point of leaving quickly.

Imagine that you are now visiting an automobile factory for the first time. You have a strong sense of déjà vu. Here's what happens.

You enter the factory and are confronted with the strong odor of metal, a rather pleasing scent given your interest in mechanics. You look ahead and are astonished to see an entire factory filled with rows of robots assembling cars. The foreman turns to you and says in a stern voice, "Can I help you?" You explain that you are new to this site. However, this exchange has left you a bit uncomfortable, and you cut your visit short.

Note that your bakery and factory experiences have completely different content—bread vs. cars and robots. However, they evoked the same track of cognitive and affective processes: Sense of smell—feelings of delight—sense of vision—astonishment—unexpected question—verbal processing in brain—emotion of discomfort—decision to leave. Your factory visit evoked the same sequence of processes evoked by your bakery experience, and thereby evoked a strong sense of familiarity. Searching your memory you could find no recollection of having visited a factory, contributing to a sense of déjà vu (Osborn, 1884).

Déjà vu and memory

A déjà vu experience can itself implant a false memory. For example, imagine you are visiting your Aunt Mimi for the first time. Upon entering her cottage, you have an intense feeling of having been there before. Perhaps you recognize that ugly brown sofa (an unconscious memory fragment from a recent television documentary on ugly sofas). In addition, some new details catch your attention, including scratches, coffee stains, and cat hair. The next day you recount your remarkable déjà vu experience: "It was amazing! Not only did I remember the ugly brown sofa, but I actually remembered specific details, like the scratches, stains, and cat hair!" Here a source memory error has occurred. You incorrectly label details experienced for the first time as mysterious memories of some previous visit.

The Déjà vu Reality Check

What type of experiment would support a paranormal interpretation of a déjà vu experience? For the sake of illustration, imagine you are visiting a castle for the first time and have the strong feeling you have visited before, perhaps in a previous life. Here are some of the issues we should consider.

- First, your memories would have to be concrete and specific, as confirmed by neutral outside observers. You could not claim that a certain room in a castle is "creepy." You would have to name specifics, the number of tables and chairs, their composition and placement.
- Second, your claimed recollections would have to be unique. You could not claim that the castle is made out of stone or is on a hill, characteristics that fit many castles.
- Third, your recollections would have to be prospective and identify specific facts not available, otherwise your recollections could be based on conversations, what you've seen or read, or **stimulus leakage** (Chapter 5). You might select a vault, sealed for hundreds of years, with no information concerning contents. Of course, you would have to identify the contents before (not after) the vault is opened.
- Fourth, you would have to rule out chance. Given that 60% of the population has had a déjà vu experience, one might suspect that many have had experiences that involve concrete and unique details. It is possible that a large number of people have had prospective déjà vu recollections involving long buried or hidden items. By chance alone we would expect some recollections to be right (Chapter 6). To minimize chance identifications, we would have to publicly record a déjà vu-based prediction of hidden information before the unveiling event. This might be hard to do given that déjà vu experiences occur unpredictably.
- Finally, you would have to apply the FEDS Standard and ensure that each step is free from any possibility of fraud, error, deception, or sloppiness (Chapter 5).

In everyday life we may not have time for such extensive scientific reality checking. Experts in memory suggest that we can do much to sort truth from fantasy through *source monitoring* (Johnson et al., 1993), a set of processes whereby we identify the origins of our memories (including knowledge and beliefs). One might conclude that a memory is not imagined but is based on an external event (a) if it is rich in perceptual detail, and you can vividly recall details such as sounds, colors, and smells, (b) contains contextual information, that is, specific recollections as to when and where an event happened, (c) seems coherent and plausible (for example, if you recalled floating out of your bed, walking through walls, becoming invisible, and speaking to your great-great-grandmother, such recollections would represent an incoherent and disconnected jumble, that is not particularly plausible given what humans can and cannot do), and (d) contains recollections of cognitive efforts used to create an idea or commit an experience to memory ("I can't remember deliberately trying to compose this tune; therefore, it must be something I heard on the radio.").

REALITY CHECK Imagine that someone has had a strong déjà vu experience, perhaps of having visited a certain site in a previous life. Such a dramatic experience might understandably prompt one to search for evidence and explanations. What perceptual processes (Chapter 7) might lead one to the wrong conclusion?

Repressed Memory Therapy

The popular press abounds with cases of false memory. Some stories are amusing, such as those who recall living past-lives as ancient slaves or kings. There can be only so many reincarnated Cleopatras or Napoleons. Then there are those poor souls who have been abducted, and probed, by aliens from outer space. Appropriately, these stories are particularly popular in science fiction. Many people have been falsely accused and incarcerated because of erroneous witness recollections. Today, juries are wisely suspicious of testimonies based only on recollection. But perhaps the most instructive examples are from the pseudoscientific world of **repressed memory therapy**.

Repressed memory therapy (RMT) derives from Freud's notion that threatening memories are automatically repressed in the unconscious, where they can do great harm. Specifically, RMT claims that traumatic childhood memories of sexual abuse are repressed, but can be uncovered and released through special therapeutic techniques including imagery and hypnosis (see Chapter 7). This approach is highly controversial, partly because its basic idea is probably false. Traumatic memories are actually more likely to be remembered than buried. But RMT therapists claim again and again that their patients recall vivid incidents of sexual abuse. Critics claim that many of these recollections are simply cases of **false memory syndrome**.

Repressed memory therapy has led to some very costly tragedies. Elizabeth Loftus (1997) has recounted numerous cases. For example, in 1986 a Wisconsin nurse's aid, Nadean Cool, was in therapy with a psychiatrist. Cool claimed she had buried memories of childhood sexual abuse, and indeed after several sessions of hypnosis, she recalled fantastic memories of rape, being in a satanic cult, eating babies, and having sex with animals. Eventually Cool realized that her memories were false and sued. In 1997 she settled for $2.4 million.

In a similar example, in 1992 a Missouri church counselor helped Beth Rutherford uncover childhood memories of being repeatedly raped by her father, a pastor. On further exploration, she recalled that she had two pregnancies, both of which were terminated by her father through abortion. When these accusations were made public, Rutherford's father resigned as pastor. However, it was eventually determined that she was a virgin at age 22. She sued the counselor and received $1 million in 1996.

From 1986 to 1992, Patricia Burgus underwent psychiatric therapy in a major Chicago hospital by a respected psychiatrist. Through drugs and hypnosis, she recovered a variety of memories, including participating in a satanic cult, rape by her father and cult members, and cannibalizing body parts of up to 2,000 people, including her own aborted children (Belluck, 1997). These recollections were so convincing that her husband had a hamburger from a family picnic tested for human content. Burgus grew suspicious of her own recollections and searched for corroborative evidence. Finding none, she decided that her recollections were false, sued, and won the lawsuit, including a settlement of $10.6 million (the largest ever). The director of the trauma unit called the settlement a "travesty."

In general, cases such as these have a number of features in common.

- lack of accurate external corroborative evidence for a memory claim;
- use of imagery or hypnosis to evoke or "enhance" memories;
- instructions to recall after a time delay;
- initial suggestion (even indirect, through media accounts) of specific memory content and source;
- encouragement, group support, and reinforcement for accepting memories as true;
- failure to request critical and skeptical reconsideration of memory claims and their sources.

In the waning years of the 20th century, repressed memory therapy was in its heyday. However, after hundreds of successful lawsuits, this approach waned in popularity. Today the consensus is that the foundations of repressed memory therapy are a "pernicious bit of psychiatric folklore" (McNally, 2004).

REALITY
CHECK   Numerous psychics and faith healers have been repeatedly and publicly revealed as frauds (Chapters 7, 14). Yet their popularity persists and grows. What memory processes might explain this?

Reality Checking for the Placebo Effect

Every decade has its cancer fad. In the 1950s it was Krebiozen, a worthless treatment made from horse blood. I am particularly fond of the Krebiozen story because it involves a treatment administered by a doctor whose Chicago office was in the very same building I work (two decades before my arrival). This story has been presented with little modification in many medical texts, although its source is Klopfer (1957).

We begin with Mr. Wright, a desperate patient suffering from cancer of the lymph nodes (lymphosarcoma) who was not responding to traditional treatment. Orange-sized tumors were growing on his neck, armpits, chest, abdomen, and groin. They had metastasized. His spleen, liver, and chest were filled with fluid, requiring two quarts of draining a day. Mr. Wright had little time left and demanded the new wonder drug Krebiozen.

His skeptical physician relented. The pace of recovery was unexpected, indeed miraculous. After one dose, tumors "melted like snowballs on a hot stove" to half their size. After 10 days, Mr. Wright appeared to be cured and was able to return to most of his normal duties. He remained cancer free for about two months until the media reported that Krebiozen may not work.

Mr. Wright was despondent and his cancers returned. In desperation, his physician decided on a placebo and a bit of deception. He claimed that Krebiozen worked but some of the initial shipments had deteriorated. He went on to say that he had a new and concentrated supply. Then, using an elaborate procedure, he injected his patient with a placebo, simple water. The experiment worked dramatically. Again, tumor masses melted and Mr. Wright enjoyed life free of symptoms. But it was a short cure. Two months later the American Medical Association announced that nationwide research had shown that Krebiozen was completely worthless. Mr. Wright's cancer returned and he died two days later (Klopfer, 1957).

The story of Mr. Wright is practically a legend in medicine. It illustrates a potent dimension of treatment called the placebo effect. Alternatively, it may illustrate how perceptions, of patients, physicians, and presumed outside experts, distort the facts and contribute to pseudoscientific medical myths. Indeed, we will probably never know if Mr. Wright's treatment in fact lengthened his life (Carroll, 2008).

What are Placebos?

A **placebo** is a pharmacologically or physiologically inactive substance or procedure that can have a therapeutic physiological and psychological effect if administered to a patient who has the expectation that it is effective (adapted from Bausell, 2007; Benedetti, 2009; and Shapiro & Shapiro, 1997). A placebo is the proverbial "sugar pill," "dummy treatment," or in Mr. Wright's case, water injection. It is an inert preparation whose medical effect, the placebo effect, is due to suggestion. But a placebo doesn't have to be a pill. It can include any intervention, whether it be a form of psychotherapy, ritual, dietary prescription, pill, rehabilitation activity, or form of surgery. A placebo is *nonspecific* in that it is not targeted to a specific disorder and works for a wide range of problems. In contrast, medical drugs or procedures are *specific* in that they are carefully designed to work for targeted conditions. This distinction is easy to miss. All placebos are nonspecific. But, as we shall see later, not all nonspecific interventions are placebos.

The word placebo derives from the Latin word for "I shall please." The term entered English by way of a mistranslation of the 116th Psalm as "I will please the Lord" (correct version: "I will walk before the Lord."). In medieval times, this psalm was sung at religious ceremonies honoring the dead. In time, you could avoid such dreary duties by hiring professional mourners to sing your placebos for you. Not surprisingly, the "placebo" acquired a derogatory connotation that continues today—something superficial and not genuine. In the 1800s the term placebo entered the medical vocabulary as a treatment given "more to please than to benefit the patient" (Hooper, 1822).

Contrary to popular opinion, placebos can work. As seen with Krebiozen, the effects can appear miraculous. But just how effective are treatments based on suggestion? In medical lore, about one-third of the medical effect of a therapeutic intervention is attributable to the placebo effect. This claim is generally attributed to Beecher (1955). Beecher also defined the placebo in terms of suggestion as well as all nonspecific effects. Beecher's claim is no longer accepted; in fact placebo response rates vary considerably from a low of 0% to up to 100% (Benedetti, 2009).

The placebo effect appears stronger for problems with a strong psychological component, such as pain or depression. However, research suggests that the effect is broad. Physicians have removed warts by painting the

Figure 9.1   Snake oil

skin with harmless dye, induced airway dilation in asthmatics through fake bronchodilators, and reduced intestinal inflammation in colitis patients using simple placebos (Talbot, 2000). Some evidence appears to show a placebo effect for "postoperative swelling, movement disorders, vital signs such as oral temperature and pulse, blood pressure, weight loss, exercise tolerance among heart patients, healing of ulcers, cholesterol reduction, blood sugar ..." (Bausell, 2007, p. 138). Placebos can even evoke the negative side effects of drugs they are claimed to be, including headaches, drowsiness, decreased respiration, and cortisol levels (Bausell, 2007).

The placebo effect has even been demonstrated for surgery. Although pharmaceutical companies routinely compare new drugs with placebos, it is rare for new surgical interventions to receive such comparisons. A surgical placebo would be a form of sham surgery involving realistic incisions but no treatment. The two best examples involve a type of heart surgery and knee surgery.

Angina chest pains are caused by a narrowing of arteries in the heart, depriving the heart of blood. Today, this condition is treated with medication, and occasionally by more invasive measures such as open heart surgery. In the 1940s and 1950s thousands of angina patients received an experimental form of heart surgery called internal mammary ligation. This involved surgically opening the chest and actually tying knots in some of the arteries leading to the heart. The speculation was that by reducing blood flow, the heart would be stimulated to grow new arteries, thereby reducing angina pains. Seventy-five percent of patients improved and the treatment appeared to work.

In the late 1950s Cobb tried something revolutionary (Cobb, Thomas, Dillard, Merendino, & Bruce, 1959). He selected a group of angina patients, surgically opened their chests, but did not tie knots in arteries. Astonishingly, this sham surgery was just as effective as actual surgery. The practice of internal mammary ligation is no longer practiced because of this demonstrated placebo effect.

A more recent example involves surgery for osteoarthritis of the knee. Arthroscopic surgery involves making a small incision around the knee, and then cleaning and scraping the diseased bone. About 650,000 such procedures are done each year at a cost of over $3 billion. Moseley (Moseley et al., 2002) created a stir in the surgical community by comparing actual arthroscopic surgery with surgery plus washing (no scraping), and simply sham surgery (cuts but no treatment). In a study involving 165 patients and lasting over 2 years, sham surgery was found to be just as effective as actual arthroscopic surgery.

Most research on placebos has focused on pain reduction or depression. Here we find very high levels of efficacy, with up to 60% reporting significant improvement (again, different studies report different numbers). Given the huge pain and antidepressant medication industry, drug companies take considerable care to compare new medications with placebos. So much rides on the magnitude of the placebo effect that disputes often arise.

Weak and Strong Placebos

Not all placebos are equal. It is not enough simply to compare an experimental treatment with a sugar pill described as a treatment. Placebos appear to work better for patients highly motivated to improve their health. That is, patients who are conscientious about complying with treatment have better recovery rates, even with worthless treatments. Similarly, patients do better if they have been given strong reasons to expect that a placebo will work. Placebos presented in an "authoritative and/or positive" way work better than those given with a neutral or equivocal message (Bausell, 2007).

Even the type of pill can make a difference. Color pills work better than white pills, capsules better than pills, big pills better than small pills, and injected placebos better than oral placebos. Placebos administered frequently are more effective than those given infrequently (Bausell, 2007). Expensive placebos work better than cheap placebos (Waber, Shiv, Carmon, & Ariely, 2008).

Placebos are actually more effective if those giving them have been deceived into believing they work. This necessitates what is termed a **double-blind** (see Chapter 5) design. Here neither the patient nor the person giving the drug knows if the treatment they are giving is the drug under question or the placebo. Failure to adequately "blind" research participants is one of the most serious problems plaguing placebo research, especially for studies on approaches to complementary and alternative medicine such as acupuncture

(Madsen, Gøtzsche, & Hróbjartsson, 2009). For example, the rituals of "correct" acupuncture needle insertion are quite complex, requiring a trained acupuncturist. However, when an acupuncture expert administers a treatment, it is no longer blinded. His or her enthusiasm could be a potent nonspecific therapeutic ingredient.

Placebos with built-in negative side effects are more effective. These are called **active placebos** and can be created by spiking sugar pills with harmless substances designed to produce symptoms such as sweatiness. Such fake side effects can be perceived as "signs" that the placebo is actually working. (A placebo accompanied by a verbal suggestion of a negative effect is sometimes called a **nocebo**.)

The complexity and plausibility of a placebo treatment can influence its efficacy. A good placebo has a complicated explanation as to why it works (the explanation can be complete rubbish, but it has to sound plausible, with lots of technobabble; see Chapter 4). Similarly, placebo procedures are more effective than placebo pills. Indeed, surgical placebos may well be extremely potent (Bausell, 2007).

Finally, (at least for pain), the recalled effect of a placebo may well be greater than the actual effect experienced at the time of treatment. In one study, pain was induced artificially by a special heat pad. As expected, a placebo could reduce the pain. However, a few minutes after the end of the experiment, participants were asked how much their pain was relieved. Recollections of degree of pain-reduction were greater than the actual reductions reported while the placebo was administered (Price et al., 1999). The implications of such findings are considerable, especially in light of what is known about the distorting effects of memory (Chapter 8).

REALITY CHECK How might memory errors described in Chapter 8 increase distorted recollections of effectiveness of a placebo?

When considering the possibility of a placebo effect, it is useful to understand underlying mechanisms that might make placebos work. Armed with these tools you can examine the conditions associated with a claimed treatment and ask if "placebogenic" mechanisms may be at play.

How Placebos Work

At first it might seem mysterious that a simple suggestion can have a physical effect. But it happens all the time. A police officer tells you to stop, and you stop walking. That's a physical effect. He asks to see your wallet and your heart starts to beat hard, also a physical effect. A friend describes in detail a delicious steak and your mouth begins to water. You watch a horror movie and your stomach feels queasy. Someone tells a joke, and you blush. Our brains and bodies constantly react to suggestions. Research on placebos and hypnosis simply shows us other ways that this happens.

Both hypnosis and placebos often involve explicit, concrete, verbal suggestion. A practitioner of hypnosis might state "When you open your eyes, your headache will go away." A nurse giving a placebo might explain "This pill (a placebo) will make your headache go away." Neither placebos nor hypnosis require a special "trance state" (Chapter 7). Both can have a measurable physiological effect on a fully conscious and awake individual. Both have been used as an analgesic and even anesthetic for surgery with little more than the simple utterance "you no longer feel pain." Some of the medical research on hypnosis is very similar to research on placebos; indeed, hypnosis has been applied to many of the same medical conditions targeted in placebo studies.

Research to differentiate placebogenic from hypnotic suggestion has yet to be conducted. We do not know if the variables often postulated to enhance hypnotic suggestion (reduced stimulation and instructions to focus and relax) also enhance the placebo effect. (I suspect they do.) We do not know if the placebo-enhancing variables listed in this chapter can also enhance hypnosis, as measured through objective tests. An explicit, concrete, verbally presented placebo may well be the same thing as a waking hypnotic suggestion (Chapter 7).

A placebo is defined in terms of suggestion. However, one might suggest improvement without administering any treatment ("You are feeling more relaxed" vs. "This pill will make you feel more relaxed."). Such direct suggestion is a nonspecific treatment. Various other nonspecific processes, such as classical conditioning, the opioid system, and reduced self-stressing, can augment placebo suggestion. Some have suggested that they may be a defining component of some placebo responses (Benedetti, 2009).[1]

Classical Conditioning

The concept of **classical conditioning** was introduced by Russian researcher Ivan Pavlov, who taught dogs to salivate to a bell simply by ringing a bell whenever they were fed. Eventually, the bell was enough. Similarly, classical conditioning may partly explain the placebo effect. If you feel better after taking a prescribed pill or receiving a medical procedure, eventually the pill (any pill) or procedure can become a conditioned stimulus and evoke feelings of improvement. This has been demonstrated in a number of careful research studies. Nitroglycerine is a heart medication that induces changes in heart rate. When participants are first given actual nitroglycerine pills, and then similar pills not containing nitroglycerine, they continue to display changes in heart rate (Lang & Rand, 1969). Mice injected with harmless sugar water, and then with an immunosuppressive drug, display a reduced immune response (fewer antibodies). Then, when sugar water is injected alone, they display a classically conditioned immunosuppressive response (Cohen, Moynihan, & Ader, 1994). Through classical conditioning placebos have been demonstrated to evoke the physiological effects of caffeine, nicotine, alcohol, interferon, bronchodilators and bronchoconstrictors, stimulants, and immunosuppression and nausea associated with cancer chemotherapy (Bausell, 2007; Benedetti, 2009). Benedetti (2009) suggests that classical conditioning is a central component to placebo effects when unconscious physiological processes are involved, such as with hormone secretion and the immune system.

Is a claimed treatment a placebo? Consider if the conditions are present for possible classical conditioning. For example, a patient undergoing acupuncture treatment for pain might enter the office of a medical professional and meet a practitioner wearing a medical gown. The practitioner touches the patient as part of the treatment. It is quite likely that, in the past, a patient may have entered a doctor's office and met a doctor who proceeded with an examination before administering a powerful pain-killing pill or procedure. If so, the reduction of pain might conceivably be classically conditioned to the medical setting and augment any explicit treatment claim. Note that when classical conditioning explains a treatment response, and no placebo expectation is given, I prefer to state that we have a nonspecific non-placebo response. In contrast, Benedetti (2009) would claim it is an "unconscious" placebo response.

The Opioid System

Different neurophysiological mechanisms may contribute to the placebo response for different medical conditions (Benedetti, 2009). Recent research suggests that the brain's reward system, the **opioid system** (and perhaps dopamine activation), may be essential to the placebo effect for pain and perhaps anxiety and depression. Its role in interventions for conditions with few overt symptoms (glaucoma, some early cancers, HIV infection) and surgical treatments is much less clear. First, a bit of pharmacology. Morphine is an extremely powerful analgesic and falls into the same class of such addictive opioid-based drugs as heroin. The brain's opioid system produces its own morphine-like substances, called endorphins, which can block pain and evoke feelings of euphoria. This is one reason why long-distance runners can persist in spite of fatigue, and football players can continue playing in spite of painful injury. **Naloxone** is an opioid antagonist, which means it can block the effects of opioids. Indeed, naloxone is sometimes used to treat heroin overdose.

If the placebo effect is associated with the brain's opioid system, then naloxone should block this effect. Often the effect is dramatic. For example, Benedetti, Arduino, and Amanzio (1999) injected capasalcin (the substance that makes chili peppers hot and burn) under the skin in the left and right hands and feet. Participants were given a placebo cream for one burning body part. The cream was described as a powerful local anesthetic. The cream worked as expected and eliminated the pain in the one hand or foot to which it was applied. However, when naloxone was injected, the effect was completely eliminated, illustrating a purely expectation-driven effect mediated by the opioid system. However, the opioid system may not be involved in all types of pain. Vase, Robinson, Verne and Price (2005) injected patients suffering from irritable bowel syndrome with either a saline solution (placebo) or naloxone. Both worked equally well. Here if pain-reduction were mediated by the opioid system, the naloxone group should have reported no effect.

Is it possible to actually see the placebo effect in the brain? Researchers are coming close (Lidstone & Stoessl, 2007). A number of studies have used advanced brain-imaging techniques to examine what happens in individuals who are experimentally subjected to pain and then given a placebo. Positron emission tomography (PET) is an advanced technique for producing a three-dimensional image of processes in the body and brain. A small amount of a radioactive substance is injected into the body and, as it decays, it releases subatomic particles called positrons and eventually photons. These are detected and sophisticated computers produce an ongoing image of what happens in the body or brain as it occurs. Zubieta et al. (2005) applied a type of PET scan to participants subjected to experimental pain (evoked by immersing a hand for about an hour in icy salt-water). At times participants were informed that they were also receiving an analgesic (actually a placebo). When individuals were told they were receiving a pain-killer, their pain was reduced through the placebo effect. This was expected. Remarkably, PET scans revealed increased activity in those parts of the brain associated with the release of opioids. Similar brain changes have been observed in individuals receiving fake acupuncture (Kong et al., 2006).

Many things can trigger the brain's opioid system, including the positive loving care and attention provided by an empathic health provider. To this we can add conceivably any form of exertion, stress, strong positive affect, or the strongly reassuring statement "this substance or procedure will make you feel better." Running up a flight of stairs can do it. So can good music or a good joke. If a claimed medical treatment requires effort or simply feels very good, there's a good chance it is triggering the brain's reward or opioid system.

Self-Stressing Theory

Benedetti (2009) has proposed that placebo and placebo-like effects that involve suggestion may emerge from our brain's ability to suppress negative emotion. If a placebo expectation feels good, that positive feeling may underlie the placebo's effect. To extend and somewhat revise this line of thinking, I propose that a broad array of brain processes associated with self-regulation may reflect nonspecific processes that can supplement placebos. The exact physiological processes are only partly understood and are certainly beyond the scope of this chapter. However, a psychological explanation is possible.

We begin with stress. The link between stress and illness is profound and well documented (Grady, 2007; Sapolsky, 2004). Chronic activation of our body's stress trigger (sometimes called the hypothalamus–pituitary gland–adrenal arc) evokes a primitive and pervasive physical "fight or flight" response, involving the release of dozens of stress hormones (such as adrenalin and cortisol). This response has a measurable impact on physiological wear and tear and immune system functioning, potentially impacting just about any medical condition. Stress increases your risk of getting and the rate you recover from heart disease, the common cold, some forms of cancer, ulcers, allergies, and so on. Stress even slows your rate of recovery from surgery. All of this has been carefully documented in thousands of well-designed medical studies (Lehrer, Woolfolk, & Sime, 2007; Sapolsky, 2004).

What has not been clearly articulated is how placebos may be part of the picture. I have devoted over 30 years of my professional life to researching and writing on stress management. Recently I developed a theory that might help us understand placebos. *Self-stressing theory* (Smith, 2005, 2007) states that there are six ways that people trigger and maintain their physiological "fight or flight" stress response. These six forms of self-stressing include:

Stressed posture and position. When confronted with stress, people often assume a variety of defensive or aggressive postures or positions (standing, crouching, bending over a desk) for an extended time. This, combined with sustained immobility, can evoke skeletal muscle tension, joint stress, and reduced blood flow and contribute to tension, fatigue, and decreased energy.

Stressed skeletal muscles. When threatened, one clenches, grips, and tightens skeletal muscles to prepare for attack or escape. When chronic, such tension can contribute to pain and fatigue.

Stressed breathing. Under stress one is more likely to breathe in a way that is shallow, uneven, and rapid, deploying greater use of the intercostals (ribcage) and trapezius (shoulder) muscles and less use of the diaphragm.

Stressed body focus. Simply attending to and evoking thoughts and images about a specific body part or process can evoke related neurophysiological changes. An individual facing a threat may notice her rapidly beating heart or churning stomach. Attending to and thinking about these somatic reactions can aggravate them.

Stressed emotion. We often motivate and energize ourselves for a stressful encounter with affect-arousing cognitions. We entertain fantasies and repeat words and self-statements that can evoke anxiety, anger, or depression.

Stressed attention. When dealing with a threat, we actively and effortfully concentrate on attacking, defending, or running. In addition, we often direct our attention to multiple targets, including competing tasks (as in multitasking), a targeted task versus worried preoccupation, or self-stressing efforts (thinking how one is breathing, maintaining a stressed posture or position, thinking about relaxed fantasies or negative emotions, etc.) rather than the task at hand. (2005, 42–43)

Self-stressing theory proposes that professional relaxation techniques (the most widely used approaches in stress management) reduce different types of self-stressing, and thereby reduce stress arousal. Indeed, most forms of professional relaxation can be described in terms of which specific form of self-stressing they address. For example, stretching reduces stressed posture and position; simply letting go, stressed muscles; slowly and deeply breathing, stressed breathing; entertaining positive and pleasant images or thinking positive thoughts, stressed emotion; and quietly diverting attention from a source of stress to a simple non-stressful stimulus can reduce stressed attention. The effects of professional relaxation on stress have been well documented (Lehrer et al., 2007).

Of interest to us is the possibility that many placebos may to a limited extent reduce self-stressing in the same way as professional stress-management treatments. This would result in a limited reduction of stress arousal and stress-related symptoms. It is very important to note that professional relaxation techniques do much more than turn off stress arousal by moderating stress triggers; in addition they evoke a profound physiological state of deep relaxation called the *relaxation response* as well as important psychological relaxation states of mind (called *R-States*) (Smith, 2005). Here a placebo can be seen as a form of *negative reinforcement*; the relaxation response and deep relaxation states are forms of *positive reinforcement* (Skinner, 1974). Negative reinforcement involves getting rid of something aversive or unwanted ("It felt so good when I walked out of the stuffy, overheated office!"). Positive reinforcement involves getting something that is desired ("It felt so good when I jumped into the cool, refreshing pond!").

The next time you encounter a treatment that seems like a placebo, ask if it might evoke any of the six forms of self-stressing. Let's consider Mr. Wright's experience with Krebiozen (assuming his reported improvement was genuine). Before treatment we might suspect he was quite worried about his dire condition (stressed emotion). Indeed, he may well have devoted much of his attention to this condition (stressed attention). It is conceivable that the resulting self-stressing subjected his body to substantial wear and tear and may have contributed to suppressed immune system functioning. Reading about and receiving a "miracle cure" could have reduced his stressed emotion, eased and diverted his stressed attention, resulting in a rebound of physical health and immune system activity. This in turn may have contributed to his astonishing patterns of improvement and deterioration. In other words, if a placebo enables you to cease self-stressing, that in itself may be enough to free your body's self-healing powers to do their job.

Self-Generated Placebos and Extraneous Nontreatment Variables

As we have seen, a placebo is defined in terms of patient expectations. These expectations are typically **exogenous**, that is, come from "outside the patient," from explicit and concrete verbal suggestions presented by a physician or printed on a pill bottle. These suggestions can be enhanced through classical conditioning, the opioid system, and reduced self-stressing.

Furthermore, when classical conditioning, the opioid system, and reduced self-stressing are presented as the actual active treatment ingredient, we are no longer speaking of placebos (suggestions) but of nonspecific effects. To illustrate, a physician who says "this pill (a sugar pill) will reduce your pain" has presented a placebo, because there is no credible rationale why the pill should work. However, when the physician says "simple distraction can often reduce pain. Try chewing on this simple sugar pill and see if focusing on its sweetness can divert your attention," she has administered a nonspecific treatment, not a placebo. When presented without a suggestion of benefit, a nonspecific process is not a placebo. A headache sufferer may divert attention to watching a movie, and experience unexpected and unplanned relief.

Sometimes an explicit external suggestion is not necessary for placebo expectations to emerge. When this happens, a patient develops an **endogenous** or **self-generated placebo expectation**. This can emerge quite unexpectedly. For example, a depressed patient may go to a health spa that involves a vegetarian diet, vigorous physical recreational activity, and daily sunbathing. Let's imagine that the diet and physical activity divert attention from distress and induce brain changes that alleviate depression. However, because these changes occur at roughly the same time the patient sunbathes, he links daily exposure to sun as the antidepressive component of the spa visit. Through classical conditioning, sunbathing reduces depression. Our patient acquires his expectation on his own, in the absence of any explicit, concrete, verbal claim. Similarly, a patient may experience reduced anxiety after talking to a joking psychic, even when no suggestion is offered that laughter may evoke anti-anxiety opioids. The patient may acquire the expectation that psychics possess a magic power for reducing depression. And a hypertension patient may not realize that she is contributing to her own high blood pressure by overworking. She may take a week off and visit her relatives. The reduction in workload may reduce blood pressure, even though the patient may acquire the expectation that her relatives are therapeutic.

Extraneous nontreatment variables have nothing to do with placebos or treatments. Patients can appear to improve because of **initial misdiagnosis**, that is, they may not have been seriously ill to begin with. (Indeed, one might argue that Mr. Wright, our dramatic opening example, may have suffered from problems different from or in addition to the reported cancer.) The **normal recovery pattern** is such that most people get better over time. If you present a placebo before a person is about to spontaneously recover, it might look like the placebo worked. Similarly, many serious diseases display a **cyclical course** in which patients improve for weeks, months, and even years, and then get worse. Again, if you give a placebo at the low point in a disease cycle, chances are the patient will get better, and the placebo will appear to be effective. Finally, **aggravating external conditions** can contribute to a variety of illnesses. Asthma is worse for those who live in polluted cities. People with digestive problems may suffer when eating a fat-rich diet. Simply removing an aggravating external condition may lead to symptom relief. An asthma patient may try a new drug while vacationing in unpolluted Arizona, and attribute her improvement to the drug.

Repeated test taking can give an erroneous impression that a treatment is working. Imagine that a nurse measures your blood pressure several times during an experiment testing the effects of a hypertension drug. Your first measure is high, partly because of the excitement of starting the experiment and unfamiliarity with the blood pressure cuff. After three or four measures, you get used to all of this and your blood pressure is no longer elevated. If you happened to be taking the experimental drug, you might be fooled into thinking that the drug, rather than adaptation, caused your blood pressure to decline.

Statisticians refer to a phenomenon called **regression to the mean** (Gilovich, 1991). Put simply, it means that if you have an extreme run of bad or good luck, chance alone says this won't continue. If you score high because of a statistical "fluke," chances are this won't be immediately repeated—that's why it's called a "fluke." If you pick three winning lottery tickets in a row, the laws of probability haven't changed a bit; the likelihood that your next ticket will be a winner is the same odds as for every other ticket, perhaps one out of a million. At this time, if your witch doctor friend casts a spell for you to lose the lottery, you might be fooled into believing that the spell actually caused you to lose when in fact your scores simply display regression to the mean.

Finally, medical science is always making new discoveries. A patient might improve because of an **undiscovered ordinary extraneous variable**. Perhaps it was the change of seasons, something in the drinking water, atmospheric pressure, a dietary change, fluctuations in the immune system due to sunlight, and so on—the list of potential extraneous variables is immense. As we saw in Chapter 1, just because we have yet to explain something doesn't mean the paranormal is involved. Note that at one time Christian theologians argued that "God is in the gaps" (Bube, 1971)—whenever we encounter an unexplained mystery, that is evidence of God's handiwork. This notion became less popular as science relentlessly explained more and more "gaps." Either God is shrinking or one needs to look to other theological arguments for God. Advocates of complementary and alternative medicine who claim that the absence of a scientific explanation for a presumed treatment effect is evidence for a mystery energy, qi, karma, and so on, are engaging in God-in-the-gaps thinking. In this sense early fundamentalist Christians, traditional acupuncturists, astrologers, and holographic urine therapists are all bedfellows.

Placebos and Superstitious Beliefs

Psychologist B. F. Skinner (1948) has suggested that **operant conditioning** may explain why people may mistake placebos and nonspecific treatment variables for actual treatment. Skinner did much of his research on caged pigeons (and in World War II invented a pigeon-piloted suicide "smart bomb"). Caged pigeons sometimes display strange repetitive behavior, such as nonstop pecking, flapping their wings, and turning their heads over and over. Skinner discovered that this was actually a type of superstition. If a pigeon happened to display a certain behavior, pecking for example, accidentally just before feeding, the bird would associate this behavior with food and do it again. Eventually, when more food is given the behavior is reinforced (through "operant conditioning"). Soon, pigeons are pecking, flapping, and turning all the time, as if they were expecting food. (Of course, they had no way of knowing that food was randomly presented.)

Skinner believed that such repetitive pigeon behavior was analogous to superstitions in humans. An accidental reinforcement fools one into believing a causal link. Imagine you are suffering from the flu. Eventually just about everyone gets over the flu, in a week or two. Let's say that one week into your illness you start consuming chicken soup, and get better. Of course, this is the natural course of the disease. However, you may be fooled into thinking that the chicken soup cured your flu, just as Skinner's pigeons behaved as if compulsive pecking produced food.

Placebo Controversies

Picking the Right Placebo

Many, if not most, placebo studies select inappropriate placebos to compare with experimental treatments. As we mentioned earlier, not all placebos are the same. There is nothing wrong with comparing a tasteless, colorless antibiotic capsule with a capsule containing a tasteless and colorless sugar pill. However, if we were to compare a complex acupuncture procedure involving a sophisticated ritual for selecting proper "acupuncture points," and inserting and twisting a needle for a precise duration with a sugar pill, acupuncture would surely emerge as more effective. One could argue that the acupuncture was a "pumped up" or "super" placebo. A proper placebo should be as complex and credible as the treatment under consideration, and incorporate every element of the treatment that might arguably augment suggestion. This is rarely done in medical research.

This is notoriously illustrated in Sun and Gan's (2008) flawed review of acupuncture treatment of pain. They concluded that acupuncture involving precise needle insertion in points dictated by ancient Chinese medicine is more effective than "sham acupuncture" and traditional medication. Sham acupuncture is one of the most elaborate placebo strategies in acupuncture. Here one deceives patients into believing that they are actually receiving needle-prick acupuncture by gently tapping or slightly pricking the skin in a way that mimics the full insertion of a needle. In such studies patients are prevented from viewing the actual procedure and claim that they cannot tell the difference between an actual acupuncture prick and a sham prick (Sun & Gan, 2008). However, few studies have carefully evaluated whether sham acupuncture in fact replicates *all* facets of acupuncture that might augment the placebo effect. In addition, few studies have been properly double-blinded (in which the individual giving real acupuncture doesn't know it is real). When this is done, the results are different. The most careful current review (Madsen et al., 2009) finds no difference between sham and actual acupuncture. Medical researchers can take an important lesson from acupuncture research. Summarizing different sham interventions as equivalent placebo controls (or ignoring the importance of rigorous double-blinding) is "misleading and scientifically unacceptable" (Dincer, 2003, p. 235).

Placebos Versus Cognitive-Behavioral Strategies

Often it is difficult to differentiate a placebo effect from nonspecific *cognitive-behavioral* strategies to think and act in a way designed to alleviate a problem (Wampold, Minami, Tierney, Baskin, & Bhati, 2005). For example, perhaps you have burned your hand and wish to reduce the pain. Psychologists may recommend a variety of strategies, including redefining the pain sensation as a more tolerable sensation ("imagine the burn as the sensation of cold ice touching the skin"), giving the pain a meaningful interpretation that makes it more bearable ("this pain will teach you to tolerate adversity," "give the pain to God"), or simply focus on the pain ("meditate on the sensation of pain, without trying to push it away or think about it"). Are these placebos? Or imagine a nurse trained in cognitive behavioral techniques who suggests that you imagine a very peaceful and happy place and explains that this can trigger pain-reducing brain opioids. Is this a placebo? Such imagery, like a placebo, may well be nonspecific. However, as long as there is no explicit or implied attribution of the pain-reduction to an agent or activity that theoretically should have no effect, there is technically no placebo effect. So, if a nurse says "Take this pill (a sugar pill) and it will reduce your pain. Imagine a peaceful place so you can swallow the pill more easily," he has given a placebo. He has claimed that an inert agent (the sugar pill) will have an effect (pain reduction). However, if a nurse says "Take this pill (a sugar pill) and imagine a peaceful place. At the very least, imagining a peaceful place may evoke brain opioids which might counter your pain," he has not administered a placebo (at least in pure form), but a nonspecific cognitive-behavioral pain-reduction strategy.

Finally, all mental health professionals, including cognitive-behavioral therapists, must entertain hypotheses about their troubled clients. What is the cause of a student's depression? What might be the best strategy to help a suicidal war veteran talk about her traumatic experiences? Should this patient receive medication or behavioral treatment for his anxiety? In a typical therapy session, a good counselor may entertain hundreds of specific hypotheses. Obviously, it would be possible for every one to be subjected to a double-blind placebo study. Such real-life hypotheses are informed by theory, research, and practice, and an awareness of popular interventions that simply do not survive the empirical test (Norcross, Koocher, & Garofalo, 2006; Lilienfeld, Lynn, & Lohr, 2003; Lilienfeld, Ruscio, & Lynn, 2008).

A good therapist is always cognizant of the possibility that his or her prized insight or intervention may in part be a placebo. Or it might work. He or she must not be paralyzed by such possibilities when the well-being, even the life, of a client may be at stake.

Placebos and Remembered Wellness

Another placebo controversy elevates simple suggestion to a borderline paranormal phenomenon. Indeed, it has been argued that because placebos demonstrate the power of "mind over matter," the placebo effect is a paranormal (specifically psychokinetic) effect (Irwin & Watt, 2007). Alternative medicine often claims that such powers can contribute to healing if tapped through meditation or faith (Benson, 1996). Benson calls this "remembered wellness," associated with a "faith factor." This is typically presented with some fanfare as if some remarkable neuropsychological capacity is demonstrated, one in which our brains and bodies are somehow "hard wired" for healing, especially when we engage in some religious or meditative ritual or assume a certain selfless or faithful attitude. This may or may not be the case. However, any hypothesized capacity for self-healing has yet to be shown to be any more effective than, well, a placebo.

> REALITY CHECK
>
> The placebo effect demonstrates the effect of mind over matter (suggestion over physiological processes). One claimed paranormal process, psychokinesis (Chapter 12), is the direct influence of thoughts on physical objects through nonphysical means. Therefore, the placebo effect is a paranormal effect. Discuss the logical error this illustrates (Chapter 4).

An entire industry of positive thinking books and videos has emerged. If you cut out the mystical jargon (see Chapter 4), positive thinking advocates are essentially talking about the same thing as those who study placebos. How is the statement "Your mind can cure" any different from "Suggestion-based interventions can cure"? When such thinking is combined with subjective relativism (Chapter 2) one introduces logical ambiguities that enable the advocate to make a claim and hide from it at the same time. Let me elaborate upon this bit of technobabble.

In Chapter 2 we considered subjective relativism, the notion that all perspectives are personal and equally valid. Reality is based on what you believe, not objective fact. A similar perspective is that science is not the only way to "truth," in which the word "truth" becomes a convenient weasel word that can mean "truly beautiful," a "moral truth" or an "empirical fact." Here is an argument I frequently get from a true believer when I suggest that their favorite paranormal "treatment X" may be a placebo. (See if you can identify subjective relativism and the use of weasel words.)

ADVOCATE: Treatment X is based on an X energy that science cannot detect.

QUESTIONER: Then how do you know it's real?

ADVOCATE: Because practitioners of Treatment X report numerous successes.

QUESTIONER: But maybe it's the placebo effect. Surely one could do a simple study and compare Treatment X with a worthless fake version that looks like Treatment X.

ADVOCATE: Can't do that. The beauty of Treatment X is that it depends on the master giving it. Each master has a different approach, and uses it in a different way. The power of X depends on the person using it. Your "Placebo" Treatment X might actually be a version practiced by some X master we don't know about. So any comparison between "real Treatment X" and some "Placebo Treatment X" would be meaningless.

QUESTIONER: Then how does a master know that Treatment X is working because of X energy, and not the placebo effect?

ADVOCATE: He intuits it in a way we can never understand. There are truths that Western science cannot detect. The placebo effect is simply a different term for deep mystical powers we do not understand.

QUESTIONER: Surely we could study a master in a controlled laboratory and see if his application of X energy works any better than when he doesn't apply X energy. That would be a start.

ADVOCATE: The very harshness and sterility of the scientific method would block and contaminate X energy, eliminating its impact. The beauty of Treatment X is that it relies on a personal bond between the master and his student. This truth can never be measured by Western science.

Placebos and Performance

Can placebos affect your performance? Can a worthless pill help you study better? The impact of placebos on performance is currently an important issue in sports psychology. Astonishingly, up to 75% of athletes can recall instances in which their performance actually improved after taking a hyped-up food supplement, procedure, or preparative ritual later revealed to be a worthless placebo (Beedie, 2007).

Some of the variables that may underlie enhanced sports performance parallel research on sources of the placebo effect. In hypnosis research, archers display improved performance when given active suggestions for increased body awareness, imagery, appropriate task focus, and smooth automatic execution of activities (Robazza & Bortoli, 1994; Wark, 2006). Brain-generated opioids may give long-distance runners extra endurance (and evoke a "runner's high"). One can easily hypothesize the involvement of classical conditioning. A cheering coach may motivate a basketball player to do her best. Eventually, simply the presence of the same coach may evoke the same effect. Athletes routinely engage in various breathing and stretching rituals before a contest, activities which may minimize the interference of self-stressing.

There is actually a growing lore of sports placebos. We have space for what is perhaps the most infamous account. Willy Voet is a well-known Belgian sports physiotherapist deeply involved in the notorious 1998 Tour de France. Voet tricked French cyclist Richard Virenque into taking a placebo, claiming it to be a performance-enhancing drug. Here is Voet's (1999) account:

> I was supposed to inject this rubbish into Richard's backside one hour before the start ... At the given moment I gave Virenque his injection. That day he rode the time trial of his life, finishing second on the stage to Ullrich. The German started 3 minutes after Richard and caught him, after which the pair had a memorable ding-dong battle all the way to the finish. "God I felt good! That stuff's just amazing" he bubbled. "We must get hold of it." His result did have something to do with the magic capsule—but there is one thing he doesn't know, unless he reads this. I had got rid of the fabulous potion and swapped it for one which contained a small amount of glucose. There is no substitute for self belief ..." (p. 104)

This is an anecdotal account. What does the research show? I count six published empirical studies on the placebo effect in sports. These have involved fake anabolic steroids (Ariel & Saville, 1972; Maganaris, Collins, & Sharp, 2000), fake carbohydrates (Clark, Hopkins, Hawley, & Burke, 2000), fake caffeine (Beedie, Stuart, Coleman, & Foad, 2006), a fake nostrum called the "new ergogenic" (Foster, Felker, Porcari, Mikat, & Seebach, 2004), or a fake respiratory training device (Sonetti, Wetter, Pegelow, & Dempsey, 2001). In each instance, those receiving a placebo performed better than baseline or controls.

REALITY CHECK Studies find that acupuncture is more effective at reducing pain than a worthless sugar pill. Does such a comparison adequately rule out the placebo effect? Why or why not?

REALITY CHECK For the sake of discussion, let's entertain the hypothesis that urine therapy (Chapter 3) is a placebo. What features of this treatment might contribute to a placebo effect?

How to Pump up Your Placebo

Imagine that you want to create a placebo treatment for, say, itching feet. You cannot use any treatment that has a specific demonstrated effect targeted to itchy feet. The only ingredient you have is simple suggestion.

You could begin with a sugar pill and simply claim that it works. But why stop there. Here's how to pump up your placebo:

- Motivate your subject to want to get better. Give exciting testimonials of others who have benefited from the treatment. Cite some supportive research and experts. Give a motivational pep talk on the hidden powers in all of us.
- Use a capsule rather than a pill, and make it large and colored. Better yet, have a nurse inject salt-water. Give the treatment frequently.
- Find a nurse to administer the treatment. Deceive them into thinking the treatment is real and highly effective. Hope the nurse's enthusiasm will rub off.
- Give it a complicated explanation or rationale that sounds plausible and uses scientific-sounding terms. For example "The esoteric elixir in

this vial [note the jargon] may appear clear, but it has been formulated to disrupt molecular discordancies that contribute to what is commonly known as 'itchy feet.' The clarity of this elixir is caused by the fact that its ingredients are in perfect biometric harmony. Science says that we experience a sensation of 'itchiness' whenever two neurophysiological processes exist in convolution, thereby contributing to subdermal irritation, or the itch. This is the reason we giggle when tickled, and why it is so hard to tickle yourself."

- Introduce a complicated and sophisticated procedure. Put the water in a chemistry flask, surrounded by tubes that run through an imposing electronic device with lots of knobs, dials, and lights (maybe an old VCR player). Explain that this device is an "extractor/purifier."
- Alter the placebo so that it has a slight negative side effect. You might spike the water with vodka so it stings a bit when applied to the itch. Give it a slightly unpleasant medicinal odor. You can say that the sting means it is working. No pain, no gain.
- Enhance your placebo with hypnotic suggestion [optional]. Have victims close their eyes, focus, and relax.
- When the treatment is over, wait a few minutes before asking how well it worked.
- Be prepared to take everyone out for dinner once you unveil your deception.

Of course, if you were doing a scientific experiment, you could not be so blatant in your deceptions. You would have to explain to everyone that a placebo is involved, although you would not have to identify the placebo until after you had collected data.

10

Reality Checking for Sensory Anomalies and Hallucinations

Most people realize that certain drugs can make you hallucinate. Schizophrenics sometimes hear voices. A patient suffering a severe fever can become delirious. A parched desert hiker may have visions of an oasis. These are just a few examples of sensory anomalies and hallucinations that can be mistaken for paranormal phenomena.

Sensory Phenomena

Ordinary neurophysiological states can evoke experiences easily misidentified as paranormal. You can demonstrate this just about any evening. Go outside and look at a darkened area of the sky, one with only one or two stars. Now gaze at a star for five minutes. In time you will see it move. Of course, the star isn't actually moving. And it isn't a flying saucer or a winking ghost. Here is a famous literary example of this from H. G. Wells' *War of the Worlds* (1898):

> Looking through the telescope, one saw a circle of deep blue and the little round planet swimming in the field. It seemed such a little thing, so bright and small and still, faintly marked with transverse stripes, and slightly flattened from the perfect round. But so little it was, so silvery warm—a pin's-head of light! It was as if it quivered, but really this was the telescope vibrating with the activity of the clockwork that kept the planet in view.
>
> As I watched, the planet seemed to grow larger and smaller and to advance and recede, but that was simply that my eye was tired. Forty millions of miles it was from us—more than forty millions of miles of void. Few people realize the immensity of vacancy in which the dust of the material universe swims. (Wells, 1898, p. 9)

Wells is describing a well-known sensory phenomenon called the **autokinetic effect**. Here a small point of light on a dark and featureless background appears to move because of minor involuntary eye movements, eye fatigue, and simple suggestion.

The autokinetic effect is a perfectly ordinary and minor aberration of physiological functioning. But it can easily trigger extraordinary paranormal experiences. Imagine that you are outside at night. You have read about UFO sightings. The sky is slightly overcast, and only one star appears. With great curiosity you stare at it for many long moments. Perhaps uncomfortable with your persistent observation, it moves. Others with you also see it move. Or imagine that you are in an old and dark abandoned house, again at night. A small light shines through a crack in the walls. You hold your breath, so as not to scare anyone away. The light moves. Or a friend claims that you can move small distant objects by simply looking at them. She stares at a shiny penny on the sidewalk several yards away. You stare too. Both agree it moves. In none of these cases did anything move.

The autokinetic effect is one of many unusual sensory phenomena most of us experience. Another is the eye's **pupil response**. In darkness the pupils dilate to let in light and in bright conditions constrict to keep light out. This is a simple reflex to protect the retina from overexposure. However, sounds, positive or negative emotion, relaxation, and focused attention are also factors that can cause dilation or constriction (Bradshaw, 1967; Partala & Surakka, 2003). An unexpected noise, someone whispering, fear, surprise, interest, a decision to focus one's attention, or simply uttering a sigh of relief after a few words of assurance can unexpectedly trigger a pupil response. When pupils constrict and less light enters the eyes, it might seem as if the lights were being turned down or the shades drawn. Shaded areas may suddenly emerge, and dark areas grow darker. Lacking an explanation, one might readily think of shadowy ghosts, spirits, or other paranormal goings on. When pupils dilate and let in more light, shaded areas may disappear or shrink, as if they were moving. One might notice things previously obscured in darkness. I suspect this process is accentuated in conditions of poor illumination. Here the retina's black-and-white detectors, the rod cells, are dominant while color detectors, cone cells, are relatively inactive. As a result, in conditions of low illumination our eyes are much more sensitive to subtle changes in shading brought about by the pupil response. So, the next time you are in a haunted house and someone surprises you by whispering "look, a ghost!" you may well see a shadowy form emerge and move, all because of the pupil response. And if, when looking at the night sky, you suddenly think you see a flying saucer, bright shining objects may well appear from nowhere because an excitement-triggered pupil response has let in more light.

Entoptic phenomena are visual experiences caused by what happens in the eye itself rather than from external light. For example, **floaters** are slowly drifting translucent strings or dots that appear when one looks at the sky.

They are caused by harmless debris in the eye's fluid. When looking at a blank blue screen you may notice the **blue field entoptic phenomenon**, points of light that dart about. Actually, the lights are white blood cells in retinal blood vessels. During an eye exam, an ophthalmologist may shine a light into your eye. Briefly you might actually see your own retinal blood vessels, the **vascular figure**. This image quickly disappears because of adaptation. By gently pressing against your closed eyes, you can evoke spots of light, **phosphenes**, simply caused by pressure-induced retinal activation. Serious paranormal investigators routinely attempt to rule out the possibility of entoptic phenomena when exploring various psychic visions.

Synesthesia is an unusual neurological condition in which stimulation of one sense can evoke a response in another sense. In letter–color ("grapheme → color") synesthesia one actually sees different black-and-white letters tinged in color, each letter colored differently. In music–color synesthesia different tones (or even timbres or keys) evoke the perception of color. In emotion–color synesthesia, emotional states (often evoked by other people) evoke colorful auras. A synesthetic might see an irritating person as surrounded by an aura of red light, a friendly person by blue light, and so on. Day–color synesthesia (seeing days as colors) is most common (Ward, Huckstep, & Tsakanikos, 2006).

Synesthesia is caused by "cross-talk" between brain centers responsible for sensation and emotion. In other words, for an emotion–color synesthetic, brain centers responsible for the experience and color might be somewhat cross-wired. Although occasionally associated with drugs and strokes, synesthesia is harmless, and is sometimes a useful tool in creativity. Of course, to the uninformed, having a synesthetic experience might seem like evidence that one can see paranormal "auras," or has "x-ray vision" (Ward, 2004). Synesthesia is relatively common, perhaps occurring in 1 out of 23 (Simner et al., 2006). It is inherited and is more common among women.

Migraines

I was playing in the garden when a brilliant, shimmering light appeared to my left—dazzlingly bright, almost as bright as the sun. It expanded, becoming an enormous shimmering semicircle stretching from the ground to the sky, with sharp zigzagging borders and brilliant blue and orange colors. Then, behind the brightness, came a blindness, an emptiness in my field of vision, and soon I could see almost nothing on my left side. I was terrified—what was happening? My sight returned to normal in a few minutes, but these were the longest minutes I had ever experienced.

(Sacks, 2008)

Is this a paranormal experience? Perhaps a vision of a ghost or spirit? An unidentified flying object? In fact, it is nothing more than a migraine head-ache, a childhood experience reported by one of the experts in the field, Oliver Sacks (2008).

A migraine headache is characterized by intense pulsing or throbbing pain, usually with extreme sensitivity to light and sound, nausea, and vomit-ing (NINDS, 2007). Students of the paranormal are interested in not so much the migraine, but the preceding aura, reported by 20–30% of patients (Evans & Matthew, 2005; Young & Silberstein, 2004). The aura lasts 5–20 minutes and includes typically changes in visual and sensory experience, and on occasion minor involuntary movements. Visual experiences can include **photopsia**, or flashes (usually white or black), **scintillating scotoma**, or bril-liant neon-like zigzag lines, or **fortification illusion**, or brilliant abstract shapes of lights shaped like the battlements of a castle or fort. All of these dramatic visual aura experiences can occur on their own, without a subse-quent headache. All can readily be misinterpreted as psychic energies, UFOs, ghosts, and the like. Religious visions at times look very much like fortifica-tion illusions. (Sacks, 1999, 2008).

Tunnel Experiences

You are resting in bed sinking into a state of deep relaxation. Your eyes are closed. Suddenly you have the sensation of sinking. Your attention turns to your eyes. Even though they are closed, faint lights appear. They seem to move. As you sink deeper, the lights move away as if you were floating deep into space, down a deep tunnel.

Your eyes-closed visual light show is known as a tunnel experience. The precise form of this experience can vary and includes soaring through space, sinking, or moving through a hallway. The whole world may be seen as rushing past as one races toward a bright light. One might even have the sensation of leaving one's body. You may clearly recognize it as something happening "in your head," although given the right context and suggestion you might be convinced of a more paranormal interpretation (moving to a different dimension, moving into someone else's mind, etc.). Tunnel experi-ences can emerge while relaxing, falling asleep, or simply applying pressure to the eyeballs. They can be associated with fainting, migraines, epileptic seizures, and ingestion of drugs such as LSD, psilocybin, mescaline, or ketamine.

Although there are several theories of tunnel experiences, Blackmore and Troscianko's (1989) explanation has received considerable attention. Central

Figure 10.1   Tunnel experience

to their idea is the basic visual illusion that a set of flickering lights will be seen as apparently moving, even though they are not. There are a number of websites that show how real this illusion of movement can be (see Illusion Forum).

Now imagine two light bulbs. When the first one lights, we see this:

$$\textcircled{0} \qquad \bigcirc$$

When the second one lights up, we see:

$$\bigcirc \qquad \textcircled{0}$$

If they light up in rapid sequence, we have the illusion that the light is moving from left to right, even though the flickering light bulbs are actually stationary:

$$\bigcirc \rightarrow \quad \textcircled{0}$$

Now we move to the brain. Nerve signals from the retina are transmitted to and processed by the brain's visual cortex. What we see is actually not in the eye, but nerves firing in the brain (like flashbulbs). Fortunately, these nerve cells do not fire all at once, but are kept in order by nerve cells that inhibit unnecessary activity. Unfortunately, trauma, oxygen deprivation, too much CO_2, drugs, sleep, meditation, and even relaxation can prevent inhibiting nerve cells from functioning. As a result, more visual neurons are *disinhibited* and start firing. With all these neural light bulbs going off, you might expect your visual world would turn into a blinding bright light (as if thousands of cameras took flash photos of you at once). This isn't quite what happens. Gradually, more and more neurons fire, producing a sort of increasing "neural noise." (Imagine more and more flashbulbs going off during an evening football game as the home team enters the field.)

Because of how visual neurons are organized in the cortex, as more and more fire, you experience concentric rings or spirals of light. This will look like a tunnel. Why do we experience movement in this tunnel? The neurons are not constantly on, but flicker.

We have already seen that quickly flickering lights create the illusion of movement, just as flickering light bulbs on a movie marquee. The sensation of movement is accentuated because neurons are more densely packed in the center of our retinas. So when disinhibited neurons increase their rate of firing, the light in the center will grow in size and brightness, as if we were getting closer. This may seem like a strange explanation for an experience that can be extremely dramatic. If this theory is correct, then people who are blind (but still have a visual cortex) should also have tunnel experiences. They do.

Hallucinations

> **REALITY CHECK**   We see with our brains, not our eyes. How is this perspective different from subjective relativism outlined in Chapter 2?

The word *hallucination* (from the Latin *hallucinari* for "to wander in mind" or "to talk idly") was first used in English to refer to "ghostes and spirites walking by nyght" (Sarbin & Juhasz, 1975). Today, hallucinations are generally defined as false perceptions that occur while awake. David (2004) offers a formal popular contemporary definition:

> A sensory experience which occurs in the absence of corresponding external stimulation of the relevant sensory organ, has a sufficient sense of reality to resemble a veridical [accurate perception of what is real] perception, over which the subject does not feel s/he has direct and voluntary control, and which occurs in the awake state. (p. 108)

Hallucinations can occur in any modality, including auditory (hearing nonverbal sounds), verbal (voices), visual (seeing visions), olfactory (smelling things), kinesthetic (sensed body position, movement, weight), gustatory (taste), tactile (touch and temperature), or multimodal (involving multiple senses).

Hallucinations appear in various clinical groups and are not restricted to one diagnostic category. Generally these include (a) psychotic disorders such as schizophrenia, severe forms of depression, and posttraumatic stress disorder; (b) neurological conditions such as brain tumors and injury, epilepsy, migraines; (c) degenerative (and ageing-related) disorders such as Parkinson's and Alzheimer's disease; (d) deficits in or injury and deterioration of sense organs such as blindness; and (e) substance abuse (Aleman & Larøi, 2008).

It is beyond the scope of this book to discuss the role of hallucinations in various clinical conditions. However, two very important points must be made. A significant minority of the nonclinical (normal) population has had hallucinations, with estimates generally ranging from 10 to 15% (Tien, 1991). Second, hallucinations in normal and disturbed individuals are *qualitatively the same* (Aleman & Larøi, 2008). There is essentially no difference between the hallucination of a schizophrenic patient and a normal college student who falsely hears his lover calling at night. Both involve the same processes and mechanisms. When differences appear they are *quantitative* and reflect how various groups react to their hallucinations. In other words, hallucinations exist along a continuum perhaps defined in terms of how strongly one believes one's false perceptions are real, one's degree of preoccupation with the hallucination, the degree of distress associated with a hallucination, and how well one functions and copes (Aleman & Larøi, 2008).

Sleep- and Rest-Related Hallucinations

Among the most common and dramatic hallucinations are those that occur just before or after sleep, or while one is simply resting in a reclining position. Of course, dreams are false perceptions that occur during sleep; however, because we are not awake, they are generally not categorized as hallucinations. Similarly, we might engage in vivid fantasy while resting. Such imagery is voluntary and therefore not considered hallucination.

Sleep hallucinations

Sleep-related hallucinations occur in wakeful moments just before or after sleep. Consider this experience of a young anthropology student (who later became a noted scholar and scientist):

As a college student in 1964, David J. Hufford met the dreaded Night Crusher. Exhausted from a bout of mononucleosis and studying for finals, Hufford retreated one December day to his rented, off-campus room and fell into a deep sleep. An hour later, he awoke with a start to the sound of the bedroom door creaking open—the same door he had locked and bolted before going to bed. Hufford then heard footsteps moving toward his bed and felt an evil presence. Terror gripped the young man, who couldn't move a muscle, his eyes plastered open in fright.

Without warning, the malevolent entity, whatever it was, jumped onto Hufford's chest. An oppressive weight compressed his rib cage. Breathing became difficult, and Hufford felt a pair of hands encircle his neck and start to squeeze. "I thought I was going to die," he says.

At that point, the lock on Hufford's muscles gave way. He bolted up and sprinted several blocks to take shelter in the student union. "It was very puzzling," he recalls with a strained chuckle, "but I told nobody about what happened." (Bower, 2005, p. 27)

Professor Hufford's experiences as a student illustrate several common sleep-related phenomena, including hallucinations and sleep paralysis. Just before falling asleep, some people experience auditory or visual **hypnogogic hallucinations**. These typically include faces, landscapes, and natural or social scenes and may be **pseudohallucinations** (although they appear real, one senses they are not real) or actual hallucinations (falsely experienced as real). Hypnogogic hallucinations are typically static images. They can appear in daytime periods of drowsiness and fatigue, or in situations of reduced stimulation, and can be superimposed over what one really sees. They are relatively common, experienced frequently by 37% of the population. Similar **hypnopompic hallucinations** can emerge in the twilight state just before waking up. Typically such hallucinations are more often fragments of recent dreams.

Sleep paralysis is a related and more dramatic condition in which one is unable to speak or move just before or after sleep. One might sense someone or something is "out there" and be unable to speak or scream. Visual, auditory, or tactile hallucinations are common. Physiologically, when we dream our bodies become temporarily immobilized, our skeletal muscles (used for moving, gesturing, and speaking) are paralyzed. This is so that we don't actually act out our dreams. In sleep paralysis the brain awakens from a neurophysiological sleep state, but the body remains very briefly paralyzed. The person is fully aware, but can't move or talk. In addition, one might experience dream-like hallucinations. To the uninformed, sleep paralysis, as well as hypnogogic and hypnopompic hallucinations, can be quite terrifying. Many people experience sleep paralysis only a few times in a lifetime, although those suffering from the sleep disorder narcolepsy experience it more often. It is quite possible that many experiences of ghosts, alien inductions, and angels reported throughout history and around the world are actually examples of sleep paralysis and the terror sometimes associated with it.

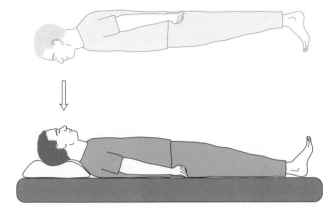

Figure 10.2   Out-of-body experiences

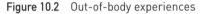

Out-of-body experience

An out-of-body experience (OBE) is the sensation of leaving and floating outside one's body, often while seeing one's body. Sometimes this experience is presented as evidence for a nonmaterial and disembodied "astral body," "spirit," or "soul," capable of paranormal journeying through "astral projection" or "spiritual travel."

Perhaps one of the most dramatic accounts is that of a leading OBE researcher, Susan Blackmore. She recounts a breathtaking journey of leaving the comforts of her Oxford apartment; floating over the Mediterranean; flying over Italy, Switzerland, and France; zooming between the skyscrapers of New York; sliding down the coastline of South America; returning to Oxford; expanding to the size of the earth, then the solar system, and then the entire universe; then shrinking back to normal and resuming a normal life as a prominent, normal-sized paranormal researcher (Blackmore, OBE).

OBEs are quite common, although usually not as dramatic as Blackmore's trip. Typically one has the sensation of floating overhead, perhaps looking down on oneself. OBEs are common in dreams. From 8 to 50% (for marijuana users) have had waking OBEs (Blackmore, 1991, 2004; Schroeter-Kunhardt, 1993).

Although an OBE can be spontaneous, it is more often associated with near-death experience, stroke, epilepsy, the ingestion of psychedelic drugs (which Blackmore reports was the case for her experience), or the emergence of hypnogogic states. Direct brain stimulation can evoke an OBE in waking subjects, and some can elicit OBEs through relaxed visualization and meditation. Researchers Ehrsson (2007), Lenggenhager (Lenggenhager, Tadi, Metzinger, & Blanke 2007), and their colleagues have achieved OBEs using little more than a set of virtual-reality goggles.

An OBE can seem more real than a fantasy or dream and many people actually believe that their "minds" or "souls" are leaving their body, perhaps to travel great distances. However, such ideas lack research support (Morris, Harary, Janis, Hartwell, & Roll, 1978). Perhaps floating above the body one can see objects deliberately hidden in the ceiling. There is no evidence for this. A century ago, researchers attempted to measure the weight of the soul as it left a dying body. At first it appeared that the soul weighed about an ounce, although later research could detect no change in body weight at the moment of death. Recently, researchers have measured changes in ultraviolet and infrared light, magnet fields, temperature, and weight of living individuals having OBEs. Again, research has shown nothing.

> **REALITY CHECK** Often we see things that are not there. Sometimes this is the result of expectations and manipulations (Chapter 7). In this chapter we see how simple body processes can also lead to errors in perception. How might expectations, manipulations, and distortions combine to create convincing illusions?

Hallucinations in General

The range of hallucinations extends far beyond hypnogogic, hypnopompic, and out-of-body experiences. Most common are visions and voices. History provides us with many dramatic paranormal claims that some hypothesize can be interpreted as hallucinations, including the secular visions and voices of Galileo, Freud, Jung, Pascal, Pythagoras, and Mozart as well as the spiritual visions of Joan of Arc, Martin Luther, Saint Paul, and Mohammed. Of course, one might claim that a hallucination, whatever its source, is an alternative window to truth. But then, there are the guiding visions and voices of Attila the Hun, Idi Amin, and Charles Manson (Aleman & Larøi, 2008; Ritsher, Lucksted, Otilingam, & Grajales, 2004).

We have noted that a hallucination can occur in any sense modality and that just about any hallucination can be mislabeled a paranormal experience. While exploring a haunted house you may hallucinate the sound of a breathing ghost (auditory hallucination). While you are deep in prayer, the divine may utter a loud command (verbal hallucination). When in the presence of someone you believe to be possessed by the devil, you may smell fire and brimstone (olfactory hallucination). While meditating in a cross-legged position, you may feel like you are becoming lighter and levitating in air (kinesthetic hallucination).

You may relish the savory sweet flavor of tap water mislabeled as special exotic spring water (gustatory hallucination). While visiting a shrine, you may feel the touch of a departed holy person (tactile hallucination). You and your fellow believers may actually see and hear a flying saucer crash, feel the vibration of an explosion, and smell the smoke of burning metal (multimodal). While grieving a loved one, you may encounter your departed in a forest, engage in conversation, and even feel his touch and breath (multimodal).

Hallucinations: When and Who?

Some people are more likely to experience hallucinations than others. However, it is a mistake to think of some sort of hallucination trait, some type of latent attribute (like a defective heart valve) that, once manifest, can affect one for the rest of one's life. Instead, Aleman and Larøi (2008) prefer to use the term *hallucination proneness*, a capacity one may have expressed from childhood, is generally controllable, and emerges only when triggered.

A substantial body of research has identified five types of hallucination triggers:

Deprivation
- Food deprivation and fasting
- Oxygen deprivation (and too much or too little carbon dioxide)
- Sleep deprivation and fatigue

Reduced sensory input
- Sensory loss (blindness, loss of hearing)
- Social isolation
- Sensory deprivation or isolation

Stimulus overload
- Increased external stimulation
- Prolonged and repetitive religious ritual
- Repetitive background noise

Stressful and strenuous situations
- Trauma
- Bereavement and grief

Consumption of certain substances
- Alcohol
- LSD, cannabis, mescaline
- Opiates
- PCP, amphetamine, and cocaine
- Hallucinations can occur while the substance is in one's bloodstream, or as a flashback memory of a previous "trip."

Of these, we focus on deprivation and reduced sensory input.

Food deprivation

A religious group requires a highly restricted fast for several weeks. Members report seeing visions. Campers searching for flying saucers track a mysterious sighting for two days. Involved in their quest, they eat little. They discover their elusive UFO, actually a vivid hallucination. A prisoner in solitary confinement hasn't eaten for days. He hears voices from ghosts of departed inmates.

When considering a paranormal report, sometimes one must rule out the psychological effects of starvation and extreme diet. Severe reductions in food intake can be accompanied by a number of physiological alterations in brain functioning and lead to hallucinations (Maddox & Long, 1999; Peterson & Mitchell, 1999).

Anoxia, hypercapnia, and hypocapnia

The brain needs oxygen to survive and function. Deprivation of oxygen, **cerebral anoxia**, can lead to impaired functioning and hallucination. This can occur in many traumatic situations, including having a stroke, anesthesia, and drowning. And on the internet one can readily find NASA videos of astronauts training in whirling centrifuge merry-go-round devices in which rapid acceleration forces blood out of the brain, and triggers dramatic hallucinatory near-death experiences, including OBEs, tunnel experiences, sensations of seeing a brilliant light, and strong mystical feelings (Birbaumer et al., 2005; Lutz & Nilsson, 1997).

When we inhale the body absorbs oxygen, and when we exhale, carbon dioxide (CO_2) is expelled. Oxygen is required for metabolism, and CO_2 is a waste product which in large quantities can be toxic. The brain detects how much CO_2 is in the blood. Excessive CO_2 is a condition called **hypercapnia** whereas too little CO_2 (sometimes triggered by rapid deep breathing or hyperventilation) is called **hypocapnia**. CO_2 disruption can be triggered by anxiety and panic (where one "freezes," holds one's breath, or conversely breathes deeply and rapidly); deep breathing relaxation, yoga, and meditation exercises; and ritualistic dances. The effects vary and include dizziness, simple visual and auditory hallucination experiences (seeing lights, hearing roars and screams), impaired awareness, disorientation, weightlessness, detachment, and loss of control over one's muscles (Birbaumer et al., 2005). These can be aggravated by feelings of anxiety, including chest pain, numbness or tingling, fear of losing control, or loss of sense of self (depersonalization).

Sensory deprivation

In everyday life we are bombarded with stimulation. It is rare to encounter a situation in which sound, light, smell, and touch have been turned down.

Even during sleep there is the pressure of the sheets, the weight of our bodies against a mattress, and if lucky, a partner. Sensory deprivation is an extreme condition in which sensory input is reduced to a minimum. In a similar condition, sensory homogenization, sensory input has been rendered bland, featureless, and unchanging. Instead of specific sounds, we hear the constant "woosh" of white noise. We see nothing but a blank, colorless screen. If in outer space, or in a special tank of water, we might feel weightless.

Something interesting happens in situations of reduced sensory input. The brain attempts to compensate for low levels of sensory stimulation by creating more. We think and fantasize more. Things seem more vivid. Hypnogogic imagery is more likely to appear. When reality testing is compromised, these experiences may become full-blown hallucinations (Grassian, 1993).

Sensory input can be reduced in the laboratory, and the shopping mall, through special chambers and floatation tanks. Floatation tanks (also called sensory deprivation tanks, float tanks, and floatation baths) are shaped like large, enclosed bathtubs filled with lukewarm salt water. Inside, one is isolated from sound and light. The water is skin temperature, so the sensation of touch is reduced. Because one is floating in salt water, one has the sensation of weightlessness. People rent quiet time in floatation tanks for relaxation, meditation, and perceived increased creativity.

When an individual claims a paranormal experience, especially one that is described as vividly experienced and resembles hypnogogic hallucinations, look for signs of reduced sensory input. Consider these examples:

- Channelers sit silently in a darkened quiet room waiting for communications with the dead.
- UFO watchers sit in a quiet field at night silently awaiting the arrival of spacecraft.
- Haunted house investigators sit in the basement, at night, with all the lights turned off so as not to scare off expected ghosts.
- A psychic healer sits silently with a patient engaged in healing meditation.

Explaining Hallucinations: The Aleman/Larøi Model

What is the difference between a false and a real perception, an accurate percept versus something you incorrectly experience and believe to be "really out there"? One obvious place to look is in the brain. Perhaps a hallucinated voice involves a different part of the brain than a voice you actually hear. Remarkably, advanced brain imaging studies have shown that hallucinations of one modality involve the same sensory cortical areas (that is, brain areas) linked to processing actual sensations of that modality (Aleman &

Larøi, 2008). Indeed, *regardless of whether you are having a deliberate fantasy, spontaneously hallucinating, or actually seeing something that really exists, the same sensory cortical areas are active.* Auditory parts of the brain are linked to auditory hallucinations as well as the perception of actual sounds. Vision areas are linked with both visual hallucinations and sensations. However, differences between hallucinations and veridical perceptions emerge when we examine parts of the brain linked not so much with perception as with more basic processes involved in attention, monitoring sources and errors, emotion, and memory.[1]

What causes a hallucination? Again, the very same thing that causes a real-life percept. Put simply, anything that activates, or switches on, a sensory cortical area responsible for a specific sensory experience will evoke that very experience. This was demonstrated a half-century ago in a dramatic and classic experiment. While performing surgery on an epileptic patient, Penfield (1955) inserted a small electrode in the brain's temporal lobe and stimulated it with a faint and harmless electric current. Immediately the patient vividly heard orchestral music. When another area was stimulated, the patient saw a man and a dog walking along a road, as clear as if it were actually happening. The point again is that a percept, whether a deliberate image, hallucination, or reality-based perception, is the same in the cortex. Instead of saying "I saw it with my very own eyes," one might more accurately say "I saw it with my very own brain" (Beyerstein, 1996). So what causes a hallucination? The same thing that triggers any percept, a "Penfield patch" or specific cortical area responsible for a sense experience.

Aleman and Larøi (2008) have proposed a comprehensive model of hallucinations that identifies various physiological and psychological processes that can have the same triggering effect as Penfield's electrodes. I offer a version slightly modified for students of critical thinking. We begin with the observation that generally our sensory experiences are the result of stimuli that are "really out there" (modified by perceptual factors noted in Chapter 7). For this reason we usually don't have to worry about whether a sensory experience corresponds to objective reality. Put technically, everyday perceptual processing is *bottom-up* or data-driven. However, under certain circumstances this process can go awry.

Some hallucinations are primarily of physiological origin, the result of disruption of perceptual areas of the brain. This can have many causes, ranging from actual brain deterioration, disease, or damage to alterations of body chemistry through fasting, fever, oxygen and carbon dioxide imbalances, or the ingestion of pharmacological substances.

However, most hallucinations, as well as deliberate fantasy images, are primarily the result of *top-down* perceptual processes or conceptual processes in the brain. Real percepts are externally driven, whereas hallucinations are internally driven (even though both may involve the exact same sensory cortical areas or "Penfield patches"). Disruption of the balance of bottom-up and top-down processes can set the stage for, or lead to, false percepts, hallucinations. These are the same top-down processes we have already considered in our discussion of perception and memory: (a) the *attentional searchlight*, (b) *reality checking (or metacognition)*, (c) *emotion and motivation*, and (d) *expectations* and *prior knowledge*.

Attentional searchlight

Our brain's attentional searchlight focuses on and highlights specific external stimuli, and ignores others. Ordinarily this process is driven by our sense organs (and parts of the brain directly linked to the sense organs), modified by beliefs, expectations, and past experiences. However, there are times when the searchlight can be directed away from the external world to internal sensory experiences such as memories and fantasized images. For example, under conditions of sensory deprivation, our sense organs simply present insufficient data to process. Our searchlight must point inward in a search for cues as to what is real. Blindness, loss of hearing, or degradation of any sense organ can have a similar effect. Strong emotion, motivation, stress arousal, extreme external stimulation, or the ingestion of psychoactive substances can disrupt how the searchlight operates. Overcharged, like a blinding headlight, it may target stimuli and leave us unaware of informative contextual cues that may be useful in revealing if a percept is imagined. For any of these reasons, the attentional searchlight may target and stir a memory or image, making it as vivid as real.

Reality checking

In Chapter 8 we saw that through source monitoring we identify whether a memory is internally or externally based. Hallucination-prone individuals display an external source-monitoring bias. That is, they tend to misattribute experiences they have conjured up as having an external source. I propose that such a person does not or cannot deploy the reality checking outlined in our Critical Thinker's Toolkit. For example, a shaman priest may come from a spiritual tradition that teaches that a healer's soul can temporarily leave one's body and accompany the soul of a newly deceased individual to the afterlife. Firmly accepting this traditional source, the priest may uncritically hallucinate leaving his body during a spiritual ritual. A college student may visit a haunted house and hallucinate what appears to be a ghost walking through a wall, not realizing the logical error in believing that two objects can be at the same place at the same time. A grieving widower may have a hypnogogic hallucination of his spouse standing next to him. He may not think of performing a simple experiment to see if the image is real (like tossing a book at the figure).

Emotions and motivations; expectations and prior knowledge

In previous chapters we have considered how our emotions and motivations as well as our expectations and prior experiences (or knowledge) can lead to perceptual and memory errors. These very same processes can contribute to hallucinations. One may experience emotions of strong love toward the Virgin Mary, joy over the prospects of living in heaven, fear toward the Devil, and excitement toward the prospect of visitations of alien spaceships. Such strong emotions might prime one to experience hallucinations of the Virgin, voices from the afterlife, attacks from the Devil, and alien abductions. These hallucinations may be intensified by strong motivations to serve the Virgin Mary, do what is necessary to go to heaven, fight the Devil, and discover aliens. One may be in the presence of like-believers or belong to a group or culture that assumes the reality of the Virgin, afterlife, Devil, and aliens, all contributing to expectations and prior knowledge that further enhance one's hallucinations. Finally, strong emotion or motivation (positive and negative) can distract and disrupt strategies that one might ordinarily deploy to discern whether a hallucination is internal or external. Under conditions of high stress arousal, attention narrows to information that is simple and concrete, and complex verbal processing is reduced. The hallucinator under stress may be struck by the vividness of the hallucination and be less likely to engage in reality checking (Benton, 1999).

Cross-cultural research provides interesting support for the role of emotions, motivations, expectations, and prior knowledge. Some non-Western cultures prize hallucinations and do not make a rigid distinction between reality and fantasy (Aleman & Larøi, 2008). Bourguignon (1970) studied anthropological data from 488 societies and found that hallucinations play an important part in 62% of religious and healing rituals. Here hallucinations were best understood in terms of local beliefs and expectations rather than the ingestion of psychoactive substances. Other studies have found auditory hallucinations to be more common in the West and visual hallucinations in Africa and Asia. Auditory hallucinations in Saudi Arabia have religious and superstitious content, whereas hallucinations by those in the United Kingdom involve instruction and running commentary. Perhaps the most vivid illustration of the role of emotional and cognitive factors in hallucination is the frequent finding that hallucinations involving the loss of loved ones typically involve the deceased individual.

> **REALITY CHECK** The components of the Aleman/Larøi model do not operate in isolation, but can influence each other. For example, how might selective deployment of the "attentional spotlight" affect reality checking in such a way as to contribute to the emergence of a hallucination? How might strong emotion or motivation direct the attentional searchlight? How might expectations and prior knowledge influence one's motivations and contribute to hallucinations?

Hallucinations and the Critical Thinker's Toolkit

What we perceive is more-or-less what is "out there." However, research on hallucinations shows dramatically that we see with our brains, not our eyes. This perhaps is the most important lesson to be gained from the Critical Thinker's Toolkit. A paranormal claim may be vivid and convincing, based on something genuinely experienced as "really real." A pseudoscientific misuse of sources, logic, and scientific observation may well provide spurious support for such claims. However, common sense suggests that we carefully consider alternative explanations. To what extent can our convincing visions be explained as misperception and misunderstanding of oddities of nature and numbers, errors of perception and memory, the placebo effect, and sensory anomalies and hallucinations? Before betting the farm on some gambling superstition, making dating decisions on the basis of psychic forecasts, forgoing medical treatment for an ancient herbal nostrum, enlisting the assistance of a priest to exorcise evil spirits, voting to restrict the rights of a currently unfavored minority group, or engaging in yet another holy war, let us at least take pause. In the following chapters we examine paranormal claims of consequence and practice our tools of reality checking.

Psychiatric Conditions and Disorders and the Paranormal

A number of recognized psychiatric conditions have been mislabeled as paranormal phenomena, particularly demon or spirit possession. I will not go into these in detail because today the risk of such mislabeling is less than in the past. For example, although the Catholic and some Protestant churches accept that individuals can be possessed by the Devil, they routinely require that the possibility of a psychiatric disorder first be explored professionally and ruled out. Also, I am not sure it is helpful for readers of this book to run around labeling UFO and ESP believers as schizophrenics.

Dissociative Identity Disorder

Once termed multiple personality disorder, the dissociative identity disorder is a rare condition in which one reports experiencing two or more (sometimes up to 20) separate and distinct identities. Each personality has its own perceptions, emotions, and memories. From time to time, a different personality may take over, with no memory of other personalities. This diagnostic category is highly controversial, partly because it is based almost entirely on the subjective report of the patient. Often a patient has considerable incentive to display multiple personalities, especially given that such reports can make good plot material for movies (Phelps, 2000). Mediums who communicate with the dead often display dramatic "trance" states in which they appear to assume the personality of the deceased. One might readily interpret this as an example of dissociative identity disorder. However, a simpler explanation is that such mediums are good at role-playing what they think are "trance" and "possession" behaviors.

Seizures

An epileptic seizure is a neurological event involving a rapid and extensive neuroelectrical activity in the brain. Seizures may have a variety of causes, including injury or stroke. Most often the cause is unknown. Many seizure patients experience a pre-seizure aura. Auras can include unusual body sensations, feelings of derealization, déjà vu, depression, irritability, nausea, and headache. Mild seizures are described as partial whereas more severe seizures are generalized. Partial seizures can cause sense distortions, repetition of certain actions or utterances, or staring blankly without awareness. One might report an experience of "tunnel vision" or reduced awareness.

Partial seizures in different parts of the brain can evoke different experiences. For example, if you have a seizure in the part of the brain linked with sense experience, you might experience smells, hear music, or see flashes of light. If part of the motor cortex is involved, you may experience involuntary movement or spasms in various muscle groups. Temporal lobe seizures can evoke extremely pleasant mystical and ecstatic peak experiences. Indeed, individuals who report such altered states of consciousness are more likely to have a history of seizures. Such seizure patients are more likely to report numerous religious conversions (Geschwind, 1983).

Generalized seizures are more severe and often involve an interruption of consciousness. One might appear to be vacant or unresponsive, and display twitching for half a minute. In more severe forms, muscles may contract involuntarily and rhythmically ("epileptic fit" or "convulsions"). In primitive times those suffering generalized seizures might be tagged with a diagnosis of demon possession. Because such seizures are time-limited, they would invariably cease after a ritual incantation or exorcism, perhaps contributing to a superstitious belief in the efficacy of such rituals.

Tourette's Syndrome

Tourette's syndrome is a neurological disorder characterized by various types of involuntary tics, vocalizations, coughing, throat clearing, sniffing, and movement. On rare occasions it is associated with the uncontrollable and inappropriate exclamation of obscenities and insults. Many examples of demon possession may well involve Tourette's syndrome. During the Inquisition, the defining characteristics of witches resemble the diagnostic criteria for Tourette's syndrome (Goodman & Murphy, 1998). Even today, many Tourette's syndrome patients have been subjected to exorcisms (Shapiro, Young, Shapiro, & Feinberg, 1988).

Schizophrenia

Schizophrenia is a psychiatric disorder defined in terms of impaired perception of self and external reality, auditory hallucinations (hearing voices), strange delusions, and disorganized and incoherent speech and thinking. Schizophrenics are seriously impaired and often withdraw or do not function or communicate well in social settings. For this reason I suspect it is rare that public advocates of paranormal phenomena are schizophrenic. It should be noted that schizophrenics may experience frightening and mysterious alterations in perception and mood. In a desperate attempt to make sense out of such unexplained events, they may resort to paranormal explanations ("I hear voices because ... aliens are communicating with me," "Things seem strangely vivid because ... I am possessed by ghosts.").

Dissociative States

In psychiatric terms, dissociation is an extreme mental state in which certain intense thoughts, emotions, sensations, and memories are cut off or removed from awareness. For example, you temporarily can't remember the name of your irritating neighbor; this memory has been dissociated or split off from consciousness. Dissociation can be a psychological defense against experiencing or re-experiencing severe trauma. It can also be induced through a prolonged emotionally intense ritual such as a ceremonial religious dance or chant. Migraines can evoke dissociative states, as can recreational drugs. In addition, some people can spontaneously enter dissociative states with little effort.

Clinically, dissociation can be manifest in several ways (American Psychiatric Association, 2004).

Psychic (or "Psychological") Numbing

This has nothing to do with "psychics" or the occult. "Psychic numbing" is a state in which you feel numb, detached, uninvolved in life. You may have difficulty loving, crying, laughing, caring, or even feeling anger. You may no longer find fun and pleasure in activities you used to like. Numbing can be a psychological defense mechanism in which one tunes out all feelings in order to "tune out" painful feelings related to a trauma.

Reduced Awareness of Surroundings

You simply might not notice or respond to other people or events. People might say you seem to be "in a daze," "spaced out," or "in one's own private world." As with numbing, this is a way to tune out traumatic pain. If you are less aware of everything, you are less aware of memories and reminders of your trauma.

Derealization

Derealization is a psychiatric term for a perceptual distortion in which the world seems strange and unreal. Consider the following accounts from a website of a community of individuals dedicated to those seeking to understand depersonalization in themselves and others (dpselfhelp.com):

> In a split second, the world seems to tilt. I am suddenly a stranger in my own neighborhood.

> Reality seems to vanish, or is closing in, as if the literally edge of the world is right beyond the horizon.

> Everything looks 'off,' like it turned into a stage set or fake replica of how it should really look …

> The world looks like I'm dreaming, or like I have unwittingly taken LSD …

Many experience mild episodes of derealization. Have you ever seen a long, engaging, and strange movie, walked into the daylight sun, and found that things and people seemed different—perhaps more vivid, perhaps unfamiliar, strange, unreal, dreamlike, or mechanical? Your perception of what's real has been slightly altered, and you experience derealization. Maybe you overslept, and when waking up felt a little confused. You may have wondered, "What day is this? What time is it?" Again, you have tasted a bit of derealization, in that parts of the normal ordinary world seem different. And perhaps you have witnessed a friend having a mildly distressing reaction to marijuana or some other drug. They may say they feel detached from their familiar world. Things might seem like they are not real, or not really happening. They may feel like they are a stranger or an outsider, even in familiar places. Maybe events seem speeded up or slowed down. Again, one's reality has been altered, and one is experiencing a type of derealization.

Depersonalization

My hands feel like they're made of paper, or like they belong to someone else.

My own face in a mirror seems foreign, like I have never really seen it before this moment ...

I cannot feel my body, not truly numb, but it is as if I have disappeared into myself, beyond my own flesh and blood ...

Sometimes I literally wonder if I am already dead and existing as a ghost ... it feels like my soul is trying to leave its shell and I am fighting with all my strength to hold it inside this body. I don't know if I'm dreaming or awake; I must be going insane ... to feel my self wafting away ... I know it is only a matter of time ... (dpselfhelp.com)

These remarkable accounts describe the experience of depersonalization. Depersonalization is a little like derealization, except that your experience of your body or self is distorted. An OBE is an example of depersonalization. In other manifestations, one's body might seem like it's split into parts, or one part of the body might feel numb, warm, or cold. In addition, one might experience multiple personalities, or a sense of being under the control of outside forces or spirits.

Both derealization and depersonalization experiences are very common. Up to 74% of the population has one such experience in a lifetime, and between 31 and 66% during a traumatic event (Hunter, Sierra, & David, 2004).

Amnesia

Amnesia is both a psychiatric term and a word in everyday language. When you experience amnesia, you simply can't remember something. This is common in times of stress. You often read or hear of people who can't remember details of a traumatic crime, attack, or accident. Often, memory returns.

Dissociation and the Paranormal

As we can see in our examples, dissociation, especially derealization or depersonalization, can readily be misconstrued as paranormal. For example, we might consider dissociation as an alternative hypothesis for the following accounts:

- After intense chanting, a medium enters a "trance" and is no longer aware of his surroundings (dissociation). He then communicates with a dead relative.
- A gifted psychic holds a pointer over the alphabet printed on the surface of an ouija board. Automatically her hand is guided over the board (dissociation; loss of awareness of deliberately moving hand) and the touched letters spell a message.
- A psychic is taken over by a spirit from her past-life as an Egyptian queen (dissociation; ordinary experiences are outside of awareness). She puts on a convincing show and is herself quite convinced of the validity of her experience.
- A victim of an alien abduction vaguely remembers fragments of this weird, otherworldly encounter (dissociation: one is cut off from familiar everyday experiences and is immersed in memories that feel strange).
- After repeating a special magical chant, you feel like you have been transported into a strange and unknown world. Nothing seems familiar.

Part III

The Paranormal Files

11

Spiritualism and the Survival Hypothesis

Does some aspect of our humanity survive death? Perhaps an immaterial soul, one's personality, or consciousness. Such claims reflect the life after death or *survival hypothesis*. Although people have believed in life after death for thousands of years, we begin in the 19th century with a spiritual movement called spiritualism. Spiritualism is a collection of beliefs based on the claim that spirits or departed souls live in a realm beyond our material universe. In the 19th century, **séances**, ceremonies in which **mediums** communicated or **channeled** with the dead, became fashionable winter-night parlor entertainment. In time spiritualism became a social movement that offered hope of an afterlife for those grieving the slaughter of the civil war and skeptical of a Christianity newly challenged by science, especially Darwin. In the United States, spiritualists fought against slavery (in the afterlife all are equal) and provided women with a rare public role not unlike that enjoyed by male priests (mediums were female). This movement set the stage for current widespread interest in channeling, psychics, parapsychology, and faith-healing. Organized scholarly research into the paranormal began with serious investigations of spiritualist claims.

Spiritualism

History of Spiritualism

Before the onset of astrology, humans believed in spirits of the dead. However, the contemporary spiritualist movement began in 1848—with a hoax. Two teenage sisters from Hydesville in upstate New York, Margaret and Katie Fox, had a special talent; just as most people can occasionally "crack" their fingers, the Fox sisters could crack their toes or ankle joints (Brandon, 1983; Kurtz, 1985; Stuart, 2005). Secretly using this ability, they claimed that the

Figure 11.1   The Fox sisters

spirit of a murdered peddler, "Mr. Splitfoot" (a name given to the Devil in the mountains of New England), could be heard tapping around the house. Furthermore, the girls proclaimed a remarkable ability to communicate with the departed peddler. Katie would tell Mr. Splitfoot, "Do as I do," and clap her hands. Simultaneously, the spirit would reply with the same number of raps. Then, Maggie would ask, "Now do just as I do; count one, two, three, four," while clapping. Again, Splitfoot replied with four raps (Mulholland, 1938, 30–33). Quickly the Fox sisters became a sensation and neighbors flocked to hear their popping performances. A third sister, Leah Fox Fish, saw a marketing opportunity in all of this and launched Maggie and Katie as performance mediums (the first rap group?).

The Fox Sisters were a hit. Within 5 years there were perhaps 30,000 mediums in the United States and up to 1,000,000 were attending séances. Spiritualist churches sprouted in America and Europe, although most mediums practiced independently. Famous politicians, feminists, abolitionists, writers, and entertainers climbed on board.

Eventually, Maggie fell in love with a dashing Arctic explorer, Elisha Kent Kane, and abandoned spiritualism. Unfortunately, he died an early death and left Maggie destitute. She was forced to resume her work as a medium, but began drinking heavily. Meanwhile, sister Katie continued work as a performance medium, but also began drinking heavily and was even arrested for drunkenness, and welfare workers took custody of her sons. In 1888 alcoholism had taken its toll on Maggie. At a public appearance at the New York Academy of Music she confessed that the Fox act was a complete fraud (probably hoping to launch a new career by giving talks on her "exposé"):

> I consider it my duty, a sacred thing, a holy mission, to expose it (Spiritualism). I want to see the day when it is entirely done away with. After I expose it I hope Spiritualism will be given a death blow. I was the first in the field and I have a right to expose it.
>
> My sister Katie and I were very young children when this horrible deception began … We were very mischievous children and sought merely to terrify our dear mother, who was a very good woman and very easily frightened. (Rhodes, 2007)

Sitting nearby, Katie appeared to agree. Later, Katie claimed that the act was not a fraud, and eventually Maggie recanted her confession and returned to her rap act (people displayed little interest in hearing exposés). Meanwhile, Leah married into wealth and abandoned her embarrassing sisters. Both Maggie and Katie died penniless.

Although the first séances of the Fox sisters involved fancy footwork, mediums quickly developed a wide variety of colorful and possibly odiferous techniques to support a full range of paranormal claims. Physical phenomena included spirit photography, automatic writing, apports, acoustic messages, glowing lights, levitation and floating objects, telekinesis, and psycho-physical phenomena such as ectoplasm, stigmata, trances, and elongation of the body. Mental phenomena included telepathy, clairvoyance, clairaudience, divination, and speaking a presumed unknown foreign language through xenoglossy (Stein, 1996a).

The primary tool of spiritualism was the séance. Here a group of people would sit around a table in a dark room, often holding hands. The medium, perhaps in a "trance," would dramatically sway, groan, speak, and provide information and messages from the dead. At times mediums would produce ectoplasm, a typically sticky substance from the spirit world secreted through various bodily orifices (just about every orifice was used, even the vagina). I suspect the heir of ectoplasm may be such products as "space mucus," "slime," and "ghost goo" designed to delight kids and disgust parents. Mediums specializing in ectoplasm would often secretly ingest (or insert) strips of gauze, which could be magically retrieved (regurgitated, excreted) in the darkness and privacy of a séance chamber. More discrete and sanitary mediums preferred to conjure up "apports," or objects and trinkets (flowers, toys) associated with the departed. Others received spirit messages through drawings or trick double-exposed photographs. Of all demonstrations, perhaps the spirit trumpet was among the most complex and dramatic. This device consisted of a tall cone of tin through which departed spirits could speak by means of an ectoplasm voice box. The trumpet was often covered with luminous paint to create the illusion of floating in air. Unknown to séance participants, a hidden flexible tube connected the mouth of the trumpet to the mouth of the medium, rendering unnecessary the need for an ectoplasmic audio attachment.

Although some still claim that a few mediums were genuine, the vast majority were crude frauds. Mediums were frequently challenged in court and ridiculed in the press. Rude séance participants ("sitters") would grab out at ghostly apparitions, only to capture an embarrassed accomplice dressed in a ghost costume. Spiritualists eventually resorted to performing in cabinets, or body-sized wooden boxes designed to create objective "test conditions" and eliminate cheating. Clever magicians delighted in demonstrating how such boxes were worthless in preventing trickery.

Impact of Spiritualism

Although interest in spiritualism declined in the 1920s, it did have a major impact on the serious exploration of paranormal claims. Magicians, with their unique insight into the tools of deception, acquired a new and important reality-checking role. This role continues with such famous debunking magicians as James (The Amazing) Randi, Banachek (Steve Shaw), Milbourne Christopher, Penn and Teller, Ian Rowland, Johnny Thompson (The Great Tomsoni), and Derren Brown. To this list we can add accomplished magicians Criss Angel, David Blaine, Apollo Robins, and Lance Burton. Unfortunately, many physicists and psychologists, untrained in the skills of sleight of hand, continue to be duped.

The investigative role of magicians can be traced to Joseph Dunninger (1892–1975) and Harry Houdini (1874–1926). Dunninger was a mentalist, an entertainer who pretended to read minds, see the future as well as distant and hidden objects, and alter matter through thought. Today, we would call such phenomena extrasensory perception and psychokinesis (see Chapter 12).

Figure 11.2   Harry Houdini

He became very well known and performed for celebrities and presidents. He consistently claimed that his psychic feats were simple tricks, and actively sought to expose paranormal fraud.

Harry Houdini (Erich Weiss), the world's best-known escape artist, began his career with a sensational European performance tour as "The Handcuff King." In England, Scotland, the Netherlands, Germany, France, and Russia, Houdini challenged police to lock him up with handcuffs or put him in jail. In the United States Houdini proceeded to increase the danger and drama of his routines and added escapes from locked large milk cans filled with water, wooden boxes submerged in a river, bank vaults, coffins, and straightjacket constraints while suspended upside-down 75 feet from the ground. He achieved this through exceptional trickery as well as brute physical strength, small size, agility, and flexibility. His escapes thrilled audiences and astonished local authorities.

In the latter part of his life, Houdini dedicated his work to tirelessly exposing spiritualist fraud. Often he would take on a disguise and follow well-known mediums and dramatically out their underlying trickery. His interest appears to have come from a desperate desire to contact his beloved mother, who died while he was in Europe, and by his contempt for fraudulent mediums and "fortune tellers" (Houdini, 1924). This may have been fueled even more by an incident involving his friend, Conan Doyle (author of the Sherlock Holmes detective stories), in which Doyle's wife arranged for a séance for Houdini to contact his mother. Although the Doyles were convinced that the contact was successful, Houdini was appalled at the obvious deception. In the séance, Mrs. Doyle generated a long letter from Houdini's mother in English. Unfortunately, she spoke only Hungarian and German (Ernst & Carrington, 1932). The Doyles complained that although mediums can receive messages in any language, they can communicate only in English. Unimpressed, Houdini broke off the friendship, although Doyle continued to believe that Houdini actually possessed paranormal powers.

Mediums were subjected to numerous scientific investigations, many including psychologists as well as magicians. From 1923 to 1926 a Boston medium nicknamed Margery achieved national fame for her spectacular séances. In 1922 *Scientific American* magazine offered an award of $5,000 ($60,000 today; Williamson, 2007) to anyone who could demonstrate a valid psychic feat before their committee of six experts, including two psychologists, a physicist, and Harry Houdini. Margery appeared before the team and members (in Houdini's absence) were inclined to pronounce her genuine. Houdini discovered this fact when a newspaper falsely proclaimed that he was stumped by Margery's demonstrations. After angrily complaining, he attended subsequent séances, and concluded they were fraudulent. The case of Margery represents an early scientific investigation of the paranormal. Perhaps its main lesson is that famous psychologists and physicists can be fooled. Often it takes an expert, a magician, to unveil the tricky truth of paranormal claims (Stein, 1996b).

Houdini died suddenly in 1926 of appendicitis. Before his death, he devised a test to see if people could indeed survive death. He and his wife Bess agreed upon a coded message which he would transmit during séances conducted on the anniversary of his death. Bess declared the test a failure before she died in 1943. However, Houdini séances continue to this day.

REALITY CHECK   Why were early psychologists fooled by mediums? How would you test the validity of claims of mediums?

Spiritualism Today

Traditional spiritualism exists today (sometimes called "survivalism"). However, it is a faint shadow of its early popularity. Over a dozen spiritualist camps, such as Camp Chesterfield in Indiana, provide comfortable settings for the elderly to communicate with the departed (Keene, 1976). Most are affiliated with the National Spiritualist Association of Churches, an organization with nearly 100 member spiritualist churches in the United States. Spiritualist churches have formal services, often with opening prayers, a sermon, hymns, and a medium-related ritual.

Better known are freelance psychics and channelers not affiliated with any religion. Every generation seems to yield a new crop. Today it is James van Praagh, Sylvia Browne, John Edward, Uri Geller, Rosemary Altea, Allison Dubois, and the recently departed Jeane Dixon. Following the tradition of Houdini, every single one has been publicly challenged, often by magicians. One can find online ample examples of cold reading and missed predictions, as well as lavish praise from followers. Many have served as consultants for leading movies and television documentaries. And many are bestselling authors.

Research on Life after Death

Although the claims of spiritualists spanned a wide range, the most important focused on ghosts, haunted houses, near-death and out-of-body experiences, and mediums. Research on ghosts and haunted houses has typically involved unsubstantiated anecdotal accounts or poorly controlled experiments. Applying Occam's razor, a variety of alternative explanations are available for sightings. Normal settling of older buildings or changes in air pressure and temperature can cause doors to slam and walls to creak. Reflected lights from passing cars or aircraft can appear as ghostly flashes. Random patterns, especially in low-light conditions, can be construed into meaningful patterns through pareidolia. Sound frequencies lower than 20 hertz are inaudible, but may well cause one to sense a nonspecific "presence" or anxiety. Carbon monoxide poisoning can evoke hallucinations and fear. Cameras used to detect ghosts are notorious for producing various strange optical distortion effects. Devices designed to detect electromagnetic fields can pick up readings from hidden wiring (Taylor, 2007).

Near-death and Out-of-Body Experiences

Swiss psychiatrist Elizabeth Kübler-Ross (1926–2004) helped popularize the link between near-death experiences (NDE) and out-of-body experiences (OBE). Her famous five stages of dying (1969; Denial, Anger, Bargaining, Depression, Acceptance) spawned a death and dying movement, and may have contributed to more humane treatment of the very ill. Unfortunately, these stages were not based on research and do not correspond to what people actually experience (Shermer, 2008). However, in the final decades of the second millennium, Kübler-Ross had become something of a guru, evoking cult-like reverence, and perhaps laying the foundation for a flurry of death-obsessed television dramas (*Touched by an Angel*, *Dead like Me*, *Six Feet Under*, *CSI*, *Curb your Enthusiasm*, etc.).

Kübler-Ross's credibility was drawn into question by an odd incident at a Kübler-Ross death and dying retreat for grieving widows. A turban-wearing male medium enabled widows to communicate directly with their dear departed, in a dark room, through sex. During one conjugal visit, the lights were accidentally turned on, revealing a naked medium (still wearing his turban). He later explained that the afterlife entity had "cloned" him to facilitate the encounter. It is entirely possible that this satisfied his grieving clients, at least temporarily. However, several widows later came down with identical vaginal infections (Rosenbaum, 2004).

Kübler-Ross fell prey to unscrupulous mediums, and began issuing fantastic claims about otherworldly body repair shops for the dead in which one could, for free, receive replacements for defective body parts. Today, researchers on death and dying tend to ignore the contributions of Kübler-Ross.

The term "near-death experience" was coined by physician and psychologist Raymond Moody (1975), considered by many to be the father of today's NDE movement. His most influential claims are that (1) people who have had a brush with death report a similar sequence of experiences including the out-of-body experience, (2) OBEs are genuine and enable the dying to actually view objects that are out of sight, and (3) NDEs are often profound and life-changing. However, his claims are based on anecdotal and testimonial evidence.

Several studies involving thousands of participants suggest that people do appear to report similar experiences near death. Perhaps the most widely quoted is the work of psychologist Kenneth Ring (1980). After interviewing 102 cases, Ring has proposed five NDE stages (not to be confused with Kübler-Ross's stages):

1. peace and a sense of well-being;
2. separation from the body;
3. entering the darkness;
4. seeing the light;
5. entering the world of light.

The early experiences are most often reported. The entire set appears to be nearly universal, reported in different cultures around the world. Furthermore, van Lommel and his colleagues report some patterns (van Lommel, van Wees, Meyers, & Elfferich, 2001). Having an NDE is not related to length of heart attack, duration of unconsciousness, use of medication, or fear of death. However, women, those resuscitated outside of a hospital, and those who fear death tend to have deep and profound NDEs.

What about Moody's claim that OBEs reflect actual transportation of the soul or spirit outside of the body? We have seen in Chapter 10 that dramatic experiences of intense euphoria, tunnels, white lights, and leaving the body are not uncommon, and have been associated with physical trauma, euphoria-inducing brain endorphins, stress, ingestion of mind-altering medications, sleep, and even simple illusion-evoking tricks. At the moment of death, nothing measurable leaves the body. Disembodied spirits are unable to identify and report hidden objects in the room. Occasional claims of brain-dead individuals coming back to life are almost certainly indicators that current brain-monitoring devices are often insensitive and cannot detect hidden sources of brain activity.

Moody's claim that NDEs can be profound and life-altering may be one of his most important contributions. First, one does not have to leave one's body, or encounter death, to have a life-altering experience. A good book, talk with a counselor or friend, or life-altering catastrophe can be deeply moving. But Susan Blackmore (1991), perhaps the leading serious expert on NDEs, notes that brushes with death may involve something more. Although this may be her most important observation concerning NDEs, it is one that reviewers tend to miss:

> NDEs provide no evidence for life after death, and we can best understand them by looking at neurochemistry, physiology, and psychology; but they are much more interesting than any dream. They seem completely real and can transform people's lives. Any satisfactory theory has to understand that too—and that leads us to questions about minds, selves, and the nature of consciousness. (1991, p. 34)

And what are those questions?

> We all too easily assume that we are some kind of persistent entity inhabiting a perishable body. But, as the Buddha taught we have to see through that illusion. The world is only a construction of an information-processing system, and the self is too. I believe that the NDE gives people a glimpse into the nature of their own minds that is hard to get any other way. Drugs can produce it temporarily, mystical experiences can do it for rare people, and long years of practice in meditation or mindfulness can do it. But the NDE can out

of the blue strike anyone and show them what they never knew before, that their body is only that—a lump of flesh—that they are not so very important after all. And that is a very freeing and enlightening experience. (1991, p. 45)

Let me attempt to put it differently. We are something like addicts when we feel that our most important concerns are a permanent "given," somehow locked into our bodies. Teenage lovers "cannot live" without their soulmate passions. "Life can't go on" after receiving a diagnosis of cancer. "Everything is ruined" when we lose a job. What is important to note is that at their peak such self-centered cries are genuine and catastrophically real. We are utterly convinced that something at the very core—perhaps "life" itself—has been destroyed. Of course, in time we gain perspective and realize that life does go on, that our utter conviction of complete personal catastrophe was nothing more than a self-centered delusion. We learn that our attachment to a love-object, perfect health, or a certain job was not permanent or written in stone. It was an attachment, or more precisely, an exaggerated belief. Our permanent, life-destroying catastrophe was just a thought.

What Blackmore is saying is that NDEs have the potential for briefly dissolving delusional attachments and showing us that they are not permanent, but just thoughts. And thoughts can be forgotten or put aside. Put differently, NDEs can jolt us into taking a radical new, less self-centered, perspective on life. Our urgent concerns aren't so important after all.

But Blackmore takes one more step. Our feeling of who we are, our sense of "identity," "agency," "self," or "I," represents an experience that is obviously quite real. If I ask you to point to who you are, few would have difficulty pointing to themselves. Now, close your eyes, and in the quiet of your mind, point to the "I," the "inner agent," your "you." Most people have little difficulty with this experiment. You would probably point to something in your head. This "I" sees out of your eyes and hears through your ears—the "windows" of your body. This "I" is locked inside the body. That's how it feels.

In Chapter 10 we noted a recent and ground-breaking self-concept experiment in which a simple set of virtual-reality goggles can literally change your view of yourself and your environment. Suddenly you are standing outside of your body looking at yourself (Ehrsson, 2007; Lenggenhager, Tadi, Metzinger, & Blanke, 2007). This experiment is much more than a parlor trick. It shows that the most central and core experience of your life, who you are, your "I," need not be subjectively locked into your body, but can subjectively exist outside of your body (yet not in some ethereal ghost). You cannot claim that your "I" is permanently housed in your body while you are outside looking at your body, looking at the very house windows you believe you are looking through. Confused?

If you see, hear, touch, or smell something outside your body that isn't really there, the object of your experience is an illusion. If ancient peoples actually saw a rabbit in the moon (Chapter 7), or a starry fish in the night sky, what they viewed were clearly illusions. If a hand amputee actually senses that her hand is still attached, that phantom hand is an illusion. If while asleep you have a terrifying and utterly real nightmare of being chased by a dragon, your nightmare is just a dream, an illusion. If while wearing virtual-reality goggles you actually experience your very self, your "I," as external to your body, then your very identity is also made of the stuff of illusion. You are a "cognitive construct." You are a thought, yet you are not dreaming. And thoughts can be put aside. Thoughts can be forgotten. Nothing is permanent.[1]

Students of world philosophy will recognize the central idea of Buddhism, a religion that (in its contemporary Western incarnation) often posits no god, no afterlife, no disembodied spirits. "Soft Buddhism" offers the gentle suggestion that life's miseries are the result of needless self-centered attachments, thoughts. "Hard Buddhism" states that self-centered attachments become attachments only when we hold the erroneous belief that our sense of "I" or "self" is permanent, locked to our body, and absolutely necessary for life itself. If you are indeed made of the stuff of illusions, a thought, and if thoughts are temporary, then all attachments to your thought-up identity must also be temporary. Buddhists call this experience *enlightenment.*

REALITY CHECK

Irwin and Watt (2007) argue: 1. Currently science has no way of testing whether heaven (or presumably hell) exists, and what its characteristics are. 2. Many people report near-death experiences in which they feel like they are approaching or entering the afterlife, and then return to this world. 3. There are a variety of nonparanormal neuropsychological and psychological theories that attempt to account for NDEs. For example, perhaps they are a result of oxygen deprivation in the brain. 4. Flaws can be found for each of these explanations. For example, some people display higher brain oxygen levels (not lower) while having an NDE. 5. If it is shown that there are flaws in existing theories of NDEs, we must accept the "separationist" interpretation that the soul travels to a paradisal environment beyond our world (p. 168). Explain how this is an example of an argument from ignorance (Chapter 4). Does it display any other logical problems?

Research on Channeling and Mediums

In the popular press, communication with the dead is now called **channeling**. Those who claim such communication skills can acquire rapid fame, perhaps because the source of communication (Jesus, Moses, Queen Elizabeth, Einstein, etc.) is already famous, and the actual communications are typically unprovable and reflect what people want very much to hear ("You are loved ... there is an afterlife ... you will join your loved one in peace ... everything will turn out fine."). Sometimes the term "channeling" is used to refer to direct communication with the deity, as when Mohammed was given the Koran or Joseph Smith the Book of Mormon (Baker, 1996). It is difficult to objectively determine when a channeled message is from a deity, a departed mortal, a mortal pretending to be a deity, or a mortal conveying a message from the deity. We have to rely solely on the unverified claims of the source ("This is God speaking ... This is Jack the Ripper ... This is Saint John conveying a message from God ...").

In spite of these challenges, serious scientific research continues. Studies have appeared primarily in journals such as the *Journal of the Society for Psychical Research* and the *Journal of Scientific Exploration*; typically such journals are ignored by mainstream scientists. Researchers face two obvious issues: presenting a single unambiguous example of an individual communicating with the departed, and demonstrating that this communication is not the result of some other paranormal ability. This latter point merits elaboration. Near the end of the 19th century, researchers recognized that a medium who claimed to obtain information from a departed subject might actually be reading the mind of a living relative or friend. For example, a psychic might claim to have contacted your departed great grandfather, and correctly reports that he died in a dirigible accident. Perhaps you already knew this, and your psychic was simply reading your mind.

Today this idea has evolved into the "super-ESP" or "super-psi" hypothesis (Hart, 1959). As we shall see in Chapter 12, ESP or psi is a general term for a wide range of paranormal powers, including telepathy (mind-reading), clairvoyance (seeing things that are out of sight), precognition (seeing in the future), and retrocognition (seeing into the past). A person with super-ESP is claimed to possess all of these abilities. Furthermore, such remarkable individuals may display "pseudo split personalities" which might take on the apparent identity of a deceased individual. In other words, a medium might not be communicating with an actual spirit of a departed individual, but with his or her own personality, psychologically split off (see page 221, Dissociative States) so it falsely appears to be a separate entity.

How does one test a medium? First attempts were pseudoscientific and simply involved having a medium talk to a relative of the deceased, contact the deceased through channeling, and then report on the otherworldly communication. Television psychics, such as James van Praagh, Sylvia Browne, and John Edward, still make millions using this technique. Although their performances are often edited (introducing the opportunity to weed out failed reading), many transcripts and video clips are available online. An informed student will find that most deploy the cold reading techniques listed in Chapter 7.

Research is a bit more rigorous. A typical study deploys a medium and a "sitter," usually a friend or relative of the deceased. The sitter provides the medium with the first name of the departed. The medium then contacts the departed and records any information obtained. This is presented to the sitter who determines whether or not it is accurate. Hyman (2003) has pointed out one fatal flaw of this design, the possibilities of perceptual and memory error. A sitter can easily distort a reader's "reading" to fit the departed, and selectively and erroneously recall information about the departed to confirm readings. For example, a reader might claim that the dearly departed reports having "died a painful death in the company of a few others, was not really understood in her community, was greatly respected, and had the capacity to evoke considerable irritation." The processes of perceptual and memory error could easily prompt a sitter to agree to the uncanny accuracy of this reading. Indeed, we can view it as a cold reading reflecting all the potential for manipulation of a psychic reading.

✓ **REALITY CHECK**   Take any of the illustrations of cold reading in Chapter 7 and rewrite them as if they were "readings" concerning a departed individual. Explain how perceptual and memory error might lead one to erroneously believe these "readings" to be accurate.

Clearly, any study on mediumship readings must introduce some basic controls. First, the medium and sitter should be prevented from viewing each other. The medium may even be in a different state and never communicate with or view the sitter. A more rigorous strategy would involve a "proxy sitter," a disinterested third person who does not know the original sitter or departed. These strategies prevent the medium from obtaining subtle cues as to when readings are correct or in error. Second, the medium should be given several names to contact, one secretly associated with the sitter. Several readings are produced and the sitter has to select which are from his or her departed friend or relative. Similarly, several mediums may produce several readings for different individuals, and a sitter has to select which one is from his or her contact. Even when such controls are introduced, there are numerous opportunities for stimulus leakage and fraud (Hyman, 2003). Frequently, controls are not carefully introduced and this is not reported. Researchers may well have discarded disconfirming trials, and reported only the successes (Hyman, 2003).

Gary Schwartz is one of the most popularized medium researchers. Indeed, he is my all-time favorite paranormal researcher, unmatched for perseverance and creativity. Schwartz is a Harvard-trained professor of psychology at the University of Arizona and has published hundreds of scientific articles and many texts, impressive credentials that give him some weight among paranormal researchers. He has claimed to have verified the validity of various questionable psychics, including Uri Geller, Allison DuBois, and John Edward. For years Schwartz was co-director of the VERITAS research program, dedicated to exploring life after death.

Schwartz professes to use rigorous research controls, often including those offered by skeptics (Schwartz, 2002). However, perhaps more than most paranormal researchers, the integrity of Schwartz's work has been brought into serious question (Hyman, 2003; Carroll, 2006; see also Chapter 7) and Schwartz has been accused of deception and displaying a repeated and distressing propensity to avoid controls for subjective validation and selective reporting of results (Carroll, 2006b).

One glaring logical problem with Schwartz's VERITAS research on mediums has been the difficulty of differentiating claimed communications of a deceased person from those of spirit guides, angels, other-worldly entities, space aliens, the Universal Intelligence, God, or the Flying Spaghetti Monster. Perhaps recognizing this problem, Schwartz now heads the SOPHIA project. This effort has the expanded goal of investigating experiences of people who claim to "channel or communicate with Deceased People, Spirit Guides, Angels, Other-Worldly Entities/Extraterrestrials, and/or a Universal Intelligence/God." (Schwartz, 2009).

One study on mediums has made it into a mainstream journal. O'Keeffe and Wiseman (2005) enlisted five professional mediums and five sitters. Each sitter was given 25 readings, which included 20 fake and 5 genuine readings (one from each medium). Sitters then had to identify which of the 25 readings applied to them. Mediums were shielded from the sitters, and the sitters did not know each other. The design was rigorous and appeared to eliminate artifacts. The sitters were unable to identify readings that applied to them.

Conclusion

The possibility of life after death has mystified humanity for millennia. Yet, over a century of research has yet to provide unambiguous evidence. Even if we were to unearth a genuine ghost, a claimed reincarnation of a king (who could accurately recall remarkable historical details), or a medium who can communicate intelligently with the dead, a question would still remain. As suggested by psychic researchers over a century ago, perhaps any evidence of an afterlife is better interpreted as evidence of some other paranormal phenomena in the world of the living. We consider the paranormal claims of ESP and psychokinesis in the following chapter.

Reincarnation

Reincarnation is the belief that the spiritual essence of a person (and perhaps animals, insects, plants, and even objects like jars) lives beyond death and is reborn in a new body. Traditions differ as to the nature of a reincarnated spiritual essence, sometimes describing it as "soul," "spirit," "higher self," or "selfless consciousness." Views of the attributes of what is reincarnated also vary widely and include immeasurable nonmaterial attributes, personality and memories, even physical bodily characteristics such as scars and birthmarks. How one is reborn is determined by one's past actions, the overall effect termed "karma" in Hinduism. Misdeeds, or attachments to desires, lead to continued rebirth, perhaps in lower forms. Virtuous actions and freedom from attachment lead to better rebirthing outcomes or freedom from rebirth (Molé, 2002).

The concept of reincarnation is ancient and can be traced to Greek and Egyptian cultures. However, it has become a central doctrine in religions of India, including Hinduism, Buddhism, Jainism, and Sikhism. Christian leaders reject reincarnation, although a recent Harris poll finds that 21% of Christians do believe (Taylor, 2003). Many biblical stories of the dead coming back to life (Jesus wasn't the only one) share some key attributes of reincarnation (a person dies, an essential part lives on and returns to life). More recently, spiritualists and followers of many new age movements believe in reincarnation, focusing more on the process of rebirth than ultimate release.

Believers in reincarnation often cite the work of Ian Stevenson (1980, 1997), who devoted over 40 years to tracking down leads and claims. Many have criticized this research, including Edwards (1996) and Roach (2005). The most popular evidence includes child prodigies, strange birthmarks, déjà vu, and past-life regression. Much of this work borders on pseudoscience.

Child Prodigies

History provides numerous accounts of unexceptional parents who have children of extraordinary talent and genius. However, such events are perfectly consistent with what we know about genetics. Genes may well be recessive and not emerge for many generations.

Strange Birthmarks

Stevenson has argued that strange birthmarks are strong evidence for reincarnation and cites many examples of families who recall deceased relatives with wounds similar to birthmarks of newborn children. However, such data is nearly always based on memory of the departed rather than objective evidence. Furthermore, birthmarks are like Rorschach inkblots in that one can see in them many things (Chapter 7).

Déjà vu

A déjà vu experience is the uncanny feeling that one has been somewhere before. A reincarnationist might explain that your hunch that you've been somewhere is evidence that you have actually been there. We have seen in Chapter 8 that déjà vu experiences are common and easily explained as memory errors.

Past-Life Regression

Much of Stevenson's evidence for reincarnation is based on simple memories, usually of individuals who already believe strongly in reincarnation. A mother might claim that her infant daughter acts very much like her great-grandmother, or that her son is afraid of rats, just like a great-grandfather. Again, such evidence is extremely weak and subject to many of the distortions of perception and memory we have considered earlier (Chapters 7 and 8).

Through hypnosis it is relatively easy to evoke what might appear to be a genuine memory of a past-life event. However, as seen in Chapter 7, memories are not accurate snapshots, but partial fictions based on expectations, suggestions, and the environment. Hypnosis is sometimes believed to be a tool for uncovering the truth; in fact, it often accentuates the distortions of fictional memory. By simply asking leading questions, a hypnotist can inadvertently lead one to "recall" totally nonexistent events as real.

Perhaps the most cited example of hypnotically induced past-life regression is the case of Bridey Murphy (Bernstein, 1956). In 1952 and 1953, Morey Bernstein, an amateur hypnotist, subjected a young housewife named Virginia Tighe to six sessions of hypnosis and regressed her to a previous life in which she was a 19th century Irish woman, Bridey Murphy. Tighe was able to recall impressive and specific details, including where she was born, her husband, and her death. In addition she spoke with an Irish accent, which Bernstein recorded. Careful investigation revealed that Tighe's specific recollections were simply false or based on what she had heard years ago from her Irish friends and neighbors. The Irish accent was inauthentic.

12

Parapsychology

Parapsychology (Greek for "beyond /beside" the "mind/soul/reason") is the scientific study of paranormal psychological claims.[1] These include extraordinary perceptual abilities, the ability to affect the physical world through one's thoughts, and the ability to communicate with animals (and plants), again through thoughts. Although parapsychologists also study paranormal healing and life after death claims (mediums, ghosts, reincarnation), they often consider basic parapsychological processes as alternative explanations (are you actually receiving thought messages from a dead relative, or thoughts from a living acquaintance of the relative?). Many parapsychologists passionately dissociate themselves from astrology, witchcraft, and spiritualism (Irwin & Watt, 2007). Although early parapsychological research involved much pseudoscience, current researchers often make a genuine attempt to deploy rigorous critical thinking and apply serious reality checks.

The Language of Parapsychology

Here is the terminology parapsychologists use (from parapsych.org and Irwin & Watt, 2007). First, **psi** (and occasionally "anomalous cognition") is a general term for all parapsychological phenomena (Thouless & Wiesner, 1948). There are two types of psi:

1. **Extrasensory perception** (ESP, receptive psi, paranormal cognition, or Psi-Gamma) is the acquisition of information about, or response to, an external object or influence not using any known sensory channel.
   A. **Precognition** (premonition, fortune-telling, prophecy) is a form of ESP in which the target is a future event that cannot be known from present data.

    B.　**Retrocognition** is a form of ESP in which the target is a past event that could not have been learned or inferred by normal means. It is seeing into the past.

    C.　**Telepathy** (thought-transference) is the paranormal acquisition of information concerning the thoughts, feelings, or activities of another conscious person. When the source of information is out of range of the senses (in another room, in another country), telepathy is often called **remote viewing**.

    D.　**Clairvoyance** is the acquisition of information directly from an external object or physical event (viewing a concealed photograph), not through the thoughts or perceptions of someone else. When the source of information is out of range of the senses, clairvoyance is also sometimes called **remote viewing**.

2.　**Psychokinesis** (PK, expressive psi, paranormal action, or psi-kappa) is the direct influence of thought on physical objects or processes (moving things, bending spoons). Psychokinesis on a living system is sometimes called **BIO-PK** or 'direct mental interactions with living systems' (**DMILS**). One might use thoughts to influence the growth of seedlings or bacteria, resuscitate anesthetized mice, heal, perform surgery without cuts or knives, or influence the mood state of others. **Micro-PK** is PK at the atomic or subatomic level, that is, the subtle impact of thoughts on molecules, atoms, and electrical systems such as electronic games or random number generators. **Retropsychokinesis** refers to using thoughts (in the present) to influence events in the past.

Large numbers of people claim to have had spontaneous psi experiences, although such recollections represent data compromised by the vagaries of chance, perceptual and memory error, the placebo effect, and sensory anomalies and hallucinations. Nonetheless, at least one conceptualization proposes that people unintentionally and unknowingly use psi in everyday life. Stanford's Psi-Mediated Instrumental Response (PMIR) model suggests that because of the obvious adaptive potential of psi abilities, many of the misfortunes we may have unwittingly avoided, or rewards we may have achieved, reflect the hidden guiding hand of psi processes (Stanford, 1974, 1990).

REALITY CHECK

"You may not believe you have psi abilities. However, you are simply not aware of the many fatal accidents you have unwittingly avoided because of your unconscious ability to predict the future. Indeed, the fact that you are alive today is evidence for psi!" Can you find any logical or scientific flaws in this argument? Is this a testable hypothesis?

Most of the research on psi has focused not on its emergence in everyday life, but in the laboratory. Over a thousand studies have been conducted on psi (Irwin & Watt, 2007; Radin, 1997) and nearly 40 scientific journals (Appendix A) routinely publish psi research. Yet, psi is not accepted by much of the scientific community, and critics of psi research are often merciless in their attacks. This intense debate has persisted for over a century, and shows little sign of cooling off. A newcomer to the field might be justified in wondering what is going on. We might find brief and heated disputes in other areas of scientific inquiry. Geologists once argued over whether the continents are fixed or float on a molten earth. Astronomers once debated whether or not the universe is expanding. Psychologists once discussed whether homosexuality, or religion, is a pathology. But these areas involved specific issues within an area of study, not the validity of geology, astronomy, or psychology as a whole. For psi, the debate goes to the core. The following review builds on the work of Carroll (2007), Hines (2003), and Irwin and Watt (2007). We devote particular attention to Irwin and Watt's classic textbook on the paranormal, perhaps the most extensive and respected pro-paranormal review.

Research on Psi

Scientists have studied psi phenomena for over a century. In some respects, studies have followed a path displayed by other sciences, using many of the same methodological and statistical techniques. However, there have been some important differences. In other sciences, early studies identify a core phenomenon, and subsequent research explores the ramifications. Astronomers discovered that the earth is not the center of everything, and telescope technology eventually revealed an expanding universe of billions of galaxies. Biologists discovered that microbes, not spirits, cause disease, and today we have modern medicine. Physicists discovered the mechanics of how atoms work, and today we have computers, television, and nuclear technology. In contrast, psi researchers are still attempting to identify a core-defining psi phenomenon. In addition, science progresses when anomalies are discovered that challenge prevailing thinking. Given the difficulties in identifying a core phenomenon, it is premature to ask about anomalies in how this phenomenon works. However, that psi research has had its starting difficulties does not mean it is wasted effort. Questions about psi are genuinely important, and psi itself may well be extraordinarily difficult to pin down.

Early History and the Society for Psychical Research

We begin with spiritualism. The remarkable claims of early mediums attracted the attention of leading scientists. In 1882 Sir William Fletcher Barrett, a physicist, and philosopher Henry Sidgwick founded the Society for Psychical Research (SPR), an English organization dedicated to scientific investigation of spiritualistic and psychic phenomena. The SPR, and its American cousin, the ASPR, exist to this day (www.aspr.com). As Sidgwick (Broad, 2000) put it in his first presidential address to the SPR:

> We must drive the objector into the position of being forced either to admit the phenomena as inexplicable, at least by him, or to accuse the investigators either of lying or cheating or of a blindness or forgetfulness incompatible with any intellectual condition except absolute idiocy. (p. 106)

Ironically, 130 years later most scientists might well agree with the second option in this dichotomy. Indeed, the very first studies conducted by the SPR were quickly revealed as fraud (Carroll, 2007). In SPR's first study, Barrett examined five teenage girls who claimed that they could communicate telepathically. He devised a variety of guessing experiments using cards, persons' names, or household objects and concluded that their psi abilities were genuine. Over 6 years Barrett brought in outside scientists who, after careful examination, concluded that no trickery was involved. As Carroll (2007) asks, "What are the odds that children can fool some very intelligent scientists for 6 years? The answer is: the odds are very good." Eventually, the girls were exposed as frauds and had been faking telepathic communication by using a secret verbal code. This debacle should have raised a red flag among paranormal researchers. Unfortunately, it had no such effect. Indeed, while Barrett was being deceived, other SPR researchers were being duped by a 19-year-old telepath and entertainer, George A. Smith, and his partner, Douglas Blackburn. Blackburn eventually revealed how their impressive feats of telepathy were faked. Smith eventually became secretary of the SPR, which continues up to this day.

The ESP Research of the Rhines

In America, serious research on psi began with the card-guessing studies of John Cooper and Joseph Banks Rhine and his wife Louisa Rhine. In 1917 Cooper conducted a series of large experiments at Stanford University on telepathy and clairvoyance. He reported that his results were not conclusive, and others reworked his data (a questionable practice called data mining; see Chapter 6) with relatively little success. Eventually, J. B. Rhine

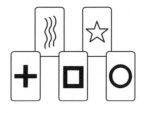

Figure 12.1   Zener cards

followed up, and is considered by most to be responsible for launching the scientific study of psi in America. Indeed, he coined the term *extrasensory perception*.

The Rhines were skeptical of the popular mediums of the day and chose a different path of investigation. They began their work at Duke University by examining the claims of a remarkable horse, Lady Wonder. Lady Wonder had the sensational ability to answer questions and over 150,000 people consulted her, paying a dollar for her wisdom. Her method of communication was to knock over alphabet blocks. It was even claimed that the horse helped the Massachusetts police find the body of a missing girl and helped discover oil. Rhine tested the horse and concluded that her talents were a genuine demonstration of animal telepathy. Later a magician concluded otherwise, after noting that Lady Wonder could not answer questions if her owner did not know the answer. Her owner apparently signaled answers with a whip (a stunt demonstrated over a decade earlier by the famous fake calculating horse, Clever Hans; Hyman, 1989). Rhine tested the horse a second time and, finding no evidence of telepathy, concluded that the desperate owner had had to resort to trickery because his horse had lost her abilities (Christopher, 1970).

Rhine began his research into ESP in 1930 with the help of his colleague, Carl Zener. Quickly the use of traditional cards was discarded (the images were too complicated), and Zener developed a deck of 25 cards in which each card had one of five simple symbols: a star, cross, circle, wavy lines, and square. In a guessing experiment, by chance one would correctly pick 5 out of the 25.

Rhine's first experiments were the most successful. Here the experimenter and subject would sit at opposite ends of a table, separated by a thin partition so that the subject could not see the cards. In a telepathy experiment, the experimenter would look at a card which the subject would try to guess. For clairvoyance, the experimenter would not look at the cards, but simply pick one up (face down) and the subject would again guess. For precognition, a subject would write down ahead of time the order in which cards would be selected from a shuffled deck. By 1934, Rhine had amassed nearly 100,000 attempts, averaging 7.1 correct identifications per run, higher than the 5 hits one would expect from chance. With great enthusiasm, Rhine announced to the world that he had finally made a world-changing discovery, a scientific demonstration of psi phenomena (Rhine, 1934). Today, researchers discount the first decade of Rhine's work with Zener cards. Stimulus leakage or cheating could account for all of his findings. Slight indentations on the backs of cards revealed the symbols embossed on card faces. Subjects could see and hear the experimenter, and note subtle but revealing facial expressions or changes in breathing. The psi effect would mysteriously disappear whenever a magician was present in the Rhine laboratory.

In the face of Rhine's initial failures, psi researchers had three options: replicate, rationalize, or cheat. Experimenters attempted to replicate Zener card studies, and failed (Crumbaugh, 1966; Beloff, 1973). Psi researchers embrace a variety of ad hoc rationalizations for negative results. Rhine suggested that psi studies are difficult to replicate because of a psi **decline effect**. Participants may initially score high, but through fatigue and boredom, eventually perform at chance levels. Students of statistics readily recognize that there is nothing paranormal about this example of **regression to the mean** (Chapter 6). A more creative ad hoc explanation is that psi works only when researchers and participants are believers, termed **sheep**. Somehow, skeptics and magicians, termed **goats**, emit some sort of mysterious influence or vibration that negates any psi effect (Schmeidler, 1945), a claim we shall consider a bit later. The resulting negative effect is termed **psi-missing**. Similarly, psi is described as a **jealous phenomenon**, one that disappears under close scrutiny.[2] Although believers claim that there is plenty of published research supporting a sheep–goat effect, skeptics counter with many cases of lifelong psi-believing researchers (Blackmore, 1996, 2008) who eventually quit, concluding no effect (Appendix C). Sheep and goats do appear to display one important difference: Blackmore (1992) has reported that sheep are more likely to be susceptible to distortions in perception and memory (Chapters 7 and 8) and mistakes in estimating probabilities (Chapter 6). Any research examining psi-missing must carefully control for the distorting effects of experimenter and participant belief.

> **REALITY CHECK**   Explain how the claimed "decline effect" might reflect regression to the mean.

Finally, scientists are uncomfortable discussing the possibility of fraudulent research. Nevertheless, psi research is not immune to cheating. One might speculate that fervent true believers are willing to bend the rules a little in order to find evidence for a world-shaking discovery that is obviously true. Indeed, the very man Rhine selected to replace him as head of his para-psychology laboratory, Walter Levy Jr., was caught meddling with auto-matic scoring equipment to produce positive results. In a more famous example, British researcher Samuel Soal decided to replace the traditional Zener card symbols with colorful pictures of animals. He reasoned that these stimuli were more interesting and would be easier to send and detect. In London between 1941 and 1943 Soal found no ESP effect. However, later he claimed to have discovered a psi **displacement effect** in which subjects could predict the card that immediately *followed* or *preceded* each card being sent. These findings caused a sensation among psi researchers. Now it is generally recognized that Soal cheated (Alcock, 1981).

Remote Viewing and the CIA Stargate Program

Did the CIA ever fund psi research? Yes. Not only that, but early test sub-jects were high-level Scientologists with special powers. Between 1969 and 1971 there were reports that the Soviet Union was engaged in extensive psi research on a variety of exotic attempts, including using psychics for long-distance assassination. In 1972 the CIA enlisted the efforts of the SRI (Stanford Research Institute, which has no connections to the university) to investigate psi phenomena in a legendary project named Project Stargate.[3] In 1990 the program was given to Science Applications International Corporation (SAIC). The overall goal of this research was to determine if talented psychics could be used as spies and obtain crucial military informa-tion not available through ordinary channels. The project was extensive and eventually cost $20 million.

Much of this research was conducted by Russell Targ and Harold Puthoff, a Scientologist. Their work focused on remote viewing and began with gifted "empaths" from the Church of Scientology who had progressed to OT (Operating Thetan) Level VII, a high achievement associated with extraordinary powers.[4] Later, Stargate focused on subjects not involved with Scientology and ultimately tested over 20 individuals.

Targ and Puthoff's remote viewing procedure typically involved a sender, a receiver, and an experimenter. The sender was instructed to visit a ran-domly selected series of locations such as an airport, bridge, park, or library (Hines, 2003) while the receiver remained in the laboratory. At specific times the sender would attempt to mentally communicate to the receiver information concerning a site he or she was currently observing. The receiver would immediately begin speaking and report any impressions received. These (as well as comments from the attending experimenter) were tape-recorded and transcribed. Thus, at the end of this phase of the project the sender had visited a specific number of sites, and the receiver had produced the same number of impressions. Then a rater, blind to the identity of the sender and receiver, was taken to each site, given transcripts of impressions for all sites, and asked to determine which transcript was associated with each site.

Targ and Puthoff (1977) report over 100 such experiments and claim spectacular support for remote viewing (Carroll claims up to 1,000; 2008). Marks (2000) examined the available transcripts and identified a serious flaw, stimulus leakage. For example, raters were told the specific order in which locations were visited. So they knew that the "university library" was first visited/transmitted and the "bridge" visited/transmitted last. You might think that this a trivial matter, except that transcripts contained clues that gave away when they were recorded. For example, one transcript might contain the phrase "Don't be nervous, you're just starting" (Hines, 2003). Thus, a rater would know this site was visited first. The Stargate project was plagued with several instances of stimulus leakage.

A distressing number of additional problems plagued the program. Occasional "hits" could have been chance occurrences, given the large number of trials (Carroll, 2008). Instances of researchers weakening claimed protocols (Marks, 2000) further compromise any findings. Finally, the fact that key researchers (in violation of accepted research ethics) refused to share raw data makes it difficult to examine possible lapses in design and analysis. Most important, claimed findings could not be replicated in independent laboratories when proper designs were deployed and possible stimulus leakage was removed (Marks, 2000; Randi, 1982). The program was abandoned in 1995 after 24 years of fruitless research. Note that even pro-psi reviewers are in disagreement. Radin (1997) views Project Stargate as a remarkable success. Irwin and Watt (2007) mention the research in one short paragraph noting the conflicting conclusions we have mentioned.

Dream and Ganzfeld Studies

One might argue that early research failed to yield results because psi phenomena are subtle and easily masked by thought and external noise. Perhaps psychic subjects should be quietly sleeping or placed awake in a setting in which sensory input is deliberately restricted, or a "psi-conducive state of mind" is evoked, perhaps through hypnosis, physical relaxation, meditation, or even drugs.

Dream telepathy

Much research on telepathy during dreams was conducted at the Maimonides Medical Center in Brooklyn in the 1960s and 1970s (Child,

1985). In these studies thoughts were transmitted telepathically while a subject was dreaming. Specifically, a receiving subject sleeps in a laboratory while brain wave electroencephalogram (EEG) activity is monitored. Generally whenever we dream we are in **REM sleep**, so named because our eyes usually dart back and forth during a dream. In psi research a sender is instructed to mentally transmit an image while the sleeping receiver is in REM sleep. When the targeted dream is over (REM activity ceases), the receiver is awoken and asked to describe any dreams. Dream transcripts are then compared to what was actually sent.

Unfortunately, when carelessly applied, this design can permit confirmation bias (Carroll, 2007). The experimenter makes a judgment as to whether a dream transcript resembles the sent stimulus. We have seen (Chapter 7) that an ambiguous stimulus can be retrofitted to fit one's expectation. In one dream experiment (Radin, 1997), the sender transmitted an image of Beckman's painting *Descent from the Cross*, which depicts Christ removed from the cross and taken downhill. The associated dream was about Winston Churchill. Radin (1997) considered this to be a hit. Why? "Churchill ... Church ... Hill ... Christ and the Christian Church ... Crucifixion on a hill ..." Just connect the dots. Subsequent dream telepathy research has permitted receivers to sleep at home, rather than in the laboratory. Subsequent research has attempted to control for confirmation bias, but the results have been weaker than those of the original Maimonides studies. In sum, sheep researchers persist in celebrating dream telepathy studies as strong evidence for psi (Child, 1985; Irwin & Watt, 2007; Sherwood & Roe, 2003), whereas skeptic goats reject this work as sloppy, compromised, unreplicated, and inconclusive (Alcock, 2003). Rarely in psychology do we find such diametrically opposed conclusions based on the same body of research. Something strange is going on in the world of psi, a point we will consider later.

Ganzfeld

A ganzfeld (German for "entire field") is a special environment in which sensory input is restricted or rendered unchanging. This involves much more than closing the door and turning down the lights. Visual stimulation can be reduced by placing halved ping-pong balls over the eyes and projecting diffuse red light on a blank screen. Receivers wear earphones in which diffuse unstructured sound (a "white noise" hiss or "pink noise" waterfall-like woosh sound) is played. The subject rests comfortably in a soft chair or bed that minimizes tactile stimulation. In such a low-stimulation environment the brain often tries to generate stimulation through imagery and hallucinations.

Figure 12.2 Ganzfeld

In a typical ganzfeld research, a receiving subject is placed in a sense-restricted environment. In a separate room a sender randomly selects a one-minute video clip (or picture in earlier studies) from a packet of four clips (selected from a pool of 40 similar four-clip packets). Then the receiver is asked to describe the images they see. Later they are given all four clips (or pictures), including the one sent, and asked to select which was transmitted. Note that in this design the transmitted picture or clip gets handled more than those left in the box, an important point we will consider.

Hyman (1985) reviewed 42 early studies (Honorton, 1985) using this technique and concluded that they were permeated with security breaches that could permit cheating, stimulus leakage, incorrect use of statistics, and data mining. For example, not all of the trials used completely soundproofed rooms, so that receivers could possibly hear revealing discussions from the experimenter. Packages containing target pictures may show tell-tale signs, including smudges and creases. More recent studies involved selecting and playing a video clip. Unfortunately, here selected videos can show evidence of fading, scratches, and dust. A receiver might correctly identify a video as sent simply because of these signs of wear and tear.

Both Hyman and Honorton agreed that the initial ganzfeld studies had to be repeated. Honorton developed an elegant autoganzfeld procedure in which care is taken to use separate sender and receiver in truly soundproofed rooms. As in previous studies, sets of four video clips are used. However, a computer randomly selects a set of four and presents a random clip to the sender on a video monitor. The reviewer sees all four clips on a monitor and judges each using a computer game controller. Outside psychologists as well as a magician have confirmed the quality of this design. Although some positive (and a few negative) results have been reported, the jury is still out. Consistent, independent replication has yet to be achieved (Hyman, 2008; Palmer, 2003). Given the troubled history of psi research, this is an area that is close to producing an airtight and replicable design, one that can be examined by outside critics, including magicians.

Neurophysiological Correlates of Psi

Perhaps psi is so subtle that the brain processes responsible for analysis and speech drown it out. Indeed, perhaps psi operates subliminally, below the threshold of detection. You may have it and not know it (Beloff, 1974). If any of these hypotheses are true, then a "direct" test of psi might involve measuring events in the body and brain, rather than your reports. Your body may well respond to a psi test, even though you believe that you do not have a psi ability.

Over 30 years of research have examined a variety of neurophysiological correlates of psi using the galvanic skin response (increased perspiration, particularly in the hands, associated with increased brain activity and mental stress), electroencephalogram (EEG; crude measures of overall brain activity measured by electrodes on the scalp), as well as heart rate and volume (amount of blood pumped with each heartbeat). Some of this research has been promising (for reviews see Beloff, 1974; Braud, Shafer, & Andrews, 1993a, 1993b; Warren, McDonough, & Don, 1992; May, 1997). However, these studies have not been accepted by the mainstream scientific community, partly because of pervasive skepticism concerning the quality of journals that typically accept such research.

Two studies have received mainstream attention. Don, McDonough, and Warren (1998) examined the responses of 22 participants to a card gambling task. Participants were not selected for any possible psi ability. Each was placed alone in a sound-isolated room and faced a monitor. Initially participants were shown a sequence of four special cards displaying images of the four suits (heart, diamond, spade, club) in random order. Then the four images were shown together and participants pointed via a joystick to which one they guessed would be randomly selected. The "winning card" was then generated and displayed. Brain EEG activity was measured by scalp electrodes.

Participants could not successfully guess cards to be presented. However, event-related brain potentials (ERPs) revealed sudden increase in brain activity at certain times during the initial exposure period in which images of four cards were presented in random sequence. Here, ERPs revealed

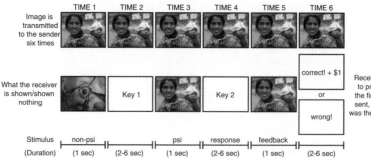

A pair of images is randomly selected. One is emotionally intense (the eye), and one neutral (woman and child). From this pair one image (woman and child) is randomly selected for the sender to psychically transmit to the receiver. The receiver has to guess which image is being sent.

Figure 12.3 One trial in Moulton & Kosslyn

a slightly different pattern of brain activity only when viewing the card that was subsequently randomly selected. In other words, the brains of participants appeared to correctly guess which card would be selected, before selection occurred, even when participant guesses were incorrect. Researchers of this study conclude that this is evidence of "unconscious" or "preconscious" psi.

Perhaps the main limitation of Don et al.'s study is that it appeared in a journal viewed with skepticism by many scientists. However, it is the only such study cited without criticism by at least one highly respected researcher in a top professional journal (Moulton & Kosslyn, 2008). Perhaps because of the apparent strengths of the Don et al. study, Moulton and Kosslyn (2008) devised a replication, a neurophysiological test for psi designed to maximize sensitivity and the chances of producing positive results. Specifically, they settled on a procedure that would detect not only precognition (such as guessing cards), but telepathy, clairvoyance, and even (although they fail to note this) psychokinesis. Furthermore, the study used emotionally related participants (e.g., twins, relatives, friends, roommates) and emotional stimuli, both features which previous psi researchers have speculated should enhance psi. In line with recommendations from psi researchers, senders were instructed to maintain a playful attitude and an active interest in their task. Target stimuli, those selected to be "transmitted," were selected to differ as much as possible in emotional valence and intensity. That is, some stimuli were highly negative (e.g., eye surgery), positive (e.g., erotic couple), neutral (e.g., a simple face or tissue box), or low negative or positive. Finally, they deployed a measure of "unconscious" and "conscious" brain activity far more sensitive than the ERP, functional magnetic resonance imaging (fMRI).

Let me attempt a simplified summary of the gist of the design. First, stimulus photos were assembled into pairs so that each pair included a positive and a neutral or negative photo. A sender and receiver were placed in different rooms, limiting the possibility of stimulus leakage. Then sender and receiver proceeded with 240 trials. The basic idea was simple. The sender transmitted (viewed) a randomly selected image. The receiver viewed two images, one being the transmitted image. MRI recordings could detect if the receiver unconsciously recognized which of the two was in fact the sent image. Now for the details (skip this complicated section if you want).

As mentioned, trials were designed to detect the presence of a variety of psi phenomena, including precognition, telepathy, clairvoyance, and even psychokinesis. In each trial, a photo pair was selected, and the sender was randomly given one image from the pair to transmit six times (from 1 to 6 seconds). As we shall see, the inclusion of six discrete transmissions of the same stimulus is an important design element. During the first transmission, the receiver was shown a photo, also randomly selected from the same pair given to the sender. Thus, it could be the exact photo transmitted, or its contrasting pair. During the second transmission, the receiver paused, viewing nothing. During transmission 3, the receiver was shown the second contrasting photo from the selected pair. During transmission 4, the receiver indicated through a key press (press "key 1" or "key 2") which of the two photos viewed were the same as the photo repeatedly transmitted. During transmissions 5 and 6 the correct answer was shown along with a one-dollar reward for a successful trial. If the participants displayed precognition (seeing into the future), the receiver should correctly detect at transmission time 1 what was transmitted later (transmission times 2–6). A clairvoyant receiver should correctly identify a photo while it is observed and transmitted. A telepathic receiver should correctly read the thoughts of the transmitter. And through psychokinesis a receiver should be able to affect ahead of time which cards are selected.

Results revealed no differences in brain activity for images correctly and incorrectly identified. That is, the brains of participants reacted the same to psi and non-psi stimuli. Finally, participants were not able to select or guess transmitted images. Although fMRI may represent the most sensitive method yet for assessing the possibility of psi, critics may note that this particular study did not include participants preselected for apparent psi abilities (as is often done in remote-viewing studies) or subjected to conditions such as sensory deprivation used in ganzfeld studies. However, it should be noted that past psi researchers have often claimed that psi phenomena can be readily displayed in ordinary participants in ordinary circumstances.

Meta-Analyses and Random Number Generators

The most distant galaxies are invisible to the naked eye. However, they can be detected by groups of powerful telescopes together, taking thousands of photographs over weeks. Combining huge numbers of photographs enables astronomers to gather enough photons, or packets of light energy, to detect the faintest of stellar objects. Similarly, some subatomic forces are so tiny that huge particle accelerators must conduct millions of trials in order to detect their operation. Perhaps psi is a star or force so faint that evidence becomes clear only after examining a huge number of participants. This can be achieved through meta-analysis. Specifically, meta-analysis is a relatively new statistical method in which the results of many studies can be treated as a single large study. Faint effects spread over many projects can be amplified when considered together. At least 14 meta-analyses have been conducted on psi phenomena, and 4 on PK (Bösch, Steinkamp, & Boller, 2006).

Early PK experiments were conducted by J. B. Rhine in the mid 1930s. He attempted to determine if participants could use their thoughts to influence the results of tossing dice. (Interestingly, this idea was first proposed in 1627 by Francis Bacon, one of the founders of the scientific method; Radin, Nelson, Dobyns, & Houtkooper, 2006.) Radin and Ferrari (1991) conducted a meta-analysis of these and over a hundred other experiments, involving 4,600 participants (and 3.6 million tosses). Although initial results appeared promising, final analyses were inconclusive due to several confounding variables. Dice do not fall randomly; "6" is the most likely throw, whereas "1" is least likely. Because die dots are drilled into each die face, the side with the most drilled dots ("6") is lightest, and the face with the fewest ("1") is heaviest, and most likely to hit the table. In addition, researchers at times deployed an **arbitrary end point,** that is, stopped tossing dice when they got the results they expected. This destroys randomization. If you were to toss a die 56 times, you might get this random result:

41632546666115266314536235462135641352143522315642124 3514

Note that this random sequence is not entirely smooth, but has occasional streaks (Chapter 6). Indeed, at the tenth throw, you have tossed "6" no fewer than four times.

4163254666115266314536235462135641352143522315642124 3514

Forty percent of your tosses have been sixes, apparently a remarkable event, if you arbitrarily stop at the tenth toss. However, you have to look at the big picture, and not stop arbitrarily when you desire.

In the mid-twentieth century researchers abandoned dice in favor of computerized procedures for generating random numbers. For example, Beloff and Evans (1961) used the rate of decay of a radioactive element as a random source. Psi participants attempted to slow the rate of decay. Other researchers used a variety of computerized random number generators (**RNG**), sometimes termed random event generators (REG), in which the output was converted to clicks or numbers (1 or 0). The use of RNGs represents an application of micro-PK, the use of thoughts to influence events at the atomic or subatomic level. The advantages of this methodology are that it permits completion of an extremely large number of trials and limits the chance of human fraud, error, or interference. However, researchers can still cheat by selecting arbitrary stop points.

Bösch et al. (2006) have conducted what may be the most comprehensive meta-analysis of RNG research. They combined the results of 380 studies and found a very small but significant effect. However, they concluded that the results are likely the result of the **file drawer effect**. Put simply, if researchers who obtain negative effects choose not to publish their results (and simply put them in the file drawer), and if journals tend not to publish negative findings, then the resulting literature will include a misleading number of positive findings. If all findings were included, the unpublished negative results would cancel out the published positive findings (see Chapter 3 for further discussion of publication bias). This is quite probably a problem for all published meta-analyses of psi phenomena. Indeed, as one highly respected statistics expert concluded, meta-analysis "elevates publication bias to an art form—to a point, in fact, that some credible research methodologists … discount this type of evidence completely" (Bausell, 2007, p. 198).

At times researchers counter that a file drawer of negative findings would have to be unbelievably large to negate a positive meta-analysis. For example, in their analysis of dice experiments, Radin and Ferrari (1991) calculated that 18,000 studies with negative results would have to have been conducted, and tossed in the file drawer, to counter the positive effects of published PK studies summarized in their meta-analysis. Other researchers, examining the data more carefully, have concluded that only 60 unpublished studies would be required (Bösch et al., 2006). Similarly, Radin (1997) has presented what might be the strongest evidence for psi (Good, 1997), a significant psi effect revealed in a meta-analysis of a half-century of 186 studies on ESP. Furthermore, Radin asserts that the file drawer of unpublished negative findings would have to include 3,300 studies to nullify this effect. Good (1997), an accomplished statistician, notes that Radin provides no justification for his file drawer claim, and in fact only 8 to 15 unpublished negative studies would be necessary. Good concludes that Radin's own evidence largely undermines his best evidence for ESP. At the very least, the frequent lack of agreement on the required sized of a presumed file drawer of negative findings is very common in psi research.

Meta-analysis is a controversial and quirky tool. It is statistically possible for a meta-analysis to combine 50 studies, none of which report significant results, and generate a spurious significant overall result (Alcock, 1981). Most researchers who conduct meta-analyses wisely either omit what they judge to be poorly designed studies, or at least give such studies less statistical weight. However, those who have attempted this in psi research rarely agree on how to rate the studies included. As a result, almost invariably two researchers who conduct meta-analyses on the same set of studies come up with quite different (and often opposing) results.

Finally, RNG methodology permits running hundreds of thousands of trials. Few humans would have the stamina to toss so many dice. Such a rigorous approach would seem like a good thing. However, statisticians routinely warn that performing statistical tests on huge samples can yield spurious positive results. With large numbers, even small sources of error (slight problems in the design of random number generating machines, temperature, "clumpiness" of data) can have an apparent effect. It has actually been demonstrated that with a very large randomly generated sample, an effect can be extremely small, *entirely spurious*, yet statistically significant (see Alcock, 1981).

In conclusion, much research and discussion has focused on the effects of PK on random number generation. Perhaps Irwin and Watt (2007) offer the most reasonable summary: It is too early to draw a firm conclusion as to the authenticity of PK from meta-analyses.

Intervening Subject Variables

Perhaps paranormal processes work for some people and not others. If so, identifying individual or subject variables associated with psi should increase the likelihood of actually demonstrating psi. Irwin and Watt (2007) believe that there are "encouraging" (see "weasel words," Chapter 4) associations between ESP performance and attitudes and beliefs, mood, personality, cognitive variables, and demographics (actually, for each dimension contradictory findings exist). Perhaps the most frequently reported is the sheep–goat hypothesis. As noted earlier, the sheep–goat hypothesis states that individuals who believe in the paranormal, "sheep," are more likely to produce paranormal effects than "goats," or those who do not believe in the paranormal (Schmeidler, 1945). Pro-paranormal researchers proclaim the sheep–goat effect to be one of the "more successfully replicated relationships in ESP research" (Irwin & Watt, 2007, p. 74). However, the only tally of existing studies reveals that the research is conflicting and the overall effect, if any, is very small (Lawrence, 1993). Even this finding is contested (Stanford, 2003). Studies on the sheep–goat effect are further compromised by the strong finding that attitudes concerning the paranormal can profoundly distort perception and memory (see Chapters 7 and 8).

Finally, a wide range of variables, including positive mood, levels of psychological adjustment, extraversion, and propensity for fantasy, may well characterize those reporting paranormal experiences. Whether or not these reports are accurate is, of course, open to question. Even though Irwin and Watt are inclined to accept evidence that psi phenomena are mediated by various individual variables, they acknowledge that:

> the determined skeptic may argue that the operation of artifacts in ESP experiments (unintentional sensory cues, subject fraud, etc.) is correlated with various psychological variables and that it is actually these correlations that process-oriented experiments have revealed. For example, ESP scores may be related to extraversion because extraverts are more inclined than introverts to seek means of cheating." (p. 81)

This observation brings us to our conclusion.

REALITY CHECK   Irwin and Watt (2007) acknowledge the skeptics' criticism that evidence for ESP may be the result of artifact. However, they go on to state: "This line of argument certainly should not be accepted without subjecting the specific claims to further empirical scrutiny" (p. 81). Where does this place the burden of proof? (Chapters 4 and 5) Compare this with "Sagan's Balance" (Chapters 2 and 5).

Conclusion: The State of Psi Research

The quest for psi has covered much ground, from spectacular séances of mediums to the microscopic clicks of random number generators. What are we to make of hundreds of studies conducted by hundreds of passionate researchers over the past century? Psi researchers often conclude that psi has been demonstrated conclusively (Irwin & Watt, 2007). Critics claim that consistent, independent replications do not exist (Hyman, 2008). The lesson I draw is simple: Extraordinary claims require extraordinary evidence. There have been too many instances of top researchers guilty of fraud, deception, sloppy research, selective reporting of positive reports, misreporting of actual methods deployed, and failing to reveal obvious design flaws. True, to some extent this happens in all research. But in paranormal studies the stakes are higher. Furthermore, in other areas of research, problems are quickly identified and dealt with in subsequent studies; in psi investigations, researchers are still making the same mistakes identified decades ago (although progress has been made).

A "Dialogue of the Deaf"?

I proposed in Chapter 5 that in order to be credible a paranormal study calls for application of the FEDS Standard, *expert independent and impartial supervision and replication to minimize fraud, error, deception,* and *sloppiness*. I doubt this will happen soon.

First, most psi researchers are convinced that they have already met the objections of critics and are conducting sound scientific research (Raz, 2008). Irwin and Watt (2007) have concluded that "the experimental evidence for ESP meets the criteria generally demanded for other psychological phenomena" (p. 60). Furthermore:

> Unless there are to be one set of rules for intuitively acceptable data and another set for parapsychological and other "radical" data, we find ourselves persuaded that the ESP studies are indicative of a genuine phenomenon. (p. 60)

Paranormal researchers are often frustrated at criticisms. As Utis (1995) complained over a decade ago, "There is little benefit in continuing experiments designed to offer proof, since there is little more to be offered to anyone who does not accept the current collection of data" (p. 290). Because of this, Alcock (2003), a rare scholar highly respected by both psi proponents and skeptics, has observed that discussions of psi research may be considered "a *dialogue aux sourds,* a dialogue of the deaf" (p. 203).

Yes, skeptics do not hesitate in drawing public attention to the embarrassing follies of paranormal researchers, an indulgence this text does not avoid.[5] Psi researchers are frustratingly persistent at ignoring and discounting reasonable requests to fix problems that prevent their research from getting into top scientific journals. They complain that mainstream science is "inflexible," "deceitful," "subversive," "suffering low self-esteem," "prejudiced" against, and even unconsciously "afraid" of psi (Irwin & Watt 2007; Radin, 1997, 2008). Dean Radin, perhaps the currently most visible psi researcher, offers a similar opinion:

> There is ample room for scholarly debate about these topics, and I know a number of informed scientists whom I respect who have reached different conclusions. But I've also learned that most of the hostile rants one reads about this topic are pure bluster proclaimed by those who don't know what they're talking about. Their rejections seem to be motivated by fundamentalist

beliefs of the scientistic or religious kind, rather than by rational, well-reasoned arguments. (Radin, 2008)

To be fair, there are instances where mainstream reviewers have misstated what psi researchers have done (Child, 1985). Perhaps this is an example of confirmation bias in which skeptical reviewers see what they have come to expect in psi research. If so, psi researchers would be well advised to clearly communicate the strengths of their studies and applications of the FEDS Standard. But a problem remains.

A challenge to Psi Researchers

Let me be blunt. Psi researchers (Irwin & Watt, 2007; Radin, 2008) are long overdue for two substantial reality checks. First, to accuse skeptical mainstream scientists of being "inflexible," "deceitful," "subversive," "suffering low self-esteem," "prejudiced," "psi-fearing," "scientistic fundamentalists" reveals a profound misunderstanding as to the very nature of science. Scientists love anomalies. Without unexplained mysteries, there would be no science. A very recent example is the notion of dark energy, that strange force that is apparently causing the universe to expand, a force which, if identified, could also require junking the prevailing and highly popular "standard model" of physics. Like the mysterious energies presumed to constitute psi phenomena, dark energy was once rejected by conventional scientists. However, it took only about 5 years of astronomical observation to reveal that indeed the universe is expanding, and this can't be explained. Today some of the most expensive pieces of scientific equipment on the planet, multi-billion-dollar successors to the Hubble telescope and the multi-billion-dollar atom-smasher, the Large Hadron Collider, are seriously invested in studying the anomaly of dark energy. In other words, scientists have no trouble dedicating huge sums of money to an anomalous energy that might require a total rewriting of physics. Contrast this with how scientists (often the same individuals studying dark energy) have ignored the hypothesized anomalous energies of psi. Why? This brings me to my second reality check—*extraordinary claims require extraordinary evidence.*

Psi researchers routinely ignore Carl Sagan's advice. Irwin and Watt (2007) fail to mention it even once. Why do we require extraordinary evidence? The energies of psi, if they exist, could have far greater implications than dark energy. Once again, think about it. The demonstration and harnessing of psi could (as correctly reasoned by top psi researchers; Chapter 2) enable us to save lives and cure illness through thought alone; solve poverty and the energy crisis; spy on enemies and prevent terrorist attack and war; abandon expensive telecommunication for direct telepathy; and enhance the course of history and evolution by selectively preventing past mistakes and disasters. It is difficult to imagine something more unethical than irrationally suppressing clear evidence that any of this could be done. Scientists who irrationally reject truly supportive psi research would be guilty of unethical behavior of historic proportions.

Coming to our senses, perhaps the unethical choice would be to embrace the glowing conclusions of psi researchers and pursue the next logical step—divert a huge portion of the world's limited treasure (and cut back efforts to combat global warming, poverty, illness, etc.) to harnessing the extraordinary powers they are convinced exist. Obviously, this isn't happening because psi researchers have yet to convincingly make their case. All it would take would be a competently designed study that meets our FEDS Standard. Again, I sincerely doubt that the mainstream scientific community would ignore such research. Of course, a modest first step would be for true-believers to pay for their own studies until they come up with a clear and convincing method for demonstrating psi. Contrary to the protests of some advocates, who claim that psi research has been inhibited by the absence of adequate funding (Irwin & Watt, 2007), this need not be prohibitively expensive.

Yes, Irwin and Watt (2007) and Child (1985) may be correct that some psi studies have met the standards traditionally applied to ordinary psychological research. Believers correctly note that a few findings have been replicated. However, replications have been inconsistent, and are generally cancelled out by other studies that find no effect. Curiously, as Hyman (2008) has frequently observed, "The effect size for psi, in every major research program in parapsychology, declines over time and reaches zero. Major attempts to directly replicate a key parapsychological finding, even when possessing adequate power, fail" (pp. 42–43). Proponents protest that psi is real, yet fleeting. Critics, looking at the same evidence, conclude that it is as fleeting as a random toss of dice. To break this impasse, psi researchers need to go the extra mile, even if this means swallowing one's pride and accepting the "higher standards" I have suggested.

Let me suggest that at the very least psi researchers address the file drawer problem (an example of "S" or "Sloppiness" in the FEDS Standard). Bösch et al. (2006) and Irwin and Watt (2007) have suggested that psi researchers publicly record the intent to conduct paranormal research before initiating a study. Such a requirement would not be excessive (and could be coordinated for virtually no cost on the web by several independent and neutral parties). Indeed, a similar procedure is currently deployed in medical research. Since 2005 the International Committee of Medical Journal Editors (editors of premier medical journals) has required registration as a condition for consideration for publication (DeAngelis et al., 2005).

In conclusion, research on psi will remain inconclusive until adequate quality controls are instituted. As stated by James Alcock (2003), parapsychologists "have *never* been able to produce a successful experiment that neutral scientists, with the appropriate skill, knowledge and equipment, can replicate ..." (p. 35). But this research will surely continue. People have and will continue to have very intense and convincing paranormal experiences, fueled by pseudoscientific misunderstood oddities of nature and the world of numbers, distortions of perception and memory, the placebo effect, and sensory anomalies and hallucinations.

Project Alpha

Research on the paranormal has been plagued with deception and foolery. Rigorous studies now include a qualified magician to identify possible sources of trickery. Project Alpha is possibly the most famous instance of deliberate deception (Randi, 1983a, 1983b). In 1979, James S. McDonnell (Chairman of McDonnell-Douglas Aircraft) gave Washington University in St. Louis a half-million-dollar grant to establish the McDonnell Laboratory for Psychical Research. Specifically the lab was interested in investigating psychokinetic metal bending (PKMB) by children. Magician James Randi ("The Amazing Randi") saw an opportunity to conduct an experiment he had contemplated for quite some time.

Randi selected two teenage magicians, Steve Shaw (Banachek) and Mike Edwards (ages 18 and 17), trained to perform a variety of tricks, and sent them off to the lab. After screening 300 applicants, the McDonnell lab selected Shaw and Edwards. For 4 years the two young men fooled a variety of scientists in more than 160 hours of experiments. They bent spoons as well as aluminum rods securely embedded in blocks of plastic, identified pictures sealed in envelopes, made digital clocks stop working, caused fuses to burn out, rotated a paper propeller isolated inside a glass dome, psychically created pictures on film inside cameras, linked two closed wooden rings, and magically drew mystical symbols out of piles of dry coffee-grounds in a locked aquarium. They achieved all of these using nothing more than standard magician's tricks easily found and explained on the internet (search "project alpha").

Amazingly, Randi wrote to the director of McDonnell lab, Dr. Peter Phillips (a physics professor) outlining eleven "caveats" they should be wary of and what to do to avoid being tricked. Randi also offered to serve as a consultant and witness for free, and to even help set up "trick-proof" experiments. Dr. Phillips refused, claiming he was quite capable of detecting deception. However, he decided to videotape many of the experiments.

Shaw and Edwards succeeded in fooling the McDonnell lab researchers and quite a few other scientists. Dr. Phillips and the paranormal community were enthralled with his "gifted psychics." Lab researchers could see no evidence of deception in the video tapes, although outside viewers found the tricks amusingly obvious. When Randi leaked stories that talented psychics might be plants, Phillips laughed it off as a joke. Of course, eventually all was revealed. Some researchers still refused to believe. One even claimed that Steve and Mike actually had psychic powers, and were lying when they claimed to be magicians. Another scientist complained that Randi's experiment had "set parapsychology back 100 years." McDonnell lab soon closed in disgrace.

Project Alpha is perhaps the best example of how a professional magician can identify deceptions that scientists and sincere psychics miss.

How to Prove You Have Psi Ability without an Expensive Lab

If you have a psychic ability, there are ample ways you can demonstrate your talents, and get rich. Play the lottery. Go to a casino. Invest in stocks. Use your powers to find hidden treasures. Write a book on positive thinking and appear on *Oprah*.

Figure 12.4   James Randi

But where are the rich psychic lottery-winners? Perhaps they are hiding their winnings for security purposes. One might argue that selfish pursuits of questionable morality cannot work because they are contrary to the spiritual nature of psi phenomena. (However, this has not prevented the Roman Catholic Church from running bingo games, or hundreds of psychics from getting rich off their schemes and books.)

Fortunately, there is a way for truly selfless psychics to demonstrate their powers, and benefit humankind. At the time of the writing of this book, over 25 public challenge tests offer substantial rewards for a demonstrated paranormal ability. Together, over $2 million is available. Perhaps the most famous is the James Randi $1 million challenge open primarily to those with claimed paranormal powers who have received media attention. Applicants must have the support of at least one person from the academic community. If your psychic powers are diminished by such materialism, give your winnings to charity. If the negative vibrations from a world-famous skeptic stifle your paranormal powers, that itself is a $1 million paranormal claim. Get tested with Randi present, and with him absent. (Hurry, because this challenge may close. As of this day, Randi plans to terminate the challenge in 2010.) To date, no one has ever passed the preliminary tests (from www. randi.org). For a recent demonstration, see Affective Computing (2008).

Finally, for psychics who must operate in isolation, far from the intrusive observations of scientists or temptations of material gain, Beloff (1985) offers a simple challenge. Produce a "permanent paranormal object" that could not be created by any means known to science. One might create a block of wood that seamlessly blends two types of timber, a living rabbit's foot with gold toes integrated at the sub-cellular level, iron that is liquid at room temperature, or pure copper wire that is superconductive at room temperature. Such an object could be taken to a lab and tested, or if the psychic prefers, simply kept for personal contemplation.

13

Energy Treatments and Complementary and Alternative Medicine (CAM)

Life could not exist without energy. We need it to run our factories, fuel our cars, and heat our homes. You feel it when you wake up refreshed and your body is excited and ready for action. On some days you may be brimming with energy, ready to conquer the world. When sick, you're listless and drained.

Many forms of complementary and alternative medicine (CAM) are based on the pseudoscientific belief in a special life energy that supports and maintains living organisms. (The best and most current reviews of CAM approaches can be found in Carroll, 2009a.) Acupuncture involves releasing blockages of life energy in the body. Feng shui involves balancing and optimizing life energies of the environment through architecture and interior design. A priest may use therapeutic touch to transfer healing energy to a patient. (See Appendix A for CAM and the National Center for Complementary and Alternative Medicine.)

What is energy? The first thing you need to know is that the paranormal use of the term bears little resemblance to its use in any of the sciences. Indeed, life energies generally cannot be measured objectively. Second, for the paranormal, the terms "energy," "force," and "power" mean pretty much the same thing and are used interchangeably. In science these terms have quite precise and distinct meanings.

Contemporary Views of Energy: The Scientific Perspective

In physics, energy is the capacity for doing work. As such it is a characteristic of something, not an entity in and of itself. To say that a party is "energized" is a way of saying that lots of people are mingling, talking, and dancing. You can't take this "party energy" and put it in a bottle. (Although you could put the guests to work to clean up their mess when the party is over.) Put a rock in a fire and it will get hot, that is, energized. Put several energized rocks in a pile and they can do work, like bake potatoes.

In an energetic party, a lot is happening. Similarly, physicists define energy in terms of motion. An object in motion (like a rolling rock or vibrating guitar string) has **kinetic energy**. An unmoving object (a rock on top of the hill or stretched-out guitar string) that can create motion has **potential energy**. Energy (motion) can be mechanical, thermal, electrical, chemical, or nuclear, as well as electromagnetic. A rolling rock has **mechanical energy**. Quickly moving molecules (such as boiling water) possess **thermal energy**. Ice molecules move less quickly and have lower levels of thermal energy. **Electrical energy** or current is the movement or flow of electrons through a conductor (such as a wire, water, or even human tissue). Chemicals bumping into and combining into new chemicals (coal combining with oxygen to produce ash) have **chemical energy**. In an atomic explosion, the very particles that comprise atoms move and break apart. This is **nuclear energy**.

Electromagnetic energy consists of all forms of radiation, including radio waves, microwaves, infrared light, visible light, ultraviolet light, x-rays, and gamma-rays. Radiation is defined in terms of packets of energy, called photons, that have no mass but move like waves at the speed of light. Different forms of radiation can be ranked according to how much energy they possess, with radio waves, microwaves, and visible light possessing the least amount of energy and x-rays and gamma-rays possessing the most.

Energy cannot be created or destroyed. However, one form can be converted into another. We burn coal (chemical energy) to create heat (thermal energy, infrared radiation) which causes water in a tank to expand into steam, powering a generator (mechanical energy) which produces electrical current (electrical energy). The capacity of energy for doing work always decreases with distance. A firecracker at close range is more dangerous than one down the street.

What is important to note is that nothing of what we know about energy can be described in any way to be "living" and certainly not something possessing "will" or "intentionality." But there is one sense in which the term "energy" can apply to life. Living systems do metabolize (or "burn") the chemicals in food into other chemicals (wastes), an example of chemical energy. Such metabolism fuels our capacity for all types of "work." As a byproduct, infrared radiation energy is released. The nervous system generates electromagnetic radiation energy that can be detected by very sensitive equipment, electroencephalographs (EEGs). However, such electromagnetic waves are very weak and indistinguishable from electromagnetic waves that can be generated by inanimate objects such as computers and cell phones.

Concepts of Energy in Children
and Western History: Vitalism

Children think differently from adults. In attempting to make sense of the world they may erroneously think of objects as possessing consciousness and agency or intentionality (Lindeman & Saher, 2007). A lucky charm has a magical "energy" that gives you luck. The clouds "want" to rain on the parade, they have intentionality. Eventually, children outgrow such simplistic thinking patterns and learn to explain the world more accurately in physical, biological, and psychological terms. Rocks don't fall because they want to touch the earth, but because of gravity.

The idea that objects possess energy and intentionality is called **vitalistic causality** or **vitalism**, a type of thinking that also characterizes adult belief in the paranormal (see Chapter 1). Vitalistic thinking also characterized early human thought and philosophy. Aristotle believed that living things possess a life-giving soul (Schubert-Soldern, 1962). In the 19th and 20th centuries physiologists proposed a vital force underlying all living things. This force was given various names, including *life force, vis essentialis, vis viva, entelechy, élan vital,* and *soul atoms* (Lindeman & Saher, 2007). Somewhat similar vitalistic concepts permeated early Eastern thoughts.

Once again, vitalism is clearly a paranormal concept. There is no evidence of vitalistic energy, much less a thinking energy with intentionality, outside the energies physics has discovered. Children give up primitive vitalistic ideas as they mature. On a larger scale, civilization abandoned vitalistic explanations for those based on science. However, vitalism persists in energy treatments of complementary and alternative medicine. We consider major approaches that have developed in the East and West.

REALITY CHECK   What logical errors characterize vitalistic views of energy?

Chinese History and Energy: The Yin–Yang School

Many oriental practices rely on vitalistic concepts. In India, yoga incorporates prana (breath energy) and chacras (energy centers in the body). We will focus on ideas that emerged from China and have considerable influence on Western energy treatments.

The Yin–Yang School of philosophy is over 2,000 years old and is a major school of ancient Chinese thought. Yin–yang philosophy offers a vitalistic view of energy that has permeated Chinese culture, including art, marriage, politics, medicine, and divination. Yin–yang thinking is central to feng shui, acupuncture, qigong, and tai chi.

In most general terms, the yin–yang school states that a single principle runs the universe, tai chi (Puro, 2002). This principle divides into two opposing but complementary "forces" or "principles," **Yin and Yang**. Things that are passive are described as yin, whereas yang is active. Additional attributes of yin include "earth, absorbing, cold, female, dark, inward, and downward." Yin is present in even numbers, valleys and streams, the color orange, and a broken line. Yang is "heaven, penetrating, hot, male, bright, outward, and upward" and exists in odd numbers, mountains, the color azure, and an unbroken line.

Everything is in constant and cyclical change. Yin eventually produces yang, and yang leads to yin. The dominance of one principle is always temporary. Illness follows health, and health follows illness. Strength leads to exhaustion, and exhaustion (and a good nap) leads to strength. Yin and yang exist in harmony, as symbolized in the popular yin/yang symbol in which dark and light halves are separated by a wavy "S" line. If you study a proper yin/yang symbol, you will note a dark dot in the light (yang) segment, and a light dot in the dark (yin) segment. This symbolizes that in every yin is the seed of yang.

Yin and yang work through a vitalistic energy, **qi** or **ch'i** (pronounced "chee" as in "cheese"). At first qi had a very simple and pungent meaning—the noxious vapors that arise from a corpse not buried deep enough (Watson, 1963). The term evolved to refer to universal vitalistic energy, one that fills the universe and is responsible for all life. It is in the environment, sunlight, and the very food we eat. Qi travels in the body through 12 major channels called **meridians**. Why 12? In Chinese thinking, there are 12 primary organs: the heart, lungs, stomach, small intestines, large intestines, spleen, urinary bladder, kidney, liver, gallbladder, pericardium, and the upper torso. Each organ has qi.

When a person is ill, yin and yang are out of balance. For example, someone with high blood pressure might have too much yang in the heart requiring a treatment that would reduce heart yang and increase yin (yin-yang, 2007). More concretely, disease is caused by a blockage or unhealthy flow of qi from one organ to another (Qi, 2007). Chinese interventions to adjust yin/yang and chi include various herbal medicines and diet (see also Ayurvedic medicine, an approach from India), physical training, martial arts, massage.

The yin–yang school provides a foundation for many paranormal systems, including Chinese astrology and the *I Ching* or *Book of Changes*. Chinese

Figure 13.1 I Ching (8 trigrams in yin–yang)

astrology is quite different from Western astrology, and is rarely applied in the West. However, the *I Ching* is popular. This book provides a way of understanding and predicting change in the universe by randomly selecting (through a complex procedure) and reading combinations of eight trigrams each of which is made of a different combination of one or two broken (yin) or unbroken (yang) lines. Each trigram has a different forecast, much like an astrological horoscope. Trigrams are often arranged in clockwise fashion around a yin-yang symbol (see Figure 13.1).[1]

We consider four Chinese approaches that have gained popularity in the West: feng shui, qigong, tai chi, and acupuncture.

Chinese Energy Treatments

Feng Shui

Feng shui ("wind water") is the art of arranging objects (from furniture to buildings and cities) in harmony with the environment to achieve health, energy, and balance. It is primarily a practice of urban planning, architecture, landscaping, and interior design (Carroll, 2009b, Wu, 2000). Major cities of China have been developed according to the rule of feng shui. Generally, the goal is to build or place structures (or furniture) in "perfect spots," places with good qi.

Contemporary feng shui combines the *I Ching* with geomancy. The *I Ching's* clock-like arrangement of trigrams, along with a compass, is used to identify the best orientation for a building (furniture, city, flower pot, etc.). Geomancy (not a Chinese term) involves "reading" or interpreting the inner meaning of hills, rivers, and various shapes in the environment. For example, if a hill looked like a dragon, one would not build a house close to its apparent mouth, or powerful, thrashing tail. Building a house next to a river might be wise because the flow of water in a river represents the flow of qi. Incidentally, one might arrange doors and furniture in a house in such a way that qi would not be blocked, but could flow freely. Obviously, geomancy is an application of the "Law of Similar" in which two properties are linked because of superficial appearances. The Law of Similar is central to ancient folklore and superstition throughout the world (see Chapters 1 and 4).

Some of feng shui is good environmental sense. Don't build a house on the beach in hurricane zones. Save on energy by orienting windows toward the sun. As a set of aesthetic stylistic principles that emphasizes balance and harmony with nature, feng shui appeals to some (just as one might prefer "traditional" or "contemporary" style). However, feng shui has nothing to do with science. Its principles are no more scientific than the principles of renaissance art, modern jazz, or Japanese flower arrangement.

Acupuncture

Acupuncture is a medical technique for unblocking qi by inserting needles at special points on body meridians. It is typically claimed to be from 2,500 to 5,000 years old, although some say it has a more recent origin (Hall, 2008).

Up to 15 million Americans spend about a half billion dollars a year for acupuncture treatments for AIDS, allergies, asthma, arthritis, bladder and kidney problems, bronchitis, constipation, depression, diarrhea, dizziness, colds, eye disorders, fatigue, flu, gynecologic disorders, headaches, high blood pressure, migraines, paralysis, PMS, respiratory problems, sciatica, sexual dysfunction, smoking, stress, stroke, tendinitis, and vision problems. It has even been used for cancer and alcoholism (Fleischman, 1998). About 4,000 U.S. physicians are trained in acupuncture.

Acupuncture procedures vary among practitioners. Generally, after an interview an acupuncturist will identify organs (from the 12 mentioned earlier) that suffer imbalance. Along the associated 12 meridians (some say 9, 10, or 11) there are about 2,000 potential target acupuncture points, of which 200 are used more frequently. Needles are inserted to manipulate qi in the appropriate meridians. Target points often have no relationship to the presumed affected organ. Sometimes needles are twirled, heated, and stimulated by mild electric current. In acupressure, pressure is applied to meridian points. A session lasts 20–30 minutes up to an hour. After an initial prick there is generally no discomfort or pain. An acupuncturist will take great care to insert needles at special meridian points. Six to 12 needles are inserted during a session (Lewith, Kenyon & Lewis, 1996; Pelletier, 2002).

Acupuncture appears to have some effect (NIH Consensus Development Program, 1997). However, evaluation of medical claims is beyond the scope of this book and many studies are conflicting (Carroll, 2009c). The most important issues in acupuncture research are:

- Is any claimed success of acupuncture due to placebo or other nonspecific effects? This is currently the most likely explanation for the effects of acupuncture (Madsen, Gøtzsche, & Hróbjartsson, 2009).
- When an acupuncture success is not due to placebo or nonspecific effects, are there any other scientific explanations? Yes, gate control theory of pain states that a stimulus in one part of the body can send nerve impulses to the spine which switch off a neurological "pain gate," preventing pain sensations from reaching the brain. A more popular hypothesis is that sticking needles into someone evokes pain-killing chemicals such as endorphins, enkephalins, and serotonin, some of which bear a chemical resemblance to morphine.
- Is needle insertion necessary? No, one can use touch, heat, or lasers.
- Must needles be inserted at precise acupuncture points? No. Poking just about anywhere works.
- Do meridian points correspond to human physiology? No consistent correspondence has been found between meridian points and any feature in human anatomy. However, with 2,000 potential needle insertion points, by chance alone one might expect some to correspond to areas of the skin dense with nerve endings.
- Do meridian points correspond to channels of qi? There is absolutely no evidence for this whatsoever. As Felix Mann (1993), founder of the Medical Acupuncture Society, has stated:

> The traditional acupuncture points are no more real than the black spots a drunkard sees in front of his eyes. (p. 14) The meridians of acupuncture are no more real than the meridians of geography. If someone were to get a spade and tried to dig up the Greenwich meridian, he might end up in a lunatic asylum. Perhaps the same fate should await those doctors who believe in [acupuncture] meridians. (p. 31)

REALITY CHECK   What characteristics of an acupuncture procedure might contribute to a placebo effect?

Qigong

Qigong (pronounced "chee gung"), or **chi kung** (Lin, 2000; Chen, 2007), is an ancient Chinese practice that freely mixes thousands of exercises including postures and stretches, martial arts training, deep breathing, imagery, and focused meditations. Many are borrowed from yoga and Buddhism. All are designed to cultivate and balance one's energy or qi. The health effects of exercises included in qi gong have been demonstrated through considerable research (Smith, 2007; Lehrer, Woolfolk, & Sime, 2007). The psychophysiological foundations for these exercises are well grounded in science and have nothing to do with qi.

Tai Chi

Tai chi is an ancient Chinese exercise involving slow and graceful dance and yoga-like movements and postures. Although originally developed as a form of self-defense, it is increasingly used in the West as an approach to stress management and a tool for enhancing balance and flexibility. Like qigong, tai chi is based on qi.

Western Energy Treatments

Western vitalistic treatments typically lack the philosophical rationale characteristic of Eastern approaches. Also lacking is a notion that vitalistic energies have purpose, intentionality, or some cosmic harmony. However, Western vitalism posits an energy of substance not detected by physical means that can be manipulated by physical means, pills and supplements, and touch.

Mechanical Devices

If you browse through your favorite tabloid newspaper, you will likely find advertisements for a wide range of devices claimed to manipulate, enhance, or protect against unwanted energies. A small computer-like chip may protect you from electromagnetic radiation emanating from power lines, or microwave ovens. Palm-sized pyramids may cure wounds and sharpen razor blades. Crystals concentrate mysterious energies to enhance health. Copper bracelets channel the mysterious forces of the universe to enhance your sex life.

Perhaps the oldest and most popular devices involve magnetism. Magnetic cures have been promoted since at least the 1770s with Anton Mesmer's notions of animal magnetism. Mesmer theorized that a strange magnetic fluid (energy) flows through the human body and, when blocked, can lead to distress and illness (Bauer, 2004). Special colorful ceremonies involving magnetized rods (Chapter 2) could free the flow of this fluid. Mesmer's treatment was eventually debunked, and he actually decided that magnets were not necessary for treating animal magnetism (Carroll, 2009d). Today, a billion-dollar industry promotes magnetic shoes, mattresses, bracelets, pendants, earrings, and hats. The most common claims are that magnets can reduce pain, facilitate the flow of blood, and enhance healing. There is absolutely no evidence that common everyday magnets can have any effect on the body. Any claims are most certainly the result of placebo or nonspecific effects.

Recent research has successfully applied one version of magnetic therapy to depression. Repetitive transcranial magnetic stimulation (rTMS) involves applying rapid intense magnetic pulses to parts of the brain for a few minutes a day over several weeks. Over 30 studies suggest that the treatment appears to be effective (Hermann & Ebmeier, 2006). Various neurophysiological explanations have been offered, including the temporary alteration of activity levels of certain parts of the brain and the increased production of serotonin in the brain. The differences between rTMS and similar treatments from magnet nostrums must be emphasized: rTMS uses extremely powerful electromagnets (in which the flow of electricity through metal produces a magnetic field; traditional treatments use weak permanent or static magnets in which no electric field is involved). rTMS involves presenting a rapidly pulsating magnetic field; traditional approaches involve a continuous magnetic field.

Dietary Supplements and Homeopathy

Health food stores are replete with pills, elixirs, and sprays claimed to have a magical effect on energy. The Food and Drug Administration is powerless as long as no precise medical claims are made. It is legal to say that a worthless supplement is good for "energy." It is illegal to call it a treatment for "liver cancer." In this sense, the law permits claims that rely on incorrect and borderline paranormal views of the human body. Indeed if a supplement claims an effect, and there is no conceivable medical way the effect could be real, then something paranormal would have to be involved.

Homeopathy is a clear example of an ineffective treatment supplement based on paranormal energy explanations. Nineteenth century medicine was primitive by today's standards. Treatments were often based on ancient Greek humoral theory, which claimed that all illnesses were due to an imbalance of the four basic fluids (blood, phlegm, black bile, and yellow bile). Humors were balanced by treating symptoms with "opposites," for example, by attempting to cool a feverish patient by draining blood. German physician Samuel Hahnemann (1755–1843) rejected this brutal approach in favor of treating symptoms with "similars" through **homeopathy.**

Hahnemann believed that a vitalistic energy directs healing, a process that can be triggered by giving a patient a minute amount of the substance presumed to be causing an ailment, the "Law of Similar." His "Law of Infinitesimals" states that the more you dilute a treatment, the more effective it becomes. Indeed, a treatment can be so diluted that not even a molecule of the single presumed active ingredient remains in solution. This is because the original ingredient leaves a sort of "memory" in the solution, and this "memory" has a curative effect. To treat arsenic poisoning, one would dilute a drop of arsenic hundreds of times, so none of the poison remains, and give the resulting water to the patient. (One can enhance, or awaken, the spiritual potency of a bottle of such watery solutions with a good slap, a process called "dynamization.")

Homeopathy has been subjected to substantial research (Carroll, 2009e). Although it is clearly better than blood-letting, there is no evidence that it is any more effective than a placebo (Barrett, 2007a; Hines, 2003). The idea of an undetectable "memory" that balances spiritual powers, can be slapped into activity, and even be transmitted over phone lines is vitalism (Jarvis & The National Council against Health Fraud, 2002). There is no evidence that it exists (Goldacre, 2007).

Touch Approaches

A variety of Western energy manipulations involve touch (or near-touch). We consider chiropractic, reflexology, Reiki, and therapeutic touch (TT).

Chiropractic is a controversial approach for preventing and treating illness that has evolved from a vitalistic understanding of the nervous system (Carroll, 2009f). In 1895 D. D. Palmer, a grocer from Iowa, proposed that most health problems could be prevented or treated by manually adjusting the spine and joints. Misaligned vertebrae, or subluxations, lead to nerve compression that interferes with nerve transition and the flow of a vitalistic innate intelligence. Because the proper flow of this intelligence is essential for maintaining health, subluxation contributes to disharmony and illness. The primary tool for unblocking energy flow is a type of massage called spinal manipulation (Haldeman, 1992; Jarvis, 2002; The Chiropractic Paradigm, 2009).

Today, a minority of chiropractors (called "straights") continue to base treatment on vitalistic thinking. Others ("mixers") incorporate modern medical thinking and use massage, exercise strength training, acupuncture-like procedures, traction (stretching), and nutrition. However, most (88%; McDonald,

2003) accept subluxation, now defined as a "complex of functional and/or pathological articular changes that compromise neural integrity and may influence organ system function and general health" (Association, 1996). Even the Foundation for Chiropractic Education and Research has observed that such a vague notion "may not be detectable by any of the current technological methods ..." (Rosner, 1997), admitting to an obviously untestable idea that clearly falls within the realm of the paranormal (Homola, 2008).

Although many chiropractors embrace an overall holistic approach to maintaining health in general, chiropractors are most often seen for lower back pain and headache. Research (Ernst & Canter, 2006) suggests that spinal manipulation for back pain is no more effective than sham (fake; see Chapter 8) placebo manipulation, simple massage, or appropriate exercise (Barrett & Homola, 2007). Physical therapists argue that they are better trained for such problems (Homola, 2008).

Reflexology is one of many massage-based treatments claimed to manipulate vitalistic energy. Unlike chiropractic, reflexologists focus on the hands and feet. In the 1930s Eunice Ingham (1889–1974) proposed that every organ and part of the body is represented on specific areas of the feet, and to some extent the hands. For example, the brain is represented by the tip of the large toe, the anus by the bottom of the right foot, and the shoulders by the area just behind the little toe. A trained reflexologist can diagnose and cure illness by feeling and massaging targeted sections of the hands and feet. This stimulates the flow of blood, nutrients, nerve impulses, and, most important, vitalistic energy. There is absolutely no evidence for the reflexology theory or the claimed specific effects of reflexology treatments (Barrett, 2007b). However, a good foot massage can be deeply pleasurable. Some of my students claim that demonstrations of reflexology are great ice-breakers at dorm parties. Perhaps relevant here is the fact that the areas of the brain that connect to the feet and genitals area are adjacent (Ramachandra & Blakeslee, 1998).

Reiki and therapeutic touch (TT) involve treating vitalistic energy by dispensing with touch, needles, or the consumption of supplements. Instead one relies on placement of hands. Reiki was developed in Japan in the early 20th century by Japanese businessman Mikiao Usui, who claimed to have received magical abilities of healing after three weeks of fasting and meditating on a mountain top. Practitioners of Reiki use a series of 12 specific hand positions placed over or on an afflicted part of the body in order to channel the unlimited flow of healing qi (ki in Japanese and Reiki) from the universe into the human body (Jarvis, 2000; Paul, 2006).

Created by nurse Dolores Krieger (1979), TT involves moving hands over a patient's energy field and aura in order to free the flow of energy, bringing

Figure 13.2   Emily Rosa's therapeutic touch experiment. By Pat Linse

it into alignment and balance. Techniques involve initial centering meditation, sweeping one's hands over the patient's body from head to feet to "unruffle stagnant energy," and actual intervention in which the healer re-patterns the patient's energy field by removing "congestion," replenishing depletion, and smoothing out energy. When the patient's energy is balanced, the body can heal itself.

There is no evidence that TT works (Rosa, Rosa, Sarner, & Barrett, 1998). Its claims are purely paranormal. In spite of this, TT is widely accepted in the nursing profession. The American Nurses' Association holds TT work-shops at national conventions, publishes articles on TT, and even grants continuing education credit for TT training.

In a classic study 11-year-old Emily Rosa became the youngest person to publish an article in the prestigious *Journal of the American Medical Association* (Rosa et al., 1998). Emily wanted to determine if 21 expert practitioners of TT could detect the presence of her hand by simply feeling its aura. To do this she sat behind a cardboard screen with one hand-sized opening. She then tossed a coin to determine whether or not to place her hand next to the opening. A TT practitioner would then reach through an opening in the screen and (without touching) determine through aura energy if Emily's hand was present. TT practitioners were able to detect Emily's hand only 44% of the time, worse than chance. Emily was subsequently recognized by the *Guinness Book of World Records* as the youngest published scientist, and appeared on the *Today Show*, *Good Morning America*, all major television news programs, and major newspapers.

Energy treatments and psychotherapy

Psychotherapy is particularly prone to unproven energy treatments (Lilienfeld, Lynn, & Lohr, 2003; Lilienfeld, Ruscio, & Lynn, 2008; Norcross, Koocher, & Garofalo, 2006). Most are loosely based on notions of qi, meridians, and energy blockage. For example, thought field therapy, or TFT (Callahan, 1997; Carroll, 2009g), claims that a wide range of psychological problems are caused by "perturbations" or blockages of "thought field" energy. Clients tap specific parts of the body presumed to be meridian points associated with the blocked energy. While tapping, one might be given a variety of additional tasks, including rolling eyes, counting eyes, humming, and thinking about a distressing image associated with the psychological problem. Tapping presumably frees and balances energy. There is no peer-reviewed evidence that TFT works, although a variety of simplified spin-off treatments have emerged (Gaudiano & Herbert, 2000).

Energy psychotherapies often incorporate a hidden ingredient that may well work. For example, exposure and desensitization treatments are among the most effective and best-validated psychological treatments for phobias and trauma (Lambert, 2004). Put simply, such approaches involve carefully structured imagined and repeated exposure to an anxiety-arousing stimulus. If you carefully examine various psychological energy therapies you may well discover that they often unwittingly include a bit of exposure and desensitization. If the energy treatment happened to work, one could argue that it was not because of freeing qi, or even the placebo effect, but because it included structured exposure to an anxiety-arousing stimulus. Indeed, this appears to be the case for TFT.

REALITY CHECK Teachers of tai chi, acupuncture, and other energy treatments persist in believing vitalistic explanations. Using the concepts of your Critical Thinker's Toolkit, discuss why vitalistic thinking persists, even in face of contrary evidence.

Conclusion

Paranormal research on energy treatments has been riddled with pseudo-science. As we observed for research on psi, initial studies may show a positive effect. However, when methodologies are improved, the effect disappears. The possibility of fraud and incompetence require replication and the over-seeing eye of a consulting magician.

Reason and Intuition: Why People Seek Complementary or Alternative Medicine

Energy treatments are a part of complementary and alternative medicine (CAM). Formally, CAM includes treatments generally not taught in medical school or used by traditional physicians, specifically (a) paranormal energy treatments considered in this chapter, (b) treatments based on insufficient research or error and (c) treatments based on substantial scientific research (see Chapter 2).

Why do people who seek out CAM often not differentiate paranormal, unsubstantiated, and erroneous treatments from those based on sound science? Saher and Lindeman (2005) suggest that one explanation may be thinking style. Dual-process theories of thinking propose two modes of information processing that underlie all reasoning. Although several versions have emerged, researchers of paranormal phenomena have focused on intuitive and rational thinking style (Evans, 2003; Lindeman & Aarnio, 2006). As viewed by Saher and Lindeman (2005),

> [I]ntuitive thinking is described as an unconscious [automatic], fast and effort-less style of thinking, making use of such information sources as personal experiences, feelings, concrete images, and narratives. Because the information processing is emotional as well as mostly unconscious, intuitive judgments are slow to change. (p. 1170)

The opposite of intuitive thinking is rational thinking, characterized by:

> Conscious reasoning and mental effort, using all available objective information to come to a true answer, and willingness to adjust the conclusion in light of new facts. (p. 1170)

Intuitive thinking develops in childhood, whereas rational thinking appears later in development. Research supports that intuitive thinking style is related to belief in alternative medicine. However, those who hold paranormal beliefs are not necessarily deficient in rational thinking ability. They simply have a preference for intuition.

Measuring Vitalistic Energy Through Kirlian Photography

Vitalistic energies are by definition beyond the natural world, meaning that they do not involve any of the forces identified by physics. Logically, they cannot be measured, because any measurement device would be based on physical principles. In spite of this, proponents sometimes borrow from Mesmer and claim that their treatments involve magnetism. There is no evidence. A somewhat more sophisticated claim is that vitalistic energy may well be nonphysical; however, paranormalists claim that it can be detected by special photographic equipment.

One does not need a camera to produce a photograph. Contact print photography involves simply placing an object directly on unexposed photographic film. The resulting image is typically a shadow. In 1939 Semyon Kirlian discovered by accident that if a photographic plate is connected to high voltage current, electrical discharges (corona discharges) emanating from the edge of an object will create a spectacular image with an electrified halo. This is similar to the sparks that fly off various charged objects viewed in the dark.

Kirlian mistakenly believed that such coronal discharges were actually paranormal energies or auras, a claim rapidly embraced by many practitioners of energy treatments. Indeed, living objects like hands, leaves, and frogs, placed on photographic plates, do create particularly vivid auras. However, this is simply because living objects are surrounded by a film of moisture, which readily conducts electricity and ionizes, leaving an image on the photographic plate. (Interestingly, Kirlian photography doesn't work in a vacuum; in a vacuum residual moisture is absent, preventing ionization.) Some practitioners of Kirlian photography have made fantastic claims of photographing missing limbs. These have not been confirmed, and do not pass the holographic urine test of credibility (Carroll, 2009h).

14

Supernatural Cures and Faith Healing

In France a young woman suffering from breast cancer seeks faith and healing at the shrine in Lourdes. An elderly woman in Malaysia has swollen feet. She seeks the assistance of a shaman, who through ritual dance enters a trance, communicates with departed souls, and attempts a cure by cutting a hole in her ankle. In Kansas a middle-aged man with arthritis attends a popular big-tent faith healing revival led by a famous televangelist. With great excitement, the evangelist invokes the power of the Holy Spirit, reaches out to his flock, and pronounces all healed. A noted researcher has brain cancer. Experts in healing prayer from Christian, Jewish, Buddhist, shaman, and secular healing energy traditions converge at her bedside to intervene. A Presbyterian congregation in Ohio prays for the rapid recovery of a family at home with the flu.

Some of these examples may resemble experiences you have had. Some may seem foreign and even laughable. However, all illustrate the same thing: asking a supernatural entity to cure a physical injury or illness. Unlike energy treatments such as acupuncture, a supernatural cure posits an entity larger or greater than ourselves that has thoughts and intentions. This entity may be a deity, the soul of a departed loved one, or a spirit. In whatever form, the entity is beyond the world that physics has revealed, and when approached, can effect cures in this world. We will examine three manifestations of supernatural cures: shamanism, faith healing, and the healing petitions of mainstream religion. We then examine the scientific evidence and implications for the faithful.

The Varieties of Healing Experience

Shamanism

Shamanism is an ancient tribal religious phenomenon that emerged around the end of the stone age (8500 BC) in central Asia and Siberia and appears around the world, including North and South America, southeast India,

Southeast Asia, Oceania and Malaysia, and Australia (Levinson, 1998; Lewis, 2003). Although it is unfair to treat diverse religious cultures as equivalent, a few central features are worth noting. Most important is the shaman (Manch-Tungus for "he who knows"), a special and revered member of the community who has the power to cure illness and communicate with gods and spirits of the dead (Krippner, 2002).

Central to many forms of shamanism are dramatic rituals in which the shaman enters an ecstatic state, induced and supported by intense and prolonged drumming, dance, fasting, intense sauna-like sweat lodges, and ingestion of alcohol and other mind-altering substances. In such altered states the shaman may quiver, struggle, yell in rage, and eventually enter an unconscious "trance." Both the shaman and participants view such displays as evidence of spirit possession, or even as a sign that the shaman's soul has temporarily departed and entered the world of the spirits.

By directly contacting spirits and gods, the shaman acquires remarkable paranormal powers. He may heal, foresee the future, retrieve lost or stolen souls, escort souls of the dead (a process called "psychopomp"), communicate and work with spirits, and appease malevolent spirits. In everyday life the shaman has great priestly authority and supervises sacred rituals, interprets dreams, finds lost animals, and assists fishing and hunting (Krippner, 2002).

Shamans are often quite comfortable using deception and sleight of hand (Krippner, 2002; Warner, 1980) and at times use tricks well known to magicians (Sternfield, 1992). Some positive reviewers view this as a gift that can be used to help others acquire a deeper understanding of reality, specifically by enhancing perception, and temporarily lifting constraints of a consensus worldview of cause and effect (Krippner, 2002; Hansen, 2001). Just how crass deception can lead to enlightenment (other than discovery that the deceiver is a fraud) is not clearly explained.

Psychic surgery, as practiced in the Philippines and to some extent Brazil, is the most publicized example of shamanistic deception. It is a practice that remains popular, and lucrative, to this day. Airlines continue to reserve special flights for large numbers of followers seeking the assistance of psychic surgeons in the Philippines (Affective Computing, 2008). Perhaps the most popular current practitioner is "John of God," a Brazilian who claims to have treated millions (Carroll, 2009a) using psychic techniques, but has been thoroughly debunked as a fraud (Nickell, 2007).[1] In psychic surgery, someone with no medical training publicly performs what appears to be an actual surgical procedure without the use of anesthesia or any medical equipment or knives. Furthermore, after surgery, the patient remarkably shows no incision or scar. The faithful leave, convinced that diseased body parts have been permanently removed. Of course, when such patients are medically examined, sadly they are still ill.

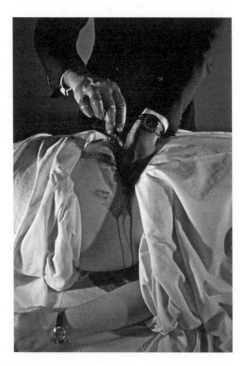

Figure 14.1   Psychic surgery

Nolen (1974) and Randi (1989) have provided classic revelations of how shamanic surgery is done. First, the surgeon needs to prepare some bloody props made to look like internal organs. He may shop at various meat markets for convincing chicken or pig livers and kidneys. Thumb-sized capsules of blood-colored iodine can prove useful. With props carefully concealed, the surgeon stands over his resting and partially disrobed victim and begins to fold and squeeze the skin over the afflicted organ. He carefully creates the illusion that he is actually inserting fingers into the victim's body (for example, by folding skin over his thumb). Suddenly, what appears to be blood gushes out (the ruptured iodine capsule) and the surgeon triumphantly plucks the diseased body part (chicken livers) and hands it to an assistant for rapid disposal. The impressed and bloodied victim sits up, and with immense gratitude pays the surgeon and departs. The creative surgeon may modify this deception. Some may use a knife to create a small, harmless, and medically useless skin incision to enhance the effect. For local patients, the surgeon may mix foreign coins and pieces of tinfoil with animal parts. Although Western patients might find the discovery of bits of metallic trash in their bodies a bit suspicious, for locals coins and foil are actually convincing signs of extracted

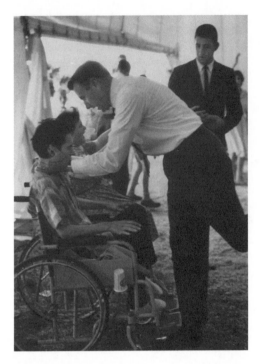

Figure 14.2   Faith healer Oral Roberts healing patient at crusade meeting

evil. Squeamish surgeons may forgo props entirely and claim to eliminate a diseased body part, leaving absolutely no trace (or incriminating evidence).

REALITY CHECK   What features of psychic surgery might enhance the placebo effect? Hypnotic suggestion?

Pentecostalism and Faith Healing

The invocation of supernatural cures is a part of Christianity. Healing is one of the nine gifts of the spirit described in Corinthians I:12. Jesus and his Apostles performed 40 healings. For millennia Christians have celebrated miraculous cures brought about by saints. Healing shrines, including the famous shrine of Lourdes in France, attract millions every year. In the 19th century, Mary Baker Eddy founded Christian Science, a denomination that stresses that illness is the result of erroneous beliefs and that faith in the healing power of God largely eliminates the need for physicians.

We focus on a particularly conspicuous example of faith healing, the American healing revival. Although psychic surgeons have made little headway in the United States, faith healing revivals are part of contemporary American Pentecostal Christian culture, frequently attracting huge television audiences. Many faith healers are household names and television personalities, including Oral Roberts, A. A. Allen, Ernest Angley, Kathryn Kulman, Richard Rossi, Benny Hinn, Peter Popoff, and Pat Robinson. One, Pat Robinson, actually ran for President.

Close examination of any of these reveals that, no matter how dramatic, these public displays of faith healing are little different from the flamboyant cures of shamans. Both are tainted with fraud and self-deception. One can find on the internet frequent outings of fake healers. James Randi's *The Faith Healers* (1989) is one of the classic exposés.

We have space to describe two famous examples. In the late 1950s, Marjoe Gortner was one of the youngest healing superstars, and the only faith healer to be enshrined in Ripley's Believe it or Not ("The World's Youngest Preacher") and the recipient of an Oscar. Marjoe (a contraction of "Mary" and "Joseph") was born of evangelists, ordained at age 3 in the Church of the Old Time Faith, and at 4½ performed his first marriage in California, dutifully recorded by a Paramount news camera. It should be noted that after this media event, California passed a law requiring that ministers who perform marriages be at least 21. For 10 years, Marjoe's parents relentlessly trotted their "miracle child" out to huge rapt audiences at Pentecostal churches and tent revivals. The little "preaching machine" (as described by his father) brought in millions of dollars. He learned well the tricks of the trade, including faking miracles, speaking in tongues, and working the crowd (Kernochan, 2007). At age 14 Marjoe had enough of this family con game and ran away, was taken on by a generous older woman, and attended college.

As a young adult, Marjoe had new college-inspired passions: smoking pot, civil rights, and revolutionary social change. Now an atheist, he returned to preaching an enlightened message, only to face indifferent and dwindling congregations. They wanted fire, blood, and brimstone, and Marjoe had changed his tune. Copying the frenzied rock 'n' roll style of the Rolling Stones he learned in college, Marjoe was again a hit. But after four and a half years he was fed up with his hypocrisy and created a movie documentary confession. *Marjoe* (the movie) won the Oscar for best documentary.

Although Peter Popoff never won an Oscar or made it into Ripley's, his story is an odd tale of renewal, and the ability of many to believe in the face of contradictory evidence. In many ways Peter Popoff is a typical faith healer. Popular in the 1980s, Popoff used many of the traditional tricks of the trade in his big-tent revivals. Elderly faithful would be wheel-chaired to Popoff, and dramatically rise and walk away. Of course, the cheering congregation was never informed that the wheel-chair riders could already walk and were simply carted to the pulpit as a courtesy. Popoff routinely showered his followers with vague prayerful promises of cure, astonishing those who later experienced recovery. Before revivals, assistants would surreptitiously obtain personal information from congregants waiting outside, information Popoff would miraculously include in his prayerful healing. Popoff was very successful, raking in 4.3 million dollars a month in 1987 (Randi, 2000).

However, Popoff's claim to fame is a remarkable encounter he had with James Randi and his assistant Steve Shaw (Randi, 1989). Frequently faith healers use the psychic trick of cold reading and offer prayers that appear specific. However, Popoff's public prayers were remarkably accurate and included names, precise diagnoses, and other personal information—all obtained from God. In 1986, Randi and Shaw performed a simple experiment that revealed that the energies used by Popoff were anything but divine. Using a secret radio receiver, Randi discovered that Popoff's wife mingled throughout the audience and casually talked with various participants. Then, using a portable radio transmitter she would tell her husband (who was wearing a miniature headphone) what to say. Popoff would then announce to thousands of thrilled worshipers the specific name, illness, and address of an actual participant. The entire charade, including wife transmissions followed by Popoff's miraculous prayers, has been recorded for posterity. First presented on Johnny Carson's *Tonight Show*, the Popoff debunking clips are popular on the internet. The Popoff ministries closed that year and Popoff declared bankruptcy. The faith healer first denied Randi's accusations, then claimed that Randi faked his recordings, and eventually claimed that he would occasionally use radio transmissions to supplement the powers of the Holy Spirit.

You might think that this would be the end of Peter Popoff. However, God works in mysterious ways. Randi presented his evidence to the United States Attorney's office, but they chose not to investigate the Popoff fraud. Since 2005 Popoff has broadcast a late-night television ministry promoting small plastic packets of his "Miracle Spring Water." Peter Popoff Ministries currently brings in $23 million a year (Charity Navigator, 2007).

Faith healing can have a dark and cruel side. Arthritis patients have discarded crutches, only to discover that their pain returns after the adrenalin (and endorphin) rush subsides. Seriously ill patients have died, after putting their faith in prayer rather than medicine. Parents have lost children they have deprived of life-sustaining medications. There is at least one documented case of a patient who may well have died of collapsed vertebrae, triggered by a faith healer's commands to run back and forth across a stage (Hines, 2003; Randi, 1989). Does faith healing work? Randi (1989) and Hines (2003) have summarized a half-dozen scientific reviews; those who have investigated claims of cure have not found a single case that stands up to scrutiny. Of course, none of this makes any difference to believers. Even Christians who

Figure 14.3   Albrecht Duerer "Study of the apostle's hands" (The praying hands), c.1508

question the reality of faith healing sometimes look aside with tolerance. However, noted physician and medical researcher Stephen Barrett, founder of quackwatch.com, sees a problem (Barrett, 2003) and argues:

- Laws to protect children from medical neglect in the name of healing should be passed and enforced. In states that allow religious exemptions from medical neglect, these exemptions should be revoked. Maybe the practice of faith healing on minors should be illegal.
- Faith healing should no longer be deductible as a medical expense.
- Reporters should be encouraged to do follow-up studies of people acclaimed to have been "healed."
- "Healers" who use trickery to raise large sums of money should be prosecuted for grand larceny.

Mainstream Christianity

Is any one of you sick? He should call the elders of the church to pray over him and anoint him with oil in the name of the lord. And the prayer offered in faith will make the sick person well.

(James 5: 14–16; New King James Version)

It is important to realize that once we put aside deliberate fraud and theatrics, the central paranormal claim of shaman priests and Pentecostal faith healers is that one can ask a supernatural entity to effect a change somewhere in the physical universe. This belief is embraced or implicitly affirmed in virtually every Christian church in America. Indeed, it is a belief held by 83% of Americans (Rice, 2003). Liberal churches frequently differentiate "cure" (restore bodily health) from "heal" (restore psychological well-being). However, even this differentiation begs the question. Most liberal churches I know have no problem praying for the psychological "wisdom," "strength," and "hope" of individuals outside of church who may have no idea they are the intended recipients of prayer. If this intervention were to work, it would be a physical miracle no less dramatic than the removal of cancer by a psychic surgeon or discarding of crutches by a faith healer. After all, "wisdom" as well as feelings of "strength" and "hope" boils down to neurophysiological events. For a distant prayer to have such a distant psychological effect, it would have to have a physical impact on the brain. However, the distinctions of liberal theologians probably fall on deaf ears, given that most Americans believe in the physical efficacy of prayer (Chapter 2).

The Evidence

If a prophet speaks in the name of the Lord and what he says does not come true, then it is not the Lord's message.

(Deut. 18: 22)

Most Americans believe that healing prayer works. Does it? This is a fair question and one that believers should not be embarrassed to ask. Both the Old and New Testaments provide numerous accounts of God-sanctioned objective tests of miracles.

The Old Testament reports at least one miracle that is actually a credible attempt at a control-group experiment. In 1 Kings (18: 20–40) the prophet Elijah challenged the prophets of Baal (a local false deity) to a test. In accordance with custom, two bulls were sacrificed, one for Baal and one for the Lord. Traditionally, worshipers would build a fire under a sacrificial bull; however, in this test no fires were set. Instead, both Baal and the Lord were called upon to provide ignition. Making the test more stringent, Elijah stood aside and exhorted the Baalites to do whatever they could to evoke supernatural intervention. They failed. He even drenched his own bull with 12 barrels of water (thereby reducing the risk of accidental spontaneous combustion or trickery). Then, in full view of everyone, skeptics and believers of both faiths, the Lord sent fire from the sky and ignited his bull. (In another experiment, reported in Daniel 1: 1–16, a vegetarian diet was found superior to a more regal meat diet. However, the involvement of the Lord in the design of this study is unclear.)

This tradition continues in the New Testament. When Thomas demanded to feel Jesus' wounds as evidence of His resurrection, Jesus had no trouble complying (John 20: 24–29). Indeed, Jesus did not command his disciples to be content with conjecture or hearsay and felt free to offer many evidential signs of His post-resurrection presence (John 20: 31). Many miracles were performed in front of hostile skeptics (even scholarly priests), with multiple witnesses, and follow-up to confirm authenticity.

Today, the identification and celebration of God's work is an important part of worship and believers offer prayers of praise and thankfulness when encountering objective evidence that prayers have been answered. Here, such evidence is celebrated. (I have yet to see a Christian thank the Lord for staging a convincing deception.) However, much of the empirical evidence for faith healing consists of testimonials. Many Christians are driven by a profound injunction to "bear witness," that is, to show in word and deed the power and truth of Jesus. In a faith healing ceremony, this may involve giving personal testimonials in front of a congregation. In activist churches this can involve helping the poor.

We have seen throughout this book that testimony is not the best type of evidence. Just as Thomas sought a verifiable empirical test, both believers and skeptics have looked beyond testimonials for evidence of the efficacy of prayer. Some of this research has appeared in serious scientific journals. Indeed, journals that have devoted special issues on spirituality and health include the *American Psychologist, Annals of Behavioral Medicine, Health Education & Behavior, Journal of Health Psychology, Psychological Inquiry*, and *Research on Aging*. Many professional organizations have special divisions devoted to spirituality and health. A surprising number of health professionals use prayer with their clients. Surveys show that a majority of social workers use intercessory prayer as a professional intervention (Hodge, 2007), a number that exceeds the number of nurses who use magical therapeutic touch (Chapter 13). I never cease to be amazed by the number of licensed healthcare professionals who believe that research has proven that distant prayer works.

Now for a reality check. What does the research say? First, we will not consider studies that examine the impact of prayer on the prayer-giver. The act of prayer may well contribute to relaxation, stress-relief, community, and personal insight in ways that do not challenge physics. Instead, we are interested in *distant intercessory prayer (IP)* where one prays for the benefit of another person. Often the prayer-giver is not in the presence of the recipient, and the recipient is often not aware that he or she is the subject of prayer. This is a legitimate paranormal topic of study given that distant intercessory prayer is encouraged and practiced in churches, and is a formal part of the liturgy in many denominations. It is among the most widely practiced forms of alternative medicine (Barnes, Powell-Griner, McFann, & Nahin, 2002).

There are at least 16 published studies on IP. Researchers have examined rheumatoid arthritis, leukemia, heart disease, substance abuse, kidney disease, fertilization, and psychological health (Masters, 2005). Masters, Spielmans, and Goodson (2006) examined 15 studies in the most comprehensive meta-analysis to date. (They chose not to include Leibovici, 2001. See page 300.) To make a long story short, *empirical evidence does not support an IP effect.*[2]

However, the popular press (and occasionally scholars who should know better) at times actually misreport negative findings as supportive (see Gerhardt, 2000; Pollack, 2001; Posner, 1998; Wallace, 1996; Chopra, 2008). Reporters often select studies of questionable merit and ignore those of quality. More frequently, the press uncritically accepts conclusions of primary authors, unaware of subsequent criticisms. Perhaps such distortions are understandable, given the emotionally charged nature of the topic and the fact that the vast majority of Americans believe in the efficacy of prayer. However, given this history of erroneous reporting, I believe it is important for a serious student of IP to be familiar with the six best prayer studies and what they actually found.

REALITY CHECK   Why might journalists and scientists misreport findings of prayer research? Discuss using the Critical Thinker's Toolkit.

The Galton Study

Francis Galton (1872), the father of modern statistics and cousin of Charles Darwin, conducted what is perhaps the first empirical study on the efficacy of prayer. He reasoned that kings, clergy, and missionaries should enjoy long lives because they are most likely the recipients of prayers. After examining the records for thousands of individuals from various occupational categories, he found no difference. Even lawyers (who he reasoned might not be the recipients of prayers, at least for health and longevity) lived as long as clergy. Galton was not particularly surprised, reasoning that insurance adjusters surely would have long ago discovered a link between piety of one's profession and longevity.

Sicher–Targ AIDS Study

The Sicher–Targ AIDS study (Sicher, Targ, Moore II, & Smith, 1998) deployed a rigorous random assignment double-blind design and is often cited as one of the better investigations on healing prayer (Bronson, 2002). On paper it looks good, convincing even to the now defunct *Western Journal of Medicine*. Indeed, the journal's editor praised this study and decided to publish in order to stimulate "more light, less dark, less heat." However, Bronson (2002) and Carroll (2009b) have uncovered a few disturbing unpublished facts that the authors left in the dark.

First, here's what the study reported. Sicher and Targ recruited 40 AIDS patients and randomly assigned them to a prayer and no-prayer control group. Participants knew prayer might be involved, but were kept blind as to which group they were in. Randomization was done by computer, and care was taken to match level of immune functioning (CD4+ level), age, and number of previous AIDS complications.

Photos were sent to a wide range of healers, including expert "professional" healers of Christian, Jewish, Buddhist, Native American, and shamanic traditions as well as practitioners from schools of bioenergetic and distant meditative healing. None met with the AIDS patients at any time during the study. The healers prayed and performed their treatments one hour a day for six consecutive days. To ensure that patients received a wide range of interventions, for each of 10 weeks they were assigned to a different mix of 10 prayer practitioners.

The results appeared to be impressive. Subjects in the control no-prayer group spent 600% more days in the hospital and contracted 300% more AIDS-related illnesses. The chances of this happening by chance are 1 out of 20. Duly impressed, the National Institutes of Health Center for Complementary and Alternative Medicine granted Targ a $1.5 million grant for additional research on AIDS patients and patients with brain cancer. (Sadly, Targ died of brain cancer in 2003, in spite of megadoses of healing prayer; Bronson, 2002.)

Four years after publication (and after the subsequent NIP grant), Po Bronson in *Wired Magazine* exposed a number of fatal deceptions in the Sicher–Targ study. These have been further elaborated by Carroll (2007). Put briefly, after data was obtained it was "unblinded" and then "reblinded" in a post-hoc attempt to scour for significant differences. To explain, the Sicher–Targ study was initially designed to compare death rates for prayer and no-prayer groups. However, one month into the study triple-drug antiretroviral AIDS therapy became popular, and worked so well that only one patient in the entire study died (not enough to make any meaningful conclusion). Disappointed, Targ and Sicher looked at AIDS-related symptoms and quality of life, and again found no differences on CD4+ levels. Finally, they looked at the last bit of data they had, hospital stays and doctors' visits, and found a significant difference. Statistically, if you keep mining the data, you will eventually find what you want.

✓

REALITY   How would you redesign the Sicher–Targ study so that
CHECK   the problems discussed are ruled out?

On the advice of a colleague Sicher and Targ obtained a list of 23 illnesses sometimes associated with AIDS and studied the files of all patients to see if any applied. Patient names were blackened out (in an attempt to "blind" the files); however, it is quite likely that Sicher could figure out the identities of patients, including whether they were in the prayer or no-prayer group, by looking at other filed information. Indeed, there are conflicting reports that Sicher at least once admitted he could figure out the identities of patients, as well as their group membership. However, he "swore he didn't remember and was therefore impartial" (Bronson, 2002). In any event, the study is no longer double-blind. Here is the fatal flaw: It is quite possible that Sicher unwittingly noticed AIDS-related illnesses in the no-prayer group, resulting in a higher illness score for this group.

None of these defects were made known to the editors of the *Western Journal of Medicine*. Had the editors been honestly and fully informed, I doubt they would have accepted the study.

Cha and Wirth Study

Cha and Wirth (2001) examined if prayer could increase the pregnancy success rate of in vitro fertilization. Two hundred and nineteen (219) Korean women were randomly divided into a treatment and no-treatment control group. Christians in Australia, Canada, and the United States prayed for successful pregnancy in the treatment group (without the knowledge of the recipients). A two-tier prayer strategy was deployed. One group of prayer-givers prayed that women in the experimental group would get pregnant. A second group of prayer-givers prayed that the prayers of the first group would be enhanced. Fifty percent of the experimental group, and only 26% of the control subjects, became pregnant, a dramatic and significant result. The study was published in the prestigious *Journal of Reproductive Medicine* and received substantial media attention.

After publication, troubling facts began to emerge concerning the study (Flamm, 2002). Wirth was convicted of 13 counts of mail fraud and 12 counts of interstate transportation of stolen money. It was revealed that he had used a variety of false identifies over the decades, including that of a dead child. Another author requested his name be removed. The *Journal of Reproductive Medicine* removed the article from their website. It appears that the study was a fraud and was never conducted (Masters et al., 2006). Yet the study is still touted as strong evidence for the efficacy of prayer.

The Krucoff MANTRA (Monitoring and Actualization of Noetic Trainings) I and II Studies

Krucoff and his colleagues (Krucoff et al., 2005) examined the effectiveness of IP presented by itself; a combination bedside treatment of prayer relaxation, imagery, music, and therapeutic touch; and no treatment on 748 patients undergoing heart surgery. After patients were randomly assigned, off-site prayers were offered by selected Buddhist, Christian, Jewish, and Muslim groups. Some patients received additional "booster prayers" in which God was asked to make the first prayers more effective. Prayer-givers were given names and medical conditions of recipients. Prayer recipients were kept blind as to whether or not they were receiving prayers. Results clearly revealed that "Neither therapy alone or combined showed any measurable treatment effect on the primary composite endpoint of major adverse cardiovascular events at the index hospital, readmission, and 6-month death or readmission" (p. 212). In other words, neither secular combination relaxation treatments nor prayer worked (Bupp, 2005).

Byrd and Harris Studies

Byrd (1988) randomly assigned 393 hospitalized cardiac patients to a prayer or no-prayer group. First names, diagnoses, and occasional clinical updates were given to "born again" intercessors. Both patients and staff were kept blind as to which group their patients were in. At least 26 medical variables were examined. Of these, the prayer patients did better on the need for diuretics, antibiotics, and ventilation therapy. The popular press frequently cites this study as strong support for the efficacy of prayer. However, critics discount it, partly because of data mining. Out of 26 variables, one might expect a handful to emerge as significant by chance alone. More seriously, this study was not, as claimed, double-blind. Byrd himself (not a neutral third party) evaluated degree of patient improvement, even though he knew which patients were prayed for. He could have unconsciously given prayer patients higher improvement scores. Finally, on the most important variables (days in hospital and use of medications), groups showed no difference.

Today, most critics have concluded that Byrd's finding was probably a spurious chance event (Tessman & Tessman, 2000).

Harris and his colleagues (1999) attempted to replicate Byrd's research using a more rigorous design. One thousand and thirteen (1,013) patients admitted to a coronary care unit were randomly assigned to a usual care control group or an IP group. Twenty-three patients were eliminated because they were hospitalized less than a day, before they could be prayed for. None of the patients or hospital staff knew the groups to which patients were assigned. Prayers were conducted by 15 intercessor teams of 5 people each on the basis of patient first name only. Prayers requested "a speedy recovery with no complications" (p. 2274). Findings were inconsistent. On none of 34 individual measures did the prayer group do better. However, when measures were combined, the IP group did better. No differences were found on the measures used by Byrd. And no differences were found on "speed of recovery," the specific request of the intervening prayer. So the prayer effect, if real, is slight.

However, one fact casts this finding into doubt. Five control and 18 prayer group patients were discharged before prayers could begin. Obviously, they were not included in the study. Why were they discharged? Because they were too healthy to be hospitalized. Note that cardiac problems are often difficult to diagnose. Frequently, simple indigestion or muscle aches may seem like a heart attack, and such patients often go to the hospital, simply to be discharged after a reassuring checkup.

Random assignment to treatment and control groups is a requirement for good research (Chapter 5). However, researchers know that because of the "clumpiness of randomness," sometimes randomization fails and one group may well start with an unexpected advantage over another. There are two strategies for dealing with this problem. First, groups can be tested after random assignment and before treatment to see if they score the same on relevant variables. If there are no initial group differences, one can feel more comfortable that random assignment has worked. Second, when initial group differences are discovered on specific variables (such as age or gender), these variables can be taken into consideration as "covariates" and factored out. Put simply, a group with an unfair starting advantage might be penalized to level the playing field. Unfortunately the Harris study suffers from an apparent flaw, failure of randomization. That over three times as many patients left the treatment group early strongly suggests that the treatment group was already healthier than the control group. This could entirely explain the obtained differences. In sum, the Harris research is fatally confounded and cannot be viewed as strong support for the efficacy of prayer (Tessman & Tessman, 2000).

Benson: The Mother of All Prayer Experiments

Herbert Benson is a well-known Harvard cardiologist, author of over 175 scientific articles and 11 books, including a number of bestselling popularizations. He is also one of the most influential scholars in stress management. Benson (1975) conducted his early work on mechanisms underlying professional relaxation techniques, arguing that clinical benefits may be due to a general anti-stress "relaxation response." Recently, he has become a passionate advocate of techniques integrating relaxation and prayer.

Given his popularity and reputation for careful, honest research, paranormal researchers took note when the Templeton Foundation honored him with a $2.4 million grant to study the effects of prayer. Aware of the criticisms of previous studies, Benson decided to conduct the most comprehensive and best-designed study ever (Benson et al., 2006). He succeeded. Indeed, David Myers, a respected scientist and self-avowed practicing Christian, summarized the excitement surrounding what could be the definitive study on prayer. Before the study was conducted, Myers proclaimed that it would be "the mother of all prayer experiments," one that "dwarfs all the others in both size and credibility" (Myers, 2000).

Benson decided to study the effects of prayer for cardiac bypass patients in six hospitals. Patients were randomly assigned to three groups: 604 received intercessory prayer but were told that they may or may not receive prayer; 597 did not receive prayer and were also told they may or may not get prayer; and 601 were told they would receive prayer and indeed were prayed for. Prayers were provided by three Christian groups who agreed to pray for "successful surgery, no complications, and quick recovery." The results were unambiguous. Groups 1 and 2 (prayer and no prayer) did not differ on any of the measured outcomes, including death rate and complications. However, something interesting happened in Group 3, those who received prayer and knew it. They were 14% *more likely* to experience complications than those who received prayer, but were not so informed. Does distant intercessory prayer work? At this point the best evidence we have is that it has no effect and may do more harm than good.

Conclusion

What are we to make of research on IP, and the Benson study? Are the negative results due to bad design? Probably not. Perhaps the results are due to the placebo effect? Not likely given that many participants were unaware that they were being prayed for. Furthermore, in the Benson study, those who knew they were receiving prayers actually did worse. Did the presence of skeptical researchers introduce a type of "negative energy" that blocked the effects of prayer? Most of the prayer researchers cited are passionate believers. Perhaps these findings call for a theological interpretation. What is God trying to tell us?

Before Benson performed his experiment, Myers (2000) predicted (as did other Christians) that he would find no prayer effect. Myers (and many learned theologians) remind believers that God is not a "celestial vending machine whose levers we pull with our prayers." The gifts we ask in prayer should be of a "spiritual" and not "material" nature.[3] After all, both the Old and New Testaments admonish us to "not put the Lord your God to the test" (Deuteronomy 6: 16; Matthew 4: 7).[4]

> **REALITY CHECK**   Work on distant intercessory prayer provides a lesson in the risks of using ancient texts as support for a claim (see Chapter 3). Discuss.

Retroactive Intercessory Prayer and a Concluding Thought on Science

One unusual prayer study deserves special note. It was published in a major medical journal by a leading medical researcher, involving the largest design ever. Furthermore, this study deployed a remarkable methodology that eliminates any possibility of a placebo effect and absolutely guarantees that the participants are unaware of the intervention they are receiving.

Yet this study has been ignored by some reviews, and celebrated by others. Indeed, the two most recent meta-analyses take opposite stances. Hodge (2007), publishing in *Research on Social Work Practice*, embraces the study while Masters et al. (2006), in the equally respected *Annals of Behavioral Medicine*, ignore it.

Leibovici (2001) examined the effects of *retroactive* intercessory prayer, that is, praying for a change to take place in the past. This intervention is a relatively recent idea and does not appear in any major holy book. It is based on the notion that an all-powerful God is not limited by the Western view that time is linear and unidirectional (past to future). In other words, God can travel (and answer prayers) back and forth in time.

Leibovici was interested in whether prayer could retroactively influence the course of bloodstream infections. First, he obtained the medical files of 3,393 patients hospitalized 4 to 10 years previously. The files were randomly divided into two groups, and one received a short prayer requesting full recovery and well-being. The patients, being in the past, were unaware that they were the recipients of prayer (a possible ethical problem because informed consent was not retroactively obtained). When Leibovici analyzed the files for both groups he found that the prayer group had spent less time in the hospital and had infections of shorter duration.

The paranormal research community has been quite comfortable with this finding, noting that it is entirely consistent with their view of the universe. The mainstream medical community has looked the other way.

I have absolutely no doubt that Leibovici performed the experiment. He is a respected scientist and his study was published in a respected journal. However, one must note that this study was published in the December issue, usually devoted to unusual and amusing articles. If one bothers to explore his work, it becomes clear what Leibovici was up to. This particular retrospective prayer study was in fact a clever, instructive parody.

Leibovici (1999) has frequently argued that much paranormal research, particularly human trials on energy and prayer-based treatments, is unethical and should not be done. He rejects the notion that all hypotheses are fair game, regardless of their origin or plausibility. The logical consequence of such a relativistic perspective is that researchers would be distracted by an unconstrained avalanche of trivial questions, and fruitful areas of study would suffer. Furthermore, empirical science was not designed to work in such an unconstrained universe and is here not particularly effective in guarding against the possibility of chance findings, bias, and fraud. Spurious yet slightly significant findings (such as the impact of a single retroactive prayer on blood infection) are inevitable.

What protects science from wasting its time with false leads is the prevailing deep model of matter and energy as described by physics. The deep model helps us pick which hypotheses to test, what tests to use, and how to interpret results. For example, a headache patient may benefit from acupuncture. The prevailing deep model of the physical universe rules out a magical energy, qi, or divine intervention, and prompts us to look for explanations consistent with the natural world, for example, the possibility of a placebo effect, distractions, or pain-reducing endorphins. The deep model does not guide us to spend millions attempting to develop a device to detect a new form of energy or consult with a shaman, televangelist, or Christian preacher for explanations.

Subjective relativists (Krippner & Achterberg, 2000) sometimes describe contemporary Western medicine as **biomedicine**, a term invented to suggest the possibility of alternative and equally valid forms of medicine not consistent with the prevailing deep model. Leibovici rejects such thinking and reminds us that Western medicine is best described as **scientific medicine**, medicine based on empirical testing and the prevailing deep model of the physical universe. He goes on to state that the deep model for paranormal alternative medicine is at best magical thinking, a strange and empty model that specifies no agreed-upon measurable entity or force (qi? God? the Devil? ghosts? quantum entanglement? the Flying Spaghetti Monster?). As such, the paranormal deep model offers little help in screening hypotheses, suggesting new hypotheses, or telling us when to stop hypothesizing. This has one fatal consequence. The paranormal deep model fails to tell us when we cannot explain away unwanted findings with a never-ending flood of ad hoc rationalizations. Whereas the prevailing physics-based deep model permits disconfirming tests, the paranormal model renders a paranormal hypothesis unfalsifiable.

REALITY CHECK   What is a good scientific theory? Compare the views of Leibovici and other experts as discussed in this book (Chapter 5). In addition, should researchers avoid studying the effects of prayer?

15

Creationism, Intelligent Design, and God

In the contemporary annals of the paranormal, perhaps the greatest story being told is the debate over creationism and evolution. "Young earth" creationists posit that God created the universe as described in the book of Genesis. The world is only 6,000–10,000 years old (or "young"), created in six days. Then came the Flood, Noah's Ark, and eventually Jesus. Creationist thinking has made considerable headway. Up to half of Americans believe its central claims. It is a view that dominates Christian publishing. Presidents Carter (2005), Reagan (Holden, 1980), G. H. W. Bush (Boston, 1988), and G. W. Bush (Mooney, 2005b) have espoused creationist views. However, creationism is controversial, rejected by serious scientific organizations, and even condemned by the European Union as a threat to individual rights (Council of Europe, 2007). Outside of Bible colleges, it is not taught in biology classes.

The Great Debate

The goal of many creationists has nothing to do with science. Instead, it is to save America from immoral, atheistic, scientific secularism by Christianizing all aspects of society, including education, business, and politics. To this end, they hope to begin by driving a "wedge" (Forrest & Gross, 2007) into the great "log" of secular biology classes. (And perhaps create a pile of secular firewood for burning troublesome murals—see later.) This mission has evolved through at least three stages. The first attempt was to inject the biblical creation story undiluted as an alternative "theory" in biology classes. This was struck down in 1987 by the U.S. Supreme court as a serious violation of the constitution's first amendment establishment clause that separates church and state ("Congress shall make no law respecting an establishment of religion, or prohibiting the free exercise thereof."). Next, creationists disguised creationism as intelligent design (ID), claiming that the universe is so complex that it must have a supernatural, and intelligent, designer. With a wink and a nod, students would assume that the ID is likely the Christian God (rather than a space alien, a being from the future, or the Flying Spaghetti Monster). This was struck down as religion in disguise in 2005 by a landmark case in Dover, Pennsylvania.

It is quite possible the next strategy will be to require that biology classes teach "controversies concerning evolution," a wedge that would permit eventual insertion of ID and creationist ideas. Similarly, some creationists advocate that biology classes teach the "strengths and weaknesses" of evolution theory (Beil, 2008), weasel words (Chapter 4) that would again permit introduction of creationism through the back door, using the argument from ignorance (Chapter 4). Perhaps such strategies will go nowhere given that they would also permit focusing on the "controversies" and "weaknesses" of all sciences, and thereby introducing astrology in astronomy class, the flat earth theory in geography, witchcraft brews in chemistry, extrasensory perception in communication class, ghost theory in architecture (haunted houses), Qi in physical education, the stork theory of reproduction in health class, and holographic urine theory in cooking class. If we follow this yellow brick road, there will be truly no time left for real science.

Kitzmiller v. Dover Area School District

It was a week before Christmas in the small and sleepy town of Dover, Pennsylvania. In a major courtroom clash between creationism and science, a federal judge barred a Pennsylvania public school district from introducing creationism in biology class. The trial was an international sensation, involving top creationists and scientists. In the end, it redefined a centuries-old debate.

We begin innocently enough with a student art project, a 16-foot mural that depicted evolution with a row of marching figures, starting with apes and ending with man (Mooney, 2005a). The Dover school board had voted to require science teachers to introduce intelligent design as an alternative to Darwin's theory of evolution, the first school board in America to do this. Teachers refused and parents sued, leading to a landmark federal court case, *Kitzmiller v. Dover Area School District*. Dover erupted in controversy, and the student mural of evaluation was mysteriously torched and destroyed.

In the trial ID creationists, biologists, and philosophers presented their best arguments. Of the many excellent books and articles on the ID creationism debate, the public television NOVA documentary, *Judgment Day: Intelligent Design on Trial* (Nova, 2007), is among the clearest and most objective. (However, by presenting the best arguments of both sides, it skims some of the less reputable tactics of ID creationists; see Forrest & Gross, 2007; Lebo, 2008; Prothero, 2007; Shermer, 2006).

Figure 15.1   Ape to man (Dover student mural destroyed by zealot arsonist)

Darwin and evolution

Here is a synopsis of the debate. Although most people have heard of Charles Darwin, few know that he entered college with the long-term aim of becoming an Anglican parson. Indeed, he believed in elements of creationism (Barlow, 1958). In 1831 Darwin joined the ship *H.M.S. Beagle* as the official naturalist and embarked on a 5-year voyage around the world. During this voyage he noted how species changed from place to place along the coast of South America, especially the Galàpagos islands. Although evolutionary ideas were a part of the Zeitgeist of Darwin's age, Darwin's honest questioning and observation led him to discover a mechanism indicating how it worked, natural selection.

In 1859 Charles Darwin published his theory of evolution in *The Origin of Species*. He proposed that different species evolve through a process of natural selection and survival of the fittest. In any particular generation, mutations can alter an organism, for example, adding a limb, subtracting an organ, modifying a process, and so on. Most mutations are fatal, but an occasional mutation is an improvement. When sea creatures mutated with fins, they could swim. Because these improved organisms were better able to survive, they were more likely to have offspring, which in turn would carry on the mutation. Over hundreds of millions of years, bad mutations are sorted out and improved mutations add up, resulting in organisms

Figure 15.2   Charles Darwin

remarkably fit for their environments. The evidence for evolution is considerable, including recently unearthed fossils of transitional "missing link" creatures (such as fish-like animals that evolved from fish and eventually into land animals), and complex genetic similarities between related species. Indeed, humans (including both evolutionists and creationists) are only a chromosome away from being chimpanzees.

ID creationists (including Darwin at one time) argue that their God created each species independently and that different species are not linked through a common ancestry. As evidence, creationists often invoke a variety of theological (not scientific) arguments, goading scientists into unfamiliar terrain. First is the **argument from design: grand watchmaker version**:

> Anything that is complicated must be the product of an intelligent designer.
> The universe is complicated.
> Therefore the universe was created by an intelligent designer.

A grand watch requires a grand watchmaker, first posed by the Roman philosopher, lawyer, and statesman Cicero (1972) who argued that the complexity of a sundial implies a purposeful and intelligent sundial designer.

REALITY CHECK   Can you find any logical problems in the argument from design: grand watchmaker version?

The argument from design can actually be applied to many paranormal claims. For example, only a remarkable mystical nonphysical energy, qi (chi), can explain such diverse treatments as healing touch, acupuncture, tai chi, psychic surgery, and kundalini yoga. Of course, this begs the question (Chapter 4). And either none of these are real, or qi exists (a false dilemma).

Those on the other side of this argument might view the universe as a "cosmos half empty" and note all the mistakes in creation, such as sickness, ignorance, species extinction, and computers that never work right. God would have to be quite inept, or malicious, to create the universe we are stuck with.

ID creationists focus on a subtle theological variation of the argument from design, **irreducible complexity**. The notion of irreducible complexity states that some biological structures are so complex that if you remove a single part they will cease to function. Furthermore, a component part is useless in itself, and therefore had no adaptive reason to survive, let alone be part of a larger evolutionary process. Thus, the complete structure must have emerged spontaneously in full final form. The most famous example presented by ID creationists is the bacterial flagellum, perhaps the only example of a living organism with an actual functioning propeller as a tail. For years this remarkable structure mystified scientists. Indeed, it appeared to be irreducibly complex. However, biologists eventually discovered that the ID creationists were wrong, and that the bacterial flagellum could indeed be partially taken apart and still work, not as a propeller but as a syringe (useful for injecting disease). ID creationists are prone to use a shotgun strategy, showering biologists with marvelously complex examples that defy explanation. How could evolution possibly lead to such miracles as the human eye or immune system? In every case, when biologists carefully study a claimed miracle of complexity, they discover how it is indeed not irreducibly complex and evolved from simpler structures.

Another variation of the argument from design is the **anthropic principle**, the notion that the universe is fine-tuned for life (Barrow & Tipler, 1988). To understand, one has to begin with the idea that in the universe there are certain constants that are the same everywhere. These include the speed of light, the amount of matter in the universe, and the strength of the force that binds atomic nuclei. Everywhere in the universe these are exactly the same. Rees (2000) argues that there are six such "cosmic numbers," and if any one of them were even slightly different, the universe could not permit life. Thus, the universe appears to be fine-tuned for life, suggesting a fine-tuning entity, a grand designer, a god at the control panel. This is a fascinating and important philosophical argument that belongs in a philosophy, not science class. Skeptics argue that there is no experiment one could perform to test the cosmic effects of adjusting the constants of physics. And one can just as easily speculate that there are an infinite number of universes, and just by chance a few pop up fine-tuned for life. Or perhaps it is not an accident that the cosmic numbers are what they are; maybe some yet-to-be-discovered grand unifying theory will show that the values of cosmic numbers are what they are for a very good scientific reason.

Creationists also cite the theological **cosmological argument: the first cause**. Here one begins with the presumption that everything has to be caused by something. So considering the entire universe, what created it? Logically, this cause would have to be larger and greater than what it caused, that is, supernatural. Skeptics reply, "Who created the first cause? Who created God?" and argue that the argument of the first cause traps us in a logical black hole, an absurd **infinite regression**, and the only way out is to apply Occam's razor by accepting the simplest explanation. The universe just is. Or maybe there are multiple universes.

Philosopher George H. Smith (1979) has noted a troublesome reason why such arguments are by definition untestable. How do we know if something is paranormal, and not the result of a natural process? Our test is to see if it differs in some important way from what we know to be natural. An artifact of intelligent design would have to contain something that does not appear in nature. But if God created everything, all of the natural world, everything is a God artifact. This means that there is nothing left to compare. One can never look for a God artifact that differs from something natural because everything is a God artifact.

An important component of the debate is a consideration of what is science. First, we have seen that creationists frequently use untestable theological arguments to support empirical claims. The arguments from design, irreducible complexity, the anthropic principle, and the cosmological argument are purely theological notions that may well belong in high school or college classes. But they are not science and should not be taught in science class. Second, creationists display a misunderstanding of the nature of science. Often they claim that Darwinian evolution is "only a theory" and should be presented fairly with other equally worthy theories, notably ID creationism. This confuses everyday and scientific uses of the term "theory." In everyday usage, a theory is a hunch. You may have a theory of who swiped the cookies. In science, a theory is the highest form of scientific explanation, one that has withstood numerous tests, and accounts for more facts than any competing theory. As we explained in Chapter 5, a theory is falsifiable (testable), productive, comprehensive, and simple. According to these criteria, the theory of evolution may well be among the best theories science has invented. It is falsifiable and productive, and has generated thousands of testable hypotheses. Sometimes these hypotheses involve real-time experiments (changing the environment for fruit flies, and observing them evolve through their fleeting generations) and careful observation of existing evidence (digging up fossils in search of missing-link transitional organisms). It is comprehensive, tying together mountains of evidence from geology, biology, chemistry, and even astronomy. As Isaac Asimov has stated, "the strongest of all indications as to the fact of evolution and the truth of the theory of natural selection is that all the independent findings of scientists in every branch of science, when they have anything to do with biological evolution at all, *always* strengthen the case and *never* weaken it" (Asimov & Gish, 1981).

In contrast, ID creationism fails miserably as a theory. It has difficulty producing testable hypotheses and some versions are probably untestable. Instead of generating hypotheses, ID creationism is essentially negativistic (arguing from ignorance), poking holes rather than proposing. Although ID creationism has wide scope in that God is posited to have created everything, this assertion explains nothing. What court would accept "the Devil did it" as a theory explaining a bank robbery? Any event, as well as its antithesis, can be explained as "God's will." Most seriously, ID creationism fails the test of simplicity. The God hypothesis begs more questions than it answers. When? Where? How? Which God? Furthermore, ID creationism has the troubling complexity that it cannot be adopted "without discarding all of modern biology, biochemistry, geology, astronomy—in short, without discarding all of science" (Asimov & Gish, 1981). In sum, ID creationism is a supernatural explanation, and as such it is a "science stopper" (Miller, 2007).

REALITY CHECK   Show how some creationist thinking involves a false dilemma and the argument from ignorance.

Things Great and Small

All of the paranormal claims discussed in this book can lead to questions about God and the supernatural. Indeed, every major textbook on the paranormal has occasionally ventured into theological discussion. We have seen that creationists often use theological arguments (calling it "theistic science" (Forrest & Gross, 2007). Parapsychological researchers (Chapter 12) have seriously hypothesized that the elusive nature of psi is due to a Higher Consciousness attempting to lead us by inducing a sense of mystery (Kennedy, 2000). However, there are problems in going where angels fear to tread. For example, eminent researchers of a Christian persuasion have argued that legitimacy of a research topic can be partly determined by Christian theological considerations ("Given that the IP [intercessory prayer] literature lacks a theoretical or *theological base* [my emphasis] and has failed to produce significant findings in controlled trials, we recommend that further resources not be allocated to this line of research"; Masters, Spielmans, & Goodson, 2006, p. 21). Clearly, when perfectly reasonable scientists let theology influence their thinking, silly things begin to happen. If this point is not already clear, I offer for your contemplation the following composite theological discussion:

> Mainline churches are comfortable proclaiming that Darwin doesn't threaten religion. God created everything, including evolution (Scott, 2004). However, this does not settle important theological issues. Did God create evolution outright, or did he create an infinite number of universes, some favoring evolution, some not (Brumfiel, 2006)? But then is God really necessary when by sheer luck an occasional universe will emerge that is conducive to life? And perhaps there are multiple multiverses (Susskind, 2006; Tegmark, 2003). Are there multiple gods?
>
> From a different perspective, perhaps Darwin's willingness to question, and not evolution, is the real challenge to religion. Questioning can reveal embarrassing gaps in our understanding. If one were to accept that biblical creationism is fair game for honest and fearless questioning, one would have to play by the same rules when considering all biblical miracle stories, from Moses and the burning bush to the virgin birth and resurrection of Jesus. But if we do this, what's left? Then again, maybe God is in the gaps, those mysterious areas science has yet to explain (Bube, 1971). But these gaps always seem to be shrinking as science advances. Is God shrinking? Maybe God can't shrink because when he created everything, gaps and all, he withdrew, never to be seen again. Of course, all of this may be completely beyond human understanding. God may work in mysterious ways, forever unknowable to us. As evolutionary biologist Haldane (1927) mused, "My own suspicion is that the Universe is not only queerer than we suppose, but queerer than we *can* suppose" (p. 286). As the weirdness of quantum physics has led a few award-winning physicists to suspect, perhaps the basics of the universe simply cannot be understood by science (templeton.org). Does this imply the existence of a deity that is inconceivably intelligent, or that humans are inconceivably stupid? Of course, there's Pascal's Wager (Rescher, 1985), which goes something like this. If there's a God, and you believe, you win. If there's no God, and you still believe, you lose nothing. If there's no God, and you don't believe anyway, you still lose nothing. But if there's a God, and you don't believe, you lose. So the best bet is to believe. This gets worse if God is a jealous God. Are the Gods of other religions equally jealous? Then Pascal's Wager becomes "Pascal's Dilemma." But then, what if God simply wants us to stop our chattering and be quiet?

Important as such questions may be, they are not science. Mixing science and theology is a risky venture, pseudoscience at its worst. Biologist and paleontologist Steven Jay Gould (1999) has offered a popular way out, one that merits some discussion. Perhaps religion and science represent Nonoverlapping Magisteria (NOMA). Specifically, science is a "magisterium" that covers the empirical world of scientific fact and theory; religion considers questions of meaning, beauty, and moral value. This position is similar to that taken by The National Academy of Sciences (Steering Committee on Science and Creationism, 2008). But this brings up more theological questions.

First, a good theory indeed can be immensely beautiful. Second, honesty, truth, and openness are powerful scientific values. Third, if religion doesn't deal with the physical world, then religious people shouldn't pray for changes in the physical world (healing, peace, etc.) or changes in the brains of distant leaders (wisdom, compassion). But they do in just about every house of worship I know.

A more serious problem with NOMA is that science most certainly can have deep implications for religious claims. To elaborate, consider one venerable religious figure, seen by many as the savior of humanity. The story, at times contested, has been around for ages. This figure was both man and God. His miraculous virgin birth was heralded by a star in the East and witnessed by shepherds. He was baptized at age 30 by a man who was later beheaded. He cast out demons, healed the sick, restored sight to the blind, and stilled the waters of the sea. He was crucified (along with two thieves), buried in a tomb, and resurrected after three days. His stirring criterion for salvation has moved humanity for millennia: give bread to the hungry, water to the thirsty, and clothing to the naked.

It may surprise you that this savior of humanity is ancient Egyptian god *Horus* (Harpur, 2004; Robinson, 2008), major falcon-headed deity who lived thousands of years BC. The pharaohs were his incarnations. However, modern scientific scholarship questions most of the claims concerning Horus. If we doubt Horus, what about the moral injunctions in his name? What about compassion? Human sacrifice? If Horus is an illusion, are we free to pick and choose? How? Perhaps compassion is an intrinsically human value developed through millennia of natural selection. Society may eventually value compassion regardless of whatever religion may or may not be popular. After all, the "golden rule" appears in virtually every system of morality. Science indeed poses troublesome moral questions to the theologically inclined. Is there anything left after the scientific explanation? If so, people still believe with great passion.

Gould's NOMA seems to raise more questions than it resolves and I do not have the answers. Yes, science has much to say about paranormal claims. Yes, such claims often ring true regardless of what science may conclude.

But when they stir theological musings, I suggest we leave it to the theologians to sort things out. However, there is a different type of question that persists, perhaps the one hopeful inhabitant that remains after Pandora's box has been emptied.

> **REALITY CHECK** "Researchers should not study questions that challenge or are inconsistent with the theology of a specific religion." Discuss.

In the back pages of the current discussions on God, one occasionally finds an interesting point of agreement between passionate atheists and believers, for example, Sam Harris (*The End of Faith*, 2004) and Christian Bishop Shelby Spong (*Jesus for the Non-Religious*, 2007). It is an invitation to take very seriously that which one experiences to be most profound and fills one with awe and mystery, perhaps even *mysterium tremendum*. For example, you might have a strong feeling of being "at one" with a lover. Reason tells you that this is not literally true for you indeed have separate brains and bodies. But in a different and very real sense it is true; you share similar values and are committed and attentive to each other's welfare.

These are spiritual states of mind. Gazing at the stars of Sagittarius, the constellation viewed by astrologers millennia ago, we might feel centered in the cosmos and at one with humanity. Such strong feelings may prompt us to think that a quantum entanglement physically links us with heavenly forces or imbues us with superhuman psychic powers. This may or may not be the case. However, a spiritual state, such as a sense of "oneness," need not be a distraction. Seen clearly, it can inspire a humble appreciation of our true place in the universe. It can guide us to handle life's onslaughts with greater equanimity. It can prompt us to care more generously for those in our human family. And perhaps, for one precious moment, it may awaken us from our daydreams of centaurs and open our eyes to things wise and wonderful, the searing beauty of the universe as it is.

The Flying Spaghetti Monster, Pastafarian Quatrains, and the Role of Parody in Paranormal Scholarship

The creationism debate took a sudden and unexpected turn in June, 2005. In a small town in Oregon, Bobby Henderson (age 24) had had enough.

Figure 15.3   Jon Smith's vision of the Flying Spaghetti Monster

Frustrated with the Kansas Board of Education's debate on teaching creationism side by side with Darwin's theory of natural selection, he wrote an open letter formally requesting that his deity, the Flying Spaghetti Monster (FSM), be given equal time. Here's his request:

> Let us remember that there are multiple theories of Intelligent Design. I and many others around the world are of the strong belief that the universe was created by a Flying Spaghetti Monster. It was He who created all that we see and all that we feel. We feel strongly that the overwhelming scientific evidence pointing towards evolutionary processes is nothing but a coincidence, put in place by Him. (www.venganza.org)

Bobby backed his request with the threat of legal action. Three members of the Board replied and strongly sympathized with his position (they were the dissenting votes in the debate). A supporter of biblical creation theory warned "It is a serious offense to mock God." This simple event gave birth to a new religion, "Flying Spaghetti Monsterism," or "Pastafarianism," complete with its own Gospel (Henderson, 2006).

Most scholars view Pastafarianism as a parody and place it in a growing tradition of faux religions that use humor to highlight the absurdities and foibles of various religions, sects, cults, or supernatural and paranormal belief systems. Some, such as Summum (www.summum.org) and the Church of Reality (www.churchofreality.org), are presented by advocates as actual religions (with tax-exempt status), although outsiders might note satirical elements. Summum has actually been the center of a heated Supreme Court debate over its right to erect a monument honoring its "Seven Aphorisms." The problem was that Summum placed its monument in a public park next to a monument of the Ten Commandments, conjuring up issues of separation of church and state (Liptak, 2008).

Notable examples of unambiguous parodies include the religion of Jedi (of Star Wars fame), the Invisible Pink Unicorn (www.invisiblepinkunicorn.com), the Great Pumpkin (a Santa-Claus holiday figure in Charles M. Schultz's *Peanuts* cartoon series), The Western Branch of American Reform Presbylutheranism (a parody from *The Simpsons* television series), and

Frisbeetarianism (a belief system invented by comedian George Carlin that posits that when you die your soul lands on a roof where it gets stuck). The Church of the Flying Spaghetti Monster is considered by outsiders to be a parody, although its founder appears to insist it is an actual religion (www. venganza.org):

> Some claim that the church is purely a thought experiment, satire, illustrating that Intelligent Design is not science, but rather a pseudoscience manufactured by Christians to push Creationism into public schools. These people are mistaken. The Church of FSM is real, totally legit, and backed by hard science. Anything that comes across as humor or satire is purely coincidental.

A Pastafarian Primer

Pastafarianism has attracted widespread popular and scholarly attention. Henderson has wagered that "the Church of the Flying Spaghetti Monster can produce more academic endorsements for our theory than Intelligent Design proponents can for theirs" (Venganza.org, 2007). Dozens of university scholars have already written support for his vision that the universe was created by the Flying Spaghetti Monster. Philosophers have argued: "Prove that it didn't happen!" Theologians provided logical evidence. ("The Flying Spaghetti Monster is a being with every perfection. Existence is a perfection. Therefore, the Flying Spaghetti Monster exists.") Scientists have pointed out that there is as much tangible evidence for the FSM as there is for creationism and ID. Biologists have noted the uncanny visual similarities between spaghetti and the convoluted wrinkles of the human brain (and squirming colonies of bacteria). Archeologists have pointed to photographs of ancient rock structures (like the many-armed dancing goddess Shiva) resembling noodles. And of course one popular understanding of the entire universe is string ("noodle?") theory. Hundreds have posted testimonial photos suggestive of the FSM's noodly handiwork. Even world-famous atheist Richard Dawkins (2006) enthusiastically announced his FSM epiphany in *The God Delusion*: "... you just *know* it's true ..." (p. 52). It is not surprising that the Flying Spaghetti Monster has received substantial media attention and appeared in *Wired News*, the *New York Times*, and *Scientific American*. Today it boasts of "millions, if not thousands of devout worshipers" (venganza.org). He has even been the focus of a scholarly presentation at a prestigious theological conference (Horn & Johnston, 2007).

The initial beliefs of the Pre-Reformation Church of the Flying Spaghetti Monster are sketchy. An invisible and undetectable Flying Spaghetti Monster created the universe, starting with a mountain, trees, and "midgit." Evidence pointing toward Darwin's theory was intentionally planted by the FSM to distract and test us. However, the existing evidence clearly shows that "global warming, earthquakes, hurricanes, and other natural disasters are a direct effect of the shrinking numbers of Pirates since the 1880s." As the number of pirates has declined, warming and disasters have increased. This fact has yet to be challenged by scientists or theologians.

Bobby has enunciated a few additional beliefs and practices:

1. The FSM guides human affairs with His "Noodly Appendage."
2. The official ending for prayers to the FSM is "Ramen," not "Amen."
3. In heaven there's a stripper factory and a beer volcano.
4. Every Friday is a religious holiday. In addition, the holidays of all religions must be observed.
5. FSM teachers must be "baptized" by "holy meat sauce."
6. It is disrespectful to teach of the FSM without wearing His chosen outfit, full pirate regalia.
7. It is polite to end conversations with the words "May you be touched by His noodly appendage."

These beliefs are outlined in the *Gospel of the Flying Spaghetti Monster* (Henderson, 2006), a must-read for serious students of the paranormal or supernatural, one that illustrates many of the concepts of this text.

The Pastafarian Quatrains

Jon Smith (a pseudonym used by the author of this book for security reasons) has discovered a remarkable fact about the Flying Spaghetti Monster, one that serves as a satirical object lesson for many of the principles discussed in this book, especially the law of very large numbers, meaningless coincidence, confirmation bias, and *reductio ad absurdum*.

Smith's scholarship is based on the anagram. An anagram, of course, rearranges the letters in one word to form another. For example, "Debit card" = "*Bad credit*," "Slot machines" = "*Cash lost in 'em*" (also "*Cash? Lost mine!*"), "Dormitory" = "*Dirty room*" (as well as "*O My! Torrid*" and "*O My! Rid rot!*"), "Christian" = "*Rich at sin*" (or "*Rich saint*"), and "Skeptic" = "*Sick pet*" (or "*It pecks*"). It is easy to see how one might think anagrams are actually a source of wisdom (anagrams are true "*as a rare argument*"). Indeed, throughout history anagrams have been linked to the mysterious and the occult (Curl, 1996; Michaelsen, 1998). Examples can be found in the Bible, the Talmudic tradition, and in the quatrains of Nostradamus.

Smith used Anagram Genius (Tunstall-Pedoe, 2007), a popular anagram-revealing program, to discover that "Flying Spaghetti Monster" yields at least 3,200,000 legal anagrams, or "spaghettigrams." Out of these, 128 spaghettigrams can be arranged into four-line quatrains to form a remarkable religious epic poem with a genuine message (Smith, 2008). At first, this discovery might appear to be of paranormal significance. However, few people realize that three words can yield so many anagrams. And with such an initial pool, one can readily select anagrams that convey a message.

The *Pastafarian Quatrains* tell the tale of a battle between "Truth" and "Illusion" (perhaps science and pseudoscience) symbolized by the "Angel" and the "Serpent." The search for truth is one of applying rational analysis and Occam's razor. The Serpent fights such efforts through obfuscating illusion, as clearly depicted in these spaghettigrams (again, each an anagram of FSM):

Sting of almighty Serpent
Temptingly fights reason
Petty mangler of insights
Floating pestering myths

Ghastly omnipresent gift
Myth generating flip/toss
Fight gentlest parsimony
Petty sign of this mangler

Armed with a set of confirmation biases consistent with the present text, it is easy to read meaning into these anagrams. Those who embrace pseudoscience "mangle" and distort the insights of science to their own end. They present their own tempting but irrational and pestering myths. Pseudoscientific myths are often the product of meaningless coincidence ("flip/toss" as with dice or a coin). Most important, such myths are not parsimonious, not in the spirit of Occam's razor.

The protagonist in this epic story is "Piggy," a figure initially tormented and confused by the Serpent's temptations. The Quatrains outline a path to truth. It involves avoiding the "two temptations" of "petty anger" (*"Angry flight to emptiness"*) and the "chains of passion" (*"Filthy G-String poets. Amen!"*). One must follow a three-step path involving virtuous study of the "gospel" (the Quatrains, of course—*"Itsy gem of plain strength"*), meditation (*"Forget simplest anything," "Ghost-empty self-training"*), and courage.

Eventually, Piggy makes a remarkable double discovery that enables him to triumph. He realizes that he is indeed "Pigasus," an iconic symbol frequently used by paranormal skeptics ("I'll believe it when pigs fly") and the inspiration behind the "Pigasus Award," James Randi's famous annual presentation of the year's best example of paranormal fraud (www.randi.org). The epic concludes with a monumental encounter between Pigasus and none other than the Flying Spaghetti Monster. The concluding spaghettigrams present the reader with an unanswered question:

> Flying Pig met Honest Star
> Flying Spaghetti Monster!
> Flying Pig's anthem … or test?

Central to Smith's scholarly analysis is the observation that each quatrain line is a precise anagram of "Flying Spaghetti Monster." As such the quatrains have apparent profundity, and (satirically) might be considered as paranormal truths, "direct from the FSM." (Note how "direct" is used as a weasel word.) Extending this parody analysis (applying *reductio ad absurdum*), Smith ponders what would happen if various sects of Monsterism were to emerge and follow the path that other world religions have taken. Would religious wars erupt over various interpretations of anagrams such as "*Mighty angel tests porn*"? (Yes, another FSM anagram.) Would rival monastic groups emerge based on conflicting interpretations of "*filthy G-string poets*"? And this is just the beginning. Again, there are at least 3,200,000 computer-generated spaghettigrams ("*Hefty, grim instant gospel*") – enough material to start a thousand religious wars. And decades of debate among paranormal researchers. (For the entire Quatrains, with commentary, see Smith, 2008).

The Message

What is the true lesson of the Flying Spaghetti Monster and the Pastafarian Quatrains? As with much wisdom literature, different people have different interpretations. Perhaps we should take spaghettigrams literally. It's been done before. Maybe they are metaphors. However, you may find it helpful to turn to this enigmatic quatrain:

Basic Information:

> Nice, insane cosmic legend?
> Concise elegance in minds?
> Angelic omniscience ends

These are not spaghettigrams. "Basic information" is an anagram of "confirmation bias." Check it out. And each of the remaining three lines is an anagram of "meaningless coincidence." I leave it to you to figure this out.

16

The Reality Checkup

Using Your Toolkit

The Critical Thinker's Toolkit is essential gear for anyone who hikes the jungle of pseudoscience and paranormal claims. In this chapter we walk through why and how to use it. Most important, the Toolkit is more than a classroom instructional aid. Scholars and scientists will find ways of tightening up paranormal research. Journalists will discover new ways of investigating fantastic claims. People of faith can use it to evaluate the authenticity of questionable supernatural claims. Specifically, here is why your Toolkit is important:

- Being smart, skeptical, or highly educated isn't enough. Throughout this text you have encountered many instances where famous and highly qualified (even Harvard educated) scientists, philosophers, and the most skeptical of journalists have been fooled. Sometimes it takes a magician to see the trick. The Toolkit helps level the playing field of the paranormal.
- Pseudoscience can be quite convincing. An apparently credible expert, with a little bit of logic and science, can persuade us not to investigate further. The Toolkit provides some protection against premature closure of inquiry.
- Confirmation bias as well as selective and constructive memory bias can prompt us to look only for support for a paranormal claim, and avoid the task of exploring disconfirming evidence. The Toolkit keeps our eyes and minds open and focused.
- Paranormal claims can overwhelm an unaided critical thinker. When a claim doesn't pass a test, a paranormal true believer may apply an unending flurry of ad hoc explanations. Each in itself may fail the test, calling for additional ad hoc explanations. The result is snowballing rationalizations. This is hard to counter piecemeal, one claim at a time. The Toolkit helps you see the bigger picture and recognize when ad hoc rationalization has gone wild.

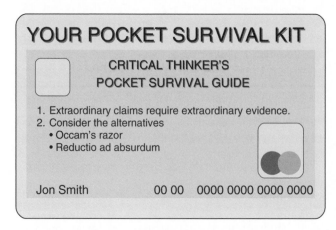

Figure 16.1   Critical Thinker's Pocket Survival Kit

- The Toolkit helps you stop. Paranormal claims may be true. However, there comes a point of diminishing returns, when we need to stop trying and go on living. The Toolkit helps you make that decision by organizing a checklist of alternative explanations.

Most important, the Toolkit encourages good habits of critical thinking. A careless thinker may apply one thinking tool, and then finish when the job isn't done. Proper Toolkit use teaches you to keep your mind open and systematically consider alternatives. Specifically, here's how to do it.

The Reality Checkup

Throughout this book we have been conducting *reality checks* by applying specific Toolkit questions. When we subject an extended paranormal claim to all Toolkit questions we perform a *reality checkup*. Start by identifying the extraordinary claim that interests you. Then apply your Critical Thinker's Pocket Survival Kit. Ask yourself if a paranormal claim requires extraordinary evidence and might have alternative explanations. In many instances, this will get you by.

After identifying your claim you may choose to evaluate someone else's presentation, perhaps a website, blog, book, article, movie, or television documentary. Alternatively, you might begin by writing a summary report of what advocates are presenting, drawing from many sources.

The Reality Checkup Report

Start your report by describing the claim in detail. What support is given by those who believe? What is the history of the claim? How prevalent is it? If the claim is paranormal, where does it fit on the Continuum (Chapter 1)? What are the actual and potential consequences of accepting this claim? Can you point to any historical consequences? What might the consequences be if the claim were true? Use extensive quotes and cite your quotes.

If you are writing a Reality Checkup Report as a class assignment, I find it useful to begin with a composite claim from the perspective of advocates. Integrate information from several websites. Jon Smith's report on Urine Therapy is an example of such a composite. If you are particularly ambitious, go on an internet scavenger hunt and see if you can find illustrations of each of the eight Toolkit reality checks. Specifically, look for websites on your chosen topic that:

1. use questionable sources;
2. make logical errors;
3. misuse observation (scientific tests and theory)
4. present information that may simply be an oddity of nature or the world of numbers and statistics;
5. present information that may have been the result of perceptual error or trickery;
6. present information that may reflect memory error;
7. present claims that may reflect the placebo effect;
8. present claims that may reflect sensory error or hallucination.

Here are some pointers on writing a report:

- Evaluate the support presented by the claimant. Consider sources, logic, and use of observation (scientific tests and theory). Do not simply label problematic claims. Describe why they are problems.
- Students often have difficulty identifying logical flaws. You may be tempted to brand a claim "illogical" simply because you disagree. Resist this urge and look for examples of the specific logical problems listed in your text.
- Sometimes advocates actually describe a scientific experiment. Usually, they won't give you enough detail to make an intelligent evaluation. If you have the time, go to the primary source, usually a research publication. Otherwise, simply note what information is missing in the report given, and why this information is important to know. When

advocates do not describe actual scientific experiments, they often present a scientific-sounding theory, or at least a disconnected collection of theoretical propositions (which you may have to gather and patch together). Here, evaluate their explanations according to our criteria of a good theory.

- Consider alternative explanations as suggested by the Toolkit. Do not simply label a claim:

Those who wear magnetic bracelets claim that the magnetism makes them healthier. This could be a **placebo effect**.

Instead, make a detailed case for your alternative explanation:

Those who wear magnetic bracelets claim that magnetism makes them healthier. This could be a placebo effect. This hypothesis is consistent with various elements of magnet therapy that also characterize effective placebos. For example, magnet therapy is presented by true believers to true believers. Belief of the presenter and recipient is known to augment the placebo effect. Magnet therapy involves a complicated treatment procedure in which specific body parts are carefully identified, magnet coils are carefully attached to the body, and so on. The complexity of a placebo is a factor that enhances effectiveness. Magnet therapy is presented with a complicated but scientific-sounding theory, just the type of theory that can enhance a placebo. Magnet bracelets often leave a metallic stain on one's wrist, sometimes described as evidence that magnet energy is working. Good placebos are active, and have negative side effects. And of course, good magnetic therapies, like good placebos, aren't cheap.

- You may not find examples of all alternative explanations. Discuss what you find.
- Most of your alternative explanations will be in the form of plausible hypotheses. You may have no evidence that your hypothesis is actually supported. However, describe in detail the type of experiment one would have to conduct to rule out your hypothesis. If the claim cannot be subjected to the type of study you suggest, explain why this is a problem. Why is your alternative hypothesis important? Why should those who are tempted to accept a paranormal claim first consider your hypothesis? Based on what you've read, can you speculate on how a true believer might discount your hypothesis, or your results if you actually conducted your experiment? How might you respond?

CTT SUMMARY

WHAT IS THE CLAIM? _____

EVALUATE APPARENT SUPPORT

Credible sources?
Clear logic? (Use the logic cheat sheet)
Good observation? (Scientific tests, theories, the FEDS Standard)

IDENTIFY ALTERNATIVE HYPOTHESES

Oddity of nature or the world of numbers?
Perceptual error or trickery?
Memory error?
Placebo, nonspecific, or non-treatment effects?
Sensory anomaly or hallucination?

CTT OUTLINE

WHAT IS THE CLAIM? _____

EVALUATE APPARENT SUPPORT

Are the sources credible? (Chapter 3)
– Weak sources
– Appeals to questionable authority
– When to be skeptical of sources and authorities

Are the claims logically clear? (Chapter 4)
– Look for examples of unfounded assertions and contradictions
– Look for examples of invalid or unsupported conclusions
– Look for questionable premises
– Use the *Logic Cheat Sheet*

Are the claims based on good observation (scientific tests, and theories?) (Chapter 5)
– Observations
– Tests
– Theories
– The FEDS Standard

Figure 16.2   Three versions of the Critical Thinker's Toolkit

IDENTIFY ALTERNATIVE EXPLANATIONS

Are we misinterpreting an oddity of nature or the world of numbers? (Chapter 6)
- Is it true?
- Availability error
- Misjudging probabilities/unreasonable/illusory optimism
- Coincidences
- Clumpiness of randomness
- Law of very large numbers
- Science and chance
- Psychic bias

Is there a potential for perceptual error or trickery? (Chapter 7)
- Barnum (Forer) effect; confirmation bias; illusions
- Magic trickery/cold reading
- Hypnotic suggestion enhancers

Is there a potential for memory error? (Chapter 8)
- False memories
- Déjà vu
- False memory syndrome warning signs

Might the placebo effect be at work? (Chapter 9)
- Weak and strong placebos

Are we being misled by sensory anomalies or hallucinations? (Chapter 10)
- Sensory phenomena
- Migraines (aura)
- Tunnel experiences
- Hallucinations
- Dissociative states
- Psychiatric conditions

CTT FULL FORM

WHAT IS THE CLAIM? _____

EVALUATE APPARENT SUPPORT

Are the sources credible?
- Weak sources:
  - ancient wisdom
  - testimonials and anecdotal evidence

- popularity
- mass media
- Appeals to questionable authority:
  - properly trained
  - experienced
  - current
  - respected by peers
- When to be skeptical of sources and authorities:
  - exaggerate
  - are gullible
  - don't differentiate good from bad research (or ignore the FEDS Standard)
  - have a record of sloppy research
  - resort to ad hominem arguments

Are the claims logically clear?
- Look for examples of unfounded assertions and contradictions
- Look for examples of invalid or unsupported conclusions
- Look for questionable premises:
  - Confusing fact with fiction:
    - jargon
    - technobabble
    - science fiction
  - fallacies of ambiguity:
    - weasel words
    - straw man
    - category errors, ontological fusion, reification
    - fallacy of similarity or analogy
    - fallacy of composition
    - fallacy of division
  - irrelevant characteristics:
    - appeal to emotion
    - ad hominem
    - appeal to personal ignorance
    - grand conspiracy theories
  - argument from temporal contiguity:
    - post hoc ergo propter hoc
    - pragmatic fallacy
  - self-terminating assumptions:
    - closed-mindedness (blind faith)
    - begging the question
    - false dilemma
  - The Logic Cheat Sheet
    - *Just because it's scientific-sounding doesn't mean it's true*
    - *Just because it's complicated doesn't mean it's true*
    - *You're mixing apples and orangutans*
    - *Just because it feels good doesn't mean it's true*
    - *Don't judge a book by its cover*
    - *Lack of negative evidence doesn't mean it's true*
    - *Just because things happen together doesn't mean they're connected*

- *Just because you believe it (or say it's so) doesn't make it true*
- *This isn't black or white, either/or (it's either true or false)*

Are the claims based on good observations (scientific tests, and theories)?
- Observations:
  - observations that are public
  - replicable
  - tests that are reliable, valid
- Tests
  - proper hypotheses
    - falsifiability/testability hypotheses;
    - ad hoc explanations
  - tests to rule out alternative hypotheses:
    - control groups
    - double-blind procedures
    - placebo controls,
    - controls for stimulus leakage
  - testing the right people
    - representative sample
    - random sample
- Evaluation of theories
  - falsifiability/testability
  - productivity
  - comprehensiveness
  - simplicity (Occam's razor)
- *The FEDS Standard. Expert independent and impartial supervision and replication to minimize:*
  - fraud
  - error
  - deception
  - sloppiness

IDENTIFY ALTERNATIVE HYPOTHESES

Are we misinterpreting an oddity of nature or the world of numbers?
- Is it true?
- Availability error
- Misjudging probabilities/unreasonable/illusory optimism
- Coincidences
- Clumpiness of randomness
- Law of very large numbers
- Science and chance:
  - alpha levels and significance/ Type 1 error
  - replication and sample size
  - control group
  - arbitrary stop point
  - publication bias
- Psychic bias

Is there a potential for perceptual error or trickery?
- Barnum effect
- Confirmation bias
- Everyday illusions
  - pareidolia
  - apophenia
  - perceptual constancy
- Magic trickery
- Cold reading tricks
  - enhancing Barnum effect and confirmation bias
    - multiple out
    - double-headed statement
    - shotgunning
    - drop and return
  - have subject feed you facts
    - questions
    - encourage cooperation
    - ask for interpretation of esoteric reading
    - draw inferences
    - 20 questions
  - draw inferences from other sources
    - read subtle cues and body language
    - base prediction on probable but unexpected statistic
    - pick a body change that is probable but unexpected
    - base prediction on pareidolia or apophenia
  - dealing with less than perfect readings
    - divert attention
    - shoehorning
    - turn misses into hits
    - blame subject
  - make a good show
    - context for confirmation bias and Barnum effect
    - make a few errors
    - tell subject what they want to know
- Hypnotic suggestion enhancers
  - close eyes
  - focus on restricted stimulus (in restricted environment)
  - relax

Is there a potential for memory error?
- False memories
  - source monitoring error
  - misinformation and implanted pseudomemories
  - familiarity is truth
  - imagination inflation / saying is believing
- Déjà vu
- False memory syndrome warning signs

Might placebo, nonspecific, or nontreatment effects be at work?
- Placebo mechanisms
  - suggestion

- classical conditioning
- opioid system
- reduced self-stressing
- Nonspecific and nontreatment effects
  - initial misdiagnosis
  - normal recovery pattern for illness
  - cyclical course of illness
  - aggravating external conditions
  - repeated test taking
  - regression to the mean
  - undiscovered ordinary extraneous variable
- How to pump up a placebo
  - motivate client
  - capsules (large, colored, frequently given), not pills
  - use "blinded" health professional to give treatment
  - complicated rationale
  - complicated procedure
  - negative side effect
  - hypnotic suggestion enhances
  - ask how well it worked after treatment

Are we being misled by sensory anomalies or hallucinations?
- Sensory phenomena
  - autokinetic effect
  - pupil response
  - entopic phenomena
  - synesthesia
- Migraines (aura)
  - photopsia
  - scintillating scotoma
  - fortification illusion
- Tunnel experiences
- Hallucinations
  - sleep and rest:
    - sleep: hypnogogic, hypnopompic, sleep paralysis
    - out-of-body experiences
  - hallucinations in general; conducive conditions (deprivation, reduced sensory input, stimulus overload, stressful and strenuous situations, substances)
  - The Aleman/Larøi model
    - attentional searchlight
    - metacognition and external bias
    - emotions and motivations
    - expectations and prior knowledge
- Psychiatric conditions and disorders
  - dissociative identity disorder
  - seizures
  - Tourette's syndrome
  - schizophrenia

- Dissociative states
- numbing
- reduced awareness of surroundings
- derealization
- depersonalization
- amnesia

- When writing a Reality Checkup Report, you may find it useful to use one of three versions of the CTT as an outline to guide your questioning. See Figure 16.2.

How to Carry on a Civilized Discussion about the Paranormal

One good way to practice your Toolkit is to talk to friends and relatives about their paranormal experiences. Try not to challenge what they claim because this might inhibit discussion. Avoid agreeing or sharing your own paranormal experiences as this may bias what they say and deprive you of opportunities to apply Toolkit concepts. I recommend playing the role of a friendly neutral journalist, simply interested in understanding the claims and getting the facts. Use the Toolkit as a source of reality-checking questions. However, I do not recommend formally proceeding through each Toolkit question. This can transform a friendly discussion into an interrogation or inquisition. Instead, simply ask what Toolkit questions come to mind. The better you know your Toolkit, the better your questions will be. Consider this discussion between Jose and Brenda, a student of Chinese medicine. Can you identify Toolkit ideas that inspired Jose's questions?

JOSE: I see you have a very large textbook and a small bag of what looks like weeds.

BRENDA: That's a sample of herbs. And this book is all about the body and acupuncture. I'm getting a degree in Chinese medicine at the Institute.

JOSE: May I ask a few questions?

BRENDA: Sure, ask away!

JOSE: As I understand it, there's an energy acupuncturists use.

BRENDA: Yes, it's called "qi."

JOSE: Qi. Where is it?

BRENDA: It travels through the body along channels called meridians.

JOSE: Are these like blood vessels or nerves?

BRENDA: Actually, they're different. By properly inserting special needles at points along meridians where qi is blocked, one can open up the flow of qi and help balance one's energy.

JOSE: How do you know when you've hit the right point with a needle?

BRENDA: Your patient will feel better. The increased energy flow makes one feel more alive and healthy.

JOSE: And what if a patient starts feeling better but the acupuncturist didn't insert at the right spot?

BRENDA: Well, I would take that as proof that the acupuncturist actually did hit a spot where qi was blocked. Sometimes an oil prospector doesn't know exactly where the oil is.

JOSE: Ah, yes. So if my qi is unblocked, I get better. If I get better, then my qi must have been unblocked. Is there any agreement as to how to look for these qi spots?

BRENDA: Actually, different acupuncture masters may insert needles in different places. If you have knee pain, some may insert needles around the knee, and others in the shoulder in order to draw excess qi away from the knee.

JOSE: So here there would be two options for knee pain?

BRENDA: What I'm saying is that each master may have their own intuitive system that works for them. It's all very intuitive and requires a lot of training and experience, more than I have!

JOSE: Is there evidence for the effectiveness of acupuncture?

BRENDA: There are thousands of doctors who use acupuncture around the world, and they would stop using it if their patients didn't get better. There are millions of patients who have received acupuncture. Personally I can point to people who have been cured by acupuncture.

Parting Words: Pandora's Challenge

We conclude our journey with where we began. My initial interest in things paranormal began with what appeared to be a tempting treasure chest of extraordinary claims. In time I began to suspect that I had opened something of a Pandora's box. Since then I have struggled with various tools for sorting fact from fantasy. One involves helping others take a peek into the Pandora's box they may have conjured up.

To begin, different reality checks work best in different situations. However, there are times when neither a simple reality check, nor a formal reality checkup, is appropriate. I realized this point only a week ago while watching an episode of *Larry King Live*, one of many devoted to a discussion of unidentified flying objects (UFOs) of alien origin. UFO supporters included an assortment of claimed physicists, movie directors, and apparently credible witnesses. On the other side was an award-winning skeptic with scientific training. Proponents presented a flurry of claims, and the skeptic attempted to challenge each, one by one. However, for each claim he challenged, UFO believers replied with additional claims of evidence. I was left with the impression that the evidence for alien UFOs was overwhelming, and our poor beleaguered skeptic was no match. This incident illustrates the risks of applying reality checks in a high-pressure public forum. Let me suggest an alternative strategy, one I call **Pandora's Challenge**.

Pandora's Challenge is essentially the main lesson of this book:

> If we open the paranormal box just enough to let one claim out, we must accept the right of other equal-sized claims to crawl out and wander the world. If we accept one extraordinary paranormal claim that fails to meet a few sensible reality checks, we are obligated to accept all paranormal claims that have equivalent support. If you believe in ghosts, you must also believe in astrology, reincarnation, TV psychic superstars, prophetic pets, alien abductions, communication with the dead, fortune-telling, mental spoon-bending, and a Pandora's box of other treasures.

Why? All have sincere, honest, sane, intelligent, educated, articulate, famous, and passionate proponents. Most are supported by intensely convincing personal experiences. But all are based on equally substandard evidence. None have met the threshold of fact: truly scientific, public, and replicable observation. The painful truth is that no quantity of substandard evidence, intriguing and seductive as it may be, can ever meet the critical mass of truth. Millions of people, over thousands of years, believed (and still believe) in witches and demons (and put them to death)—all on substandard evidence. Yes, one can find "experts," "witnesses," and even "scientific studies" in support of witches and demons. But this enormous amount of "evidence" doesn't establish that witches and demons are demonstrated fact. *Again, there is no substitute for scientific, public, and replicable observation.*

Put into action, the paranormal challenge might begin like this:

AMY: I believe in pixies, fleeting fairy-like winged creatures with pointed ears.

JIM: Why do you believe that?

AMY: I have seen them with my own eyes and I read the account of a respected psychologist with a PhD who says they are real.

JIM: Then you must also believe in astrology, reincarnation, TV psychic superstars, prophetic pets, alien abductions, communication with the dead, fortune-telling, and mental spoon-bending.

AMY: No! What are you talking about?

JIM: There are also credible experts, with PhDs, who claim to have seen evidence for all of these claimed paranormal phenomena.

The advantage of Pandora's challenge is that it avoids the trap of endless argument over piecemeal claims and focuses discussion on the crux of the debate: What constitutes credible support? Just what is a fact? One can then consider why specific claims of support may be substandard, and what the consequences of accepting such claims are. This indeed is what we have been doing throughout my book. Hopefully my efforts will provoke, and even inspire, you to pursue this adventure beyond our short journey together.

Brief Reality Checkup Report on Urine Therapy

Urine Therapy

(Based on "The Miracle Urine Therapy" by Jon Smith)

Urine therapy is an ancient treatment for enhancing health, beauty, and spirituality by consuming one's own urine. There are many ways of doing this. For example, drink it early in the morning, put drops under the tongue, spray it in the nose, use it as eye drops, soak your feet in it, or spread it over your skin (Smith, 2009). Advocates claim that it is good for just about everything, from aging and AIDS to typhus and tuberculosis.

Support

What is the support for this unusual treatment? Most is pseudoscientific. Smith relies heavily on testimonial data, although we can find examples of other forms of support, some used incorrectly.

Sources

Advocates rely on unsubstantiated anecdotes and testimonials, both from practitioners and presumed health professionals. For example, Smith (2009) cites:

> Boy (age 9) suffering from enuresis. Treated by many physicians using all available methods. Failed. Fasted on urine for 11 days and completely cured.

> Woman (40) suffering from severe kidney disease. Given two days to live by doctors. Difficult breathing, blood in urine. Started urine therapy, and as much tap water as she desired. Cured in about a month.

> Woman (40) with gangrene in right leg. Amputation recommended. One week of urine therapy and no sign of gangrene and completely cured.

No external confirmation is given for these remarkable claims. They could be based on false memories, the placebo effect, or a variety of extraneous nonspecific effects. Who knows if these patients were misdiagnosed or simply would have recovered given the normal course of illness. Perhaps they simply made it up.

Advocates (Smith, 2009) frequently present as support ancient history and famous practitioners. Indeed, urine therapy may be 5,000 years old, and may have been used in various ancient cultures around the world, but that doesn't mean it works. Many false ideas have persisted for thousands of years. Also, former Indian Prime Minister Morarji Desai, as well as Gandhi, Jim Morrison, John Lennon, and Steve McQueen, are some of the famous people claimed to have used it. Famous as these people are, they are not medical experts. We have no evidence of who this author who goes by the pseudonym "Jon Smith" really is (although an author posing with the same name has written questionable religious material; Smith, 2006). I find 190,000 Google hits for "Jon Smith."

Advocates also claim three million Chinese practitioners. Again, popularity is not proof of effectiveness. You could probably find three million people who do all sorts of worthless things. The fact that there have been three international world conferences on urine therapy only shows that there are some people willing to pay money for a hotel room and advertising.

Observations (tests and theories)

Observational scientific support is weak. Smith lists over 50 conditions that urine is good for, which, taken together, involve a long list of different biological causes. AIDS is caused by a virus, allergies from allergic reactions, broken bones from physical trauma, fever from viral or bacterial infection, Karposi's sarcoma from cancer, poisoning and snake bite from toxics, and aging from life itself. In other words, urine therapy would seem to be unique among treatments in that it is claimed to have an impact on just about every human biological process. This makes urine therapy virtually unfalsifiable because any biological change that occurs after the consumption of urine can be a claimed effect. The range of negative side effects (presumably evidence that the treatment is working) is just about as long. Just about anything, desirable or undesirable, that happens after consuming urine is evidence. You can't lose.

   Finally, the scientific theory underlying urine therapy sounds sophisticated. As reported by Smith (2009), urine is seen as a hologram of some sort of one's body condition. This liquid hologram can trigger the body's self-healing powers. As a scientific theory, this fails miserably. It is not simple because it raises more questions than it answers. For example, if urine is so good for you, why bother to drink it? You already have it in your body. Holograms require lasers to work, but where are the lasers in the body? Lasers or holograms have never been shown to have an effect on the body's immune system.

Logic

Advocates sometimes make logical errors. During WWI troops may have used urine-coated eye patches to protect against chlorine gas. Pergonal and Urokinase are legitimate drugs based on urine. And urine itself may be somewhat antibacterial. But to claim wide-reaching curative powers from this is a logical stretch. For example, advocates sometimes make the error of arguing from similarity (some medications are made from urine, urine treatment also involves urine, therefore urine therapy should be therapeutic). We see examples of argument from temporal contiguity (just because someone felt better after drinking urine doesn't mean that urine was the cause). They sometimes use ad hominem arguments (urine therapy must work because the medical community is suppressing it). Enthusiastic advocates can get carried away and risk arguing from emotion ("It is exciting to contemplate what the future may bring. Once urine therapy is accepted by medicine, politics, and religion, stigmas concerning urine excretion may be flushed away."). Examples of valid, but false, deductive reasoning can be found (Anything with vitamins in it is good for you. Urine has vitamins in it. Therefore urine must be good for you.).

Alternative Explanations

There are a variety of alternative explanations for the claimed effects of urine therapy.

Statistics

First, from the laws of probability one would expect an occasional person to improve after treatment. Improvement could simply be regression toward the mean, or the occasional statistical anomaly that emerges when a large number of cases are considered. With three million claimed Chinese practitioners, one might expect at least three "once in a million" miracles—just by chance.

Perceptual and memory error

Testimonial and anecdotal accounts are easily contaminated by perceptual and memory error. We have no idea if an uncorroborated account was simply misperceived in the first place, or embellished on recall. Indeed, one could speculate what the conditions for such errors might be. True believers could well display confirmation bias and experience the Barnum effect, selectively noticing only supportive evidence—all of the conditions that might contribute to implanted memories and imagination inflation. The "saying makes it true" effect might easily be seen in proponents who eagerly share and write about their cures to enthusiastic believers and fellow patients, perhaps at an "international urine therapy conference." Proponents describe some uncomfortable side effects from drinking urine (nausea, for example). An expert at cold reading would redefine this as a sign that urine therapy is indeed working. As Smith reports, advocates have claimed that the anecdotal support is so strong that no science is needed. This would seem to be a type of denial.

Sensory anomalies and hallucinations

Are claims of cures the result of sensory anomalies or hallucinations? Some toxins can evoke hallucinations, and urine is a secretion of toxins. And if you had earlier consumed a mind-altering drug, and are now excreting it, drinking your own urine might conceivably give you a free "high." This is pure speculation and I have never tried it.

The placebo effect

One could make a good case that urine therapy is a placebo. As I have shown, Smith claims it is good for just about everything, ranging from aging and AIDS to typhus and tuberculosis. This alone makes one suspect that urine therapy is not particularly specific in its effect, a defining characteristic of placebos. Generally, placebos work best when they are presented by true believers, involve complicated procedures, have rationales rich in technobabble, are given to motivated patients, and have some negative side effects. It is quite likely that health professionals who advocate urine therapy believe in what they are doing. We see such enthusiasm in Smith's piece. Surely it would take a certain level of patient belief and motivation to consume one's own urine. The procedures are indeed complicated, involving drinking early in the morning, carefully consuming the initial flow, fasting for 15 minutes, getting enough sleep, and engaging in various urine rituals such as placing 1–5 drops under the tongue, spraying urine in the eyes, or applying it in the nostrils. Like any good placebo, urine therapy has negative side effects, described as a "healing crisis." This can involve almost any form of discomfort or distress (headaches, nausea, vomiting), which could also simply be the result of performing the disgusting act, rather than from any presumed healing power of urine.

Pandora's Principles and the Paranormic Propensity

We concluded this chapter with Pandora's Challenge. You might be interested in an extended version of this challenge, Pandora's Principles. Put simply, these state that if you accept a paranormal claim, and wish to remain intellectually honest, you must accept other paranormal claims. To elaborate:

1. **The Weak Support Principle.** If you accept one claim on the basis of weak support (sources, logic, scientific observation), and you wish to remain intellectually honest, you must accept other claims based on equivalent support.

Example: John believes in ghosts because he saw one. It walked through walls, became invisible, and caused far-away doors to squeak. Sherry believes in werewolves because she saw one. She also saw one die when stabbed by a silver dagger and shapeshift into human form. To be intellectually honest, John must also believe in werewolves, and Sherry in ghosts.

2. **The Strong Support Principle.** If you accept one claim even though it lacks "strong support," you must accept other claims equally lacking in strong support.

Example: There is no replicated account of a scientist conjuring up a ghost (who could walk through walls, become invisible, and cause far-away doors to squeak) in an electronically shielded laboratory in the presence of a trained magician. There is no replicated account of a werewolf dying only when stabbed by a silver dagger, or shapeshifting into human form in an electronically shielded laboratory in the presence of a trained magician. If you believe in ghosts, you must believe in werewolves, and vice versa.

3. **The Catastrophic Implications Principle.** If you continue to accept a claim, even if its full implications would be catastrophic to the laws of physics as we know them, such implications should not prevent you from accepting other equally catastrophic claims.

Example: If a paranormal ghost entity exists, who could walk through walls, become invisible, and instantaneously cause doors to squeak at a long distance, laws of physics concerning the speed of light and the basic forces would have to be wrong. If werewolves really existed, never died (except when stabbed by a silver dagger), and shapeshifted, several basic laws of physics would be wrong. If the catastrophic implications of believing in ghosts does not limit your acceptance of ghost claims, then the equivalent catastrophic implications of believing in werewolves should not limit your acceptance of werewolf claims.

A Closing Hypothesis: The Paranormic Propensity

I propose that individuals who embrace paranormal claims can be sorted into two groups. Some harbor one or two isolated beliefs and are quite willing to apply critical thinking skills. Then there are those who display something of an expansive and free-floating *paranormic propensity*, a suspension of, or hostility to, critical thinking combined with a willingness and eagerness to embrace a wide range of paranormal claims. Such *paranormic thinking* is fostered by four processes:

1. *Belief in a paranormal claim and extended inclusive but reverse application of Pandora's Principles*. Paranormic individuals do not apply reality-checking skills; indeed, they are quite willing to accept the logical consequences of accepting a paranormal claim (and open the box to all equal claims). Central to this process is the abandonment of a commitment to critical thinking (honest and fearless questioning). This simple act transforms Pandora's Box from warning into an invitation (see subjective relativism, Chapter 2).
2. *Social reinforcement*. Family, friends, and support group members share and reinforce the paranormic processes identified here.
3. *Subjective confirmation*. Paranormic individuals may have intense and personally convincing paranormal experiences that in fact reflect misunderstanding of oddities of nature and numbers, perceptual error, memory error, the placebo effect, and sense anomalies and hallucinations.
4. *Supportive belief system*. Paranormic individuals embrace an encompassing belief system that accommodates (or does not limit) the above processes.

I suspect that both religious and secular individuals can display a paranormic thinking. One's religious belief system may define a specific domain of acceptable paranormal claims. However, within this domain, paranormic individuals accept a larger number of claims. Thus one might find paranormic Christians, paranormic Buddhists, and paranormic secular humanists.

Finally, this proposal makes no claims concerning the relative healthiness or desirability of the paranormic propensity. It is quite possible that researchers inclined to accept paranormal claims may hypothesize that such a propensity predicts actual paranormal skills. Skeptics may view the paranormic propensity as contributing to distortion and error. These are empirical questions.

I am currently developing a Paranormic Propensity Inventory. Email me for details at the Pseudoscience and Paranormal Laboratory at Chicago's Roosevelt University: jsmith@roosevelt.edu. I plan to make all versions of my inventory available to researchers without charge.

Appendix A

Complementary and Alternative Medicine

The National Center for Complementary and Alternative Medicine, a division of the National Institutes of Health, groups CAM practices into four domains, recognizing that there can be some overlap. In addition, NCCAM studies CAM whole medical systems, which cut across all domains. It is instructive to consider that the position of NCCAM (NCCAM, 2008) blurs the distinction between paranormal and nonparanormal approaches.

Whole Medical Systems

Whole medical systems are built upon complete systems of theory and practice. Often, these systems have evolved apart from and earlier than the conventional medical approach used in the United States. Examples of whole medical systems that have developed in Western cultures include homeopathic medicine (originated in Europe. Homeopathy seeks to stimulate the body's ability to heal itself by giving very small doses of highly diluted substances that in larger doses would produce illness or symptoms (an approach called "like cures like")) and naturopathic medicine (originated in Europe. Naturopathy aims to support the body's ability to heal itself through the use of dietary and lifestyle changes together with CAM therapies such as herbs, massage, and joint manipulation). Examples of systems that have developed in non-Western cultures include traditional Chinese medicine (a Chinese system based on the concept that disease results from disruption in the flow of qi and imbalance in the forces of yin and yang. Practices such as herbs, meditation, massage, and acupuncture seek to aid healing by restoring the yin–yang balance and the flow of qi) and Ayurveda (a whole medical system that originated in India. It aims to integrate the body, mind, and spirit to prevent and treat disease. Therapies used include herbs, massage, and yoga).

Mind–Body Medicine

Mind–body medicine uses a variety of techniques designed to enhance the mind's capacity to affect bodily function and symptoms. Some techniques that were considered CAM in the past have become mainstream (for example, patient support groups and cognitive-behavioral therapy). Other mind–body techniques are still considered CAM, including meditation, prayer, mental healing, and therapies that use creative outlets such as art, music, or dance.

Biologically Based Practices

Biologically based practices in CAM use substances found in nature, such as herbs, foods, and vitamins. Some examples include dietary supplements, herbal products, and the use of other so-called natural but as yet scientifically unproven therapies (for example, using shark cartilage to treat cancer).

Manipulative and Body-Based Practices

Manipulative and body-based practices in CAM are based on manipulation (the application of controlled force to a joint, moving it beyond the normal range of motion in an effort to aid in restoring health. Manipulation may be performed as a part of other therapies or whole medical systems, including chiropractic medicine, massage, and naturopathy) and/or movement of one or more parts of the body. Some examples include chiropractic or osteo-pathic manipulation (a type of manipulation practiced by osteopathic physi-cians. It is combined with physical therapy and instruction in proper posture) and massage (pressing, rubbing, and moving muscles and other soft tissues of the body, primarily by using the hands and fingers. The aim is to increase the flow of blood and oxygen to the massaged area).

Energy Medicine

Energy therapies involve the use of energy fields. They are of two types:

- **Biofield therapies** are intended to affect energy fields that purportedly surround and penetrate the human body. The existence of such fields has not yet been scientifically proven. Some forms of energy therapy manipulate biofields by applying pressure and/or manipulating the body by placing the hands in, or through, these fields. Examples include qigong (a component of traditional Chinese medicine that combines movement, meditation, and controlled breathing. The intent is to improve blood flow and the flow of qi), reiki (a therapy in which practitioners seek to transmit a universal energy to a person, either from a distance or by placing their hands on or near that person. The intent is to heal the spirit and thus the body), and therapeutic touch (a therapy in which practitioners pass their hands over another person's body with the intent to use their own perceived healing energy to identify energy imbalances and promote health).

- **Bioelectromagnetic-based therapies** involve the unconventional use of electromagnetic fields, such as pulsed fields, magnetic fields, or alternating-current or direct-current fields.

Source: NCCAM (2008). Retrieved April 1, 2008 from: nccam.nih. gov/health/whatiscam/

Appendix B

Critical Thinking and Paranormal Resources

If you are interested in exploring the topics of this text, the following websites and journals are a good place to begin.

Skeptical Sources

skepdic.com

This site contains *The Skeptic's Dictionary*, the most useful online source of definitions, arguments, and essays on paranormal claims. Its primary focus is skeptical. The site includes many useful links and a large bibliography.

www.randi.org/site/index.php/encyclopedia.html

Encyclopedia of claims, frauds, and hoaxes of the occult and supernatural. Online version of James Randi's encyclopedia.

csicop.org

This is the official website for the Committee for Skeptical Inquiry (CSI). The CSI encourages the responsible, critical, and scientific investigation of paranormal claims and the dissemination of factual information about paranormal research. The site includes useful links and a large bibliography. The CSI publishes the *Skeptical Inquirer*, a very readable journal of paranormal claims. A transnational umbrella organization, the Center for Inquiry, encompasses the CSI as well as the Council for Secular Humanism and the Center for Inquiry—On Campus.

skeptic.com

This is the official website of The Skeptics Society, "a scientific and educational organization of scholars, scientists, historians, magicians, professors and teachers, and anyone curious about controversial ideas, extraordinary claims, revolutionary ideas, and the promotion of science." Its official journal, *Skeptic,* provides a thorough and readable inquiry into various paranormal topics. The website has a free reading room with interesting articles and essays, as well as a free collection of podcasts and video downloads.

skepticreport.com

This is Chris Larson's compendium of news articles, essays, and links on paranormal topics. Skepticreport contains much information, including transcripts of psychic cold readings, difficult to obtain elsewhere.

quackwatch.org

Quackwatch, Inc., is a "nonprofit corporation whose purpose is to combat health-related frauds, myths, fads, fallacies, and misconduct. Its primary focus is on quackery-related information that is difficult or impossible to get elsewhere." It offers useful links to other sites and a forum where experts can answer questions.

randi.org

The James Randi Educational Foundation was founded by author, magician, and skeptic James Randi. It promotes "critical thinking by reaching out to the public and media with reliable information about paranormal and supernatural ideas so widespread in our society today." The Foundation offers classroom demonstrations and educational seminars, supports and conducts research into paranormal claims, maintains a library of print, audio, and video resources, and assists those critical of paranormal excesses who have been the victim of attack. To increase public awareness of paranormal issues, the Foundation offers a $1 million prize to anyone demonstrating "any psychic, supernatural or paranormal ability of any kind under mutually agreed upon scientific conditions." The website has many useful links and audio and video downloads. It is not shy about presenting heated discussion from both skeptics and non-skeptics.

Theskepticsguide.org

The Skeptics Guide to the Universe is a weekly Podcast talk show produced by the New England Skeptical Society and the James Randi Educational Foundation. Programs discuss the latest news and topics from the world of the paranormal, fringe science, and controversial claims from a scientific point of view.

Neutral Sources

www.answers.com

Shepard, L. A. (2003). *Encyclopedia of Occultism and Parapsychology* (5th ed.). Detroit, MI: Gale Research Co.

This two-volume encyclopedia contains more than 5,000 entries covering recent phenomena, concepts, cults, personalities, organizations, and publications. For controversial topics, evidence for and against is presented.

www.pbs.org/wgbh/nova/id

Here is a classic presentation of the Dover school board trial on teaching intelligent design in biology class. An excellent review of evolution as well as the nature of science.

Non-skeptical Sources

parapsych.org

The Parapsychological Association is an "international professional organization of scientists and scholars engaged in the study of '*psi*' (or 'psychic') experiences, such as telepathy, clairvoyance, psychokinesis, psychic healing, and precognition ('parapsychology')." This website describes the organization, discusses how to conduct parapsychological research, and provides links to groups conducting such research. Try out the fun do-it-yourself online psi game/experiments.

http://www.koestler-parapsychology.psy.ed.ac.uk/

The website of the Koestler Parapsychology Unit of the University of Edinburgh consists of scholars and students interested in parapsychology. Their site provides useful information on research and links to journals and other laboratories doing research on the paranormal.

Paranormal Laboratories

Koestler Parapsychology Unit at the University of Edinburgh
Parapsychology Research Group at Liverpool Hope University
SOPHIA Research Program at the University of Arizona
Consciousness and Transpersonal Psychology Research Unit of Liverpool John Moores University
Center for the Study of Anomalous Psychological Processes at the University of Northampton

Anomalistic Psychology Research Unit at Goldsmiths, University of
London

Princeton Engineering Anomalies Research (PEAR) laboratory in Princeton
is often cited in paranormal circles, but yielded little supportive evidence
(Odling-Smee, 2007). It closed in February, 2007.

Paranormal Research Organizations

American Society for Psychical Research (*Journal of the American Society
for Psychical Research*)

Australian Institute of Parapsychological Research (*Australian Journal of
Parapsychology*)

ISAR International Society for Astrological Research

National Council of Geocosmic Research

Parapsychological Association

Parapsychology Foundation (*International Journal of Parapsychology*)

Rhine Research Center and Institute for Parapsychology (*Journal of
Parapsychology*)

Society for Psychical Research (*Journal of Society for Psychical Research*)

Scientific Journals

Below are 39 journals that have often published paranormal research:

Arbeitsberichte Parapsychologie der Technischen Universität Berlin
Australian Journal of Parapsychology
Australian Parapsychological Review
Bulletin PSILOG
Consciousness and Physical Reality
Cuadernos de Parapsicologia
Electronic Journal for Anomalous Phenomena
European Journal of Parapsychology
Frontier Perspectives
*Il Mondo del Paranormale. Rivista di parapsicologia, tematiche affini,
insolito*
International Journal of Parapsychology
Japanese Journal of Parapsychology
Journal of the American Society for Psychical Research
Journal of Consciousness Studies
Journal of Indian Psychology
Journal of International Society of Life Information Science
Journal of Near-Death Studies

The Journal of Paraphysics
Journal of Parapsychology
Journal of Scientific Exploration
The Journal of the American Society for Psychical Research
Journal of the Society for Psychical Research
Journal of the Southern California Society for Psychical Research
La Revue de Parapsychologie (1971–1989)
Luce e Ombra
Metapsichica the Italian Journal of Parapsychology
Proceedings of the Parapsychological Association Annual Convention
Psyche
Quaderni di Parapsicologia
Research in Parapsychology
Research Letter of the Parapsychological Division of the Psychological Laboratory University of Utrecht
Revista Argentina de Psicología Paranormal
Revue Française de Parapsychologie
Revue Métapsychique
Subtle Energies and Energy Medicine Journal
Tijdschrift voor Parapsychologie
Zeitschrift für Parapsychologie und Grenzgebiete der Psychologie

The following focus on objective analysis of paranormal claims:

Enquêtes Z (in French)
Indian Skeptic (The Indian C.S.I.C.O.P.)
Scienza & Paranormale (C.I.C.A.P.)
Skeptical Inquirer (C.S.I.C.O.P.)
The Skeptic magazine
The SWIFT Bulletin (James Randi Educational Foundation)
The Skeptic Quebec (in French)

General Websites

About.com

About.com is a source for original consumer information and advice. It is owned by the New York Times and written by a network of 600 journalists (called Guides) who are experts in their fields. Content includes articles, online courses, interactive quizzes, and videos. About.com provides many useful articles on paranormal topics.

Religioustolerance.org

Religioustolerance.org is the official website of the Ontario Consultants for Religious Tolerance (OCRT), a group whose goal is to promote religious tolerance and provide information about world religions, morality, spirituality, religious tolerance, and new religious movements, and many paranormal topics. It takes the perspective that there is no one true religion and all religions have their positive and negative aspects.

Beliefnet.com

Beliefnet.com provides information about various religious and spiritual beliefs and includes interviews of various scholars and advocates, articles, and blogs. It also provides a forum for religious information and inspiration, spiritual tools, and discussions and dialogue groups. Beliefnet.com is not affiliated with a particular religion or spiritual movement. Discussion groups are available for couples, teens, and other groups on topics ranging from abortion to sexism, and spiritual growth. Paranormal topics are included.

Sites with Passionate Agendas

Venganza.org

Bobby Henderson presents his satirical vision (with evidence) for the Flying Spaghetti Monster, a presumed deity who created the universe 4,000 years ago and erased all evidence of his existence in order to test our faith.

Whywontgodhealamputees.com

Perhaps the best irreverent online resource for those exploring supernatural claims such as the efficacy of prayer and miracles as well as the validity of religious sources. This entertaining site definitely has a point of view.

sprott.physics.wisc.edu/Pickover/esp.html

The Pickover ESP Experiment claims an accuracy of 98%. Unlike other online PSI tests, the Pickover Experiment provides a "quantum consistency" assessment for each trial. Developed by Clifford Pickover, an author with a PhD from Yale in Molecular Biophysics and Biochemistry.

Professional Organizations

Various professional scientific organizations have websites that occasionally cover paranormal or related topics. These include:

apa.org (The American Psychological Association)
Nature.com (Nature magazine)
Newscientist.com (New Scientist magazine)
www.sciam.com (Scientific American magazine).

Personal Databases

It is amazing how much personal information you can find for just about anyone using the internet. Several online personal databases have amassed a huge collection of information for nearly everyone in the United States. Information includes: criminal and civil court records, marriage and divorce records, property records, criminal history, and even phone numbers and addresses. This information is useful for law enforcement, businesses assessing the potential risks of potential and current employees as well as customers, government agencies, journalists, and academics. An unscrupulous psychic with a smart cell phone can in seconds access a wealth of personal detail for an unsuspecting client. This should improve the accuracy of psychic readings considerably.

Wikipedia.com

Wikipedia.com can provide good leads to discussions of esoteric paranormal topics. However, articles can be inaccurate, incomplete, and biased. An article that appears today can be revised by nearly anyone at any time. I recommend that students and researchers always cross-check and verify any claims and citations presented on wikipedia.com.

Appendix C

Susan Blackmore on Paranormal Research

Blackmore, S. (2008). The paranormal. *The Edge*. Retrieved February 18, 2008 from www.edge.org/q2008/q08_13.html

Noted paranormal researcher Susan Blackmore recounts her lifelong interest in the paranormal. Her account is typical of the handful of highly capable researchers who have actually devoted substantial time and effort to studying paranormal claims. Note the sources of her early enthusiastic embrace of the paranormal, her initial hostility toward skeptics, her unusual dedication to replication and quality research methodology, her persistence with ad hoc explanations for null results, her search for new explanations and tests that might reveal PSI just around the corner, her reaction to the ad hoc explanation of the "psi-inhibitory" researcher, and above all her continued commitment to question honestly and fearlessly.

Susan Blackmore
Psychologist and Skeptic; Author, Consciousness:
An Introduction

The Paranormal

Imagine me, if you will, in the Oxford of 1970; a new undergraduate, thrilled by the intellectual atmosphere, the hippy clothes, joss-stick filled rooms, late nights, early morning lectures, and mind-opening cannabis.

I joined the Society for Psychical Research and became fascinated with occultism, mediumship and the paranormal—ideas that clashed tantalisingly with the physiology and psychology I was studying. Then late one night something very strange happened. I was sitting around with friends, smoking, listening to music, and enjoying the vivid imagery of rushing down a dark tunnel towards a bright light, when my friend spoke. I couldn't reply.

"Where are you Sue?" he asked, and suddenly I seemed to be on the ceiling looking down.

"Astral projection!" I thought and then I (or some imagined flying "I") set off across Oxford, over the country, and way beyond. For more than two hours I fell through strange scenes and mystical states, losing space and time, and ultimately my self. It was an extraordinary and life-changing experience. Everything seemed brighter, more real, and more meaningful than anything in ordinary life, and I longed to understand it.

But I jumped to all the wrong conclusions. Perhaps understandably, I assumed that my spirit had left my body and that this proved all manner of things—life after death, telepathy, clairvoyance, and much, much more. I decided, with splendid, youthful over-confidence, to become a parapsychologist and prove all my closed-minded science lecturers wrong. I found a PhD place, funded myself by teaching, and began to test my memory theory of ESP. And this is where my change of mind—and heart, and everything else—came about.

I did the experiments. I tested telepathy, precognition, and clairvoyance; I got only chance results. I trained fellow students in imagery techniques and tested them again; chance results. I tested twins in pairs; chance results. I worked in play groups and nursery schools with very young children (their naturally telepathic minds are not yet warped by education, you see); chance results. I trained as a Tarot reader and tested the readings; chance results.

Occasionally I got a significant result. Oh the excitement! I responded as I think any scientist should, by checking for errors, recalculating the statistics, and repeating the experiments. But every time I either found the error responsible, or failed to repeat the results. When my enthusiasm waned, or I began to doubt my original beliefs, there was always another corner to turn—always someone saying "But you must try xxx". It was probably three or four years before I ran out of xxxs.

I remember the very moment when something snapped (or should I say "I seem to ..." in case it's a false flash-bulb memory). I was lying in the bath trying to fit my latest null results into paranormal theory, when it occurred to me for the very first time that I might have been completely wrong, and my tutors right. Perhaps there were no paranormal phenomena at all.

As far as I can remember, this scary thought took some time to sink in. I did more experiments, and got more chance results. Parapsychologists called me a "psi-inhibitory experimenter", meaning that I didn't get paranormal results because I didn't believe strongly enough. I studied other people's results and found more errors and even outright fraud. By the time my PhD was completed, I had become a sceptic.

Until then, my whole identity had been bound up with the paranormal. I had shunned a sensible PhD place, and ruined my chances of a career in academia (as my tutor at Oxford liked to say). I had hunted ghosts and poltergeists, trained as a witch, attended spiritualist churches, and stared into crystal balls. But all of that had to go.

Once the decision was made it was actually quite easy. Like many big changes in life this one was terrifying in prospect but easy in retrospect. I soon became "rentasceptic", appearing on TV shows to explain how the illusions work, why there is no telepathy, and how to explain near-death experiences by events in the brain.

What remains now is a kind of openness to evidence. However firmly I believe in some theory (on consciousness, memes or whatever); however closely I might be identified with some position or claim, I know that the world won't fall apart if I have to change my mind.

Notes

Chapter 1

1 The "continuum mysteriosum" is my invention, borrowing from Rudolf Otto's *mysterium tremendum*. Otto was a famous 20th century German theologian. His *The Idea of the Holy* is one of the most important books on God in the century. Otto proposed that one can have a religious experience of God that is *numinous*—non-rational, non-sensory, and outside the "self." The numinous is a mystery (Latin: mysterium) that is terrifying (tremendum) and fascinating (fascinans). Otto's idea is important because it challenges us to look at religion and God in terms of subjective experience, not science or logic. Do not confuse this with *theridion mysteriosum*, which is a type of spider.

2 One might define as paranormal any anomalous event that cannot be explained by the laws of chemistry, or biology (as well as physics). Thus a psychic who claims to see through your eyes is making a claim that is inconsistent with what we know about the biology of eyes. An acupuncturist who claims to cure heart disease by inserting pins in specific parts of the body is doing something for which there is no biological explanation. However, on close examination such paranormal claims reduce to violations of physics. Yes, the psychic who claims to see through someone else's eyes claims a power not supported by any detectable chemical or biological process in his body. He simply doesn't have what it takes. If he could indeed see in such a remarkable way, he would have to be using some entity or process that is undetectable but nonetheless has an influence on biological and chemical processes. But such a miracle would require a type of matter and energy unknown to physics. In other words, his claim violates physics. The acupuncturist who cures heart disease is making a claim for which there is no biological or chemical explanation. No chemical or biological process in the human body would permit a simple needle prick to alter blood lipid levels, dissolve arterial plaque, and heal injured blood vessels. If pin pricks could do this, unknown and undetectable chemical or biological processes would have to be at work. Again, this would require a violation of physics, the

presence of nonmaterial (non-detectable) entities that nonetheless have a material effect. Every paranormal claim in this book violates physics.

At this point it might be worth saying a few words about the term "superstition." In this text we use a very limited definition of the term "superstition" as a popular casual belief concerning a simple everyday event that seems to violate the laws of physics. Superstition can be defined more generally as a fixed belief maintained in spite of logic or evidence to the contrary. A paranormal or supernatural belief need not be superstitious, providing the holder is willing to subject it to honest questioning. A superstitious claim need not be paranormal, but simply mistaken. One may superstitiously believe that lightning never strikes twice in the same place. This more general definition can be very useful for many reasons. It focuses attention to the lack of logical or empirical support for a claim. It highlights how a rigidly held fallacious claim may be similar to obviously absurd everyday superstitions, such as a belief in magic coins. To illustrate, to say that one has a "questioning curiosity about astrology" means that one is willing to apply the tools of critical thinking to evaluate astrological claims. To say that one has a "superstitious belief in astrology" says that one holds astrological beliefs in spite of an honest application of the tools of critical thinking.

3   I use the term "entity" to refer to any set of paranormal forces or energies claimed to possess an internal complexity.

Chapter 2

1   Consider the statement "We are all interconnected." As a literal fact this might mean that we are all physically connected, for example, through our phones. Of course, this could be evaluated scientifically by simply checking to see if everyone indeed has access to phones. Or this statement could be a description of a subjective state, an emotion: "I love everyone very much and feel close to people." It could be part of a moral statement: "Be careful what you say about others because they may eventually hear about it and be hurt." Our statement could be symbolic, a metaphor: "Our society is complex and each person plays a role. Together, we keep things going." Finally, a claim of interconnectedness could be a paranormal statement that at the subatomic or quantum level the consciousness of every human is part of a larger universal consciousness.

2   You might protest that no one observed cavemen, black holes at the centers of galaxies, or tiny particles, or quarks, that make up atoms. But we have observed historical artifacts and immediate and undeniable consequences. Skid marks on the road show that a crashed car was speeding, even though we have no witnesses. Drawings on ancient caves point to cave dwellers, although we have never talked to one. Atoms smashed in accelerators produce a visible spray of energy, fireworks signaling the existence of quarks. Stars disappear in a shower of light, the beacon of an invisible black hole. Objective facts leave objective footprints.

3   Maybe one "knows" through "unknowing." I think this is beyond dispute.

4   Cognitive psychologists would call such questions **metacognition** (Flavell, 1979), or considering and questioning what we perceive and believe. In practical terms, a simple "cognition" is one's comprehension of a claim. ("My astrological horoscope says that because I am a Taurus I am bull-headed and do not listen to others. I understand.") A metacognitive question goes one step further and asks if a claim helps one understand the world more clearly and effectively. If not, what changes should one make to lead to increased understanding? ("How could a horoscope, based on the position of the stars, possibly say anything about my specific personality? Has anyone tested whether all 'Taurus' individuals are bull-headed? How would one go about doing this?")

Chapter 3

1   This may be confusing until you realize that our calendar year (the Georgian calendar) is not defined by the exact time it takes to circle the sun. Instead it is set up so that months are properly aligned with seasons (in July the earth is always tilted toward the sun, causing summers to be consistently warm in the northern hemisphere). But because of precession wobble, the earth is not exactly in the same place in its orbit around the sun each time it is tilted toward the sun. So each time summer comes, the earth is in a slightly different cosmic neighborhood with respect to all the stars in the heavens. The stars you see overhead today in July aren't the same as the stars your ancestors saw 2,000 years ago. In technical terms, the tropical year (from the longest day this summer to the longest day next summer) is not exactly the same as the sidereal year (when the earth, like the hand of a clock, makes one full circle around the sun). Still confused? Try this. Imagine the earth and sun are part of a giant clock, with the sun in the center and the earth at the end of a hand. This summer the longest day may occur when the sun is in the, say, "2 o'clock position" with respect to the sun. Two thousand years from now, because of the effects of precession tilt shift, the longest day may occur when the sun is in the "3 o'clock position."

2   Of course, Sagittarius A* can't "shine" because it is a black hole. What we see are surrounding stars and superheated gas before they descend into oblivion.

Chapter 4

1   For another interesting example, consider paranormal Professor Gary Schwartz's "Systemic Memory Theory" (Schwartz, 2004; Schwartz & Russek, 1999; Unfacts, 2000). According to Schwartz, Einstein came up with his famous theory of relativity by engaging in a thought experiment in which he imagined himself riding a beam of light. Inspired by this idea, Schwartz decided to imagine himself riding vibrations. Imagine two adjacent tuning forks. If you strike one, it will hum and the second fork will also hum in resonance. Furthermore, the first fork will pick up the hum of the second fork and resonate in a new way reflecting

both the original hum and the reflected hum. There are three parts to this system. The first tuning fork, the second fork, and the vibrations that travel between them. Take the forks away, and the vibrations continue through the air containing the information from each fork. (When you finally hear a lightning bolt, the lightning is actually over.) Through such feedback the recurrently interactive behavior of photons and electrons enables them to store information. Therefore any two things (electrons, cells, organs, people) that maintain an ongoing relationship evoke a dynamical info-energy system, a memory of their interactional history. Just as the photons of a dying star travel through the universe millennia after the star's demise, the informational loop between electrons, atoms, organs, and even people exists independently. Homeopathy works because such information contains memory concerning bodily systems. Psychics can read "minds" by actually tapping into information feedback loops. Life after death exists, because information loops continue even after one's demise. Systemic Memory Theory also explains out-of-body experiences, reincarnation, qi, aromatherapy, crystal healing, distant healing, spirit medicine, acupuncture, the kabala, and karma. People have their own dynamical info-energy systems, which are actually living and evolving after death. So Jesus, and Elvis, still live. This synopsis has not done justice to the subtleties of Professor Schwartz's theory.

2   Similar weasel phrases include "these findings were not significant, but suggest a trend" (translation: no effect), "initial evidence is suggestive," "emerging science suggests," "results are promising" (translation: "if we stop our study just at the right point—stop our horse race at the point our horse is ahead, we win." See Chapter 5, arbitrary stop points).

> REALITY CHECK   Apply a logic-based reality check to Systemic Memory Theory.

3   In legal circles, this is the "innocent until proven guilty" standard. Scientists refer to it as the "null hypothesis," or the hypothesis that effect or difference does not exist (and when observed is simply the result of chance). In court the prosecutor is responsible for providing evidence for a claim of guilt. In a research study, a scientist sets up a test to determine if an expected effect or difference exists. It is the responsibility of the prosecutors and scientists to support their claims.

4   This is also an example of affirming the consequent. If you win the lottery, soon you will get a large check. If you stop eating, you will lose weight. When one event causes another, the two events reliably appear together. However, the opposite is not necessarily true. If two events reliably appear together, it is not proof that they are causally related. Receiving a large check is not proof that you won the lottery, and losing weight is not proof that you stopped eating.

5   Do deductive arguments beg the question? This issue has been debated for some time. However, I find it useful to recognize that in a good deductive argument,

the only component at issue is usually the conclusion, not the premise. However, if an argument begs the question, at least one of its premises is questionable (Unfacts, 2000).

Chapter 6

1   Note that the probability of obtaining the exact sequence TTTTT is the same as the probability of obtaining any exact clumped sequence, say THHTT or THTHT. However, the probability of obtaining any clumped sequence (in which two, three, or four "Ts" or "Hs" appear together) is greater than a non-clumped sequence. There are two ways of obtaining a purely unclumped sequence: TTTTT or HHHHH. However, there are 10 ways of getting a clumped sequence: TTHHH, THHHT, HHHTT, HHTTT, HTTTH, TTTHH, THHHH, HHHHT, HTTTT, TTTTH.

2   Suggested headline for tabloid newspaper reports on my discovery: "PSYCHOLOGIST STICKS THUMB IN PI AND FINDS GOD"

Chapter 7

1   Phineas Taylor Barnum was a famous 19th century showman known for his entertaining hoaxes and for founding what became the Ringling Brothers and Barnum and Bailey Circus. He was one of the first professional debunkers (preceding Harry Houdini, see Chapter 11), although he had no problem with using shameless hype to make money. He is associated with the phrase "There's a sucker born every minute" (actually there is no agreement as to the true author, although Barnum never denied making the statement).

2   For interesting optical illusions, see: www.michaelbach.de/ot/; www.colorcube.com/illusions/illusion.htm

Chapter 9

1   At this point it is useful to emphasize that we define a placebo behaviorally, as an inert intervention presented with a suggested benefit. We presume that such suggested benefit induces an expectation of symptom relief. One might also assume that expectations can be defined in terms of neurophysiological events, just as visual imagery or strong affect can be traced to certain areas of the brain. Neurophysiological processes that define placebo expectations are complex and may differ according to symptom (Benedetti, 2009). They are beyond the scope of this chapter.

Chapter 10

1 It is beyond the scope of this book to consider the roles of the thalamus, dorso-lateral prefrontal cortex, amygdala, and dorsal anterior cingulate as well as neurotransmitters such as dopamine, acetylcholine, serotonin, and glutamate. If you are interested, see Aleman & Larøi (2008).

Chapter 11

1 Of course, if you believe that your sense of "I" is indeed a permanent body inhabitant, you would have to conclude that in a virtual-reality goggle experiment the out-of-body identity you are genuinely experiencing is a hallucination or dream, and that you have lost consciousness of the "real you" inside your body. But if the "real you" is in your body, unconscious, how can you simultaneously be unconscious and conscious, at least sufficiently conscious to ask the question? How can a dream or hallucination be more self-aware than the unconscious "real you" in your body? It gets messy. You are left with the worrisome task of figuring out just when the "real you" is a mental construct and when it is an actual body inhabitant. If you want to have fun with a thought experiment, think of yourself as a salami. Start cutting away slices. After each subtraction, point to yourself and ask "where am I?" Don't stop. When finished, put yourself together and proceed to the next chapter.

Chapter 12

1 Irwin and Watt (2007) have insisted upon an alternative definition: "*Parapsychology* is the scientific study of experiences which, if they are as they seem to be, are in principle outside the realm of human capacities as presently conceived by conventional scientists" (p. 1). In contrast, the Parapsychological Association (parapsych.org) defines parapsychology as the scientific study of paranormal phenomena. Irwin and Watt claim that defining parapsychology in terms of what is experienced ("This feels like it can't be explained") rather than a claimed process ("This can't be explained by current science") adds credibility to the field. This may be true, but an experiential definition of the paranormal always contains an implicit paranormal claim. Otherwise the countless delusions of psychotics, the confused otherworldly dreams of children, and drug-induced trips would merit the same attention as a psychic who claims to have the ability to read thoughts. The current definition of the Parapsychological Association does not clearly differentiate paranormal and parapsychological.

2 This curious and revealing choice of words is reminiscent of the Christian notion of a "jealous god" in which the Christian deity is the only god worthy of worship (and is "jealous" of those who worship idols or lesser gods). Whatever its origin, the notion of jealous phenomena begs for ruthless elaboration. Do some

researchers bring with them a certain "negativity" that interferes with psi? If so, what is this negativity? Let me offer three possibilities. First, is it a certain anti-psi bias or hostility? We have seen that this is inconsistent with findings that psi-believing researchers also obtain negative results. Also, believers often claim that psi phenomena such as remote viewing are not affected by distance. One can read minds around the world. Yet distance suddenly becomes a factor with negativity. Otherwise angry skeptics in New York could interfere with psi research in Arizona. Second, perhaps the presence of a cold laboratory environment puts the damper on psi. But then positive results have been reported in sterile laboratories. Finally, psi is less likely to appear when research is careful, error-free, and honest (Hines, 2003). Perhaps caution, accuracy, and honesty constitute psi-inhibiting "negativity." If so, psi-enhancing "positivity" would involve sloppiness, error, and the possibility of fraud. Continuing this line of thinking quickly reaches the hinterlands of the absurd. Taking the plunge, many who study paranormal phenomena view their research as providing a window into nonmaterial worlds perhaps of a spiritual nature. Indeed, paranormal research is often blatantly religious in nature (see Chapters 13 and 14 on spiritual energies and prayer). This invites a troubling theological question. What type of god would create a universe where careless, mistaken, and dishonest people are most likely to find evidence of his or her existence? Why would he or she create a universe in a way that conscientious, accurate, and honest people are least likely to find such supernatural evidence? This is my modest contribution to the never-ending "argument from design" (Chapter 15).

3   In 1988 (Druckman & Swets, 1988) the U.S. Army Research Institute commissioned the National Research Council to form a committee to assess techniques claimed to enhance performance. Although many fantastic claims were explored, ranging "from the incredible to the outrageously incredible" (171), the committee concluded that the evidence did not support the existence of psi phenomena. They argued strongly for more rigorous research that includes skeptical observers.

4   Other OT VII achievers appear to include actor Tom Cruise (Verini, 2005). Although this level is shrouded with mystery, Verini (2005) provides this account: "According to experts and the church's own literature, OT-VII ("OT" stands for Operating Thetan, "thetan" being the Scientology term for soul) is the penultimate tier in the church's spiritual hierarchy—the exact details of which are fiercely guarded and forbidden to be discussed even among top members. It is where a Scientologist learns how to become free of the mortal confines of the body and is let into the last of the mysteries of the cosmology developed by the church's longtime leader, science fiction novelist and 'Dianetics' author L. Ron Hubbard. This cosmology also famously holds that humans bear the noxious traces of an annihilated alien civilization that was brought to Earth by an intergalactic warlord millions of years ago."

5   Following the model of religious self-disclosure offered by Masters (Masters, 2005; Masters, Spielmans, & Goodson, 2006; see Chapter 15), I affirm that my

religious affiliation is Reformed Pastafarianism, a spiritual path that calls upon followers to draw a spotlight to evidence of the absurd.

Chapter 13

1   Hexagrams originated from an earlier practice in which yes–no questions were written on a turtle shell, which was then heated and dropped in cold water. The shell would crack, and a broken crack (– — —) was interpreted as "no" whereas a solid crack (——) indicated "yes." Shell cracks were replaced by the lines of the trigram.

Chapter 14

1   Gary Schwartz (Schwartz & Simon, 2007) has conducted research that he claims supports the claims of John of God. After noting the criticisms, he cites his own research: "Nonetheless, ongoing experiments in my laboratory for Advances in Consciousness and Health provide some surprising evidence that is remarkably consistent with spiritual healers' most controversial claims involving John of God" (p. 192).

2   Pro-paranormal researchers Irwin and Watt (2007) conclude that prayer search is "inconclusive."

3   Thus one should pray only for things that are totally unmeasurable and completely outside of the known universe? If so, we should restrict ourselves to prayers for things in the fifth dimension? Things before the Big Bang? After death? The wellbeing of inhabitants of Heaven, Hell or possibly Limbo? Remember, offering a distant request for someone else's happiness or wisdom is actually asking for a magical physical change in someone else's brain. Of course, there are many other spiritual reasons to pray, including asking for forgiveness, committing oneself to various ideals, and giving thanks for the intellectual faculties to figure things out.

4   Note: Galton's early study on prayer (previously described) appears to circumvent theological problems of "putting God to the test." Recall, he did not ask participants to pray.

References

Chapter 1

Bauer, H. H. (1996). Cryptozoology. In G. S. Stein (Ed.), *The encyclopedia of the paranormal* (pp. 199–214). Amherst, NY: Prometheus Books.

Einstein, A., Podolsky, B., & Rosen, N. (1935). Can quantum-mechanical description of physical reality be considered complete? *Physical Review, 47,* 777–780.

Frazer, J. G. (1911–1915). *The golden bough: A study in magic and religion* (3rd ed.). London: Macmillan.

Heuvelmans, B. (1962). *On the track of unknown animals.* London: Rupert Hart-Davis.

Hitchens, C. (2007). *God is not great: How religion poisons everything.* New York: Twelve.

Lindeman, M., & Aarnio, K. (2007). Superstitious, magical, and paranormal beliefs: An integrative model. *Journal of Research in Personality, 41,* 731–744.

Kuhn, R. L. (2007). Why this universe? Toward a taxonomy of possible explanations. *Skeptic, 13,* 28–39.

Monk, W. H. (1875). *Hymns ancient and modern* (2nd ed.). London: W. M. Clowes and Sons.

Otto, R. (1923). *The idea of the holy.* Oxford: Oxford University Press.

Radin, D. (2006). *Entangled minds: Extrasensory experiences in a quantum reality.* New York: Simon & Schuster.

Ryle, G. (1949). *The concept of mind.* Chicago: University of Chicago Press.

Truzzi, M. (1976). Editorial. *The Zetetic, 1*(1), *Fall/Winter,* 4.

Chapter 2

Angell, M., & Kassirer, J. P. (1998). Alternative medicine—the risks of untested and unregulated remedies. *New England Journal of Medicine, 339,* 839.

Bader, C. D., Froese, P., Johnson, B., Mencken, F. C., & Stark, R. (2005). *The Baylor Religion Survey.* Waco, TX: Baylor Institute for Studies in Religion. Retrieved March 25, 2007 from www.baylor.edu/content/services/document.php/33304.pdf

Barnes, P. M., Powell-Griner, E., McFann, K., & Nahin, R. L. (2004). *Complementary and alternative medicine use among adults: United States.* Washington, DC: National Center for Health Statistics.

Bausell, R. B. (2007). *Snake oil science: The truth about complementary and alternative medicine.* Oxford: Oxford University Press.

Einstein, A. (1936). *Physics and reality.* Reprinted in A. Einstein (1950). *Out of my later years.* New York: Philosophical Library, p. 59.

Farha, B., & Steward, G. (2006). Paranormal beliefs: An analysis of college students. *Skeptical Inquirer, 30*(1), 37–40.

Flavell, J. H. (1979). Metacognition and cognitive monitoring: A new era of cognitive-developmental inquiry. *American Psychologist, 34,* 906–911.

Fontanarosa, P. B., & Lundberg G. D. (1998). Alternative medicine meets science. *Journal of the American Medical Association, 280,* 1618–1619.

Gallup (2008). *Evolution, creationism, intelligent design.* Retrieved March 24, 2008 from www.gallup.com/poll/21814/Evolution-Creationism-Intelligent-Design.aspx

Gilovich, T. (1991). *How we know what isn't so.* New York: Free Press.

Glenday, C., & Friedman, S. T. (1999). *The UFO investigator's handbook.* Philadelphia, PA: Running Press.

Gordon, J. E. (Ed.). (1967). *Handbook of clinical and experimental hypnosis.* New York: Macmillan.

Gould, S. J. (1999). *Rocks of ages: Science and religion in the fullness of life.* New York: Ballantine Books.

Hall, T. (1972). Sociological perspectives on UFO reports. In C. Sagan & T. Page (Eds.), *UFOs—a scientific debate* (pp. 213–223). Ithaca, NY: Cornell University Press.

Harris Poll. (2005). *The religious and other beliefs of Americans 2005.* The Harris Poll #90, December 14. Retrieved March 24, 2008, from www.harrisinteractive.com/harris_poll/index.asp?PID=618

Harris, S. (2004). *The end of faith: Religion, terror, and the future of reason.* New York: Norton.

Hitchens, C. (2007). *God is not great: How religion poisons everything.* New York: Twelve.

Huxley, T. H. (1880). *The crayfish: An introduction to the study of zoology.* London: C. Kegan Paul & Co.

Irwin, H. J., & Watt, C. A. (2007). *An introduction to parapsychology* (5th ed.). Jefferson, NC: McFarland.

Kroger, W. S. (1977). *Clinical and experimental hypnosis in medicine, dentistry, and psychology.* New York: Lippincott.

Lynn, S. J., & Kirsch, I. (2006). *Essentials of clinical hypnosis: An evidence-based approach.* Washington, DC: American Psychological Association.

McCullough, M. E., & Willoughby, B. L. B. (2009). Religion, self-regulation, and self-control. Associations, applications, and implications. *Psychological Bulletin, 135* (1), 1–25.

Moore, D. W. (2005). Three in four Americans believe in paranormal. Gallup News Service, June 16. Retrieved March 25, 2008 from http://www.gallup.com/poll/16915/Three-Four-Americans-Believe-Paranormal.aspx

Newport, F. (2007). *Americans more likely to believe in God than the Devil, heaven more than hell.* Gallup News Service, June 13. Retrieved March 24, 2008 from www.gallup.com/poll/27877/Americans-More-Likely-Believe-God-Than-Devil-Heaven-More-Than-Hell.aspx

Newport, F., & Strausberg, M. (2001). *Americans' belief in psychic and paranormal phenomena is up over the past decade.* Retrieved March 24, 2008 from www.gallup.com/poll/4483/Americans-Belief-Psychic-Paranormal-Phenomena-Over-Last-Decade.aspx

Newsweek/Beliefnet. (2005). *Newsweek/Beliefnet poll results.* Retrieved March 27, 2008 from www.beliefnet.com/story/173/story_17353_1.html

New York Times. (2001). *Massachusetts clears 5 from Salem witch trials.* November 2. Retrieved March 24, 2008 from select.nytimes.com/search/restricted/article?res=F30815F63A540C718CDDA80994D9404482

Niewyk, D. L., & Nicosia, F. R. (2000). *The Columbia guide to the Holocaust.* New York: Columbia University Press.

Parapsych.org. (2008). *Parapsychological Association.* Retrieved March 24, 2008.

Pattie, F. A. (1994). *Mesmer and animal magnetism: A chapter in the history of medicine.* Hamilton, NY: Edmonston.

Paydarfar, D., & Schwartz, W. J. (2001). An algorithm for discovery. *Science Express,* March 8, 292(5514), p. 13.

Rice, T. W. (2003). Believe it or not: Religious and other paranormal beliefs in the United States. *Journal for the Scientific Study of Religion, 42,* 95–106.

Robbins, R. (1959). *Encyclopedia of witchcraft and demonology.* New York: Crown Publishers.

Saher, M., & Lindeman, M. (2005). Alternative medicine: A psychological perspective. *Personality and individual differences, 39,* 1169–1178.

Schwartz, G. E. (2003). *The afterlife experiments: Breakthrough scientific evidence of life after death.* New York: Atria Books.

Shakespeare, W. (1598). *Love's labour's lost.* London: Cuthbert Burby.

Truzzi, M. (1996). Pseudoscience. In G. Stein (Ed.), *The encyclopedia of the paranormal* (pp. 560–574). Amherst, NY: Prometheus Books.

Vyse, (1997). *Believing in magic: The psychology of superstition*: New York: Oxford University Press.

Chapter 3

Atkinson, D. R., Furlong, M. J., & Wampold, B. E. (1982). Statistical significance, reviewer evaluations, and the scientific process: Is there a statistically significant relationship? *Journal of Counseling Psychology, 29,* 189–194.

Bausell, R. B. (2007). *Snake Oil Science: The Truth about Complementary and Alternative Medicine.* Oxford: Oxford University Press.

Broad, W., & Wade, N. (1983). *Betrayers of the truth.* New York: Simon & Schuster.

Carroll, R. T. (2005). Anecdotal (testimonial) evidence. *Skepdic.* Retrieved August 14, 2007 from: www.skepdic.com/testimon.html

Culver, R, & Ianna, P. (1984). *The Gemini Syndrome*. Amherst, NY: Prometheus Books.

Hoskin, M. (2003). *The Cambridge Concise History of Astronomy*. Cambridge: Cambridge University Press.

Hume, D (1958). *An Enquiry Concerning Human Understanding*. Chicago: University of Chicago Press. Originally published 1758.

Irion, R. (2008). Homing in on black holes. *Smithsonian Magazine*, April. Retrieved November 6, 2008 from: www.smithsonianmag.com/science-nature/black-holes.html?c=y&page=1

Kohn, A. (1988). *False Prophets*. New York: Blackwell.

Melia, F. (2007). *The Galactic Supermassive Black Hole*. Princeton, NJ: Princeton University Press.

Shepard, L. A. (2003). *Encyclopedia of occultism and the paranormal* (5th ed.). Detroit, MI: Gale Research Co.

Tester, J. (1989). *A History of Western Astrology*. New York: Ballantine Books.

van Gent, R. H. (2004). *Isaac Newton & Astrology*. Skeptic Report, July. Retrieved December 10, 2007 from: www.skepticreport.com/predictions/newton.htm

Chapter 4

American Heritage Dictionary of the English Language, Fourth Updated Edition (2003). New York: Houghton Mifflin. Retrieved February 22, 2008 from: www.thefreedictionary.com/faith

Asimov, I. (1969). *Opus 100*. New York: Houghton Mifflin.

BBC News. (2003). Pill changes women's taste in men. January 20. Retrieved August 1, 2007 from: news.bbc.co.uk/1/hi/health/2677697.stm

BBC News. (2006a). Housework cuts breast cancer risk. December 29. Retrieved August 2, 2007 from: news.bbc.co.uk/2/hi/health/6214655.stm

BBC News. (2006b). Sex 'cuts public speaking stress'. August 26. Retrieved August 2, 2007 from: news.bbc.co.uk/2/hi/health/4646010.stm

Brooks, D. (2007). Goodbye, George and John. *New York Times*, August 7. Retrieved August 7, 2007 from: select.nytimes.com/2007/08/07/opinion/07brooks.html?hp

Burns, W. C. (1997). Spurious correlations. Retrieved August 8, 2007 from: www.burns.com/wcbspurcorl.htm

Carroll, R. C. (2006). False analogy. Retrieved May 19, 2008 from: www.skepdic.com/falseanalogy.html

Carroll, R. C. (2007). Occult statistics. Retrieved August 8, 2007 from: www.skepdic.com/occultstats.html

Carroll, R. T. (2003). *The skeptic's dictionary*. Hoboken, NJ: Wiley.

CNN (1999). Night-light may lead to nearsightedness. May 13. Retrieved October 10, 2007 from: www.cnn.com/HEALTH/9905/12/children.lights/index.html

Davies, P. (2007). Taking science on faith. Op-ed contribution. *New York Times*, November. Retrieved February 22, 2008 from: www.nytimes.com/2007/11/24/opinion/24davies.html?_r=1&oref=slogin

Gledhill, R. (2005). Societies worse off "when they have God on their side." *The Times*. September 27, 2005. Retrieved January 25, 2008 from: www.timeson-line.co.uk/tol/news/uk/article571206.ece.   See   also: moses.creighton.edu/JRS/2005/2005-11.html

Hare, W. (2009). What open-mindedness requires. *The Skeptical Inquirer, 33*(2), 36–39.

Irwin, H. J., & Watt, C. A. (2007). *An introduction to parapsychology*. Jefferson, NC: McFarland.

Johnson, C. K. (2007). Panic attacks may raise risk of heart failure, stroke in women. *Oakland Tribune*, Oct 2, 2007. Retrieved April 4, 2009 from: findarticles.com/p/articles/mi_qn4176/is_20071002/ai_n21021006/

Lindeman, M., & Aarnio, K. (2007). Superstitious, magical, and paranormal beliefs: An integrative model. *Journal of Research in Personality, 41,* 731–744.

Mueller, J. (2007). Correlations or causation. Retrieved August 2, 2007 from: jonathan.mueller.faculty.noctrl.edu/100/correlation_or_causation.htm

Nowak, R. M., & Walker, E. P. (2005). *Walker's carnivores of the world*. Baltimore: Johns Hopkins University Press.

Park, R. L. (2008). Two meanings of 'faith' confuse even scientists. *Skeptical Inquirer, 32,* 14.

Peer trainer. (2007). New study sponsored by General Mills says that eating breakfast makes girls thinner. Retrieved August 2, 2007 from: www.peertrainer.com/LoungeCommunityThread.aspx?ForumID=1&ThreadID=3118

Radin, D. (1997). *The conscious universe—the scientific truth of psychic phenomena*. New York: HarperCollins.

Radin, D. E. (2006). *Entangled minds: Extrasensory experiences in a quantum reality*. New York: Simon & Schuster.

Randi, J. (1982). *The truth about Uri Geller*. Buffalo, NY: Prometheus Books.

Ryle, G. (1949). *The concept of mind*. Chicago: University of Chicago Press.

Schwartz, G. (2004). Feedback and systemic memory: Implications for survival. Survival of Bodily Death: An Esalen Invitational Conference, May 2–7, 2004. Retrieved November 26, 2007 from: www.esalenctr.org/display/confpage.cfm?confid=19&pageid=149&pgtype=1

Schwartz, G. E. R., & Russek, L. G. S. (1999). *The living energy universe*. Charlottesville, VA: Hampton Roads.

Science Daily. (2007). Surgeons with video game skill appear to perform better in simulated surgery skills course. Retrieved August 2, 2007 from: www.sciencedaily.com/releases/2007/02/070220012341.htm

Sokal, A. D. (1996). Transgressing the boundaries: Towards a transformative hermeneutics of quantum gravity. *Social Text*, 46/47, 217–252. Retrieved April 1, 2008 from: www.physics.nyu.edu/faculty/sokal/transgress_v2/transgress_v2_singlefile.html

Springen, K. (2007). Newsweek online. Retrieved March 28, 2008 from: www.newsweek.com/id/41945

Tanner, L. (2006). Sexual lyrics prompt teens to have sex. Associated Press, August 6, 2006. Retrieved August 2, 2007 from: www.sfgate.com/cgi-bin/article.cgi?f=/n/a/2006/08/06/national/a215010D94.DTL

Townes, C. H. (2005). Statement by Charles Hard Townes at the Templeton Prize News Conference, March 9. Retrieved February 22, 2008 from: www.templeton. org/newsroom/press_releases/archive/050309townes.html

Unfacts. (2000). Book review: Living energy universe. Retrieved November 27, 2007 from: unfacts.org/archive/psychics/leureview.html

Yewchuck, B. (2008). The Star Trek Techno-Babble generator. Retrieved March 28, 2009 from: www.robotplanet.dk/humor/startrek_babble_generator.html

Chapter 5

Bassi, Agostino. (2008). In *Encyclopædia Britannica*. Retrieved January 17, 2008, from: www.britannica.com/eb/article-9013676

Bausell, R. B. (2007). *Snake oil science: The truth about complementary and alternative medicine*. Oxford: Oxford University Press.

Black, J. G. (1996). *Microbiology. Principles and applications* (3rd ed.). Upper Saddle River, NJ: Prentice Hall.

Blackmore, S., & Seebold, M. (2001). The effect of horoscopes on women's relationships. *Correlation, 19* (2), 17–32.

Carlson, S. (1985). A double-blind test of astrology. *Nature, 318,* 419–425.

Crowe, R. A. (1990). Astrology and the scientific method. *Psychological Reports, 67,* 163–191.

Culver, R. B., & Ianna, P. A. (1984). *The Gemini syndrome: A scientific evaluation of astrology*. Buffalo: Prometheus Books.

Dean, G. (2002). Is the Mars effect a social effect? A re-analysis of the Gauquelin data suggests that hitherto baffling planetary effects may be simple social effects in disguise. *Skeptical Inquirer, 26,* 33–38. May, 2002 Retrieved December 15, 2007 from: findarticles.com/p/articles/mi_m2843/is_3_26/ai_85932618/pg_2

Dean, G., Mather, A., & Kelly, I. W. (1996). Astrology. In G. Stein (Ed.), *The Encyclopedia of the Paranormal* (pp. 47–99). New York: Prometheus.

Eysenck, H., & Nias, D. (1982). *Astrology: Science or superstition?* New York: St. Martin's Press.

Forlano, G., & Ehrlich, V. (1941). Month and season of birth in relation to intelligence, introversion-extroversion, and inferiority feelings. *Journal of Education Research, 32,* 1–2.

Gauquelin, M. (1974). *Cosmic influences on human behavior*. London: Garnstone Press.

Hartshorne, C., & Weiss, P. (Eds.). (1932). *Collected papers of Charles Sanders Peirce, Volumes I and II, Principles of philosophy and elements of logic*. Cambridge, MA: Belknap Press.

Hines, T. (2003). *Pseudoscience and the paranormal* (2nd ed.). Amherst, NY: Prometheus Press.

Irving, K. (2003). The Gauquelin planetary effects. *Planetos: An online journal*. Retrieved December 27, 2007 from: www.planetos.info/index.html

Irwin, H. J., & Watt, C. A. (2007). *An introduction to parapsychology* (5th ed.). Jefferson, NC: McFarland.

Jerome, L. E. (1977). *Astrology disproved*. Amherst, NY: Prometheus Books.

Kelly, I. W. (1998). Why astrology doesn't work. *Psychological Reports, 82,* 527–546.

Kuhn, T. S. (1970). *The structure of scientific revolutions*. Chicago: University of Chicago Press.

Metchnikoff, E., & Berger, D. (1939). *The founders of modern medicine: Pasteur, Koch, Lister*. New York: Walden.

Nienhuys, J. W. (1997). The Mars effect in retrospect. *Skeptical Inquirer, 21,* 24–29. Retrieved April 1, 2008 from: www.skepticfiles.org/skeptic/marsef18.htm

Popper, K. (1959). *The logic of scientific discovery*. New York: Basic Books.

Schick, T., & Vaughn, L. (2005). *How to think about weird things: Critical thinking for a new age* (4th ed.). New York: McGraw-Hill.

Vaughn, L. (2008). *The power of critical thinking: Effective reasoning about ordinary and extraordinary claims* (2 ed.). New York: Oxford University Press.

Chapter 6

Anderson, D. (1996). Pi-search page. Retrieved April 1, 2008 from: www.angio.net/pi/piquery

Bausell, R. B. (2007). *Snake oil science: The truth about complementary and alternative medicine*. Oxford: Oxford University Press.

Blackmore, S., & Troscianko, T. (1985). Belief in the paranormal: Probability judgments, illusory control, and the "chance baseline shift." *British Journal of Psychology, 76,* 459–468. Retrieved April 1, 2008 from: www.susanblackmore.co.uk/Articles/BJP%201985.htm

Bollobás, B. (Ed.). (1986). *Littlewood's miscellany*. Cambridge: Cambridge University Press.

Bonferroni, C. E. (1935). Il calcolo delle assicurazioni su gruppi di teste. In *Studi in Onore del Professore Salvatore Ortu Carboni*. Rome, Italy, pp. 13–60.

Chopra, D. (2003). *The spontaneous fulfillment of desire*. New York: Harmony/Random House.

Elmo, Gum, Heather, Holly, Mistletoe, & Rowan. (2002). *Notes towards the complete works of Shakespeare*. Retrieved August 3, 2007 from: www.vivaria.net/experiments/notes/publication/NOTES_EN.pdf

Frazier, K. (Ed.). (2009). The new UFO interest: Scientific appraisals. [Special issue]. *Skeptical Inquirer, 33*(1), January/February.

Gauquelin, M. (1974). *Cosmic influences on human behavior*. London: Garnstone Press.

Gilovich, T. (1991). *How we know what isn't so*. New York: The Free Press.

Hines, T. (2003). *Pseudoscience and the paranormal*. Amherst, NY: Prometheus Books.

Holt, J. (2004). Throw away that astrological chart. *New York Times,* April 29, D10.

Kittel, C., & Kroemer, H. (1980). *Thermal physics* (2nd ed.). New York: W. H. Freeman.

Leavy, J. (1992). Our spooky presidential coincidences contest. *Skeptical Inquirer, 16,* 316–320.

McGaha, J. (2009). The trained observer of unusual things in the sky (UFOs?). *Skeptical Inquirer, 33*(1), 55–56.

McKenna, F. P., & Albery, I. P. (2001). Does unrealistic optimism change following a negative experience? *Journal of Applied Social Psychology, 31,* 1146–1157.

Morewedge, C. K., & Norton, M. I. (2009). When dreaming is believing: The (motivated) interpretation of dreams. *Journal of Personality and Social Psychology, 96,* 249–264.

Murray, H. A., & Wheeler, D. R. (1936). A note on the possible clairvoyance of dreams. *The Journal of Psychology, 3,* 309–313.

Myers, D. G. (2004). *Intuition: Its powers and perils.* New Haven, CT: Yale University Press.

Paulos, J. P. (2001). *Innumeracy: Mathematical illiteracy and its consequences.* New York: Hill and Wang.

Redfield, J. (1993). *The Celestine prophecy.* New York: Warner Books.

Sanbonmatsu, D. M., Posavac, S. S., & Stasney, R. (1997). The subjective beliefs underlying probability overestimation. *Journal of Experimental Social Psychology, 33,* 276–295.

Schick, T., & Vaughn, L. (2005). *How to think about weird things: Critical thinking for a new age.* New York: McGraw-Hill.

Tversky, A., & Kahneman, D. (1973). Availability: A heuristic for judging frequency and probability. *Cognitive Psychology, 5,* 207–232.

www.veegle.com. Substantiated true facts—the odds. Retrieved April 30, 2008 from: www.veegle.com/odds.htm?submit2=The+Real+Odds

Weinstein, N. D. (1980). Unrealistic optimism about future life events. *Journal of personality and social psychology, 39,* 806–820.

Weinstein, N. D., & Klein, W. M. (1996). Unrealistic optimism: Present and future. *Journal of Social and Clinical Psychology, 15,* 1–8.

Chapter 7

Baker, R. A. (1990). *They call it hypnosis.* Buffalo, NY: Prometheus Books.

Bányai, É., & Hilgard, E. (1976). A comparison of active-alert hypnotic induction with traditional relaxation induction. *Journal of Abnormal Psychology, 85*(2), 218–224.

Beloff, R. (1999). Bent on Uri Geller. *The Jerusalem Post Magazine,* December 6, 1999. Retrieved 27 November, 2007 from: www.uri-geller.com/jpostfriday.htm

Browne, S. (2005). *Secrets & mysteries of the world.* Carlsbad, CA: Hay House.

Browne, S. (2006). *Exploring the levels of creation.* Carlsbad, CA: Hay House.

Browne, S., & Harrison L. (2000). *Life on the other side: A psychic's tour of the afterlife.* New York: New American Library.

Carroll, R. T. (2003). *The skeptic's dictionary.* Hoboken, NJ: Wiley.

Carroll, R. T. (2006). Mass media funk. Retrieved April 4, 2009 from: skepdic.com/refuge/funk44.html

Carroll, R. T. (2007a). Cognitive dissonance. In *The skeptic's dictionary.* Retrieved April 1, 2008 from: skepdic.com/cognitivedissonance.html

Carroll, R. T. (2007b). Uri Geller. *The skeptic's dictionary.* Retrieved April 1, 2008 from: skepdic.com/geller.html

Cherry, E. C. (1953). Some experiments on the recognition of speech, with one and with two ears. *Journal of the Acoustic Society of America, 25,* 975–979.

Crick, R. (1984). Function of the thalamic reticular complex: The searchlight hypothesis. *Proceedings of the National Academy of Sciences USA, 81,* 4586–4590.

Dickson, D. H., & Kelly, I. W. (1985). "The Barnum Effect" in personality assessment: A review of the literature. *Psychological Reports, 57,* 367–382.

DuBois, Allison. Allisondubois.com

Dulin, D. (2005). "Soul Advice." *A&U Magazine,* December. Retrieved April 1, 2008 from: www.aumag.org/coverstory/December05cover.html

Edward, J. (1998). *One last time.* New York: Berkley Trade.

Edward, J. (2001). Crossing Over. San Diego, CA: Jodere Group.

Edward, J. (2003). *After life.* New York: Princess Books.

Endersby, A. (2002). *Talking the John Edward Blues.* SkepticReport. Retrieved April 1, 2008 from: www.skepticreport.com/psychicpowers/jeblues.htm

Festinger, L. (1957). *A theory of cognitive dissonance.* Stanford, CA: Stanford University Press.

Garb, H., Lilienfeld, S., Wood, J., & Nezworski, M. (2002, October). Effective use of projective techniques in clinical practice: Let the data help with selection and interpretation. *Professional Psychology: Research and Practice, 33*(5), 454.

Geller, U. (2007). *Uri Geller's Full Biography.* Retrieved 27 November, 2007 from: site.uri-geller.com

Gilovich, T., Savitsky, K., & Medvec, V. J. (1998). The illusion of transparency: Biased assessments of others' ability to read our emotional states. *Journal of Personality and Social Psychology, 75,* 332–346.

Glick, P., Gottesman, D., & Jolton, J. (1989). The fault is not in the stars: Susceptibility of skeptics and believers in astrology to the Barnum effect. *Personality and Social Psychology Bulletin, 15,* 572–583.

Glick, P., & Snyder, M. (1986). Self-fulfilling prophecy: The psychology of belief in astrology. *Humanist, 46,* 20–25, 50.

Goldstein, E. B. (2007). *Sensation and perception.* Belmont, CA: Thomson Wadsworth.

Hyman, R. (2003a). How *not* to test mediums: Critiquing the afterlife experiments. *Skeptical Inquirer, 27.* Retrieved April 1, 2008 from: www.csicop.org/si/2003-01/medium.html

Hyman, R. (2003b). Follow up reply. Skeptical Inquirer, 27. Retrieved April 1, 2008 from: www.csicop.org/si/2003-05/follow-up-hyman.html

Kihlstrom, J. F. (1962). *Stanford Hypnotic Susceptibility Scale.* Palo Alto, CA: Consulting Psychologists Press.

King, L. (2001). Are psychics for real? *Larry King Live,* March 6, 2001. Retrieved April 1, 2008 from: transcripts.cnn.com/TRANSCRIPTS/0103/06/lkl.00.html

Kirsch, I., & Braffman, W. (2001). Imaginative suggestibility and hypnotizability. *Current Directions in Psychological Science, 4*, 57–61.

Lancaster, R. (2007). Stop Sylvia Browne. www.stopsylviabrowne.com

Lilienfeld, S. O., Lynn, S. J., & Lohr, J. M. (Eds.). (2003). *Science and pseudoscience in clinical psychology*. New York: Guilford.

Lilienfeld, S. O., Ruscio, J., & Lynn, S. J. (Eds.). (2008). *Navigating the mindfield: A guide to separating science from Pseudoscience in mental health*. Amherst, NY: Prometheus Books.

Martinez-Conde, S., & Macknik, S. L. (2008). Magic and the brain. *Scientific American, 299*(6), 72–79.

McClain, C. (2005). Varied readings on Arizona psychic. *Arizona Daily Star*, January 17. Retrieved April 4, 2009 from: web.archive.org/web/20060507055430/www.azstarnet.com/dailystar/dailystar/57187.php

Memorable Quotes. (1999). Memorable quotes for "Family Guy". Retrieved April 1, 2008 from: stopsylvia.com/home/

Nickell, J. (2004). Psychic Sylvia Browne once failed to foresee her own criminal conviction. *Skeptical Inquirer, 28*(5), November/December, p. 11.

Nickerson, R. S. (1998). Confirmation bias: A ubiquitous phenomenon in many guises. *Review of General Psychology, 2*, 175–220.

Novus Spiritus. Retrieved April 1, 2008 from: www.novus.org/home/faq.cfm

Pronin, E., Gilovich, T., & Ross, L. (2004). Objectivity in the eye of the beholder: Divergent perceptions of bias in self versus others. *Psychological Review, 111*, 781–799.

Pronin, E., Lin, D. Y., & Ross, L. (2002). The bias blind spot: Perceptions of bias in self versus others. *Personality and Social Psychology Bulletin, 28*, 369–381.

Randi, J. (1982a). *Flim Flam!*. Buffalo, NY: Prometheus Books.

Randi, J. (1982b). *The truth about Uri Geller*. Buffalo, NY: Prometheus Books.

Randi, J. (1993). *The mask of Nostradamus: The prophecies of the world's most famous seer*. Amherst, NY: Prometheus.

Randi, J. (2006). John Edward Revisited. Swift: Online newsletter for the JREF. April 21. Retrieved April 1, 2008 from: www.randi.org/jr/2006-04/042106edward.html#i1

Randi, J. (2007). *An encyclopedia of claims, frauds, and hoaxes of the occult and supernatural*. Uri Geller. Retrieved April 1, 2008 from: www.randi.org/encyclopedia/Geller,%20Uri.html

Religioustolerance. (2007). Retrieved April 1, 2008 from: www.religioustolerance.org/end_wrld.htm

Rowland, I. (2005). *The Full Facts Book of Cold Reading* (4th ed.). London: Ian Rowland, Ltd.

Schick, T., & Vaughn, L. (2005). *How to think about weird things: Critical thinking for a new age* (4th ed.). New York: McGraw-Hill.

Schwartz, G. (2003a). *The Afterlife Experiments*. New York: Atria Books.

Schwartz, G. (2003b). *How not to review mediumship research: Understanding the ultimate reviewer's mistake*. Retrieved April 1, 2008 from: www.enformy.com/Gary-reHymanReview.htm

Shermer, M. (2002). *Why people believe in weird things: Pseudoscience, superstition, and other confusions of our time*. New York: Henry Holt.

Shermer, M. (2005). *Science friction*. New York: Henry Holt.

Shor, R. E., & Orne, E. C. (1962). *Harvard Group Scale of Hypnotic Susceptibility*. Palo Alto, CA: Consulting Psychologists Press.

Sternberg, R. J. (2006). *Cognitive psychology* (4th ed.). Belmont, CA: Thomson/ Wadsworth.

Stone, J. (2001). Behavioral discrepancies and the role of construal processes in cognitive dissonance. In G. B. Moskowitz (Ed.), *Cognitive social psychology: The Princeton symposium on the legacy and future of social cognition* (pp. 41–58). Mahwah, NJ: Erlbaum.

The Two Percent Company. (2005). *Medium: The dubious claims of Allison DuBois*. March. Retrieved April 1, 2008 from: www.twopercentco.com/rants/ archives/2005/03/medium_the_dubi_4.html

The Two Percent Solution. (2005). Retrieved April 4, 2009 from: www.twoper centco.com/rants/archives/2006/07/polar_opposites.html

Time. (March 12, 1973). The magician and the think tank. Retrieved April 1, 2008 from: www.time.com/time/magazine/article/0,9171,944639,00.html?promoid= googlep

Turnbull, C. M. (1961). Some observations regarding the experiences and behavior of the BaMbuti Pygmies. *American Journal of Psychology, 74,* 304–308.

Vorauer, J. D. (2001). The other side of the story: Transparency estimation in social interaction. In G. B. Moskowitz (Ed.), *Cognitive social psychology: The Princeton symposium on the legacy and future of social cognition* (pp. 371–385). Mahwah, NJ: Erlbaum.

Vorauer, J. D., & Claude, S. (1998). Perceived versus actual transparency of goals in negotiation. *Personality and Social Psychology Bulletin, 24,* 371–385.

Wark, D. M. (2006). Alert hypnosis: A review and case report. *American Journal of Clinical Hypnosis, 48,* 291–300.

Watson, P. C. (1960). On the failure to eliminate hypotheses in a conceptual task. *Quarterly Journal of Experimental Psychology, 12,* 129–140.

Chapter 8

Ackil, J. K., & Zaragoza, M. S. (1998). Memorial consequences of forced confabulation: Age differences in susceptibility to false memories. *Developmental Psychology, 34,* 1358–1372.

Atkinson, R. C., & Shiffrin, R. M. (1968). Human memory: A proposed system and its control processes. In K. W. Spence & J. T. Spence (Eds.), *The psychology of learning and motivation: Vol. 2. Advances in research and theory*. New York: Academic Press.

Begg, I., & Armour, V. (1991). Repetition and the ring of truth: Biasing comments. *Canadian Journal of Behavioral Science, 23,* 195–213.

Begg, I. M., Anas, A., & Farinacci, S. (1992). Dissociation of processes in belief: Source recollection, statement familiarity, and the illusion of truth. *Journal of Experimental Psychology, 121,* 446–458.

Belluck, P. (1997). "Memory" therapy leads to a lawsuit and big settlement. *The New York Times,* Page 1, Column 1, November 6. Retrieved April 1, 2008 from: query.nytimes.com/gst/fullpage.html?res=9B04E7D91F30F935A35752C 1A961958260

Boyd, R. (2008). Do people only use 10 percent of their brains? *Scientific American.* Retrieved April 1, 2008 from: www.sciam.com/article.cfm?id=people-only-use-10-percent-of-brain&page=1

Brown, A. S. (2004). *The Déjà vu experiences: Essays in cognitive psychology.* East Sussex, England: Psychology Press.

Cutler, B. L., & Penrod, S. D. (1995). *Mistaken identification: The eyewitness, psychology, and the law.* New York: Cambridge University Press.

Echterhoff, G., Higgins, E. T., Kopietz, R., & Groll, S. (2008). How communication goals determine when audience tuning biases memory. *Journal of Experimental Psychology: General, 137,* 3–21.

Gloor, P. (1990). Experiential phenomena of temporal lobe epilepsy: Facts and hypotheses. *Brain, 113,* 1673–1694.

Hasher, L., Goldstein, D., & Toppino, T. (1977). Frequency and the conference of referential validity. *Journal of Verbal Learning and Verbal Behavior, 16,* 107–112.

Hicks, J. L., & Marsh, R. L. (2001). False recognition occurs more frequently during source identification than during old-new recognition. *Journal of Experimental Psychology: Learning, Memory, and Cognition, 27,* 375–383.

Higgins, E. T. (1992). Achieving "shared reality" in the communication game: A social action that creates meaning. *Journal of Language and Social Psychology, 11,* 107–131.

Hyman, I. E., & Pentland, J. (1995). The role of mental imagery in the creation of false memories. *Journal of Memory and Language, 35,* 101–117.

Johnson, M. K. (2006). Memory and reality. *American Psychologist, 61,* 760–771.

Johnson, M. K., Hashtroudi, S., & Lindsay, D. S. (1993). Source monitoring. *Psychological Bulletin, 114,* 3–28.

Loftus, E. F. (1996). *Eyewitness testimony.* Cambridge, MA: Harvard University Press.

Loftus, E. F. (1997). Creating false memories. *Scientific American, 277,* 70–75.

Loftus, E. F., & Ketcham, K. (1994). *The myth of repressed memory.* New York: St. Martin's.

McNally, R. J. (2004). The science and folklore of traumatic amnesia. *Clinical Psychology: Science and Practice, 11,* 29–33.

Moskowitz, G. B. (2005). *Social cognition.* New York: Guilford Press.

Osborn, H. F. (1884). Illusions of memory. *North American Review, 138,* 476–486.

Radford, B. (1999). The ten-percent myth. *Skeptical Inquirer, 23,* 52–53. Retrieved February 28, 2008 from: csicop.org/si/9903/ten-percent-myth.html

Schacter, D. L. (1996). *Searching for memory—the brain, the mind, and the past.* New York: Basic Books.

Skurnik, I., Yoon, C., Park, D. C., & Schwartz, N. (2005). How warnings about false claims become recommendations. *Journal of Consumer Research, 31,* 713–724.

Squire, L. R. (2004). Memory systems of the brain: A brief history and current perspective. *Neurobiology of Learning and Memory, 82,* 171–177.

Sternberg, R. J. (2006). *Cognitive psychology.* Belmont, CA: Thompson.

Stevenson, R. L. (2004). *Essays in the art of writing.* Adelaide: Ebooks.

Sutton, J. (2003). Memory, philosophical issues about. In L. Nabel (Ed.), *Encyclopedia of cognitive science, Vol. 2* (pp. 1109–1113). London: Nature Publishing Group.

Tulving, E., & Wayne, D. (1972). *Organization of memory.* Oxford: Oxford University Press.

Wade, K. A., Sharman, S. J., Garry, M., Memon, A., Mazzoni, G., Merckelbach, H., et al. (2006). False claims about false memory research. *Consciousness and cognition, 16,* 18–28.

Wilson, K., & French, C. C. (2006). The relationship between susceptibility to false memories, dissociativity, and paranormal belief and experience. *Personality and Individual Differences, 41,* 1493–1502.

Zuger, B. (1966). The time of dreaming and the déjà vu. *Comprehensive Psychiatry, 7,* 191–196.

Chapter 9

Ariel, G., & Saville, W. (1972). Anabolic steroids: The physiological effects of placebos. *Medicine and Science in Sport and Exercise, 4,* 124–126.

Bausell, R. B. (2007). *Snake oil science: The truth about complementary and alternative medicine.* Oxford: Oxford University Press.

Beecher, H. K. (1955). The powerful placebo. *Journal of the American Medical Association, 159*(17), 24 December, 1602–1606.

Beedie, C. J. (2007). Placebo effects in competitive sport: Qualitative data. *Journal of Sports Science and Medicine, 6,* 21–28.

Beedie, C. J., Stuart, E. M., Coleman, D. A., & Foad, A. J. (2006). Placebo effects of caffeine in cycling performance. *Medicine and Science in Sport and Exercise, 38,* 2159–2164.

Benedetti, F. (2009). *Placebo effects: Understanding the mechanisms in health and disease.* New York: Oxford University Press.

Benedetti, F., Arduino, C., & Amanzio, M. (1999). Somatotopic activation of opioid systems by target-directed expectations of analgesia. *Journal of Neuroscience, 9,* 3639–3648.

Benson, H. (1996). Harnessing the power of the placebo effect and renaming it "remembered wellness." *Annual Review of Medicine, 47,* 193–199.

Bube, R. H. (1971). Man come of age: Bonhoeffer's response to the God-Of-The-Gaps, *Journal of the Evangelical Theological Society, 14,* 203–220.

Carroll, R. (2008). Book review: The cure within: A history of mind-body medicine (Anne Harrington). In *The skeptic's dictionary.* February 18. Retrieved June 13, 2008 from: skepdic.com/refuge/harrington.html

Clark, V. R., Hopkins, W. G., Hawley, J. A., & Burke, L. M. (2000). Placebo effect of carbohydrate feeding during a 4-km cycling time trial. *Medicine and Science in Sport and Exercise, 32,* 1642–1647.

Cobb, L. A., Thomas, G. I., Dillard, D.H., Merendino, K.A., & Bruce, R.A. (1959). An evaluation of internal mammary artery ligation by a double-blind technic. *New England Journal of Medicine, 20,* 1115–1118.

Cohen, N., Moynihan, J. A., & Ader, A. (1994). Pavlovian conditioning of the immune system. *International Archives of Allergy and Immunology, 105,* 101–106.

Dincer, F. (2003). Sham interventions in randomized clinical trials of acupuncture—a review. *Complementary Therapies in Medicine, 11*(4), 235–242.

Foster, C., Felker, H., Porcari, J. P., Mikat, R. P., & Seebach, E. (2004). The placebo effect on exercise performance. *Medicine and Science in Sport and Exercise, 36*(Suppl.), S171.

Gilovich, T. (1991). *How we know what isn't so.* New York: The Free Press.

Grady, A. M. (2007). Psychophysiological mechanisms of stress: A foundation for stress management therapies. In P. M. Lehrer, R. M. Woolfolk, & W. E. Sime (Eds.), *Principles and practice of stress management* (3rd ed.). New York: Guilford Press.

Hooper, R. (1822). *Hooper's lexicon-medicum.* New York: Harpers and Brothers.

Hróbjartsson, A., & Gøtzsche, P. C. (2001). Is the placebo powerless? An analysis of clinical trials comparing placebo with no treatment. *The New England Journal of Medicine, 344,* 1594–1602.

Irwin, H. J., & Watt, C. A. (2007). *An introduction to parapsychology.* Jefferson, NC: McFarland.

Kaptchuk, T. J., Stason, W. B., Davis, R. B., Legedza, A. R. T., Schnyer, R. N., Kerr, C. E., et al. (2006). Sham device v inert pill: Randomised controlled trial of two placebo treatments. *British Medical Journal, 332,* 391–397.

Klopfer, B. (1957). Psychological variables in human cancer. *Journal of Projective Techniques, 21*(4), 331–340.

Kong, J., Gollub, R. L., Rosman, I. S., Webb, J. M., Vangel, M. G., Kirsch, I., et al. (2006). Brain activity associated with expectancy-enhanced placebo analgesia as measured by functional magnetic resonance imaging. *The Journal of Neuroscience, 26,* 381–388.

Lang, W., & Rand, M. A. (1969). A placebo response as a conditional reflex to glyceryl trinitrate. *Medical Journal of Australia, 1,* 912–914.

Lehrer, P. M., Woolfolk, R. M., & Sime, W. E. (2007). *Principles and practice of stress management* (3rd ed.). New York: Guilford Press.

Lidstone, S. C. C., & Stoessl, A. L. (2007). Understanding the placebo effect: Contributions from neuroimaging. *Molecular Imaging and Biology, 9,* 176–185.

Lilienfeld, S. O., Lynn, S. J., & Lohr, J. M. (Eds). (2003). *Science and pseudoscience in clinical psychology.* New York: Guilford Press.

Lilienfeld, S. O., Ruscio, J., & Lynn, S. J. (Eds.). (2008). *Navigating the mindfield: A guide to separating science from pseudoscience in mental health*. Amherst, NY: Prometheus Books.

Madsen, M. V., Gøtzsche, P. C., & Hróbjartsson, A. (2009). Acupuncture treatment for pain: Systematic review of randomized clinical trials with acupuncture, placebo acupuncture, and no acupuncture groups. *British Medical Journal*, March, 3115. Retrieved March 3, 2009 from www.bmj.com/cgi/reprint/338/jan27_2/a 3115?maxtoshow=&HITS=10&hits=10&RESULTFORMAT=&fulltext=sham +acupuncture&searchid=1&FIRSTINDEX=0&resourcetype=HWCIT

Maganaris, C. N., Collins, D., & Sharp, M. (2000). Expectancy effects and strength training: Do steroids make a difference? *The Sport Psychologist, 14,* 272–278.

Moseley, B. J., O'Malley, K., Petersen, N. J., Menke, T. J., Brody, B. A., Kuykendall, D. H., et al. (2002). A controlled trial of arthroscopic surgery for osteoarthritis of the knee. *The New England Journal of Medicine, 347*(2), 81–88.

Norcross, J. C., Koocher, G. P., & Garofalo, A. (2006). Discredited psychological treatments and tests: A Delphi poll. *Professional Psychology: Research and Practice, 37*(5), 515–522.

Price D. D., Milling L. S., Kirsch, I., Duff, A., Montgomery, G. H., & Nicholls, S. S. (1999). Analysis of factors that contribute to the magnitude of placebo analgesia in an experimental paradigm. *Pain, 83,* 147–157.

Robazza, C., & Bortoli, L. (1994). Hypnosis in sport: An isomorphic model. *Perceptual and Motor Skills, 79*(2), 963–973.

Sapolsky, R. M. (2004). *Why zebras don't get ulcers* (3rd ed.). New York: Henry Holt.

Shapiro, A. K., & Shapiro, E. (1997). *The powerful placebo: From priest to modern physician*. Baltimore, MD: Johns Hopkins University Press.

Skinner, B. F. (1948). 'Superstition' in the pigeon. *Journal of Experimental Psychology, 38,* 168–172.

Skinner, B. F. (1974). *About behaviorism*. New York: Random House.

Smith, J. C. (2005). *Relaxation, meditation & mindfulness: A mental health practitioner's guide to new and traditional approaches*. New York: Springer.

Smith, J. C. (2007). The psychology of relaxation. In P. M. Lehrer, R. L. Woolfolk, & W. E. Sime (Eds.), *Principles and practice of stress management* (3rd ed., pp. 38–56). New York: Guilford Press.

Sonetti, D. A., Wetter, T. J. Pegelow, D. F., & Dempsey, J. A. (2001). Effects of respiratory muscle training versus placebo on endurance exercise performance. *Respiration Physiology, 127*(2–3), 185–199.

Sun, Y., & Gan, T. J. (2008). Acupuncture for the management of chronic headache: A systematic review. *Anesthesia and Analgesia, 107*(6), 2038–2047.

Talbot, M. (2000). The placebo prescription. *New York Times Magazine*, January 9. Retrieved April 1, 2008 from: www.nytimes.com/library/magazine/home/ 20000109mag-talbot7.html

Vase, L., Robinson, M. E., Verne, G. N., & Price, D. D. (2005). Increased placebo analgesia over time in irritable bowel syndrome (IBS) patients is associated with desire and expectation but not endogenous opioid mechanisms. *Pain, 115,* 338–347.

Voet, W. (1999). *Breaking the chain: Drugs and cycling, the true story.* London: Random House/Yellow Jersey Press.

Waber, R. L., Shiv, B., Carmon, Z., & Ariely, D. (2008). Commercial features of placebo and therapeutic efficacy. *Journal of the American Medical Association, 299,* 1016–1017.

Wampold, B. E., Minami, T., Tierney, S. C., Baskin, T. W., & Bhati, K. S. (2005). The placebo is powerful: Estimating placebo effects in medicine and psychotherapy from randomized clinical trials. *Journal of Clinical Psychology, 61,* 835–854.

Wark, D. M. (2006). Alert hypnosis: A review and case report. *American Journal of Clinical Hypnosis, 48,* 291–300.

Zubieta, J-K., Bueller, J. A., Jackson, L. R., Scott, D. J., Xu, Y., Koeppe, R. A., et al. (2005). Placebo effects mediated by endogenous opioid activity on æ-opioid receptors. *The Journal of Neuroscience, 25,* 7754–7762.

Chapter 10

Aleman, A., & Larøi, F. (2008). *Hallucinations: The science of idiosyncratic perception.* Washington, DC: American Psychological Association.

American Psychiatric Association. (2004). *DSM-IV-TR.* Washington, DC: American Psychiatric Association.

Beyerstein, B. L. (1996). Believing is seeing: Organic and psychological reasons for hallucinations and other anomalous psychiatric symptoms. *Medscape Psychiatry & Mental Health ejournal, 1.* Retrieved April 1, 2008 from: www.medscape.com/viewarticle/431517

Birbaumer, N., Gruzelier, J., Jamieson, G. A., Kotchoubey, B., Kübler, A., Lehmann, D., et al. (2005). Psychobiology of altered states of consciousness. *Psychological Bulletin, 131,* 98–127.

Blackmore, S. (1991). Near-death experiences: In or out of the body? *Skeptical Inquirer, 16,* 34–45.

Blackmore, S. (2004). *Consciousness: An introduction.* New York: Oxford University Press.

Blackmore, S. (n.d.). OBE. Retrieved April 1, 2008 from: www.issc-taste.org/arc/dbo.cgi?set=expom&id=00075&ss=1

Blackmore, S. J., & Troscianko, T. S. (1989). The physiology of the tunnel. *Journal of Near-Death Studies, 8,* 15–28.

Bourguignon, E. (1970). Hallucinations and trance: An anthropologist's perspective. In W. Keup (Ed.), *Origins and mechanisms of hallucinations* (pp. 83–90). New York: Plenum Press.

Bower, B. (2005). Night of the crusher. *Science News, 168,* p. 27. Retrieved April 1, 2008 from: www.sciencenews.org/articles/20050709/bob9.asp

Bradshaw, J. (1967). Pupil size as a measure of arousal during information processing. *Nature, 216,* 515–516.

David, A. S. (2004). The cognitive neuropsychiatry of auditory verbal hallucinations: An overview. *Cognitive Neuropsychiatry, 9,* 107–124.

Depersonalization Support Community. Retrieved April 1, 2008 from: www.dpself help.com/

Ehrsson, H. E. (2007). The experimental induction of out-of-body experiences. *Science, 317,* 1048.

Evans, R. W., & Matthew, N. T. (2005). *Handbook of headache* (2nd ed.). Philadelphia: Lippincott Williams and Wilkins.

Geschwind, N. (1983). Interictal behavioral changes in epilepsy. *Epilepsia, 24,* 23–30.

Goodman, W. K., & Murphy, T. K. (1998). Obsessive-compulsive disorder and Tourette's syndrome. In S. J. Enna & J. T. Coyle (Eds.), *Pharmacological management of neurological and psychiatric disorders* (pp. 177–211). New York: McGraw-Hill Health Professions Division.

Grassian, S. (1993). Psychiatric effects of solitary confinement. Declaration submitted September 1993 in Madrid v. Gomez, 889F. Supp. 1146. Retrieved April 1, 2008 from: www.prisoncommission.org/statements/grassian_stuart_long.pdf

Hunter, E. C., Sierra, M., & David, A. S. (2004). The epidemiology of depersonalisation and derealisation. A systematic review. *Social Psychiatry and Psychiatric Epidemiology, 39,* 9–18.

Illusion Forum. Retrieved March 23, 2008 from: www.brl.ntt.co.jp/IllusionForum/basics/visual/index-e.html

Lenggenhager, B., Tadi, T., Metzinger, T., & Blanke, O. (2007). Video ergo sum: Manipulating bodily self-consciousness. *Science, 317,* 1096.

Lutz, P. L., & Nilsson, G. E. (1997). *The brain without oxygen.* Austin, TX: Landes Bioscience.

Maddox, R. W., & Long, M. A. (1999). Eating disorders: Current concepts. *Journal of the American Pharmacological Association, 39,* 378–387.

Morris, R. L., Harary, S. B., Janis, J., Hartwell, J., & Roll, W. G. (1978). Studies of communication during out-of-body experiences. *Journal of the Society for Psychical Research, 72,* 1–22.

NINDS. (2007). National Institute of Neurological Disorders and Stroke. Migraine information page. Retrieved April 1, 2008 from: www.ninds.nih.gov/disorders/migraine/migraine.htm

Partala, T., & Surakka, V. (2003). Pupil size variation as an indicator of affective processing. *International Journal of Human-Computer Studies, 59,* 185–198.

Penfield, W. (1955). The twenty-ninth Maudsley lecture: The role of the temporal cortex in certain physical phenomena. *Journal of Mental Science, 101,* 451–465.

Peterson, C. B., & Mitchell, J. E. (1999). Psychosocial and pharmacological treatment of eating disorders: A review of research findings. *Journal of Clinical Psychology, 55,* 685–697.

Phelps, B. J. (2000). Dissociative identity disorder: The relevance of behavior analysis. *The Psychological Record, 50,* 235–249.

Ritsher, J. B., Lucksted, A, Otilingam, P. G., & Grajales, M. (2004). Hearing voices: Explanations and implications. *Psychiatric Rehabilitation Journal, 27,* 219–227. Retrieved April 1, 2008 from: repositories.cdlib.org/postprints/1597

Sacks, O. (1999). *Migraine*. New York: Knopf.

Sacks, O. (2008). Patterns. *New York Times,* Thursday, February 14. Retrieved February 14, 2008 from: migraine.blogs.nytimes.com/2008/02/13/patterns/index.html

Sarbin, T. R., & Juhasz, J. B. (1975). The historical background of the concept of hallucination. In R. K. Siegel & L. J. West (Eds.), *Hallucinations: Behavior, experience and theory* (pp. 214–227). New York: Wiley.

Schroeter-Kunhardt, M. (1993). A review of near death experiences. *Journal of Scientific Exploration, 7,* 219–239.

Shapiro, A. K., Young, J. G., Shapiro, E., & Feinberg, T. E. (1988). Gilles de la Tourette syndrome. Philadelphia, PA: Lippincott Williams and Wilkins.

Simner, J., Mulvenna, C., Sagiv, N., Tsakanikos, E. Witherby, S. A., Fraser, C., et al. (2006). The prevalence of atypical cross-modal experiences. *Perception, 8,* 1024–1033.

Tien, A. Y. (1991). Distribution of hallucinations in the population. *Social Psychiatry and Psychiatry Epidemiology, 26,* 287–292.

Ward, J. (2004). Emotionally-mediated synaesthesia. *Cognitive Neuropsychology, 21,* 761–772.

Ward, J., Huckstep, B., & Tsakanikos, E. (2006). Sound-colour: To what extent does it use cross-modal mechanisms common to us all? *Cortex, 42*(2), 264–280.

Wells, H. G. (1898). *War of the worlds*. New York: Bartleby.com.

Young, W. B., & Silberstein, S. D. (2004). *Migraine and other headaches*. St. Paul, MN: AAN Press.

Chapter 11

Baker, R. (1996). Cryptomnesia. In G. Stein (Ed.), *The encyclopedia of the paranormal* (pp. 186–199). Amherst, NY: Prometheus Books.

Bernstein, M. (1956). *The search for Bridey Murphy*. New York: Doubleday.

Blackmore, S. (1991). Near-death experiences: In or out of the body. *Skeptical Inquirer, 16,* 34–45.

Brandon, R. (1983). *The spiritualists: The passion for the occult in the nineteenth and twentieth centuries*. New York: Alfred A. Knopf.

Carroll, R. C. (2006a). What if Gary Schwartz is right? *The skeptic's dictionary*. Retrieved April 1, 2008 from: skepdic.com/essays/schwartz.html

Carroll, R. C. (2006b). Gary Schwartz and intelligent design. The Skeptic's Dictionary Newsletter 67. May, 2006. Retrieved April 1, 2008 from: skepdic.com/news letter67/html#5

Edwards, P. (1996). *Reincarnation: A critical examination*. Amherst, NY: Prometheus Books.

Ehrsson, H. E. (2007). The experimental induction of out-of-body experiences. *Science, 317,* 1048.

Ernst, B. M. L., & Carrington, H. (1932). *Houdini and Conan Doyle: The story of a strange friendship*. New York: Albert and Charles Boni.

Hart, H. (1959). *The enigma of survival*. London: Rider & Co.

Houdini, H. (1924). *A magician among the spirits*. New York: Harper.

Hyman, R. (2003). How *not* to test mediums: Critiquing the afterlife experiments. *Skeptical Enquirer*, January/February 2003. Retrieved April 1, 2008 from: www.csicop.org/si/2003-01/medium.html

Irwin, H. J., & Watt, C. A. (2007). *An introduction to parapsychology*. Jefferson, NC: McFarland.

Keene, M. (1976). *Psychic mafia*. New York: St. Martin's Press.

Kübler-Ross, E. L. (1969). *On death and dying*. New York: Simon & Schuster.

Kurtz, P. (1985). Spiritualists, mediums, and psychics: Some evidence of fraud. In P. Kurtz (Ed.), *A skeptic's handbook of parapsychology* (pp. 177–223). Amherst, NY: Prometheus Books.

Lenggenhager, B., Tadi, T., Metzinger, T., & Blanke, O. (2007). Video ergo sum: Manipulating bodily self-consciousness. Science, *317*, 1996.

van Lommel, P., van Wees, R., Meyers, V., & Elfferich, I. (2001). Near death experience in survivors of cardiac arrest: A prospective study in the Netherlands. *Lancet, 358*, 2039–2045.

Molé, P. (2002). Reincarnation. In M. Shermer (Ed.), *The skeptic encyclopedia of pseudoscience* (pp. 204–212). Santa Barbara, CA: ABC-CLIO.

Moody, R. A., Jr. (1975). *Life after life*. New York: Bantam.

Mulholland, J. (1938). *Beware familiar spirits*. Reprinted New York: Charles Scribner's Sons, 1979.

O'Keeffe, C., & Wiseman, R. (2005). Testing alleged mediumship: Methods and results. *British Journal of Psychology, 96*, 165–179.

Rhodes, E. (2007). Signed confession of Margaret Fox Kane October, 1988. Retrieved April 5, 2009 from: www.emmalouiserhodes.com/articles/fox-statement.php

Ring, K. (1980). *Life at death*. New York: Coward, McCann and Goeghegan.

Roach, M. (2005). *Spook: Science tackles the afterlife*. New York: W.W. Norton.

Rosenbaum, R. (2004). Dead like her: How Elisabeth Kübler-Ross went around the bend. Retrieved April 1, 2008 from: from: slate.com/id/2107069/

Schwartz, G. E. R. (2002). *The afterlife experiments: Breakthrough scientific evidence of life after death*. New York: Pocket Books.

Schwartz, G. E. R. (2009). The Sophia Project. Retrieved February 26, 2009 from: lach.web.arizona.edu/sophia/

Shermer, M. (2008). Stage theories of human behavior have little evidentiary support. *Scientific American, 299*(5), 42.

Stein, G. (1996a). Spiritualism. In G. Stein (Ed.), *The encyclopedia of the paranormal* (pp. 713–716). Amherst, NY: Prometheus Books.

Stein, G. (1996b). Harry Houdini and the paranormal. In G. Stein (Ed.), *The encyclopedia of the paranormal* (pp. 329–332). Amherst, NY: Prometheus Books.

Stevenson, I. (1980). Twenty cases suggestive of reincarnation (2nd ed., rev. and enlarged). Charlottesville: University of Virginia Press.

Stevenson, I. (1997). *Where reincarnation and biology intersect*. Westport, CT: Praeger.

Stuart, N. R. (2005). *The reluctant spiritualist: The life of Maggie Fox*. New York: Harcourt.

Taylor, H. (2003). *The religious and other beliefs of Americans 2003*. The Harris Poll #11, February 26, 2003. Retrieved April 1, 2008 from: www.harrisinterac tive.com/harris_poll/index.asp?PID=359

Taylor, T. (2007). Prairieghosts.com

Williamson, S. H. (2007). *Six ways to compute the relative value of a U.S. dollar amount, 1774 to present*. Retrieved April 1, 2008 from: www.measuringworth. com/calculators/uscompare/index.php

Chapter 12

Affective Computing. (2008). Million dollar challenge. Retrieved April 29, 2008 from: affect.media.mit.edu/milliondollarchallenge/

Alcock, J. E. (1981). *Parapsychology: Science or magic?* Burlington, MA: Elsevier.

Alcock, J. E. (2003). Give the null hypothesis a chance: Reasons to remain doubtful about the existence of psi. *Journal of Consciousness Studies, 10*, 29–50.

Bausell, R. B. (2007). *Snake oil science: The truth about complementary and alternative medicine*. Oxford: Oxford University Press.

Beloff, J. (1973). *Psychological sciences*. London: Crosby Lockwood Staples.

Beloff, J. (1974). ESP: The search for a physiological index. *Journal of the Society for Psychical Research, 47*, 403–420.

Beloff, J. (1985). Research strategies for dealing with unstable phenomena. In B. Shapin & L. Coly (Eds.), *The repeatability problem in parapsychology* (pp. 1–21). New York: Parapsychology Foundation.

Beloff, J., & Evans, L. (1961). A radioactivity test of psycho-kinesis. *Journal of the Society for Psychical Research, 41*, 41–46.

Blackmore, S. (1992). Psychic experiences: Psychic illusions. *Skeptical Inquirer, 16*, 367–376.

Blackmore, S. (1996). *In search of the light: Adventures of a parapsychologist*. Amherst, NY: Prometheus Books.

Blackmore, S. (2008). The paranormal. *The Edge*. Retrieved April 1, 2008 from: www.edge.org/q2008/q08_13.html

Bösch, H., Steinkamp, F., & Boller, E. (2006). Examining psychokinesis: The interaction of human intention with random number generators—a meta-analysis. *Psychological Bulletin, 132*, 497–532.

Braud, W., Shafer, D., & Andrews, S. (1993a). Reactions to an unseen gaze (remote attention): A review, with new data on autonomic staring detection. *Journal of Parapsychology, 57*, 373–390.

Braud, W., Shafer, D., & Andrews, S. (1993b). Further studies of autonomic detection of remote staring: Replications, new control procedures, and personality correlates. *Journal of Parapsychology, 57*, 391–409.

Broad, C. D. (2000). *Religion, philosophy and psychical research: Selected essays* (p. 106). Oxford, UK: Routledge.

Carroll, R. C. (2007). A short history of psi research. From *The skeptic's dictionary*. Retrieved April 1, 2008 from: skepdic.com/essays/psihistory.html

Child, I. L. (1985). Psychology and anomalous observations: The question of ESP in dreams. *American Psychologist, 40,* 1219–1230.

Christopher, M. (1970). *ESP, seers & psychics.* New York: Thomas Y. Crowell Co.

Crumbaugh, J. (1966). A scientific critique of parapsychology. *International Journal of Neuropsychiatry, 5,* 521–529.

DeAngelis, C. D., Drazen, J. M., Frizelle, F. A., Haug, C., Hoey, J., Horton, R., et al. (2005). Is this clinical trial fully registered? A statement from the International Committee of Medical Journal Editors. *Lancet, 365,* 1827–1829.

Don, N. S., McDonough, B. E., & Warren, C. A. (1998). Event-related brain potential (ERP) indicators of unconscious psi: A replication using subjects unselected for psi. *Journal of Parapsychology, 62,* 127–145.

Druckman, D., & Swets, J. (1988). *Enhancing human performance: Issues, theories, and techniques.* Washington, DC: National Academy Press. Retrieved April 1, 2008 from: books.nap.edu/openbook.php?record_id=1025&page=3

Good, I. J. (1997). Where has the billion trillion gone? *Nature, 389,* 806–807. See also Pedersen, M. M. Book Review: The conscious universe. *SkepticReport.* Retrieved April 1, 2008 from: www.skepticreport.com/pseudoscience/radinbook.htm

Hines, T. (2003). *Pseudoscience and the paranormal* (2nd ed.). Amherst, NY: Prometheus Books.

Honorton, C. (1985). Meta-analysis of psi ganzfeld research: A response to Hyman. *Journal of Parapsychology, 49,* 51–86.

Hyman, R. (1985). The ganzfeld psi experiment: A critical appraisal. *Journal of Parapsychology, 49,* 3–49.

Hyman, R (1989). *The elusive quarry: A scientific appraisal of psychical research.* Buffalo, NY: Prometheus Books.

Hyman, R. (2008). Anomalous cognition: A second perspective. *Skeptical Inquirer, 32*(4), 40–43.

Irwin, H. J., & Watt, C. A. (2007). *An introduction to parapsychology* (5th ed.). Jefferson, NC: McFarland.

Lawrence, T. (1993). Gathering in the sheep and goats: A meta-analysis of forced-choice sheep/goat ESP studies, 1947–1993. *Proceedings of Presented Papers: The Parapsychological Association 37th Annual Convention,* 261–272.

Marks, D. (2000). *The psychology of the psychic* (2nd ed.). Amherst, NY: Prometheus Books.

Masters, K. S. (2005). Research on the healing power of distant intercessory prayer: Disconnect between science and faith. *Journal of Psychology and Theology, 33,* 268–277.

Masters, K. S., Spielmans, G. I., & Goodson, J. T. (2006). Are there demonstrable effects of distant intercessory prayer? A meta-analytic review. *Annals of Behavioral Medicine, 32,* 21–26.

May, E. C. (1997). Anomalous cognition in the brain: The search continues. *Proceedings of Presented Papers: The Parapsychological Association 40th Annual Convention,* 202–213.

Moulton, S. T., & Kosslyn, S. M. (2008). Using neuroimaging to resolve the psi debate. *Journal of Cognitive Neuroscience, 20,* 182–192.

Palmer, J. (2003). ESP in the ganzfeld: Analysis of a debate. *Journal of Consciousness Studies, 10,* 51–68.

Radin, D. (1997). *The conscious universe – the scientific truth of psychic phenomena.* New York: HarperCollins.

Radin, D. (2008). Deanradin.com. Retrieved April 1, 2008 from www.deanradin.com

Radin, D., Nelson, R., Dobyns, Y., & Houtkooper, J. (2006). Reexamining psychokinesis: Comment on Bösch, Steinkamp, and Boller (2006). *Psychological Bulletin, 312,* 529–532.

Radin, D. I., & Ferrari, D. C. (1991). Effects of consciousness on the fall of dice: A meta-analysis. *Journal of Scientific Exploration, 5,* 61–83.

Randi, J. (1982). *Flim-Flam!* Amherst, NY: Prometheus Books.

Randi, J. (1983a). The Project Alpha experiment: Part one: The first two years. *Skeptical Inquirer,* Summer. Reprinted in Frazier, K. (Ed.). (1986). *Science confronts the paranormal.* New York: Prometheus Books, 1986. Retrieved 24 August, 2007 from: www.banachek.org/nonflash/project_alpha.htm

Randi, J. (1983b). The Project Alpha experiment: Part two: Beyond the laboratory. *Skeptical Inquirer,* Fall. Retrieved April 1, 2008 from: www.banachek.org/nonflash/project_alpha.htm

Raz, A. (2008). Anomalous cognition: A meeting of the minds? *Skeptical Inquirer, 32*(4), 36–39.

Rhine, J. B. (1934). *Extra-sensory perception.* Boston: Boston Society for Psychic Research.

Schmeidler, G. R. (1945). Separating the sheep from the goats. *Journal of the American Society for Psychical Research, 39,* 47–50.

Sherwood, S. J., & Roe, C. A. (2003). A review of dream ESP studies conducted since the Maimonides dream ESP studies. In J. Alcock, J. Burns, & A. Freedman (Eds.), *PSI wars* (pp. 85–110). Charlottesville, VA: Imprint Academic Press.

Stanford, R. G. (1974). An experimentally testable model for spontaneous psi events. I. Extrasensory events. *Journal of the American Society for Psychical Research, 68,* 34–57.

Stanford, R. G. (1990). An experimentally testable model for spontaneous psi events: A review of related evidence and concepts from parapsychology and other sciences. In S. Krippner (Ed.), *Advances in parapsychological research,* Vol. 6 (pp. 54–167). Jefferson, NC: McFarland.

Stanford, R. G. (2003). Research strategies for enhancing conceptual development and replicability. *Journal of Parapsychology, 67,* 17–51.

Targ, R., & Puthoff, H. (1977). *Mind-reach: Scientists look at psychic ability.* New York: Delacorte Press.

Thouless, R. H., & Wiesner, B. P. (1948). The psi processes in normal and "paranormal" psychology. *Proceedings of the Society for Psychical Research, 48,* 177–196.

Utis, J. (1995). An assessment of the evidence for psychic functioning. *Journal of Parapsychology, 59,* 289–320.

Verini, J. (2005). Missionary man. Salon.com. June 27. Retrieved April 1, 2008 from: dir.salon.com/story/ent/feature/2005/06/27/cruise/index.html?pn=1

Warren, C. A., McDonough, B. E., & Don, N. S. (1992). Event-related brain potential changes in a psi task. *Journal of Parapsychology, 56,* 1–30.

Chapter 13

Association of Chiropractic Colleges. (1996). A position paper on chiropractic. *Journal of Manipulative Physiological Therapeutics, 19,* 633–637.

Barrett, S. (2007a). Homeowatch. Retrieved April 1, 2008 from: www.homeowatch. org/

Barrett, S. (2007b). Reflexology: A close look. Retrieved April 1, 2008 from: www. quackwatch.org/01QuackeryRelatedTopics/reflex.html

Barrett, S., & Homola, S. (2007). Chirobase. Retrieved April 1, 2008 from: www. chirobase.org/

Bauer, H. H. (2004). *Science or pseudoscience: Magnetic healing, psychic phenomena, and other heterodoxies.* Urbana: University of Illinois Press.

Callahan, R. J. (1997). Thought field therapy: The case of Mary. *Electronic Journal of Traumatology, 3*(1). Retrieved April 1, 2008 from: www.fsu.edu/ trauma/ T039.html

Carroll, R. T. (2009a). *The skeptic's dictionary.* www.skepdic.com

Carroll, R. T. (2009b). *Feng shui.* Retrieved April 6, 2009 from: www.skepdic.com/ fengshui.html

Carroll, R. T. (2009c). *Acupuncture.* Retrieved April 6, 2009 from: www.skepdic. com/acupuncture.html

Carroll, R. T. (2009d). *Magnet therapy.* Retrieved April 9, 2009 from: www.skep dic.com/magnetic.html

Carroll, R. T. (2009e). *Homeopathy.* Retrieved April 6, 2009 from: www.skepdic. com/homeo.html

Carroll, R. T. (2009f). *Chiropractic.* Retrieved April 6, 2009 from: www.skepdic. com/chiro.html

Carroll, R. T. (2009g). *Thought field therapy.* Retrieved April 6, 2009 from: www. skepdic.com/thoughtfield.html

Carroll, R. T. (2009h). *Kirlian photography.* Retrieved April 6, 2009 from: www. skepdic.com/kirlian.html

Chen, K. (2007). Qigong therapy for stress management. In P. M. Lehrer, R. L. Woolfolk, & W. E. Sime (Eds.), *Principles and practice of stress management* (3rd ed., pp. 428–448). New York: Guilford Press.

Dietary Supplement and Nonprescription Drug Consumer Protection Act of 2006. S.3546, 2006. 109th Cong., 1st session (2006). Retrieved April 1, 2008 from: www.fda.gov/cder/regulatory/public_law_109462.pdf

Ernst, E., & Canter, P. H. (2006). A systematic review of spinal manipulation. *Journal of the Royal Society of Medicine, 99,* 192–196.

Evans, J. S. B. T. (2003). In two minds: Dual-process accounts of reasoning. *Trends in Cognitive Science, 7,* 454–459.

Fleischman, G. F. (1998). *Acupuncture: Everything you ever wanted to know.* New York: Barrytown.

Gaudiano, B. A., & Herbert, J. A. (2000). Can we really tap our problems away: A critical analysis of thought field therapy. *Skeptical Inquirer* online. Retrieved April 1, 2008 from: www.csicop.org/si/2000-07/thought-field-therapy.html

Goldacre, B. (2007). The end of homeopathy. *The Guardian,* Friday, November 17, 2007. Retrieved April 1, 2008 from: www.badscience.net/2007/11/a-kind-of-magic/

Haldeman, S. (Ed.). (1992). *Principles and practice of chiropractic* (2nd ed.). Norwalk, CT: Appleton & Lange.

Hall, H. (2008). What about acupuncture? *The Skeptic, 14*(3), 8–9.

Hermann, L. L., & Ebmeier, K. P. (2006). Factors modifying the efficacy of transcranial magnetic stimulation in the treatment of depression: A review. *Journal of Clinical Psychiatry, 67,* 1870–1876.

Hines, T. (2003). *Pseudoscience and the paranormal* (2nd ed.). Amherst, NY: Prometheus Books.

Homola, S. (2008). Chiropractic: A profession seeking identity. *Skeptical Inquirer, 32,* 19–22.

Jarvis, W. T. (2000). *Reiki.* National Council against Health Fraud. www.ncahf.org/articles/o-r/reiki.html

Jarvis, W. T., & The National Council against Health Fraud. (2002). Homeopathy. In M. Shermer (Ed.), *The skeptic encyclopedia of pseudoscience* (pp. 347–356). Santa Barbara: CA: ABC-CLIO.

Krieger, D. (1979). *The therapeutic touch: How to use your hands to help or to heal.* Englewood Cliffs, NJ: Prentice Hall.

Lambert, M. J. (2004). *Bergin and Garfield's handbook of psychotherapy and behavior change.* New York: Wiley.

Lehrer, P. M., Woolfolk, R. L., & Sime, W. E. (2007). *Principles and practice of stress management* (3rd ed.). New York: Guilford Press.

Lewith, G., Kenyon, J., & Lewis, P. (1996). *Complementary medicine: An integrated approach.* Oxford: Oxford University Press.

Lilienfeld, S. O., Lynn, S. J., & Lohr, J. M. (Eds.). (2003). *Science and pseudoscience in clinical psychology.* New York: Guilford Press.

Lilienfeld, S. O., Ruscio, J., & Lynn, S. J. (Eds.). (2008). *Navigating the mindfield: A guide to separating science from pseudoscience in mental health.* Amherst, NY: Prometheus Books.

Lin, Z. (Ed.). (2000). *Qigong: Chinese medicine or pseudoscience?* Amherst, NY: Prometheus Books.

Lindeman, M., & Aarnio, K. (2006). Paranormal beliefs: Their dimensionality and correlates. *European Journal of Personality, 20,* 585–602.

Lindeman, M., & Saher, M. (2007). Vitalism, purpose and superstition. *British Journal of Psychology, 98,* 33–44.

Madsen, M. V., Gøtzsche, P. C., & Hróbjartsson, A. (2009). Acupuncture treatment for pain: Systematic review of randomized clinical trials with acupuncture, placebo acupuncture, and no acupuncture groups. *British Medical Journal,* March, 3115. Retrieved March 3, 2009 from: www.bmj.com/cgi/reprint/338/jan27_2/a 3115?maxtoshow=&HITS=10&hits=10&RESULTFORMAT=&fulltext=sham +acupuncture&searchid=1&FIRSTINDEX=0&resourcetype=HWCIT

Mann, F. (1993). *Reinventing acupuncture: A new concept of an ancient medicine.* Oxford: Butterworth-Heinemann.

McDonald, W. K. (2003). How chiropractors think and practice: The survey of North American chiropractors. Ada, OH: Institute for Social Research, Ohio Northern University.

NIH Consensus Development Program. (November 3–5, 1997). *Acupuncture—Consensus Development Conference Statement.* National Institutes of Health. Retrieved April 1, 2008 from: consensus.nih.gov/1997/1997Acupuncture107html.htm

Norcross, J. C., Koocher, G. P., & Garofalo, A. (2006). Discredited psychological treatments and tests: A Delphi poll. *Professional Psychology: Research and Practice, 37*(5), 515–522.

Paul, N. L. (2006). *Reiki for dummies.* Hoboken, NJ: Wiley.

Pelletier, K. R. (2002). *The best alternative medicine.* New York: Simon & Schuster.

Puro, J. (2002). Feng shui. In M. Shermer (Ed.), *The skeptic encyclopedia of pseudoscience* (pp. 108–112). Santa Barbara: CA: ABC-CLIO.

Qi. (2007). In *Encyclopædia Britannica.* Retrieved September 17, 2007 from: www.britannica.com/eb/article-9023931

Ramachandra, V. S., & Blakeslee, S. (1998). *Phantoms of the brain.* New York: Quill, William Morrow.

Rosa, L., Rosa, E., Sarner, L., & Barrett, S. (1998). A close look at therapeutic touch. *Journal of the American Medical Association, 279*(13), 1005–1010.

Rosner, A. (1997). *A role of subluxation in chiropractic.* Des Moines, IO: Foundation for Chiropractic Education and Research.

Saher, M., & Lindeman, M. (2005). Alternative medicine: A psychological perspective. *Personality and Individual Differences, 39,* 1169–1178.

Schubert-Soldern, R. (1962). *Mechanism and vitalism.* London: Burns & Oates.

Smith, J. C. (2007). The psychology of relaxation. In P. M. Lehrer, R. L. Woolfolk, & W. E. Sime (Eds.), *Principles and practice of stress management* (3rd ed., pp. 39–52). New York: Guilford Press.

The Chiropractic Paradigm. (2009). Retrieved April 6, 2009 from: www.chirocolleges.org/paradigm_scopet.html

Watson, B. (1963). *Mo Tzu: Basic writings.* New York: Columbia University Press.

Wu, B. (2000). *Lighting the eye of the dragon: Inner secrets of taoist feng shui.* New York: St. Martin's Press.

yin-yang. (2007). In *Encyclopædia Britannica.* Retrieved September 17, 2007, from: www.britannica.com/eb/article-9077972

Chapter 14

Affective Computing. (2008). Million dollar challenge. Retrieved April 29, 2008 from: affect.media.mit.edu/milliondollarchallenge/

Barnes, P., Powell-Griner, E., McFann, K., & Nahin, R. (2002). CDC Advance Data Report #343: Complementary and alternative medicine use among adults: United States, 2002. Washington, DC: U.S. Government.

Barrett, S. (2003). Some thoughts about faith healing. Retrieved April 1, 2008 from: www.quackwatch.com/01QuackeryRelatedTopics/faith.html

Benson, H. (1975). *The relaxation response*. New York: Morrow.

Benson, H., Dusek, J. A., Sherwood, J. B., Lam, P., Bethea, C. F., Carpenter, W., et al. (2006). Study of the therapeutic effects of intercessory prayer (STEP) in cardiac bypass patients: A multicenter randomized trial of uncertainty and certainty of receiving intercessory prayer. *American Heart Journal, 151,* 934–942.

Bronson, P. (2002). A prayer before dying. *Wired*. December. Retrieved April 1, 2008 from: www.wired.com/wired/archive/10.12/prayer_pr.html

Bupp, N. (2005). *Follow-up study on prayer therapy may help refute false and misleading information about earlier clinical trial.* Press release from the Commission for Scientific Medicine and Mental Health, Amherst, NY, July 22. Retrieved April 1, 2008 from: www.godlessgeeks.com/LINKS/PrayerTherapy.htm

Byrd, R. C. (1988). Positive therapeutic effects of intercessory prayer in a coronary care unit population. *Southern Medical Journal, 81,* 826–829.

Carroll, R. T. (2007). Faith healing. *The skeptics dictionary*. Retrieved 17 October, 2007 from www.skepdic.com

Carroll, R. T. (2009a). *John of God*. Retrieved April 6, 2009 from: skepdic.com/johnofgod.html

Carroll, R. T. (2009b). Sicher-Targ distant healing report. Retrieved April 7, 2009 from: skepdic.com/sichertarg.html

Cha, K. Y., & Wirth, D. P. (2001). Does prayer influence the success of in vitro fertilization-embryo transfer? *Journal of Reproductive Medicine, 46,* 781–787.

Charity Navigator. (2007). Retrieved April 1, 2008 from: www.charitynavigator.org/index.cfm?bay=search.summary&orgid=5206

Chopra, D. (2008). Taking the afterlife seriously. *Skeptic, 13,* 55–57. Argues that there are 11 studies showing that "prayer works."

Flamm, B. L. (2002). Faith healing by prayer: Review of Cha, KY, Wirth, DP, Lobo, RA. Does prayer influence the success of in vitro fertilization-embryo transfer? *Scientific Review of Alternative Medicine, 6(1),* 47–50.

Galton, F. (1872). Statistical inquiries into the efficacy of prayer (letter). *The Fortnightly Review, 68,* 125.

Gerhardt, P. (2000). Saying a prayer for science: Studies of the healing power of prayer pose challenges some call divine. *Washington Post,* December 19. Retrieved April 1, 2008 from: pqasb.pqarchiver.com/washingtonpost/access/65284393.html?dids=65284393:65284393&FMT=ABS&FMTS=ABS:FT&date=Dec+19%2C+2000&author=Pamela+Gerhardt&pub=The+Washington+Post&edition=&startpage=Z.08&desc=FINDINGS+OF+FACT

Hansen, G. P. (2001). *The trickster and the paranormal*. New York: Xlibris.

Harris, W. S., Gowda, M., Kolb, J. W., Strychacz, C. P., Vacek, J. L., Jones, P. G., et al. (1999). A randomized, controlled trial of the effects of remote, intercessory prayer on outcomes in patients admitted to the coronary care unit. *Archives of Internal Medicine, 159,* 2273–2278.

Hines, T. (2003). *Pseudoscience and the paranormal*. Amherst, NY: Prometheus Books.

Hodge, D. R. (2007). A systematic review of the empirical literature on intercessory prayer. *Research on Social Work Practice, 17,* 174–187.

Irwin, H. J., & Watt, C. A. (2007). *An introduction to parapsychology.* Jefferson, NC: McFarland.

John of God. Retrieved April 1, 2008 from: www.johnofgod.com/article.htm

Kernochan, S. (2007). Retrieved April 1, 2008 from: www.sarahkernochan.com/documentaries/index.html. See also (retrieved October 23, 2007): www.huffingtonpost.com/sarah-kernochan/sympathy-for-the-evangeli_b_46731.html

Krippner, S., & Achterberg, J. (2000). Anomalous healing experiences. In Cardeña, E., Lynn, S. J., & Krippner, S. C. (Eds.), *Varieties of anomalous experience: Examining the scientific evidence* (pp. 353–395). Washington, DC: American Psychological Association.

Krippner, S. C. (2002). Conflicting perspectives on shamans and shamanism: Points and counterpoints. *American Psychologist, 57,* 962–977.

Krucoff, M.W., Crater, S.W., Gallup, D., Blankenship, J.C., Cuffe, M., Guarneri, M., et al. (2005). Music, imagery, touch, and prayer as adjuncts to interventional cardiac care: The Monitoring and Actualisation of Noetic Trainings (MANTRA) II randomized study. *The Lancet, 366,* 211–217.

Leibovici, L. (1999). Alternative (complementary) medicine: A cuckoo in the nest of empiricist reed warblers. *British Medical Journal, 319,* 1629–1632.

Leibovici, L. (2001). Effects of remote, retroactive intercessory prayer on outcomes in patients with bloodstream infection: Randomised controlled trial. *British Medical Journal, 323,* 1450–1451.

Levinson, D. (1998). *Religion: A cross-cultural dictionary.* New York: Oxford University Press.

Lewis, I. M. (2003). *Ecstatic religion: A study of shamanism and spirit possession* (2nd ed.). London: Routledge.

Masters, K. S. (2005). Research on the healing power of distant intercessory prayer: Disconnect between science and faith. *Journal of Psychology and Theology, 33,* 268–277.

Masters, K. S., Spielmans, G. I., & Goodson, J. T. (2006). Are there demonstrable effects of distant intercessory prayer? A meta-analytic review. *Annals of Behavioral Medicine, 32,* 21–26.

Myers, D. G. (2000). Is prayer clinically effective? *Reformed Review, 53,* 95–102. Retrieved April 1, 2008 from: www.davidmyers.org/Brix?pageID=53

Nickell, J. (2007). "John of God": Healings by entities? *Skeptical Enquirer.*

Nolen, W. (1974). *Healing: A doctor in search of a miracle.* New York: Random House.

Pollack, G. (2001). How faith heals: An increasing amount of evidence is convincing doctors. *Readers Digest.* Retrieved April 1, 2008 from: www.readersdigest.ca/mag/2001/07/prayer.html

Posner, G. P. (1998). Has science proven the "divine" health benefits of religion? Retrieved April 1, 2008 from: www.infidels.org/secular_web/feature/1998/prayer-USAToday.html

Randi, J. (1989). *The faith healers.* Amherst, NY: Prometheus Books.

Randi, J. (2000). James Randi in a speech made at Australian Skeptics Convention in 2000. Retrieved April 1, 2008 from: video.google.com/videoplay?docid= 3178853788754765978 (at 50:57 mark).

Rice, T. W. (2003). Believe it or not: Religious and other paranormal beliefs in the United States. *Journal for the Scientific Study of Religion, 42*, 95–106.

Schwartz, G. E., & Simon, W. L. (2007). *The energy healing experiments: Science reveals our natural power to heal.* New York: Artria Books.

Sicher, F., Targ, E., Moore II, D., & Smith, H. S. (1998). A randomized double-blind study of the effect of distant healing in a population with advanced AIDS. *Western Journal of Medicine, 169*, 356–363.

Sternfield, J. (1992). *Firewalk: The psychology of physical immunity.* Stockbridge, MA: Berkshire House.

Tessman, I., & Tessman, J. (2000). Efficacy of prayer. *Skeptical Inquirer, 24*(2), 31–33.

Wallace, C. (1996). Faith and healing. *Time.* Monday, June 24. Retrieved April 1, 2008 from: www.time.com/time/magazine/article/0,9171,984737,00.html

Warner, R. (1980). Deception and self-deception in shamanism and psychiatry. *International Journal of Social Psychiatry, 26*, 41–52.

Chapter 15

Asimov, I., & Gish, D. (1981). The Genesis war. *Science Digest, 89* (October), 82–87.

Barlow, N. (Ed.). (1958). *The autobiography of Charles Darwin, 1809–1882.* New York: W.W. Norton.

Barrow, J. D., & Tipler, F. (1988). *The anthropic cosmological principle.* Oxford: Oxford University Press.

Beil, L. (2008). Opponents of evolution adopting new strategy. *New York Times,* June 4. Retrieved June 4, 2008 from: www.nytimes.com/2008/06/04/us/04evolution.html?hp

Boston, R. (1988). God, country, and the electorate. *Church and State,* October, 8–15.

Brumfiel, G. (2006). Our universe: Outrageous fortune. *Nature, 439*, 10–12.

Bube, R. H. (1971). Man come of age: Bonhoeffer's response to the God-Of-The-Gaps. *Journal of the Evangelical Theological Society, 14*, 203–220.

Carter, J. (2005). *Our endangered values: America's moral crisis.* New York: Simon & Schuster.

Cicero. (1972). *The Nature of the Gods* (trans. H. C. P. McGregor). Harmondsworth: Penguin.

Council of Europe. (2007). *Resolution 1580, "The dangers of creationism in education. Council of Europe Parliamentary Assembly.* Retrieved April 1, 2008 from: assembly.coe.int/Main.asp?link=/Documents/AdoptedText/ta07/ERES1580.htm

Curl, M. (1996). *The anagram dictionary.* London: Robert Hale.

Dawkins, R. (2006). *The God delusion*. New York: Mariner Books.

Forrest, B., & Gross, P. R. (2007). *Creationism's Trojan horse: The wedge of intelligent design*. New York: Oxford University Press.

Gould, S. J. (1999). *Rocks of ages: Science and religion in the fullness of life*. New York: Ballantine Books. See also Gould, S. J. (1999). Non-overlapping magisterial-special issue: Science and religion: Conflict or conciliation?—Religion and science have their own respective domains of teaching authority. *Skeptical Inquirer*, July-August. Retrieved March 24, 2008 from: findarticles.com/p/articles/mi_m2843/is_4_23/ai_55208055/pg_7

Haldane, J. B. S. (1927). *Possible worlds and other papers*. New York: Harper & Bros.

Harpur, T. (2004). *The Pagan Christ: Recovering the lost light*. Toronto, ON: Thomas Allen.

Harris, S. (2004). *The end of faith: Religion, terror, and the future of reason*. New York: W. W. Norton.

Henderson, B. (2006). *The Gospel of the Flying Spaghetti Monster*. New York: Villard.

Holden, C. (1980). Republican candidate picks fight with Darwin. *Science, 209*, September 12, 1214.

Horn, G. V., & Johnston, L. (2007). Evolutionary controversy and a side of pasta: The Flying Spaghetti Monster and the subversive function of religious parody. *Golem: Journal of Religion and Monsters, 2*(1), Spring. Retrieved October 1, 2008 from: www.golemjournal.org/van%20horn%20spaghetti%20monsters.pdf

Kennedy, J. E. (2000). Do people guide psi or does psi guide people? Evidence and implications from life and lab. *Journal of the American Society for Psychical Research, 94*, 130–150.

Lebo, L. (2008). *The devil in Dover: An insider's story of dogma v. Darwin in small-town America*. New York: New Press.

Liptak, A. (2008). Justices grapple with a question of church monument as free speech issue. *New York Times*, November 12. Retrieved November 12, 2008 from: www.nytimes.com/2008/11/13/washington/13sect.html

Masters, K. S., Spielmans, G. I., & Goodson, J. T. (2006). Are there demonstrable effects of distant intercessory prayer? A meta-analytic review. *Annals of Behavioral Medicine, 32*, 21–26.

Michaelsen, O. V. (1998). *Words at play; quips, quirks & oddities*. New York: Sterling.

Miller, K. (2007). In defense of evolution. Judgement day: Intelligent design on trial. Retrieved April 1, 2008 from: www.pbs.org/wgbh/nova/id/defense-ev.html

Mooney, C. (2005a). The Dover monkey trial: Chris Mooney reports on how intelligent design is hijacking science. Seedmagazine.com. October 1. Retrieved April 1, 2008 from: seedmagazine.com/news/2005/10/the_dover_monkey_trial.php?page=all

Mooney, C. (2005b). *The republican war on science*. New York: Basic Books.

Nova. (2007). Judgment day: Intelligent design on trial. www.pbs.org/wgbh/nova/id/

Prothero, D. R. (2007). *Evolution: What the fossils say and why it matters*. New York: Columbia University Press.

Rees, M. (2000). *Just six numbers: The deep forces that shape the universe*. New York: Free Press.

Rescher, N. (1985). *Pascal's Wager: A study of practical reasoning in philosophical theology*. Notre Dame, IN: University of Notre Dame Press.

Robinson, B. A. (2008). *Parallels between Jesus & Horus, an Egyptian god*. Retrieved October 31, 2008 from www.religioustolerance.org/chr_jcpa5.htm

Scott, E. (2004). *Evolution vs. creationism: An introduction*. Los Angeles: University of California Press.

Shermer, M. (2006). *Why Darwin matters: The case against intelligent design*. New York: Owl Books.

Smith, G. H. (1979). *Atheism: The case against God*. Amherst, NY: Prometheus Books.

Smith, J. (2008). *GOD SPEAKS! The Pastafarian Quatrains: A scholarly analysis and critique of the flying spaghetti monster*. www.lulu.com/content/4537362

Spong, J. S. (2007). *Jesus for the non-religious: Rediscovering the Divine at the heart of the human*. San Francisco: HarperCollins.

Steering Committee on Science and Creationism, National Academy of Sciences. (2008). Science, evolution, and creationism. Washington, DC: The National Academies Press.

Susskind, L. (2006). *The cosmic landscape: String theory and the illusion of intelligent design*. New York: Little Brown.

Tegmark, M. (2003). Parallel universes. *Scientific American*, May. Retrieved April 1, 2008 from: www.mukto-mona.com/science/physics/ParalellUniverse2003.pdf

Tunstall-Pedoe, W. (2007). Anagram Genius. Anagramgenius.com

Chapter 16

Smith, J. (2006). *The Bible's true words on your deepest secret*. Raleigh, NC: Lulu Press.

Smith, J. (2009). The miracle of urine therapy. In J. C. Smith (2009). *Pseudoscience and extraordinary mysteries of the paranormal: A critical thinker's toolkit*. Boston: Wiley-Blackwell.

Appendix B

Odling-Smee, L. (2007). The lab that asked the wrong questions. *Nature, 446*(7131), 10–11.

Name Index

Subject Index